AF560835

CONTESTING MARGINALITY

ETHNICITY, INSURGENCY AND SUBNATIONALISM IN NORTH-EAST INDIA

CONTESTING MARGINALITY

Ethnicity, Insurgency and Subnationalism in North-East India

SAJAL NAG

MANOHAR
2026

First published 2002
Reprinted 2025, 2026

ISBN 978-81-7304-427-4 (hardbound)
ISBN 978-93-6080-719-1 (eBook)

Published by

Ajay Kumar Jain for
Manohar Publishers & Distributors
4753/23 Ansari Road, Daryaganj
New Delhi 110 002

Printed and bound in India

For
RIA (Upasana), BABU (Siddhant),
CHHOTU (Saptarshi)
and my
MUM (Niharika)
who all are growing up
as Rejected people in
North East India

'. . . *historians are to nationalism what poppy-growers in Pakistan are to heroin-addicts; we supply the essential raw material for the market. . . . So a historian who writes about ethnicity or nationalism cannot but make a politically or ideologically explosive intervention.*'

ERIC HOBSBAWM, 'Ethnicity and Nationalism in Europe', *Anthropology Today*, Vol. 8, No. 1, February 1992, p. 3.

Contents

Preface

One of the criticisms about my first book (*Roots of Ethnic Conflict: Nationality Questions in North-East India*) has been that though it claims to tackles the nationality question in north-east India its focus is only on the Brahmaputra and Barak Valley. The criticism was indeed valid and I immediately decided on a sequel to the book. Since Brahmaputra and Barak Valley constituted the plains of the north-east, I planned to take up the hill areas in the next project. I chose Mizoram, Manipur and Nagaland as the nationality question in these areas had led to massive secessionist and insurgency movements. The proposal materialized when I joined the Centre for Social Studies (CSS) in Surat which agreed to sponsor the project. Prof. Sudhir Chandra who was the Director of the Centre then not only gave me the 'go ahead' but also sanctioned an additional contingency grant to meet the expenses of the project. The Indian Council of Historical Research also helped me with a contingency grant. My immense gratitude to both these institutions and Prof. Sudhir Chandra and Prof. Ghanshyam Shah (who succeeded him) in particular for encouraging and supporting me throughout the period. In fact, I was apprehensive about starting the project at the Centre which is far away from the north-east where my sources were. But CSS proved to be an ideal place to pursue the study. The wonderful faculty helped me by making my stay comfortable, familiarized me with the current debates and discourses on the subject, offered critical intervention in the Seminar I presented. I must acknowledge my debt particularly to Prof. S.P. Punalekar, Dr. Biswaroop Das, Prof. Lancy Lobo, Dr. Surindar Singh Jodhaka, Dr. Arjun Patel, Dr. Satyakam Joshi and Kiran Desai. I had a very fruitful interaction with Dr. Dilip Simeon who came as a Visiting Fellow at a later stage of my tenure at the Centre. His interest in the developments in north-east India enabled me to have frequent discussions with him on the subject. My friends, K.S. Raman and Esha helped me in many ways. Without the help of Sheikh Bhai, Dayanandan, Ashok, Hina Ben and above all late Mrs. Mac, this work would not have been competed.

I am also thankful to the Director and Staff of the Archives/Record room of Manipur, Assam and Mizoram. I am particularly thankful to Krishna Kant, an MA student of Manipur University then, who helped me locate some of the literature published by the banned underground outfits and introduced me to some of its leaders whom I interviewed. I am grateful to N. Lokendra Singh and Kshetri Rajendra Singh for permitting me to use their then unpublished doctoral dissertations. My thanks are due to Lalthangmuana of the Mizoram State Archives who helped me translate documents from Mizo to English and also to Dr. David Reid Syiemlieh and Dr. I.L. Iyer of the North-Eastern Hill University, and Y.K. Shimray of the National Insurance who helped me with research materials.

Lastly I would like to express my gratitude to my parents, my wife Mala and little daughter Tuntuni whose support has made the work possible.

A word or two about the book. I have refrained from interpreting statements, either written or oral, of the underground leaders or organizations due to its sensitive nature. I preferred to reproduce them in full for the reader to interpret them. This accounts for the use of large number of long quotations in the book.

Needless to say I am responsible for errors of facts or understanding.

SAJAL SAG

Abbreviations

AICC	All India Congress Committee
AIGL	All India Gorkha League
AIDS	Acquired Immune Deficiency Syndrome
AISPC	All India State Peoples Conference
ANPPC	All Naga Peoples Peace Conference
ANVC	Achik National Volunteers Council
ATTF	All Tripura Tigers Force
BSF	Border Security Force/Bodo Security Force
CPI	Communist Party of India
CPI (M)	Communist Party of India (Marxist)
CPI (ML)	Communist Party of India (Marxist-Leninist)
CONSOCOM	Consolidation Committee
CNP	Council of Naga People
CWC	Congress Working Committee
DIG	Deputy Inspector General (of Police)
DIF	Democratic Independent Front
DMK	Dravida Munnetra Kazagham
DNSF	Dimasa National Security Force
DHD	Dima Halom Daoga
EITU	Eastern India Tribal Union
HALC	Hynniewtrep Achik Liberation Council
HLU	Hill Leaders Union
HPC	Hmar Peoples Convention
IBRF	Indo Burma Revolutionary Front
IGP	Inspector General of Police
INA	Indian National Army
INC	Indian National Congress
IBM	Indo Burma Movement
JKLF	Jammu & Kashmir Liberation Front
KLA	Kashmir Liberation Front
KNA	Kuki National Assembly
KNA	Kuki National Army
KSPA	Khasi States Peoples Association
KCP	Kangleipak Communist Party

KNV	Karbi National Volunteers
KYKL	Kanglei Yowl Kanna Lup
MU	Mizo Union
MNFF	Mizo National Famine Front
MNF	Mizo National Front
MNA	Mizo National Army
NNC	Naga National Council
NNO	Naga National Organisation
NMM	Nikhil Manipuri Mahasabha
NNCB	Naga National Council of Burma
NEFA	North Eastern Frontier Agency
NYM	Naga Youth Movement
NWC	Naga Womens Convention
NPC	Naga Peace Council
NLFT	National Liberation Front of Twipra
NDFB	National Democratic Front of Bodoland
NGO	Non Governmental Organisation
NPMHR	Naga Peoples Movement for Human Rights
NSCN	National Socialist Council of Nagaland
NSCN (IM)	National Socialist Council of Nagaland (Nagalim) ISAC SWU – Th.Muivah
NSCN (K)	National Socialist Council of Nagland (Khaplang)
PHTRA	The Plains and Hills Tribes and Races Assocaition
PANMYL	Pan Manipuri Youth League
PMM	Pan Mongoloid Movement
PLA	Peoples Liberation Army (of Manipur)
PREPAK	Peoples Liberation Army of Kangleipak
RGM	Revolutionary Government of Manipur
RJC	Revolutionary Joint Committee
TNV	Tripura National Volunteers
UNO	United Nations Organisation
UNPO	Unrepresented Nations and Peoples Organisation
UNLF	United National Liberation Front (of Manipur)
ULFA	United Liberation Front of Assam
UMFO	United Mizo Freedom Organisation
UPSC	Union Public Service Commission
UDF	United Democratic Front
UNLFOSS	United Liberation Front of Seven Sisters
YLA	Young Lushai Assocaition
YMCA	Young Mens Christian Association
YMA	Young Mizo Association

Prologue

In the summer of 1989 I, as a college teacher, attended a workshop on the Indian National Movement sponsored by the Indian Council of Historical Research at the North-Eastern Hill University, Shillong. The monotonous and mundane atmosphere of the gathering suddenly livened up when one of my Mizo colleagues interrupted one of the lectures and said that the entire workshop was all about the anti-British movements that took place in Indian mainland. It did not include the century-long fight of the Nagas or Mizos against the British. He threw another shocker when he said that as far as he and his people were concerned the Mizo National Front (MNF) movement was their national movement and freedom struggle, which should be included in the curriculum. The resource-person, an eminent historian, replied that though he sympathized with his stand on the subject, since the Government of India wouldn't permit he was not in a position to include the so-called Mizo national movement in the syllabi. Moreover, as far as the historian and the Government of India were concerned the MNF movement was a secessionist movement—an insurgency.

INTERACTION OF DISCOURSES

Although the matter ended there and the course was concluded smoothly, the interaction, between my Mizo colleague and the speaker was profoundly reflective. It revealed a discourse pattern. The positions taken by the two individuals were representative of the two parties involved: the Indian State and its representatives on the one hand, and aggrieved communities on the other. The present work is about this discourse—this confrontation. What is considered as the nationalist movement and freedom struggle by the struggling Nagas, Mizos or the Meitheis is explained away in terms of 'secessionism' and 'insurgency' by the Indian State. One is reminded of a similar discourse between the colonial state and the Indian nationalists in pre-independence India wherein the latter declared themselves a 'nation' while the former denied the existence of any Indian nation. This dynamic force of history makes this discourse important. It would be futile to go into the details of the usual pattern of arguments: whether Nagaland or Mizoram really belongs to India or whether the movements were nationalist in character or not because history has proved time and again that national boundaries are not sacrosanct nor is the permanence of nation states guaranteed. Yesterday's terrorists are today's martyrs. Similarly if the Mizo 'scessionism' was a fact, the cessation of this movement is also a fact. The Mizo 'insurgents' of yesterday are not less Indian today than any other Indian. It is this aspect of the unpredictable fluidity of history, so profoundly proved by the events in Eastern as well as Central Europe in the eighties and nineties of the twentieth century, that makes history so immensely mystical and lively. Our object is to study this facet of the Naga, Mizo and Meithei movements *vis-a-vis* the Indian State from a contemporary historical perspective without bothering about predicting its future course.

But what needs to be emphasized here is that the so-called 'secessionism' is not unique to north-east India, or India as is believed.[1] In fact most of the post-colonial states and even the so-called modern nation states in Europe, Africa and America have faced such crises.

SEPARATISM AND SECESSIONISM IN INDIA

A separatist movement was visible in India as early as 1906. In fact, barely two decades after the foundation of the Indian National Congress as the representative political organization of all sections of Indians, a counter political organization was born in the form of the Muslim League (1906), which was followed by the emergence of the All India Hindu Mahasabha (1915) and Akali Dal (1920) representing Muslims, Hindus and Sikhs respectively. These developments posed a serious threat to the concept of Indian nation itself as all three components of it, e.g. the Muslims, Hindus and Sikhs claimed to be separate nations by themselves. Initially these demands for separate nationhood were brushed aside as 'insignificant' but its real strength was visible in the 1940s, when Muslims demanded Pakistan, Sikhs demanded Sikhistan and the Hindus wanted hegemony in Hindustan. The situation worsened at the imminence of British withdrawal from India. There was a move to carve out of India an independent United Bengal, Paktunisthan in North Western Frontier Province, and Gorkhasthan in the Darjeeling District of Bengal. The

Princely States of Bhopal, Hyderabad, Travancore-Cochin, Junagadh, Manipur, the tribal areas of Naga Hills, Mizo Hills and Khasi Hills in north-east India desired independence and self-rule. While Pakistan was conceded, some of the other separatist-turned-secessionist moves were suppressed and 'integration' was achieved. One of the areas where the 'integrationist' attempt had failed was in the Naga Hills. The Nagas declared themselves independent on 14 August 1947. Soon after, the Meitheis decried the merger and demanded independence from India. A number of insurgent organizations beginning with the United National Liberation Front to the People's Liberation Army were active in the north-east. The merger of Kashmir with India was also decried by certain sections. The newly created Pakistan found that without Kashmir their state was 'moth-eaten' and invaded and occupied part of Kashmir. Since then secessionist demands continued to be voiced all along the 1950s. In 1953 Sheikh Abdullah himself was arrested on charges of 'subversion'. There were underground activities headed by Jammu & Kashmir Liberation Front and Kashmir Liberation Army whose objective was to get 'Kashmir liberated from Indian occupation'. The 1980s saw a revival of secessionism in Punjab following the dismissal of the Akalis from office (1980). The movement started with a demand for autonomy on the basis of Anandpur Sahib Resolution and ended with the demand for independence and establishment of Khalistan. The insurgency and terrorism unleashed in Punjab since then, was unprecedented.

The Dravida Munnetra Kazagham (DMK) also raised a banner of revolt against the hegemony of the casteist-Hindi belt.[2] Following the attempt to introduce Hindi as the national language and the dismissal of the DMK Government in Tamil Nadu in 1976, the DMK activists campaigned for severance of ties with India and establishment of an independent Dravidastan in south India.

In March 1966, the Mizos under the leadership of the MNF followed suit and revolted. The Tripura National Volunteer began their secessionist campaign in June 1980 and the United Liberation Front of Assam in 1981. Among these only Mizoram seemed to have quietened after the Accord with the Centre in 1986 and settled down to peace for the time being.

OTHER POST-COLONIAL SOCIETIES

These secessionist tendencies are similar to those in other post-colonial states where separatist movements have been endemic too. The creation of Pakistan out of India was not the final division. Soon

East Pakistan (Bangladesh) seceded from it and the Sindhis have been fighting a battle of separation from the Punjabi dominated Pakistan. Bangladesh too has not been free from separatism, with the Chakmas as the insurgency group. There is a violent Tamil Secessionist Movement in Sri Lanka. In the African continent the Ibos have been fighting to secede from Nigeria. The Yoruba and Housa-Fulani are the other aggrieved communities in Nigeria; there is a Buganda challenge in Uganda. The Moros are fighting in the Philippines, and so are the Chins in Myanmar, the Bangalas in Zaire, Kurds in Iraq and the Meos in Thailand. There is a Muslim insurgency in Lebanon, and that of Black and Anayanza and Sudan. Besides, there is also the long drawn struggle of the Tibetans against China, the Palestinians against Israel. Even the old nation states are no exception to this. The Irish battle against British colonialism is perhaps one of the oldest. The Scots and Welsh are equally vociferous about autonomy. There are also movements such as the Basque Nationalist Movement in Spain, the Quebec Movement in Canada, and the separatist movements of the Shans in Myanmar and Eritreans in Ethiopia. The artificial creation of multinational states through conquests, agreements, negotiations and superpower manipulation has also failed against the resurgence of ethnic aspirations. The multinationalism of Russia has already fallen to pieces and has not solved the conflict between the Armenians and Azerbaijanis, the Serbs, Croats and the Muslims of Bosnia Herzegovina—all erstwhile constituents of the Yuogoslav nation—and has virtually turned into a civil war. The Czechs and Slovaks have split Czechoslovakia into two nations. This is not the end of separatist movements, there are more in the pipeline. The Kikuyu dominance in Kenya, and that of the Javanese in Indonesia, have faced serious challenges. The cracks in the relationship between the Zulus, Sotho and Xhosa in Africa is increasingly manifesting itself. The contradictory interests of the African National Congress and the Zulu-Inkata party has already jeopardized the South African nationalist unity. The unification of Germany has only reinforced the growth of Neo-Nazism and contempt for Asians. In India itself there is a Hindu resurgence while the Naga and Meithei struggle continue to challenge the might of the Indian State.

While there are scholarly studies abroad on these 'Secessionist' or Insurgency Movements, in India it is only the journalists who have been interested in the subject. Consequently, students of nationalism, secessionism and insurgency have very little material at hand that can be taken seriously.

HISTORIOGRAPHICAL RESPONSIBILITY

North-east India faces not just political, economic and cultural marginalization but even historiographical marginalization. A study on British India has pointed out that secessionism thrived in the areas which were late in becoming a part of the British Empire in India. Even the specific areas have been mentioned, but not the north-east, though it fits the argument.[3] If as an authority this scholar is forgiven considering his European nationality, our national and so-called 'history from below' also excluded the north-east, in narrating certain crucial phases of Indian history like the State Peoples' movement in Manipur or Mizo People's movement to merge with India in opposition to a section of its leaders.[4] As for the studies on secessionism they follow a pattern which is typical to north-east India. It is the historiographical pedigree that has set the pattern and is unquestioningly followed. Worse, this historiography, which was shaped by the colonial school, has only reinforced the arguments of the insurgents themselves. While the rest of India has moved ahead to reach the concept and ideology of peoples' history, north-east Indian historiography is still chained to its colonial framework set by Edward Gait's *History of Assam* (1905).

The secessionists justify their movements by saying that the Naga Hills, Mizo Hills, Manipur or even Assam were never a part of India till the British conquered them. The students of the history of north-east India are taught that each was an independent political unit in the pre-colonial period, and that it had maintained its 'splendid isolation'.[5] It is never discussed as to what was 'splendid' about this isolation, nor is it explained that the 'independence of Assam' in the pre-colonial times was not an isolated phenomenon. The entire medieval world, including India was characterized by such regionalism where autonomous units thrived. Nation, and nation states are only a modern phenomenon. Multiplicity of regional kingdoms and feudal chiefdoms, fragmentation of empire, appearance and disappearance of regional powers, regionalism and insularity in vision and political action are characteristic of the medieval times. It is a significant failure of the regional historiography to highlight the fact that Assam could not have been an exception to these medieval characteristics. Similarly tribals and subalterns are treated equally shabbily by some of the 'doyens' of this historiography. For example, a three-volume work on the Anglo-Tribal relationship in north-east India has been titled *Problems of the Hill Tribes: North East Froniter.*[6]

The laboriously collected data from India and abroad presented in these volumes depict the 'tribals' as the 'problem' which justified their being conquered by the British. No attempt has been made to appreciate the heroic resistance offered by small tribal groups like the Nagas or Lushais against a modern military power like the British. Instead the emphasis is on how the tribes created problems for the British by committing raids, plunders and kidnapping in British territory. The grip of colonial historiography is so evident in this work that instead of presenting the tribal side of the picture, British policy has been projected—dividing its course into phases such as peace-mission, punitive expedition, and non-intervention, period of indecision, forward policy, etc. No attempt has been made in this study to use folk history, oral historiography in the absence of documentary evidence to present the tribal point of view. A comparison of these early historical works with the original official imperialist documents of Alexander Mackenzie,[7] Pemberton,[8] Butler, Mills,[9] Woodthrope,[10] Needham[11] or Robert Reid[12] will perhaps not reveal much difference between the two. Such was the stronghold of colonial historiography of the northeast. It is striking that it didn't loosen its grip over historians. For example, since S.K. Bhuyan published his study, *Anglo-Assamese Relations* there has been an enormous interest in studying British relationship with various tribes of the north-east. As a result of S.K. Bhuyan's[13] study the following historians among others, worked in the tribals of this region: H.K. Barpujari on Anglo-Tribal relations, S.K. Barpujari on Anglo-Naga relations,[14] J.B. Bhattacharjee on Anglo-Garo relations,[15] S. Chatterjee on Anglo-Lushai relations,[16] Helen Giri[17] and Hamlet Bareh on Anglo-Khasi relation,[18] Laxmi Devi on Ahom-tribal relation,[19] and Milton Sangma on Anglo-Garo[20] relations. Even as late as 1989, research works on the north-east maintained the stance that the tribals of this region lived in complete political isolation. A critic discovered a strange insularity in the historiography of north-east India in the sense that it never tried to view its history against the background of developments in India as a whole.[21] He also found that there is a discernible lack of interest or information about north-east India outside the north-east.[22] So much so that an Indian History Congress volume categorized a paper on the northeast as 'non-Indian'.[23] It has also been pointed out that the British had no intention of conquering these tribes as it would not gain much economically by such a conquest[24] as these hills were 'not a land of flowing milk and honey, no glittering outcrops to raise thoughts of mineral wealth, no telling indications of reservoirs of endless oil'.[25] Such a view overlooks the fact that imperialism is its own justification. There need not always be an 'economic' motive for a conquest. The following is a representative example from a history written in the imperialist tradition.

> At least in 1866, it was resolved to take possession of the Angami country and reclaim its inhabitants from savagery. . . . The object in view was to protect the low land from the incursions of the Nagas. It was not desired to extend British rule into the interior, but when a footing in the hills had once been obtained, further territorial expansion became almost inevitable.[26]

There was a more direct version too.

> It should be first premised that for the annexation of their territory, the Nagas themselves are responsible. The cost of administration of the district is out of all proportion to the revenue that is obtained, and we only occupied the hills after a bitter experience, extending over many years, which clearly showed that annexation was the only way of preventing raids upon our villages. . . . It was impossible for any civilized power to acquiesce in the perpetual harrying of its border folk.[27]

The naivette of the regional historiography of north-east India is reflected in the contention that the annexation of the Naga or Mizo Hills was a historical accident. It only carries forward the colonial argument that the British had no intentions of conquering these hills which were not only devoid of any natural resources but proved to be a liability to the them; it is only the 'barbarism' of the tribes which forced their conquest. Colonialism had not only conquered India, it had conquered Indian minds too. While the mainstream historiography had been able to by and large decolonize itself, the regional counterpart could not yet do so. The absence of motives, plans, strategies, benefits in the conquest of Naga-Mizo Hills was seen as a legitimization of the colonial argument. It not only refuses to acknowledge the reality of 'conquests' but undermines the nature and strength of imperialism itself. The story of the conquest of the Naga/Mizo tribes lasting about a century, which imperialism described as 'one long sickening story of open insults and defiance, bold outrages and cold blooded murders on the one side and long-suffering forbearance, forgiveness, concession and unlooked favours on the other',[28] goes a long way to prove this.

In fact, an appropriate phrase to describe this historiographical situation would be missing 'the wood for the trees'. The fact that the hills were occupied and devastated was overlooked and the emphasis was on whether the British had any motive for the conquest or not. Did the British ever publicize or profess their intentions at any stage of their conquering spree in India? Similarly, imperialist concepts such as non-intervention, non-interference and non-regularizations were uncritically accepted without inquiring into their epistemological background or imperial legitimization.[29] It is said that the Inner Line Regulation Act was a device to safeguard the identity of the tribals, though their identity was never discussed in the Inner Line Regulation document.[30] The primary motive, as shown later, was to restrict the European planters from occupying and converting tribal lands into tea plantations and secondly to stop Indian merchants from encroaching on the trades that were the monopoly of the tribals like collection of rubber, ivory, tribal salt and other forest products.[31] These studies themselves have revealed that despite the claims of non-interference, the British did interfere with the life of the tribals. It is also said that the roots of the insurgency movements in north-east India lay in the fact that these tribes never participated in the nationalist movement and were isolated from the mainstream of Indian life. By doing so, this historiography only succeeded in reinforcing the ideas that colonial administrators had drilled into the minds of the tribals instead of examining or countering it.

There was this false propagation by the colonialists that to be considered a part of India one had to be either Hindu or Muslim or at least be influenced by them. It was never pointed out that the spread of Hindu culture is South-East Asia did not make them part of India. At the same time the advent of Islam has not only turned a large chunk of Indian population into Muslims but also rejuvenated Indian culture and civilization. So was the case with Christianity which arrived in India as early as AD 52, much before it did in some of the Christian States themselves and enriched Indian heritage. It is not true that Christianity came only with colonialism. In fact if the Nagas or Lushais had escaped these influences, it only proves the diversity and strength of Indian civilization. What is also to be remembered is that Hinduism spread in most far-flung areas of India not only because the monarchs of these regional kingdoms embraced it personally but adopted it as the State religion to legitimize their rule. Assam, Manipur and Tripura are classic examples of it. The tribals under discussion were yet to develop any such kingship, which could facilitate such Hinduization.

What is also a striking failure of the regional historiography was to point out that British rhetoric about the tribals of north-east India being non-Indian was a phenomenon of the 1940s, except for the two memoranda submitted to the Simon Commission in 1928 again by British Officials themselves. After the declaration of British withdrawal in the face of growing hostility from Indians, there was an increasing apprehension in the minds of the tribals about their future amidst people who, they were told were aliens. With the Plan Balkan on, the British perhaps wanted to retain as much of India as possible under their suzerainty as colonies. The 'tamed' tribals were an easy target. Picking up on the legitimate fears of the tribals, some of these imperialist administrators mooted a plan of creating a Crown-Colony Protectorate or a Trust Territory comprising the tribal areas which would be a British colony. Robert Reid, the Assam Governor (1937-42), L.S. Amery the Secretary of State for India and Myanmar, and Reginald Coupland, an Oxford professor were some of those involved in this conspiracy. They were inspired by the thesis put forward by J.H. Hutton, N.E. Parry and A.G. McCall. It is in the light of this 'Crown-Colony' that the British viewed these tribes being different from other Indians and described them as non-Indian although until then they themselves had ruled the tribals as part of India. But the Labour Government in Britain which has inherited an economy devastated by the war, did not entertain the proposals of a Crown-Colony and wanted to be rid of India as early as possible. So not only did the Crown-Colony plan fizzle out, even the declared date of British withdrawal (June 1948) was advanced to August 1947. If the 'secessionists' today appropriate the rhetoric of the imperialists and put forward the same arguments, it is not that they are historical facts, but because they were never countered by nationalist historiography. The nationalists directed their attention elsewhere thereby imposing another false historiographical consciousness on the people. Jawaharlal Nehru, for example, polularized the idea that the tribals were anti-Indian because 'they (the tribals) never experienced the sensation of being in a country called India and they were hardly influenced by the struggle for freedom or other movements in India. Their chief experience of outsiders was that of British officers and Christian missionaries who generally tried to make them anti-Indian.'[32]

The refusal to accord the Naga and Mizo anti-colonial movements—a bloody war which lasted little less than a century the status of being a part of the Indian freedom struggle was not only reflective of the 'elitist bias' of the Indian nationalist historiography but also resulted in alienating the tribals. It is high time that the understanding of Indian freedom struggle underwent some changes in the north-east Indian historiography. And that Indian freedom struggle does not merely consist of the Gandhian movements. The Khasi war against the British (1829-33), the Jaintia rebellion (1860-2) or the Naga-Lushai (1832-98) fights against the British conquerors were as anti-colonial as the Gandhian movements. In fact, when the elites of the country were organizing the first session of the Indian National Congress the Nagas and Lushais were still fighting a life and death war against the mighty British Empire.

Regional history has a specialized role in raising the consciousness of its people. But in the process it should not become 'regionalist'. K.M. Panikkar's caution is most appropriate for regional historians in this context:

> I would make one appeal to Indian Historians and that is, not lend themselves to the heresy of elevating regional glories as a result of their specialisation with certain period or certain areas. Every region of India has contributed to the evolution of the Indian people, every group added to our common heritage. Every part of India has its heroic period and forgetting this the historians have contributed to the false pride resulting from the glorified self-image of our different areas. This is the most dangerous development which one has especially to guard against.[33]

NOTES

1. Sajal Nag, 'Withdrawal Syndrome: Secessionism and Insurgency in Post-Colonial India', Occasional Paper, Surat: Centre for Social Studies, 1993.
2. Urmila Phadnis, *Ethnicity and Nation-Building in South Asia*, Delhi: Sage, 1990, pp. 133-47.
3. R.J. Moore, *Endgames of the Empire: Studies of Britain's Indian Problem*, Delhi: OUP, 1988, p. 174.
4. Sumit Sarkar, *Modern India*, Delhi: Macmillan, 1983.
5. Borrowed from European History, this expression was used in the context of Assam by H.K. Barpujari. But subsequently it was used by a number of authorities, e.g. Suhas Chatterjee, *Mizoram Under British Rule*, Delhi: Mittal, 1985, pp. 180-1.
6. H.K. Barpujari, *Problems of the Hill Tribes: North East Frontier*, Vol. I, Gauhati: Lawyers, 1970; Vol. II, Gauhati: United, 1976; Vol. III, Gauhati: Spectrum, 1981.
7. Alexander Mackenzie, *Memorandum on the North East Frontier*, Calcutta: Govt. of Bengal, 1884.

8. R.B. Pemberton, *Report on the Eastern Frontier of British India*, Calcutta: Govt. of Bengal, 1835.
9. A.J.M. Mills, *Report on the Khasi and Jaintia Hills*, Calcutta: Govt. of Bengal, 1901.
10. Woodthrope, *Lushai Expedition 1871-72*, London: C. Hurst & Blacket, 1873.
11. Niddham, *Report on the Trip into Abor Hills*, Shillong, 1885.
12. Robert Reid, *History of the Frontier Areas Bordering Assam*, Shillong: Eastern Publishers, 1934.
13. S.K. Bhuyan, *Anglo-Assamese Relations, 1717-1826*, Gauhati: Govt. of Assam, Directorate of Historical & Antiquarian Studies, 1949.
14. *Proceedings of the North East India History Association, 1980-90*, volumes, passim.
15. J.B. Bhattacharjee, *The Garos and the English*, Delhi: Radient, 1978.
16. Suhas Chatterjee, *Mizoram Under British Rule*, Delhi: Mittal, 1985.
17. Helen Giri, *Khasis Under British Rule*, Shillong: Regency, 1999.
18. Hamlet Bareh, *History and the Culture of the Khasi People*, Calcutta: Author, 1967.
19. Laxmi Devi, *Ahom-Tribal Relations*, Gauhati: Gauhati University, 1968.
20. Milton Sangma, *History and the Culture of the Garos*, Delhi: Oriental, 1981.
21. O.P. Kejariwal, 'North-East in Indian Historiography: The Need for a Corrective', *Proceedings of the North East India History Association*, Pashighat, 1987, pp. 17-84.
22. Ibid.
23. O.P. Kejariwal, 'The Indian History Congress and Historical Research in North East India', *Proceedings of the North East History Association*, Kohima, 1987, pp. 33-81.
24. David Reid Syiemlieh, *British Administration in Meghalaya: Policy and Pattern*, New Delhi: Heritage, 1989, p. 11.
25. A.G. McCall, *Lushai Chrysalis*, London: Luzac & Co., 1949.
26. Edward Gait, *History of Assam*, Calcutta: Thacker Spink & Co., 1906 (reprint 1984).
27. B.C. Allen, *Assam District Gazetteer: Nagaland and Manipur*, Shillong: Govt. of Assam, 1905.
28. John Butler, 'Rough Notes on Angami Nagas', *Journal of Asiatic Society of Bengal*, Vol. 44, No. 4, 1875, pp. 307-27. Cited in Asoso Yonuo, *The Rising Nagas: A Historical and Political Study*, Delhi: Vivek, 1974, p. 72.
29. Sajal Nag, Review of David Reid Syiemlieh, op. cit., in *Indian Historical Review*, forthcoming.
30. Ibid. Also see Innerline Regulation Act, 1873 Document.
31. Ibid.
32. Jawaharlal Nehru, 'A Note by the Prime Minister on His Tour of the North Eastern Frontier Areas', 15-18 October 1952, p. 4.
33. K.M. Panikkar quoted in Tarasankar Banerjee 'Changing Pattern of Indian Historiography and North East India: An Evaluative Approach', General President Address, North East India History Association, Imphal, 1990.

CHAPTER ONE

The Backdrop

Although it is customary to provide a general background of the area under study for the readers' benefit, India's north-east is one periphery which really needs a detailed introduction for the mainlanders. This is illustrated by the reaction of my friend on his first visit to the north-east as he exclaimed, 'it seems to be altogether a different world'. This introduction is also essential as a backdrop in understanding the developments in the late colonial and post-colonial period which we shall be examining in this study.

THE NAGA, MIZO AND MEITHEIS

Nagaland, Mizoram and Manipur are the three major units of north-east India and are among the tiniest states in the Indian Union inhabited by the Nagas, Mizos and the Meitheis respectively. According to the 1991 Census these three communities: the Nagas, Mizos, and the Meitheis who were supposed to have challenged the might of the gigantic Indian State only had a population of 12,15,573, 6,86,217 and 18,26,914 respectively. Nagaland and Manipur form the eastern-most boundary of India sharing their frontier with Myanmar while Mizoram shares its frontier with both Myanmar and Bangladesh. The present state of Nagaland with an area of 6,366 sq. km, is situated on a chain of mountains extending from the Chittagong Hill tracts to the Patkai ranges and joined by the north-eastern offshoot of the Himalayas. Adjoining a part of the Chin Hills and Arakan-Yoma mountain range, Nagaland comprises three massive mountain ranges running parallel to each other from north to south—the Barail, the Naga and the Patkai with an altitude ranging between 660 metres and 4,220 metres above sea-level. Nagaland has Assam as its neighbour on the north-west, Manipur on the south, Myanmar on the east and Arunachal Pradesh on the north-east. Mizoram shares 70 per cent of its frontier with two foreign countries on three sides, Myanmar and Bangladesh. Only portion on its west is joined by Tripura and on its north is the Barak Valley of Assam—the only road-link with the rest of India. Mizoram's territory covers an area of 21,087 sq. km. Manipur also has Myanmar on its eastern and southern borders while on the west it is bound by Assam and Nagaland on the north. Out of the 22,327 sq. km of its total area only 1,012 sq. km constitute the plain valley area, the rest of the area consists of the surrounding rugged hills. The people of all the three states are of the Indo-Mongoloid stock with variations. Although the inhabitants of Nagaland state are known as the Nagas—it is a generic name given by the plains people to them. In other words Nagas are not single tribe, there are at least thirteen tribes within Nagaland (excluding Arunachal Pradesh) who are known by their distinctive tribal names. Some of the major tribes are Ao, Angami, Sema, Chakesang, Rengma, Lotha, Chang, Konyak, Tangsa, Tangkhul, Mao, and Zeliangrong—(combining the Zemi, Liangmai and Rongmei groups). Similarly, though the inhabitants of Mizoram are Mizos to outsiders, the word Mizo does not denote one single tribe. It is a generic term given to a conglomeration of tribes, e.g. the Lushai, Pawis (Poi), Lakher, Paite, Ralte, Hmars and Chakmas. The state of Manipur is inhabited by the Naga-Kuki tribes in the hills while the plains are inhabited by the Meitheis. The Meitheis are more or less a homogeneous ethnic group with no division in ethnic terms within itself. But the hills' people belong to distinctive tribes. While many of them belong to Naga tribes/sub-tribes others claim affiliation to the Mizo group. Despite the massive diversity and heterogeneity the common feature that these tribal and ethnic groups share is their Indo-Mongoloid origin as against the Indo-Aryans of the rest of India. This made them distinguishable physical types to begin with, which is evident from the description of these people in Sanskrit literature in blanket terms as *kirats*, *asuras*, *danavas*, *kuvachas* and *mlecchas*. The Aryan perception of these groups can be seen from what is recorded in the *Padmapurana*. 'The *mlechchas* as barbarians are accustomed to eat everything. They are idiotic and kill cows and Brahamans. These other *mlechchas-kuvachas* have their birth place in the hills. Their language is of *pishacha* character. They have no (good) social practices.'[1] Thus linguistic, physiological and geographical factors were also considered to distinguish the non-Aryans from the Aryans. Although other Indo-Mongoloid tribals of the area like the Bodos, Koches, Kacharis, Chutiyas, Ahoms, Tripuris, Meitheis all gradually came into the fold of the Sanskritization and Hinduization process afoot all over India, the Nagas were not touched by this wave due to their geographical distance and strict exclusivity and so were the

Mizos who were relative late comers in the region. The Tibeto-Burmese speaking Mongolian race—loosely termed as Nagas—were a neolithic people and had come from Myanmar. They also with other allied tribes like the Karen, Kachin, Singpho, Chin, and Shan had settled in Myanmar after migrating from western China. It was the Mao, Angami, Sema, Rengma, Rongmei, and Lothas who migrated in course of the first five waves of migrations to the south Manipur-Nagaland regions. The second wave of migrations comprised the Aos Changs, Sangthams and Tangkhuls. Even when the British made their appearance on the Scene there was a marked movement of people from the Chin-Lushai Hills towards the plains of India. The exodus was believed to have begun as early as AD 1283 with the Tai invasion of Myanmar. The Mizos settled in the Kabaw Valley of Myanmar were forced to flee. The Tai invasion not only compelled the Mizos to flee Myanmar but also fragmented them into smaller groups. They wandered about in the Chin Hills looking for a place to settle down during the fourteenth century and from this point they went up further west to the Manipur Valley in the fifteenth and sixteenth centuries. In the seventeenth century they settled in the Tian Valley from and moved over during the same period to present-day Mizoram. These late migrants to the region were surrounded by the Aryan population settled in the plains which constituted an outlet for the tribes to collect scarce items of requirement as well as to prove their might. Interestingly, like the Aryans, these tribals too viewed the plains people contemptuously whom they considered weak, uncivilized and look alikes. In fact, many of these groups had their own names for the plains people, the Mizos called them *vais*, the Khasis *dkhar*, the Garos *achang*, the Meitheis *mayang*, the Minyangs *ayeng*, the Gallongs *nipak*, and the Ao Nagas *thumar*. The antipathy between these tribes in the north-eastern hills and the people of the plains was mutual, each looking down on the other but the two were hopelessly dependent on each other.

PRE-COLONIAL ECONOMIC AND POLITICAL LIFE

The integration of the distinct tribal economy of the Nagas and the Mizos into the orbit of the greater colonial economy formed the basis of the advent of a modern economy in the region and that of modern identity formation. Prior to the appearance of such a system, the Mizos and the Nagas generally operated in what can be described as a primitive economy with certain variations. Their mode of production displays a primitive form of collectivism both in production and consumption due to the underdeveloped state of productive forces. Both the tribes were still essentially food gatherers. Theoretically, the primitive mode of production is marked by the following characters (a) the orginazation of labour partly on an individual basis (the small family) and partly on a collective basis (large family, the clan, the village). The essential means of production being land, it was collectively owned by the clan and all its members were allowed to cultivate it according to the rules of assignment of plots of land to each household; (b) the absence of commodity exchanges and correlative with this: (c) the distribution of the products within the group in accordance with rules that are closely related to the kinship organization.[2] In practice however,

> The different forms of commune or tribe members' relation to the tribes land and soil to the earth where it was settled depend partly on the natural inclinations of the tribe, and partly on the economic conditions in which it relates as proprietor to the land and soil in reality, i.e. in which it appropriates its fruits through labour and the latter itself depend on climate, physical make-up of the land and soil, the physically determined mode of its exploitation, the relation with the hostile tribes or neighbour-tribes and the modifications which migrations, historic experiences, etc., introduce.[3]

Karl Marx often reiterated, that 'Primitive communes are not all fashioned on the same lines. On the contrary they form a series of social groupings which differ as much as types as by age and which represent successive stages of social evolution.'[4]

Both the Naga and Mizo economies with the exception of some advanced sub-tribes of the Nagas, by and large, had the following characteristics:

(i) A de-commercialized agricultural sector in which the organization of labour and means of production bore close resemblance to the theoretical description of primitive communes. Agriculture was most primitive (called *jhooming*) in north-east India. Those who practised wet-rice cultivation, like the advanced Naga tribes, could commercialize it to some extent as slavery was prevalent—people from the plains were captured through raids and attacks were put to work. But slavery did not play a dominant role in the mode of production. They were more to prove the power of the tribes to the plains people and sometimes for securing technology. These slaves did not constitute a major source of labour nor did they initiate a structural change facilitating a transition to a slave-owning mode of production.

(ii) A home-based industrial sector having an auxiliary role in the economy where family acted as the nuclear group.

(iii) Simple commodity relations with other tribal/sub-tribal groups; and

(iv) Raids and plunder in the outer zones.

The Mizos lived by rice cultivation and hunting. The method of cultivation was the primitive system of slash and burn, called '*jhooming*'. Since there was a paucity of plain lands in these hills, the hill people evolved a pattern of cultivation in which the elevated slopes of its ridges were usually cleared off the jungle and burnt during winter. During the next monsoon they would sow paddy and other seeds with the help of a plough stick. After the harvest the land would be left fallow for few years and another plot selected for *jhooming*. Though the method of cultivation was called *jhooming*, the Mizos did not give any name to it. In Myanmar it is called *taunya*. The following five are the characteristics of this system of cultivation: (1) Rotation of field, (2) Keeping the land fallow for a number of years, (3) Use of human labour as the chief input, (4) Non-employment of animal, and (5) Use of very crude and simple implements. This method of cultivation was the backbone of the Lushai economy, which made the Mizos a migratory tribe, their villages were not stationary. They went to changed new locations at regular intervals. Salt was produced from salt springs and often this scarce commodity led to wars between two tribes. The Mizo Hills being full of wild animals the Mizos were good hunters. Rice was the staple food and meat was a regular item on the menu. The meat of the tamed bison (mithun), deer and pigs were the favourite food of the Mizos. Barter was a prevalent system. Scarcity of land and food often made the Mizos hardpressed. The clash of economic interests led to frequent inter-tribal feuds. Economic necessity was also the reason for frequent Mizo raids on the plains from where they generally picked up necessary consumption items as well as slaves. Slaves were an important part of the Mizo economy and society. The Mizos lived in villages (*khua*) inhabited by 500-700 people. While locating a suitable site for a new village the hunters in the community would consider a variety of factors like abundance of land for *jhooming*, proximity to drinking water, protection form enemies and so on. Since the Mizos were constantly on the move, they hardly possessed any property except for their Mithun and chickens. Food production included *jhooming*, fishing and hunting.

The Nagas practised both *jhooming* and wet rice cultivation. Wet cultivation was done through the method of terracing. The lower hills were terraced in a pattern through organized cooperative labour. Each layer was irrigated by means of an effective construction of a chain of channels linked with successive layers. It retained the required amount of water and drained the excess to the next terrace. These channels were constructed along the contours of the hills through long distances and have been in use for hundreds of years. This method was used by the somewhat advanced tribes like the Angami, Mao, Sema and Tangkhuls. The less advanced tribes generally followed the slash and burn method of cultivation, same as the Mizos did. Besides cultivation, fishing and hunting was the other important feature of their mode of production. An important aspect of the Naga economy was the barter of their forest-products with the people in the Assam-plains coupled with raids on those plains.

The Meitheis being inhabitants of a plain area had a much advanced mode of production. In fact it was a transitional phase advancing towards a feudal economy. And be described as a quasi-feudal structure where features of primitive Communism had not yet disappeared. The rain-abundant alluvial valley was a rice economy, and state intervention in the production process was necessary. The state performed its function by enumerating the entire male population of the kingdom which was required to render services to the state, in turns, through public works which included the constitution of a massive irrigation network and its maintenance. Agriculture was the mainstay of the economy and the method and technology of production was fairly developed compared to those of the neighbouring communities. There were two fundamental forms of cultivation: (1) *Punghul*, in which seeds were directly sown in well-ploughed fields. (2) *Lingaba* in which the seedlings from the nurseries were transplanted in well-prepared fields. Both are extensively used in Manipur. The tools and implements of cultivation were those used in eastern Bengal. Bullocks and buffaloes were used to plough the land. Iron tipped single-hoe, *langol* or plough, *kangpat* or sledge, *ukai* or harrow, *humai* or fan for winnowing the paddy, *chairong* or paddy-thresher were among the important implements of cultivation. During the nineteenth century the king had predominant claim and authority over state land though remnants of the earlier communal forms of ownership was also prevalent. The king granted lands of various demoninations to a number of officials, sepoys, Brahmins and royalty. The *inkhol* was homestead land, and the *tauna* cultivable rice land. Although the *inkhol* lands were revenue-free these could be sold and inherited and the king could not confiscate it from the owner. But the *tauna* (*lou*) lands could not be sold. Most government employees were granted land in lieu of their salaries. The royal land grants to the nobles and spiritual aristocracy led to the growth of the rich and powerful feudal landlord class. Slaves were available to cultivate the lands of the royalty as well as the aristocracy both spiritual and temporal. The peasants were bound to render labour services to the state under the *lallup* system. Weaving, knitting, basket making were part of the cottage industry, internal commerce was extensive but external trade was minimal. The feudalization of this transitional economy was strengthened by Hinduization of the society through a process, which D.D. Kosambi described as 'feudalism from above'.[5] A new class of spiritual and temporal aristocracy—equivalent to the feudal lords—emerged after the king's adoption of Hinduism as the State religion.

The political life of the Mizos was typical of any tribal formation. It centred round the village chief, in case of the Mizos it was the *lal*. A *lal* was the head of the clan and was the most important functionary in the Mizo political system. He was assisted by the village elders like *upa* or *mantris*. Every chief had his separate cantonment, with a number of dependent villages attached to it. These cantonments consisted of strong men who could be mobilized into fighting a garrison under the order of a chief. In matters relating to public interest he would consult his brothers or subordinate chief. All public business was conducted from his *zawlbuk* or the office which was at once a public house and a protected fortress. Generally the youngest son inherited the chieftainship and other sons had the right to set up new village with their own followers. The chief had to be the best warrior in a village, a strong man who could offer people protection, judgement and guidance. Politics was based on daily life, there were some groups who would try to get special favours from the chiefs. Both warfare and raids on other villages or the plains area was a part of this political life.

The permanent political institution of the Naga society was the village. The Semas, Konyaks and Maos had hereditary chieftainship (monarchy) while the Aos had a council of elected headmen called the *tatar* which constituted the government. The Angamis, Lothas and Rengmas were nominally governed by the kings or chieftains of their respective villages who were chosen for their bravery in war, skilful diplomacy, wealth in the form of cattle, and power of oratory. This was in contrast to the hereditary system where the eldest or youngest son succeeded his father. Being the head of the village the king or chieftain—considered to be the repository of God's favour—commanded peoples' obedience and had special powers and certain privileges. The chief had to ensure the observance of the village laws which was not a command of the chief but based on the Naga customs. He was responsible for peace and tranquility in the village, and also dealt with foreigners directly.

In contrast to the Nagas and Mizos, the Meitheis had a full-fledged feudal monarchy in which the king was the head of secular and spiritual matters. The chief feature of this rule was that a wide monarchical paraphernalia consisting of the king's immediate brothers and sons played a crucial role. The 'heads' of the clans were associated with administrative tasks. The day-to-day administration of the state was vested in the *Darbar* which included most of the important officers of state. The immediate younger brother of the king would be the *yuvaraj* or heir-apparent to the throne, and the brother next to the *yuvaraja* would be the *senapati* or commander of the army. In the nineteenth century Manipuri political setup, the law and primogeniture was not observed and hence there was no specific trends of succession to the throne. Consequently there was intense rivalry among the claimants to the throne. Appointment to high offices seemed to depend virtually on the wishes of the king. Between 1834-66 there were as many as fifteen attempts to overthrow the king. There was no separation of executive and judicial powers in the strict sense. All the *Darbar* members were ex-officio members of the *cheirap* court—the highest court of justice. Traditional customary laws were the basis of judgement and the most common forms of punishment were death for murder and treason, and exile (to *loi*) for women committing adultery. There was another court called *pacha* or women's court, in which all women related disputes were dealt with. Common cases included divorce and adultery. The punishment for adultery was *khungoinaba* (social ostracization) and exile to *loi* villages. In the villages there were traditional clubs called *singlups*, and all the villagers were supposed to be members of such clubs. The *singlups* were essentially meant to serve the socio-economic needs of the villages. The village headmen, who was appointed by the king for the realization of the feudal labour service and other taxes, would take charge of such *singlups*.

Tribes or ethnic groups like the Meithies were absolutely apolitical and had no interest in modern politics introduced by the British in India. While the rest of Indians had ample time and preliminary training in preparing themselves for participation in the bourgeois political process, these groups had been confined within their own system. The British felt it unnecessary to open and train them to the new system but even the Indian State did not provide time to training to join the rest of India as we shall see later in this study.

RELIGIOUS PRACTICES

When the Naga Club submitted its memorandum to the Simon Commission in 1929, it stated that the Nagas had nothing in common with the people of India who were either Hindus or Muslims. This was quite right as can be seen from the details of their religious practices. Even though Hinduism itself in many respects an advanced form of animism and nature-worshipping, Hindus tended to look down on these tribes for their 'tribal' religious practices.

The Mizo tribes were generally 'pagan' in their religious beliefs. They believed in a supreme being known as *Pathian*, and that there were numerous *ramhuis* (demons). They also worshipped a spirit less powerful than *Pathian* named *Khuarang*. However, the Paite Kulkis who lived under the raja of Tripura had adopted Hindu religious practices. The Mizos buried their dead along with a few hunted heads as they believed that the chief would require slaves in the next world. Similarly, the Naga tribes generally were animists who believed in an invisible God as the creator of all earthly things. According to them there are white gods (lower in status) who stood for everything good and black gods who stood for everything evil. There were also gods of earth, sun, sky, light, fire, wind and so on. These gods were supposed to maintain everyday records of the words and deeds of man and assign rewards for good and punishment for evil deeds. In order to propitiate and exorcize the evil gods and spirits the Nagas would offer pigs, liquor, eggs, etc., in sacrifice. Tribal taboos were observed and also ritual ceremonies, prayers, and incantations, were performed by the Nagas to prolong life, recover from illness, ward off evil and destroy or harm enemies. They also believed in life after death, the immortality of soul and ancestor worship.

The Meitheis believed in a religion called *Sanamahi* before the Manipuri King Pamheiba adopted Hinduism in 1714 and declared it as the state religion. The imposition of Hinduism from above and the anti-caste and anti-ritualistic character of Vaishnavism helped the spread of Hinduism among the Meitheis. Though many Hindu sects were active in Manipur it was Chaintanyite Vaishnavism which was accepted by the king. By the nineteenth century Hinduism was firmly established despite opposition from the supporters of the traditional religion. Along with it the Meithei society adopted—not too stringently—some of the pollution-purification and ritualistic practices of Hinduism like the caste system, sati, purdah, prohibition on food and drink. All Manipuris became either Kshatriyas or Brahmins. Besides Hindus, a small portion of the population were Muslims as well. This was a result of the Mughal-Manipur interaction.

TRIBES IN INDIAN CIVILIZATION: THE INTERACTION

The protagonists of the separation of tribes from the Indian State often put forward the theory that these tribes have never been a part of India to legitimize their position. Despite the mutual dislike and suspicion between the tribals and the plainsmen, it would be a historical fallacy to believe that the tribes did not form a part of the Indian civilization as can be seen in this examination of their role in the Indian context.

The term 'tribe' and its subsequent conceptualization is as recent a phenomenon as the colonial period. During this period, colonialists-turned-anthropologists began categorizing social groups—based on colonialist parameters—which were in a relatively backward stage of advancement as 'tribes'.[6] Although identifying communities as tribals is a recent phenomenon, tribes have played a significant role in all the civilizations that history of mankind witnessed. In the 21 civilizations that Toynbee examines, he traces the process of civilization 'exerting influence' and 'drawing into its orbit' the 'outlying barbarian societies' which were described as its 'pre-civilizational neighbours'. Toynbee also related the process how the same group emerged as the *external proletariat* as against *internal proletariat* to bring about the collapse of many a civilization.[7]

In the Indian context, people whom we today refer to as tribals were known as '*janas*'. which mean 'communities of people'. Although most of these aboriginals were subsumed by the *jati* system of the powerful Aryans, some of the *janas*, whom we call tribe, continued to remain outside the control of the *jati* system of the social organization. The so-called 'tribals' of India were the indigenous, autochthonous people of the land before Aryans penetrated India. The Aryans in course of their settlement in India had settled as agricultural people, mastered the technology of settled agriculture, developed a highly capable language, evolved ideas and institutions of a political system as seen in *sabha samiti* and *parishad* as well as a social system (as seen in the *varna-jati* system) and a set of religious ideas, principles and institutions known as Brahmanical Hinduism. All these developments took place while some of the pre-Aryan *janas* were still in the food-gathering stage. Practising slash and burn (*jhoom*) and hoe cultivation. They lived in isolated settlements, spoke a variety of languages, belonged to a variety of physical types and practised some kind of pagan cults. The pressure of the conquering and expanding Aryans pushed them to the remote, inaccessible regions, forests, and fringe and frontier areas to escape assimilation. The task was difficult because not only the technological power of the Aryans was superior, their socio-political institutions also proved stronger than that of the aborigines. Once they were caught in the production system of the *jati* it was no longer possible for them to resist its social implication. That is what happened to Tibeto-Burmese stock of *janas* in north-east India. But some continued to live far away in the inaccessible frontier areas and continued to resist these assimilation processes. These were the *janas* who are found in the eastern and north-eastern frontier of India. Some of them were not even enumerated in the country's history or historical geography except for the Nagas who were mentioned by Ptolemy in the second century AD. The *kiratas* was the blanket name given to these frontier tribals of north-east India.

> Assam (formerly north-east) forms a part of the great land of India which could not be always in the limelight because of its geographical position in the extreme corner of vast country. . . . Yet Assam was never wholly isolated from the rest of India and at times loomed large in Indian History and politics. . . .[8]

Assam formed a highway not only for trade but also for the movement of people and exchange of ideas between India, Myanmar and south-west China from at least the closing centuries of the first millennium BC. The prehistoric stage of Indian history continued longer in the eastern frontier including Assam and since time immemorial there were movements of people in the region. Different branches of the great Sino-Tibetan speaking people from the Yang-Tse-Kiang and Hwang-Ho river areas were pushed down south and west probably 200 BC onwards and some of these tribal groups infiltrated into India mostly along the western coast of Brahmaputra.

The great Bodo tribe appears to have been established over the valley of the Brahmaputra fairly early and to have extended into the north and east Bengal, and into north Bihar. The north Assam tribes of the Abors and Akas, Dafflas and Miris and Mishmis appear to have come later and established themselves in the mountains of the Brahmputra Valley. There were some Austric and Dravidian tribes who preceded the Bodos in the area. Finally we have the incursions of some Kuki-Chin tribes into south Assam. Assam was thus open to all the tribal movements from the east, including the advent of the Tibeto-Chinese, and Tibeto-Burmese speaking Mongoloids into India, and it was in Assam primarily that this great element in the formation of the Indian people became largely Indianized. Certain Tibeto-Burmese and Sino-Tibetan speaking Mongoloid tribes become part of the settled population of Assam since time immemorial and had come within the orbit of Indian civilization at a fairly-early age. Although remotely connected with the Mongoloid people of Myanmar, China and Tibet, they have acquired a special niche in the hall of Indian *penplades* and have long been separated from the countries of origin. The Nagas belong to India as much as the Mishmis, Miris; Daflas, Akas and Abors. To the Europeans they were known as Mongoloid and to the Sanskrit-using Indians as *kiratas*, *asuras*, *danavas* and *mlecchas*. In fact, most of the important ruling clans of the region belonged to these groups. Bhagadatta, the legendary king of ancient Assam was the son of Naraka, the Asura and was the captain of the *cina-kira-mleccha*.[9] The dynasty of Pushyavarman belonged to this clan. Salasthambha was also a *mlecchadhipathi*. The Pala's also belonged to the same stock. The terms *kirata*, *danava*, *mleccha* were applied to these early rulers and their kinsmen by the Aryans to denote their non-Aryan origin.

The Meitheis were the most advanced section of the 'Kuki-Chin people' whose ultimate homogeneity with the Nagas and Kukis of the hills is undoubted. 'Two hundred year ago in internal organisation, religion, habits and manners the Meitheis were as the hills people are now.'[10] The Manipur Valley most probably had been occupied by several tribes which had come from different directions, the principal among them being the Koomal, Looang, Miorang and Meithei. For a time the Koomal appeared to have been the most powerful and with their decline the Moirang tribe takeover. But soon the Meitheis subdued the whole group which came to be known as Meithei. The successive waves of foreign invasions of the Shan, Burmese, English and Hindu each left their permanent mark on these people who have passed finally from the stage of a relatively primitive culture into one of comparative civilization.

Since then the Meitheis have been playing the role of fringe communities in Indian civilization. Similarly, although the Mizos had migrated to Mizoram only in the seventeenth century south Cachar has been home to the original forest people to which the Puranas and *Mahabharata* testify. Suniti Kumar Chatterjee feels that like the Bodos, the Kukis of the Cachar frontier are the *kiratas* of ancient Indian history. In fact, the Kacharis claim to be descendents of Hidimba, the wife of Bhima which is of course a later day idea coined during the process of Sanskritization. It is a historical fact that these Tibeto-Burmese Mongoloid groups were the earliest settlers in north-east India and as such had close socio-economic contact with the people of the plains. In fact, the Mizos (specially the Lushai clan) have more interaction with the Bengalees than any of the other frontier tribes.[11] Hindu slaves (Bengalee men and women) were brought as captives through raids by the Lushai chiefs from the Cachar plains and later integrated into the Lushai society. The Kuki chiefs of Lalchukla clan had been important frontier officers of the rajas of Tripura, and Lalchukla's *mantris* could converse in Bengalee with the officials. The Lushais of Sylhet frontier had similar connections with the Hindus of Sylhet. It is also likely that the Kukis and Dimasas of Cachar intermarried.[12] Again, every year at the Silicoorie tea estate in South Cachar a *mela* is held in the honour of a Kuki saint Baram Baba—a local Kuki godman who had disciples among the plains people too. Bengalee words were introduced into the Mizo language wherever a new word was required, e.g. *motor* (motor vehicle), *duli* (*adhuli*, half a rupee), *lekhabu* (book), *panruang* (pan, betel-leaf), *kuva* (*gua*, betel nut), *monena* (chillies), *bawlbawa* (brinjal), *alu* (potato), *mula* (radish), *mistri* (carpenter), *lekhatui* (ink), *lhekhapuan* (paper), *tangka* (*taka*, rupee), etc. Even certain food habits and cultural traits of Bengalee were adopted by the Mizos from the inhabitants of Cachar and Sylhet including the habit of chewing betel leaf, cultivation and eating of rice and vegetable cultivation. In fact, when halted by the British the Mizos were migrating for settlements towards the plains of South Cachar in the foothills.

Systematic historical records of the Nagas are not available for the pre-Ahom period, except for some stray references. The slender accounts of the period of the Hindu kings of Kamrupa, between the fourth and twelfth centuries are silent regarding the Nagas. The first tribal settlements were those of the Nagas which the Ahoms came across in AD 1228 on their way to Assam after crossing the Patkoi range. Some Nagas did attempt to resist this advance but the powerful Ahoms defeated the tribal warriors and advanced towards the Brahmaputra Valley. For a temporary period this brought the Wanchu, Nocte, Tangsa, Konyak, Ao and Lothas under the control of Ahoms. The subsequent relationship between the Nagas and the Assamese were of amity as well as of hostility. The Nagas raids on the plains, head hunting as well as fights for the salt springs were some of the issues over which there were frequent warfare between the Nagas and the Ahom state followed by periods of peace and tranquility. Nagas living in areas bordering the Brahmaputra Valley plains had to submit and pay tribute to the Ahom kings in exchange for which they were granted revenue-free lands and fishing waters on the tacit understanding that they would not carry any predatory raids on the plains.[13] These lands were known as *naga-khats* and the officer in charge were *naga-katakis*. The Buranjis, however, referred to these Nagas tribes not by their tribal names but by names assigned to them by the Assamese, e.g. Khamjangias, Aitonias, Tablungias, Namchangias, etc. Commencing from the west, between Dayang and Dikhou rivers, the Naga tribes are known as the Panihatias (those who come by water), the Torhatias or Dayangias (those who come by land), the Hatigorias, Asiringias, Dupdorias and Namchangias. The first two are the sub-tribes of the Lothas and the rest are Aos. Between the river Dikhou and Buri-Dihing, the Naga tribes are known as the Tablungias, Jaktoongias, Moloongs, Changhois or Bhitar, Namchangias, Jobokas (Abhaypurias), Banferas, Mutonias, Paniduarias and Barduarias. Besides these some Nagas were known by the name of their native villages or simply as 'Nogas'. The Assamese names of these tribes originated either from the *duars* (passes) through which the particular group of Nagas descended into the plains or from the important Naga villages or places in the plains situated at or near the entrance of the passes.[14]

During the Ahom rule, for purposes of trade, the Naga tribes bordering the plains were in constant communication with the plains men. They would offer hill products like cotton, betel leaves, ginger and salt and in exchange take goods that were scarce in the hills. In fact the so-called self-sufficiency of the tribes was a myth as they were dependent on the plains for consumer products. Even the Ahom state partially depended on the Nagas as they were in possession of quite a few salt springs; though the proprietary rights of these springs were jointly held by the Nagas and the Ahoms quite often hostility broke out over these springs. Moreover, the constant Naga raids in the Assam plains and the abduction and kidnapping of the Ahom subjects prompted the latter to send repeated expeditions into the Naga villages. The Assamese came into contact with the Nagas of the Dayang Valley during the reign of Gadadhar Singha (AD 168-96). This Naga population was made up the Lothas who lived by the river side of Dayang. These Lothas were apparently loyal to the Ahom king and accepted Gadadhar Singha as their overlord and agreed to pay annual tribute to the Ahom king. As a part of the tribute the Nagas offered two of their princesses to the Ahom king. The relation was so cordial that during a crisis Gadadhar Singha kept his two sons in a Naga village for reasons of safety and security. Moreover the custom of adoption and matrimonial alliances with the hill tribes was practised during the Ahom regime. Sometimes the adopted children were placed in high positions. The Dupgaria Nagas presented three boys, Ao, Apam and Lachit to the Burha raja. References of many marital relationships between the Ahoms and the Nagas are found in the chronicles. For example the Dihingia raja had a son by a Naga woman and this son Tyachengumg was later made a minister. Supimha, son of Suhampha handed over one of his queens to a Naga chief for her misbehaviour. Dihingia raja offered Khunbaw, a Naga, an Ahom princess as a token of gratitude. In AD 1504 a treaty was concluded in which the Nagas acknowledged the supremacy of the Ahom king and promised to pay an annual tribute. A Naga chief arranged the wedding of his daughter to Suhungmung to strengthen their mutual relations. Moreover many Rengma Nagas had 'Cacharee and Assamese wives'. Sankardeva (AD 1449-1569) made a major contribution towards the amity between the people of the hills and plains. He adopted disciples from among the hill people, Norottam—a Naga, Gobinda—a Garo, and Balai—a Mikir were prominent among them. Even today some Naga villages in Sibsagar subdivision and Tirap district follow Hindu practices. The Nagas that migrated to the plains did not speak the Naga languages. The seven Sema villages at Margherita of Dibrugarh district, Latumgaon and Ligiri-Pukhuri Gaon (Konyak) at Sibsagar are notable in this respect. Linguistically these Nagas have merged with the plains people of Assam. Similarly, during the Mughal and Burmese invasions many Assamese who took refuge in the Naga villages (in Mokokchung and Kohima districts) were also assimilated with the Nagas. Such contacts and socio-economic intercourse enabled the Nagas to speak in broken Assamese which served as the medium of communication between the Nagas and the plainsmen. During British rule Assamese language was introduced in the schools of Nagaland, this further helped to spread the Assamese language in Nagaland which soon emerged as a pidginized language. Since each Naga tribe had its own district language which was unintelligible to others, they used this language in communicating amongst themselves. Soon it came to be known as Nagamese. And is in fact a living example of the Naga-Assamese socio-economic relationship. The Nagas bartered products such as salt, cotton, ivory, wax, Naga dao and medicinal herbs for rice, clothes, and beads from the plains. The Assamese reserved some agricultural farms and fisheries for the friendly Nagas called *bori* (friendly) as distinguished from *abori* (non-friendly). In fact, whenever the Nagas came down to the Assamese villages they were protected and it was customary to keep their spears at the house of the Assamese hosts (*naga-kataki*). On the other hand, the Naga-Meithei relationship was one of hostility. The Meitheis often tried to extend their suzeranity over the unwilling Nagas which resulted in a series of conflicts. As a result of Hinduization, the Meitheis kept the Nagas outside the social system as outcastes and considered them inferior.

Manipur has been described as an 'Oasis of Civilization' implying that it had achieved a high degree of civilization despite its isolation from the rest of India. It had a settled agriculture and production technology like the rest of the Indian plains. It had regular socio-economic and cultural contacts and exchanges with the Cachar Valley. In fact it was due to these exchanges that Hinduism was introduced in the Manipur Valley and had a very firm foothold by the eighteenth century. The adoption of Hinduism as a religion brought about a change in the social fabric too. It became a Hindu society complete with the Brahmanic ideology and its hierarchical structure. But the Meithei society was not exactly as Hindu as the one in the Ganga-basin. In Manipur there was a synthesis of the Brahmanic Hinduism and the traditional Sanamahi religion. It was in the fourth century AD that Brahmins migrated to the Manipur value and by the fourteenth century Brahmin priesthood was already established. From the eighth century onwards Puranic gods like Hari, Shiva, Ganesha and Vishwakarma made their appearance in the valley. By the turn of the century Hari replaced the pre-Hindu household God Atiya-Sidaba as the supreme God and imperceptibly the Vishnu cult made its way into the valley. It received further filip during the reign of Kyaamba (1467-1508). In 1704 the ruling prince Charai Rongba embraced Vaishnavism through the influence of one Krishnacharya, whose school of

Vaishnavism centred round the Radha-Krishna worship. During the reign of his son Pamheiba, re-christened as Garib Nawaj, the Chaitanya School also became active in Manipur. Later, another preacher Shanti Das arrived in Manipur who worshipped Rama as the supreme deity. And his sect was called Ramandi-Vaishnavites. This captured the imagination of Garib Nawaj who along with a number of palace retinues and nobles joined the Ramandi School which became the state religion. However, the Vaishnavism by which the Meithei Hindus ordered their lives still looked upon Krishna as their prime deity. The synthesis of this variety of Hindu religion and culture with that of the Meitheis gave rise not only to a new form of Vaishnavism but resulted in a new and unique culture. It gave rise to distinctive dance-forms, music and musical instruments, a distinctive *gotra* system, caste system, etc. The coming of Islam in Manipur was another important development. There was a continuous Muslim migration into Manipur from the seventeenth century AD. About 1,000 Muslims, captured and held as prisoners in AD 1606[15] during the rule of King Khagemba, were settled in the state. They were then given respective occupations and permitted to attend the *lallup*. They were known as *pangal* by the Meithei Hindus.[16] Soon there were inter-marriages and social interaction, and as a result some became Meitheis Muslims. There were about 40 Muslim sub-clans and a significant number of Islamic institutions in Manipur. Since then they have been an important part of the Meithei society.

THE PLAINS: NATURAL OUTLET FOR THE TRIBES

Although historical compulsions like physical and numerical weaknesses, inability to withstand hostile attacks from stronger neighbour and search for safer living shelter had pushed migratory tribes like the Nagas and Mizos (Lushais) to the hills, they were still increasingly dependent on the plains for sustenance. The plains at the foothills provided the tribes their natural outlets. As mentioned earlier, the tribes would come down to the foothills to barter their forest, agricultural and handicraft products for salt, iron, etc., which were not available in the hills. The plains were also happy hunting ground for the tribes for the perpetration of raids, kidnapping, head-hunting and slave-procurement. By colonial parameters these acts were an expression of 'barbarism', 'inhumanism' and 'low-civilization', but for the tribes these were essential components of their mode of living. Raids, were committed to procure consumer items which they could not afford to barter or otherwise procure. Slaves were procured by kidnapping to make up for manpower shortage in a tribal economy. These slaves were also a source for improved technology. Kidnapping was also necessary to procure women for tribal chiefs who needed to prove their might by such acts. Lastly head-hunting was necessary to procure human heads for the funeral rites of chiefs. After the acquisition of the *Dewani* of Bengal (1765) the Englishmen were horrified to witness these 'barbaric' acts and sought their immediate suspension. For example when Lalrina, a powerful Lushai chief died in 1843, his son Lalchukla raided the Kachubari area of Pratapgarh in Sylhet and carried away 22 heads and 6 captives including a girl to complete the morturial rites of his late father.[17] An event which would have been condoned in pre-British days, now provoked a punitive expedition from the British ensuing in life-long deportation of Lalchukla. Since British assumption of the administration of Sylhet in 1765, this was its first contact with the raiding Lushai tribes. Cachar was incorporated into British India in 1830 which brought them into closer contact with the Lushais. Similarly the annexation of the Brahmaputra Valley (1862) brought them into confrontation with the Nagas who were committing similar raids on the foothills. The British initially left the control of these raiding tribals to the kings of Tripura, Cachar and Manipur. Even though these respective kings claimed suzerainty over these tribes they virtually had no control over them. The tribes on their part claimed themselves to be free and sovereign people who exercised authority in the plains of the foothills.

This was a crucial period of history for the Naga and Mizo tribes. There were heavy migratory movements of the Thadou, Lushai, and Naga tribes in the Cachar area.[18] J.W. Edgar reported in 1840 that around that time the Lushais entered the hills of South Cachar and Manipur and drove the original inhabitants of the area—the Thalangums, the Changsels, the Thadous and Paites—away to the Hills of Cachar, Manipur and Tripura. Among the Naga tribes too there were increasing number of violent inter-tribal feuds for supremacy leading to warfare, devastation and head-hunting. Simultaneously there was also a discernible migratory movement of the tribes towards the plains—Cachar for the Mizo tribes and Brahmaputra Valley for the Naga tribes.[19] The increasingly difficult life of the hills, an increasing population and shortage of cultivable lands prompted northward expansion of the tribes towards new settlements in the plains. The advent of the British not only halted this migratory movement, it also encroached on its suzerain areas. For example, the

Nagas and Mizos had self-assumed authority over the foothill plains and villages where they committed regular raids. They not only considered raids as a display of their authority, they even imposed tributary levies on these villages which the terror-stricken villagers paid.

> Many of them advanced claims to rights more or less definite over lands lying in the plains; others claimed tributary payments from the villages below their hills or the services of the paiks, said to have been assigned to them by the Assam authorities. It mattered of course little to us whether these claims had their basis in primeval rights from which the Shan invaders had partially ousted the hillmen or whether they were expressions of Barbarian cupidity. Certain it was that such claims existed and that had been to some event and in some places, formally recognised by our predecessors.[20]

The advent of the British in the Valleys of Surma and Barak, and their attempt to derecognized and usurp the authority of the tribals were resented both by the Nagas and Mizos. They saw the situation had changed with the advent of the 'pale people' (the British), and woke up to the fact that the plains which was the natural outlet for them was not the same anymore. It had a new breed of people who not only objected to their 'acts' which were 'natural' but even sent armed expeditions into the hills and threatened their very survival. After returning from a fact-finding mission a Sizang delegation reported to a conference of their chiefs: 'These enemies (British) were different from other people, we have ever seen. They are as white as goats. They clothe themselves from head to foot. They cover their feet with leather and we believe they will not be able to climb the slopes of the hills (unlike us).'[21]

The tribals reacted violently through a series of raids, kidnapping and carried off heads as trophies. The Paite raid in Sylhet in 1827 which resulted in the killing of a few woodcutters was one such raid, and was committed as a protest against the withholding of the annual protection fee by the British police at Pratapgarh.[22]

INTRUSION

Not only had the British blocked the migratory movement of the tribes, restricted their expansion and free movement into the plains but even begun to trespass into their territory.[23] As early as 1832 the British endeavoured to survey the Naga Hills to find an alternative route through these hills to accomplish this goal to Manipur.

Capt. Jenkins, Pemberton and Gordon with 700 Manipuri troops and 800 porters entered the Naga Hills, and marched through the Mao and Angami villages from Imphal. The Nagas viewed this unauthorized trespassing as a prelude to invasion and vehemently opposed the march. A similar survey was conducted in the Lushai Hills too. The British even encouraged Gambhir Singh, the ambitious Manipuri king to annex the western Naga Hills and amalgamate it with Manipur. In a blatant display of authority over the tribals, the British often sent expeditions inside the hills, as in the Lushai Hills during 1826-49, even when there were inter-tribal warfare which was an internal affair of the tribals. In 1849 when the Lushais killed 20 Thadou Kuki captives, the British intervened and raised a Thadou Army of 200 men as a bulwark against further Lushai attacks. Very often British officers marched to the heart of both the Naga and Lushai Hills with their men armed with modern weaponery and unleashed a counter reign of terror. Large number of villages were burnt down, crop stocks, cattle and poultry destroyed and men-women were punished indiscriminately. While the tribes considered the villagers living on the foothills as their subjects, the British felt that it would do no good to their image to stand helplessly without protecting their subjects on the foothills. The English point of view was evident from the argument presented by Henry Hopkinson the Chief Commissioner of Assam, who did not favour the idea of non-interference, in the course of his correspondences (1862) with Cecil Beadon, the Lt. Governor of Bengal. The establishment of a British outpost in Samaguting (1847) and the posting of a British police officer there, the subsequent strengthening of the outpost and the establishment of further outposts at Khonoma (1850) and Kohima (1878), the heart of the Naga territory, was the ultimate display of British intrusion and authority as far as the Nagas were considered. The same was true of Lushai Hills too. Tribal life was associated with complete freedom, unrestricted movement and action, exclusiveness and insularity. Trespasses were aggressively retaliated. This was true of the Naga and Lushai tribes as well. They had an intuition that these intrusions were just a prelude to an invasion. They had also come to realize that this was not the same 'plains' that they used to interact with. The 'half cooked people' (as the British were described by the Nagas) not only had sinister motives, they were powerful too; they could even advance to the heart of their land and devastate them through 'promenades'—the British official term for punitive expeditions. The pent-up anger at such intrusion and suppression manifested itself in instances such as the retaliatory killing of Bhogchand Daroga of the Samaguting outpost (1849), the raids and brutal killings of the people associated with the British, and the tea gardens.

THE TEA FACTOR

The suspension of the Chinese tea supply to the East India Company led the British to a desperate search for an alternative source which resulted in the discovery of wild tea plants in Assam in 1823. It was immediately taken up for experimental plantation. A tea committee was formed by the government in early 1834, a government experimental tea garden was set up in 1836 and in December 1837 the first Assam tea was successfully manufactured.[24] In 1840, two-thirds of the official experimental gardens were transferred to the Assam Company—rent-free for the initial years. To facilitate private investment in the tea industry as set of rules were formed (1838) to make wastelands available to the planters, which was revised (1854) and made more attractive (1861) from time to time. The wasteland settlement policy tempted the planters to grab more lands than what was required or what they could manage. As a result about 0.7 million acres of land had been settled by the planters in Assam by 1870-1. The planters usurped the grazing land and encroached upon the *jhoom* lands of the tribals. By 1859, the Assam Company itself had 4,000 acres of land under teal cultivation producing over 16,87,200 kg per year. Its local expenditure extended to Rs.1 lakh in 1853 by which time nine other gardens had been started in upper Assam. Soon tea was found in Chachar and Sylhet too, and in 1855 gardens were set up in Cachar. By 1872, 27,000 acres were under tea plantation in the Brahmaputra Valley, 23,000 acres in Cachar and 1,000 acres in Sylhet. Edward Gait described the land grabbing craze for tea cultivation as a 'mania'. 'Fresh gardens were opened in all directions and a period of wild excitement and speculation supervened. The mania extended to the Government officers and three Deputy Commissioners and several police officers threw up their appointments to engage in tea gardens.'[25]

As a corollary, the planters soon came into conflict with the tribals because the expanding network of tea gardens were threatening to, and in many cases actually did, encroach upon tribal land. Such land grabbing in the Brahmaputra Valley affected the Nagas while in Cachar and Sylhet it affected the Lushais. Initially the 'pale-people' (as the Lushai's called the Englishmen) objected to the raids (Nagas in the Brahmaputra Valley, Lushais in the Surma Valley) and kidnapping in the areas which the tribals considered their domain, and even sent punitive expeditions thereby trespassing on their freedom and usurping their authority over the foothills. Now the English were advancing towards the hills as a result of the advancing network of tea gardens towards the hills. Both the Nagas and Mizos soon woke up to the fact that the new pale entrants were here to stay and the situation had changed. The advancement of the English towards the hills was seen as a threat to their very existence. They foresaw that the day was not far when the English would penetrate the hills. Indeed the British were drawn towards the fertile slopes which were ideally suited for tea cultivation. 'If cultivated', it was felt 'these strongholds of tigers, leopards, elephants, etc.' would be replaced by flourishing 'gardens of tea, coffee, oranges and lemons'.[26]

As early as 1860, the Assam Company had taken land in the Naga Hills for tea cultivation and by the turn of the century there were more than 40 tea gardens on the land claimed by the Nagas, e.g. Jamguri Tea Estate (T.E.) Amuguri T.E., Nagura T.E., Wokha T.E., Gildhari T.E., Mukhrung T.E., Borhaolla T.E., Guejam T.E., Kalipari T.E., Rajabari T.E., Bossabari T.E., Modhupur T.E., Kherimea T.E., Bahuni T.E., Naga Junka T.E., Nagini Jan T.E., Laojan T.E., Singloo T.E., Deopani T.E., Ahoo T.E., Tiphook Namti T.E., etc.[27]

The government endeavour to grant lands—claimed by the Nagas as their own—to the planters resulted in a crisis situation. The Nagas took in not only as an encroachment but also an invasion into their territory. When their appeal and arguments were ignored, the helpless Nagas resorted to their own primitive means of registering objection and thwarting such invasions. To obstruct British plans the Nagas led perpetual raids on the plantations and killed people. The Lushais too faced a similar problem, under the leadership of Sukpilal they raided the Monierkhal Tea Estate in Cachar (1869).[28] The Monierkhal raid affected the tea plantation in the Surma Valley and seriously jeopardized the interest of the planters. The government had the obvious obligation to protect the tea planters. The raid was followed by more raids which aggravated the situation and threatened the plantation economy of the region. Between 1826 and 1844 about 150 persons were killed in the Lushai raids. In 1849 a violent raid has committed in Rupcherra, in which 30 persons were killed and 42 kidnapped. The tea merchants and newspapers in England raised a hue and cry over the situation. George Campbell the Lt. Governor of Bengal himself was stirred into action as he felt, 'The planation in Cahcar seems to have been more successful and the system has been put on a better footing then anywhere else and it will be a subject of very great regret if this enterprise in seriously checked (due to these tribal raids).'[29]

In Naga Hills too the raids created terror which prompted the lt. governor of Bengal of stop fresh grants of land to the planters in the disputed territory (vide letter no. 2733, dated 13 June 1871).

It was not just tea, timber too was being extracted from the tribal lands. The Lushais caught elephants as a part of their subsistence from the hills. But the Government of India began to permit non-tribals to catch elephants thereby depriving the Lushais of their traditional livelihood. The annoyed tribals expressed their anger by repeated raids which prompted the administration to abolish the operation of elephant *kheda*. In fact the raids as a result of encroachment had become so acute that the Government of India had to think of a device to control encroachment by Britishers as well as by Indian non-tribals into the Naga and Lushai territory, lest the security of their tea plantation be jeopardized and a prosperous plantation sector had to be abandoned on account of something as 'silly' as tribal raids. The device formulated to control encroachment came to be known as the Inner Line Regulations according to which the lt. governor of Bengal was empowered to draw an inner line beyond which no British subjects, specified classes or foreign residents could enter without a valid pass or licence issued by the deputy commissioner. Tea planters were not allowed to acquire land beyond the inner line either from the Assam Government or the local tribal chiefs. This came into force both in the Naga and Lushai Hills. It is another matter however that throughout the colonial period the line continued to be violated ensuing in violent repercussions.

THE CONFRONTATION

After the punitive[30] expedition under Capt. Lister (1849) there was a need for a stronger standing army that would effectively deal with the raiding tribes. But the Government of India was sceptical about the efficacy of coercive methods. It asked Lister to try to concilliate the tribes and their chiefs. However, as soon as the British left, the Lushais butchered 20 Thadou captives proving the inadequacy of conciliatory tactics. But when a levy of 200 armed Thadous were raised the area was peaceful for 12 years.

Buy the 1860s the Lushais became restive again. On 22 January 1862 the village of Adampore in Sylhet was attacked and burnt. In

1863 another raid took place in Chandraipur. In January 1867 the Lushais attacked Monierkhal and burnt down the tea garden of Loharbund in Cachar. The military expedition having failed, the British tried to concilliate the chiefs. The result was a treaty with one such chief Suakpuilala who recognized Cachar as British territory. But while Suakpuilala was negotiating the boundary between the Lushais and the British, two other Lushai groups descended on the plains of Sylhet and Cachar. One party was led by Liankhama, Buantheuva, Pawibuwaia and Lalbura and the other by Savunga, Lalphunga and Benghuaia. On 23 January 1871, the Cachari *punjee* of Ainerkhal was burnt, 25 person were killed and 37 kidnapped. The second party burnt the Alexandrapore tea garden, shot dead Winchester—the tea planter—and kidnapped his five year old daughter Mary. On 24 January 1871 Katlichera, and on 27 January Monierkhal was raided. on 27 the tea gardens of Nudigram was also raided, 11 persons were killed and three were taken as captives. On the west on the border of Sylhet, the British frontier was attacked on 23 January and the next day another outpost was overrun. The outpost at Allinagar was raided on 27 February. Some villages in Tripura were burnt down on 21 January and the next day the village of Boonbari was destroyed.

In the famous 1871 military expedition with two columns the British attacked the raiders from two sides. This brought devastation and deaths for the Lushais on a scale that they were unable to withstand. As a result of it the chiefs Lengura, Vanlula, Vanhnuaia and Vanhnuna followed by another batch of chiefs—Savunga, Lalngura, Lalzika and Bengkhuaia surrendered to the British. As a result of this surrender there were 16 years of relative peace in Anglo-Lushai relations. During this period with the death or aging of the chiefs the younger leaders who took over mere resentful of the restrictions imposed on them by the British. They realized that the only way to get back their earlier freedom was to overthrow the British. But they had not yet forgotten the proven might of the whitemen. Whenever possible they would ambush the British. And would steal cattle from the British camps, destroy vegetable gardens and cut telegraph cables—essentially to vent their resentment.

During the period 1880-95 the British were busy suppressing tribal uprisings one after another. In February 1888, Hausat, Vantuai and Dokhuai of the Thantlang clan ambushed the survey party of Lt. Lewin killing eight of its members. Around the same time a party of Lushai chiefs led by Nikhama, Khairuma and Lungliana attacked a village near Demagiri and kidnapped 15 persons. In early 1889 Lianphunga Sailo attacked 23 villages, killed 100 people and took 91 persons as captives. The British realized that the Lushai tribes were out to threaten the peace of the area again. A strong punitive expedition—which became the famous Chin-Lushai expendition (1880-9)—was planned for a multi-pronged attack on the Lushai tribes. The massive attack by the British and the counter offensive by the Lushai tribes reached the scale of a prolonged war. It finally succeeded in getting most of the chiefs to submit to British authority. It also succeeded in the building of a road connection between Chittagong and Kale and in setting up outposts at Aizawal and Lungleh. The Lushais instinctively knew that their territory had been annexed, their chiefs were deposed, and that they had lost their hunting rights in the forest, and raiding the plains was no longer possible so all the chiefs of the west Dhaleswari-Liengpunga, Rangkuper, and Mintang area decided to rise in rebellion. On 9 September 1890 a party of British political officers was ambushed which left seven persons dead. H.R. Browne the political officer succumbed to his injuries. R.B. McCabe who had distinguished himself in suppressing the Nagas was hurriedly sent to the spot and was able to restore order and secure the surrender of the guilty chiefs. Following these incidents the Government of India approved the proposal of D.R. Lyall to constitute Lushai Hills as a district together with Chittagong Hills district under a superintendent. The district was to be governed through the chiefs. But the British attempt at imposing taxes and levy of labourers aroused immense resentment and turned into a violent uprising. It was only after 1896 that relative peace dawned in the Lushai Hills. The glorious history of Lushai resistance which spanned over seven violent decades came to an end in 1898 (27 January) when the whole of Lushai Hills was placed under the charge of a superintendent with headquarters at Aizawal.

As far as the Nagas were concerned the murder of the Daroga of the Samaguting outpost, Bhogchand was an event that greatly outraged the British. An expedition under Lt. Vincent was sent to avenge the death of its official. The expedition was however called off due to a reprisal. A revitalized expedition was sent in 1850 which, amidst violent reprisals, succeeded in establishing an outpost at Khonoma village. The rescue of the stranded Lt. Vincent necessitated another expedition which was the tenth in succession. This one included a detachment of 384 men with sophisticated weapons. But after a prolonged war to enter the Khonoma fort, when the British finally got there, the Nagas had abandoned the village. Frustrated, the British troop, in order to demonstrate its might, burnt down several villages. But the villagers of Kekrima did not give in till about a 1000 of its warriors died fighting the unequal battle.

After the Kekrima battle, the British decided to try the policy of non-interference vis-à-vis the Nagas. But it proved to be one-sided as the Nagas did not believe in it. In 1851 itself there were no less than 22 Naga raids, in which 35 persons were killed, 10 wounded and 133 taken captives. In 1862, the Commissioner of Assam, Henry Hopkinson pointed out to the Lt. Governor, Cecil Beadon the ineffectiveness of the policy of non-interference arguing that it was not good for the image of British power to look so helpless in countering tribal raids and protecting their subjects living in the plains. His reference was to the period between 1854 and 1865 when there had been raids by the Angamis alone in which 292 British subjects had been killed, wounded or taken as slaves.

The subsequent discussion on the matter led to the strengthening of the outpost at Samaguting (1866) and placing it under the charge of Lt. Gregory. In 1869, Gregory was succeeded by Capt. Butler, who was successful in gradually extending his influence over the tribes.

The year 1874 marked the beginning of a significant change in British strategy—a slow and tacit process of annexation of the hill areas to British India. Capt. Johnstone who was officiating for Butler effected the submission of three villages which agreed to pay a nominal revenue to the government. In 1875 survey operations were undertaken and continued despite intermittent attacks and ambushes.

But the Angamis of Khonoma and Mezoma still remained a major source of concern for the British. In two years they had plundered as many as 6 villages and killed 384 persons. Therefore in 1877 Carnegy a British political officer, attacked the Mezoma village and destroyed it, thereby compelling it into submission. In November 1878 the Khomia village was occupied securing the submission of 16 other villages. But Khonoma continued to be the trouble spot. The British tried to assert its might by levying fines on the villagers. But the murder of Damant, the political officer of Naga Hills, whilst trying to enter the village proved fatal. The avenging British troops marched to Khonoma on 21 October 1879. A six-day-long siege of Khonoma eventually brought its downfall. But the surrender of the villagers was still along way. On 22 November 1879, Khonoma was attacked by a reinforced British force. The assault only brought about the loss of 3 more British officers and 44 other men at the hand of the Nagas who abandoned the village and retreated to the mountains. To nab the fleeing villagers, the British had to subdue 13 other villages whose resistance was countered by a ruthless use of British military power without any compunction. While the villages of Piphema, Merema, Sechuma Chipema and Pfuchama were reduced to ashes Khonoma continued to hold out till March 1880 when it finally capitulated. As a symbol of their subjugation the villagers were made to pay revenue to the British Government.

The Sema Nagas of Rotomi village were the next source of trouble as they had murdered two Lotha Nagas who were British subjects. McCabe's district officer of North Lushai Hills expedition had quietened the Semas which encouraged him to lead an expedition to the Ao areas where he met with little opposition. In April 1888, the villages of Yaju, Jesu, Noksen and Liteng in the Tuengsang area were also occupied following the tribal raids. But undaunted, these Nagas attacked the Ao villages of Mongsemdi and Lungkung killing 148 and 40 villagers respectively (June 1888). To prevent such incident a 50-men stockade was posted at Mongsemdi which itself became the target of Naga attack. The deputy commissioner had no way but to lead another punitive expedition—which devastated several villages—to procure the surrender of the offenders. But his two successive promenades met with no success.

In 1892 an Ao Nagas was killed by a Sangtham Naga in the village of Yongphang. The deputy commissioner proceeded to the village to catch the murderer. Though the DC spared the villagers and destroyed only the house of the absconding murderer the villagers attacked the villager, who had provided the British troops with necessary supplies. The retaliatory violence secured the submission of the village. A similar event took place in November 1903 when the Philashi *khel* of Tuengsang killed two Ao Nagas and followed it by conducting raids in British territory. This was followed by another punitive expedition (January 1905) which destroyed the village of the offenders thereby securing their submission.

By the turn of the century, raids were reduced as the Nagas had realized the power of the new masters of the plains, and refrained from harassing either the British or their subjects. Thus ended one of the glorious histories of peoples' resistance to British colonialism in India. In fact it is amazing that the Naga and Lushai tribes fought the British power during the entire nineteenth century.

CAPTURE OF THE JEWEL[31]

In the annals of Manipur's history 1714 marked an important year when Pamheiba alias Garib Nawaj ascended the throne. He immediately shot into prominence as a powerful monarch and warrior. Pamheiba made several unsuccessful attempts to occupy the neighbouring Burmese kingdom which was also growing as a power at that time. The murder of Garib Nawaj by one of his sons and the consequent power rivalry plunged Manipur into one crisis after another resulting in the gradual weakening of the state. This was the time when the westward expanding Burmese empire inflicted a series of invasions on Manipur. The Burmese devastated the valley and committed inhuman cruelties on the people. The reigning King Jaisingh appealed to the East India Company for help but the detachment sent to help him could not proceed beyond Kashipur in Cachar. Unable to check the Burmese attack, Jaisingh abdicated and left his sons behind who were involved in a bloody rivalry over the throne for the next 23 years. In 1812 Marjit, one of his sons, seized the throne through Burmese aid and remained in power till 1819 when consequent upon his refusal to pay the promised tribute the Burmese attacked Manipur again and this time nearly depopulated the valley. In 1823 when the first Anglo-Burmese war broke out and the Burmese invaded Cachar, the East India Company entered into an alliance of mutual assistance with King Gambhir Singh of Manipur. When the Burmese were defeated and the Treaty of Yandabo (1826) was signed, Gambhir Singh was recognized as the king of Manipur which implied that from then on the state had only a semi-independent status according to the provisions of Subsidiary Alliance. The years following Gambhir Singh's death saw another phase of internecine rivalry over the throne. Gambhir Singh was succeeded by his brother Nar Singh who abdicated in favour of his nephew Chandra Kirti Singh. But a conspiracy by Gambhir Singh's widow prompted Nar Singh to occupy the throne. On Nar Singh's death (1850) Chandra Kirti Singh proceeded to Manipur and seized the throne. But his sense of insecurity led to seek British recognition. The British Government in turn made the king accountable to it for all his actions. In other words Manipur was for all intents and purposes a British protectorate and was not to do anything that was against their interest. Chandra Kirti Singh played this role so well that he was conferred knighthood. But again during 1890-1 the royal household was rife with conspiracies and rivalries over the throne. When things really got out of hand, the new King Sura Chandra ran to the safety of the British residency in Imphal. The following day despite the advise of the Political Agent, he declared his intention to abdicate and proceed on a pilgrimage to Brindaban. But on reaching Calcutta, he changed his mind and wanted to regain his throne. In the meantime Tikendrajit Singh, the step-brother of the king persuaded his elder brother Kula Chandra Dhwaja Singh to occupy the throne and requested the British Government to recognize the succession. The British Government knew that recognizing Kulchandra was in their interest but wanted to take Tikendrajit to task for creating a crisis in the valley. But Kulchandra's inability to secure the arrest of his brother Tikendrajit prompted the British to attempt to capture him by force. The anti-British sentiment was so strong that it ended in the public beheading of British officers. Viewed as an anti-British upsurge it was tantamount to waging war against the Government of India. War was declared on Manipur, and its defeat was followed by the trial and execution of Tikendrajit and Thangal, the generals on 13 August 1891. But despite lobbying by the pro-annexationists, Manipur was not annexed. It was decided that Manipur would be a Tributary State and native rule be re-established. The great grandson of Narsingh, Churachand was selected to be the ruler of Manipur. During the period of minority of the ruler a regency administration (1891-1907) was set up. On the assumption of authority by the raja (May 1907), the Manipur Darbar was reconstituted at the instance of the British Government. According to the new pattern of administration, the president of the Darbar was the raja himself and the vice president was to be an officer from the Assam Provincial Civil Service. Besides them were six Manipuri members who were entrusted with portfolios such as judiciary, public works, civil, police and the jail. The president was given charge of education, medicine and health, and armed state police, and the vice president was made responsible for the hill tribes, finance and revenue. The members were appointed by the Government of India on the recommendation of the raja and the British Political Agent in Imphal and could be removed by an order of the government. In other words the raja was a mere pawn and real powers were vested in the Political Agent and the vice president.

DETRIBALIZATION AND WESTERNIZATION

The turbulent years of Anglo-tribal conflict soon gave way to a more peaceful life in the Naga and Lushai Hills. The emphasis of the British was to structurally detribalize the tribals while a superficial policy of non-interference in their life and culture was followed. In other worlds the British believed that the only way to 'tame' these 'savages' as the tribals were referred to, was to bring about changes in their mode of production. So trade marts were established at the foothills in order that the tribal need not raid. Three such trade marts in the Lushai foothills were set up at Tipai-Mukh, Lushai-hat and Jhalnacherra.[32] In these marts the tribals sold or bartered commodities such as rubber, ivory, etc., for salt, iron, brass-utensils, tobacco and cattle. The shifting cultivators were taught to produce potato, cabbage, etc. Links with the outside world were established through road communications.

By 1871-2 the road between Sungoo Valley and Dalekmai, and Demagiri and Lungleh was complete.[33] The Silchar-Aizawl road was completed by 1872. The East Bengal Railway was extended up to Chittagong in 1896 connecting it with Calcutta. By 1898 Silchar was connected with Calcutta and soon a branch line was opened till Lalabazar at the foothills of the Lushai district. In 1900, measures were taken against the water scarcity by establishing an elevated water reservoir at Aizawal.[34] The British rendered innumerable welfare services to the Lushais during the periodic famine that devastated the Lushais in 1881-2. Western medicines and hygiene were introduced along with education.[35] Momentous changes in the life patterns of the tribes were taking place. But interestingly the British insisted that they retain the tribal dresses and hair-cuts and not emulate the British or the Westernized Indians.

So by the beginning of the twentieth century the 'pale'[36] intruders, whom the Lushais had previously fought against, had been accepted as the Mirang Sawipa or Mikang Topa or Mirang Lalpa—the White Masters. The introduction of Christianity reinforced the detribalization process. The first missionary to the Lushai Hills came in the 1880s and it was Rev W. Williams of the Welsh Calvanistic Church. In 1893, R. Arthington of Arthington Aborigine Mission financed two missionaries to Aizawl—F.W. Savidge, and J.H. Lorraine. Despite their initial failure in the conversion of tribals to Christianity, they learnt the Lushai language, introduced the Roman script to the tribals, translated portions of the Bible into Lushai and prepared a Lushai-English dictionary. The British administration had neglected the education of the tribals. The missionaries introduced Western education in the hills and by 1944 the Lushais had their first graduate. The number of Western-educated Lushais increased giving rise to the growth of a middle class in the hills. The successive wartime changes, political upheavals, and nationalistic fervour—nationally and internationally—activated this new middle class which though lacking numerical strength was on an equal footing with those of the plains.

A similar transformation was taking place in the Naga Hills too as a result of the British initiative. The British tried to consolidate their position immediately. They realized that unless paramountcy was established, the conquered tribes might revolt again. The only way to achieve this was to introduce British administration in the Naga Hills. The Ao area was formed into the Mokokchung subdivision (1890). The area which was known as the area of political control (part of the present Tuensang) was also incorporated into the Naga Hills division (1866). Kohima was formed into a subdivision too. The tribes covered by the Naga Hills district at the close of the nineteenth century were: the Angamis, the Aos, the Kachha Nagas, the Lothas, the Rengmas and the Semas. The Sangthams, Konyaks and Changs were still living in the unadministered area. A Deputy Commissioner assisted by a European assistant was posted at Kohima whereas Mokokchung was placed under the charge of an European police officer along with an engineer and civil surgeon. The criminal and civil procedure codes of India did not apply to this district. However, Deputy Commissioner was empowered to exercise his power in cases involving life and death in consultation with the Chief Commissioner of Assam. The village headmen were given the authority to decide civil and criminal cases according to the customary laws of the respective tribes. The *dobashis* (interpreters) too had a role to play. A small police force, military battalion and a small jail were set up for law and order purposes.

Education was encouraged but left to the initiative of the Christian missionaries. The number of students recorded in 1890-1 was 297 which rose to 319 in 1900-1 and to 647 in 1903-4. By 1903-4 there were twenty-two primary schools, one secondary and two special schools in the district.[37]

The hills were then connected with the plains through modern communication system. Roads were constructed by 1903-4, 117 km of cart-roads and 757 km of bridle paths were ready. The road linking Manipur and Kohima and Dimapur was widened and a railway head installed at Dimapur.[38]

Christian missionaries, as they have done worldwide, followed the British flag to the Naga Hills. To avoid overlapping the organized Christian missionaries assigned the Naga Hills to the American Baptist Mission. Rev Miles Bronson set out for the Naga Hills and set up a Naga Mission School at Namsang in 1839-40.[39] But with Bronson's sudden departure prompted by illness, the work come to a standstill until E.W. Clark replaced him in 1869. Clark, with the help of Susongmeren, a local Ao convert and Godhula an Assamese evangelist opened the Baptist Mission Centre to Molungyimgchen village. But when the converts increased in number and a conflict grew in the village over the question of observance of tribal rituals and festivals vis-à-vis Christianity, Clark founded a new village at Molungyimchen which would be completely Christian. As soon as the Ao area came under British administration the mission was shifted to Impur (April 1894) which emerged as the centre not only for the Ao churches, but also for the Sema, Lotha, Chang, Phom and Sangtham churches. In the Kohima subdivision the American Baptist Mission Centre was opened at Samaguting. Rev C.D. King was the first missionary in the area who converted the first Angami in 1885. The mission opened a few schools. Persons of eminence like Kevichusa, Zopianga Longlang, J.B. Zasokie and Vizol were products of this mission centre. The progress of Christianity was slow initially but accelerated after the Second World War.

In Manipur too, the advent of colonialism heralded a change in every sphere of life. The land system introduced by the British was qualitatively different from the pre-colonial one. It involved a thorough monetization, commercialization of agriculture and introduction of the concept of private landownership. The state also abolished (1892) the Manipur version of slavery and the *lallup* system—a local variety of serfdom. The colonial authorities surveyed the land and introduced taxes on homestead land. Unlike the earlier system the taxes had to be paid in cash. In order to effectively implement this system and elaborate administrative structure was instituted. The valley was divided into five *panas*, and each *pana* was in charge of a *lakpa* (local revenue officer) which was a prestigious post. Due to these changes new social categories of people emerged. In the pre-British society there were only two broad social categories: the king and the feudal nobles on the one hand and peasants on the other. Colonial Manipur saw the emergence of such as rent receivers, tenant-cultivators, ordinary cultivators, and field labourers. The new system adversely affected the former nobility and even the peasants but a new category of middle rankers like the Lakpas, Amins, etc., became prominent. They formed the progeny of the modern middle class of Manipur which made its presence conspicuous in the post-war period.

The colonial policy of introducing English education in Manipur was to serve imperial interests. The emphasis was on teaching literature—Bengalee and Sanskrit, and philosophy rather than science and technology. However, the number of lower primary schools rose from 56 in 1909-10 to 82 in 1929-30.[40] The number of students increased from 3,380 in 1990-10 to 6,520 in 1929-39. The government encouraged the growth of this sector and increased its outlay from Rs.18,806 in 1909-10 to Rs.34,717 in 1929-30. There was however only one high school in Manipur—the Johnstone High School which was recognized by Calcutta University only in 1921-2. In 1921-2 a Matriculation centre was opened in Manipur. After 1930 there were three Boys High Schools and one Girls High School. These schools were opened through voluntary efforts and given grants-in-aid subsequently. But the only college, that is the D.M. College was set up after the Second World War. Nevertheless, the percentage of literacy increased from 0.9 per cent in 1901 to 3.0 per cent in 1921, and to 5.0 per cent in 1941. Between 1927-8 and 1930-1 as many as 82 students passed the matriculation exam. Between 1922-3 and 1929-30, 11 students completed graduation in the arts and science streams. Between 1930-40, two journals, *Yakairol* (quarterly) and *Lalit Manjuri Patrika* (monthly) and two daily newspapers—*Dainik Manipur* and *Manipur Matam* were published.[41] All these marked the emergence of a modern middle class from the middle ranking categories of the transformed society. Like the plains of Assam, the proselytization efforts of the Christian missions did not succeed much in the plains of Manipur. But it did much better in the Hills of Manipur which consisted of numerous Naga, Kuki and Mizo tribes.

Fruits of Transformation: Emergence of Middle Class

The emergence of a modern middle class in Manipur was late as it was among the last states to come under the influence of colonialism. A full-fledged colonial takeover of the state was only after 1891 and an embryonic middle class was visible in the post-War period. They were small in number and mostly trained in the education institutions of Calcutta and Gauhati. They were largely land based and from semi-urban areas and adopted for new professional careers like teaching in schools and colleges, administrative posts like clerks in the government offices and positions like *amins* and *lakpas* which were hitherto filled by people brought in from Assam and Bengal. They were products of the changed system and trained in Western thought and ideas which were considered modern as against the orthodox/ traditional.

> What was important was the change in their outlook. They began to look upon Europeans as models and tended to become pro-Western in taste and attitude. They also began to regard themselves as belonging to more or less different categories and assumed new leadership—political and religious. In this way the emergence of a new elite group disturbed the structures of traditional social organisation.[43]

Initially the essential concern of this class was educational development, religio-cultural change and to secure respectability for Manipuri language, literature, art and threatre.[44] They believed that reforms within the religious—structure getting rid or Brahmanic oppression and hegemony and other such ills that had crept in to Hinduism—was a sure way to reform the society. Strangely enough during the colonial rule Hinduism (Gaudiya Vaishnavism), the religion of the Meitheis was encouraged by the colonial government. The new middle class favoured this religion. It took pride in professing a faith that was the dominant faith of the subcontinent. Translation of Hindu religious scripture and literature into local languages and ways to strengthen Hindu practices without the hegemony of the Brahmins were suggested. Only a very small and feeble voice of dissension came from a group led by Naorem Phullo who wanted to do away with Hinduism and revive the pre-Hindu faith of the Meitheis, the Sanamahi. But is had a different context and originated in a place outside Manipur. A small migrant Meithei peasantry lived in Cachar which suffered discrimination as a minority and was not accepted as proper Hindus by the caste based, hierarchical majority of Cachar. Phullo's voice was that of a hurt community, of a rebel and the fact that his ideas were not accepted by the Meitheis of Manipur proved the people's tilt towards Hinduism.

The second concern was the education of its people. The new middle class advocated the necessity of modern education for the Meithei men and women and the need to work towards the goal. It also recognized the need for industrialization and adoption of trade and business as a profession by Meitheis which could help in the removal of poverty in Manipur. It was suggested that people should buy locally manufactured products rather than British manufactured goods.

In the inter-War period when the whole of India was steeped in the freedom struggle and the 'nationalist' movement had come to be termed as 'politics' the Meithei middle class too became restive. The new form of politics attracted them because in the monarchical regime common people were not allowed to participate. They now had political rights and aspirations, became aware of their rights and were determined to realize them. These people were apolitical as the medieval monarchical system of Manipur had only allowed the participation of a limited number of people in the political process. Political decision making was the domain of a select group of royal family members and their ministers. Decisions were imposed on people and orders came from above and anyone protesting or not complying with decisions was charged with 'sedition' and ruthlessly suppressed. Trained in Western political thought and processes, the new middle class saw the 'power' in democratic institutions and also the prospects of their participation in these political institutions and decision making processes. They demanded the democratization of the medieval political system with modern political institutions in which people could participate. The Meithei middle class was ready to go all out to secure the introduction of such institutions. The establishment of the Nikhil Hindu Manipur Mahasabha in 1934 was one such effort which was transformed into a political party in 1938 with a secular name—Nikhil Manipuri Mahasabha. The Indian National Congress was the avowed inspiration of the party.

NAGA MIDDLE CLASS

The various Naga tribes remained overwhelmingly tribal except for the Semas and Angamis as is evident from their views on land-ownership. Private ownership was practised by the Angamis while the Semas were vested with the 'legal ownership of their land'. Most of the other tribes practised collective ownership. These two tribes had also advanced considerably in terms of technology. Some feudal trends were already emerging in the Angami and Sema Hills. But the processes of colonization had checked such a development. Colonial rule without disturbing the land pattern prevented the break up and decline of tribalism in these hills. For example shifting cultivation was not discouraged. Commercial crops were introduced but commodity production was not encouraged. Monetization was introduced but the traditional barter system was also retained in the exchange between the plainsmen and the tribes. Trade with the plains was thoroughly discouraged not due to the fear of exploitation of the tribes by the plainsmen but to restrict the entry of outsiders to the hills which could bring about a renewal of raids and jeopardize the flourishing tea industry. In fact, the Inner Line Regulations was one such device to restrict the entry of outsiders to the hills. The regulation had nothing to do with the preservation of indigenous identity, culture, institutions, etc. It was aimed at preventing the land-hungry planters from encroaching on the Naga land and thereby creating a problem for the government. Thus the break up of the tribal society and the development of feudal relationship of production were arrested by British rule and hence the middle class that finally emerged in the Naga Hills, had its roots neither in the landed aristocracy nor did it evolve through commercial development.[45] The growth of this class in Nagaland was inextricably linked with the spread of Western education introduced by the Christian missionaries and it was composed mainly of small entrepreneurs, salaried bureaucracy and independent professionals like teachers, doctors, lawyers, etc.

The first act of the this emerging middle class seemed to have been the formation of the Naga Club in 1918. But we should not overlook the fact that the control over the club was still retained by the chiefs which was evident from the preponderance of *dobashis* (interpreters) in its membership. *Dobashis* were mostly chiefs or ersthwhile chiefs. There is very little material on the Naga Club (which seemed to have become defunct after it submitted the famous memorandum to the Simon Commission) but the very idea of club/association, cooperatives which it ran in Mokokchung and Kohima were modern and obviously the work of ex-soldiers, returning from the war, government officials, professionals like teachers who comprised the nascent middle class. The odd men were the chiefs, who seemed to have found place in the Club by virtue of their being *dobashis* which was a very important office during the British regime and had played an important role in matters relating to the Nagas vis-à-vis British India by virtue of their being chiefs.

In 1929, the Naga Club submitted a memorandum to the Simon Commission which was accepted asking the British Government to exclude the Naga areas from the prospective political reforms as the community was too backward and lacked leadership capable of representing the numerous Naga tribes.

A look at the memorandum shows that although it claimed to lack leadership capable of representing all the Naga tribes the memorandum itself was signed by representatives which included 15 Angamis, 1 Zeliang, 1 Sema, 1 Lotha, 1 Rengma, and 1 Kuki. Among the signatories there were 9 *dobashis* or interpreters, 3 teachers, 2 clerks,

1 doctor, 1 *potdar*, 1 treasurer, 1 sub-overseer, and 1 *chaprasi* which again proves the preponderance of *dobashis*. The institution of *dobashis* was instituted by the British in the Naga Hills as in the rest of India. The primary function of the *dobashis* was to interpret Naga dialects into Assamese which the British officers knew. In pursuance of its policy of giving special importance to local authorities these *dobashis* were selected from among the chiefs and rulers and in course of time were given authority to decide cases. They were allowed to establish *dobashi* courts in district and subdivisional headquarters like Kohima and Mokokchung. Cases which could not be settled at the village level were brought to these *dobashi* courts and decided according to the customary laws of the respective tribes. The British administrators generally confirmed the decisions of these *dobashi* courts and did not encourage appeals against them which meant that the *dobashis* had emerged to be a powerful institution. The fact that *dobashis* were chiefs also gave them extra authority over the tribes. The *dobashis* were allowed to go out on tour to various areas of the district to settle cases regularly. They were close to the administration and often accompanied British administrators who visited their area annually and assisted them in deciding cases. Given the context of the memorandum submitted to the Simon Commission which appealed to keep the Nagas out of modern political institutions and processes and permit them to retain their old tribal structures, and given the background of the *dobashis* who were chiefs in reality, it is likely that these chiefs feared the loss of power, privilege and hegemony which included economic assets if a new political system was imposed on them and that their appeal was only an attempt at preserving the *status quo*. The Second World War contributed towards the strengthening of the Naga middle class and led to the weakening of the Naga Club. The Naga National Council (1946) was truly an organization of the Naga middle class which took over the leadership of the Naga people from the Naga Club. The Naga National Council (NNC) emerged out of the Naga Hills District Tribal Council which was formed at the initiative of Charles Pawsey, the Deputy Commissioner of the Naga Hills. The Naga National Council primarily aimed at actively supporting of British officials working for social, economic, political and cultural development of the Nagas but in the wake of the impending British withdrawal from India, it switched over to political activity. Originally NNC consisted of 29 members representing various tribes on the basis of proportional representation from among whom the office bearers were elected. The finances were raised by contributions from

every family making them an indirect member of the NNC. The modern outlook of the NNC leaders was testified by the various reform work which it undertook for the tribes. But its support of the Naga Club Memorandum to the Simon Commission, which was the handwork of traditional chieftains was surprising. It would be explained by the retention of the overwhelmingly tribal structure from which this middle class emerged or their ambitiousness. However, under a new leadership, the Nagas were participating in the modern political process and institutions.

MIZO MIDDLE CLASS

In the Mizo Hills too the British emphasis was on structural detribalization while encouraging the retention of tribal way of life at a superficial level. In other words the Mizos were restrained from changing their dress, hair style, etc., but the production process was drastically changed. The food-gathering Mizos were introduced to commercial crop production like rubber and vegetables; cattle rearing, poultry, piggery and trading. This detribalization process was reinforced by the introduction of Christianity and Western education which came along with the modern ideas of hygiene and medicine. Certain restrictions and curtailment of the traditional rights of the chiefs were ordered by the British despite the fact that they required the institution of the chiefs and administered the district through them. As a result the power and wealth of chiefs started diminishing with the coming of the British.

> On the other hand the British as we have stated earlier, to protect their interest in governing the area with minimum expenses favoured the chiefs in contrast to the common people. This however could not check the growth of an enlightened section of the Mizos (because of education and Missionary activities) viz., traders, nurses, teachers, public men.[46]

Even though the initiative was from the British and purpose was religio-social, the Young Lushai Association (1938) was the first middle class attempt at actualizing its modern concepts. The emergence of the Mizo Union (1926) was only a logical follow-up. The former was social while the latter was fullfledgedly political. The removal of the Mizo Union office bearers, on the ground that they lacked 'college education' showed the importance of modern education among the Mizos and the movement for the abolition of 'chieftainship' showed the emergence of a modern middle class in the Mizo Hills and their Westernized perspective. The integrationist and secessionist debates also showed the dilemma between the old chiefs and the new middle class. In effect, it was the reflection of a society in transition—a society making a wild leap, from the tribal stage to that of a bourgeois society.

NOTES

1. Suniti Kumar Chatterjee, *The Place of Assam in the History and Civilization of India*, Gauhati: Gauhati University, 1970, p. 113.
2. Samir Amin, *Accumulation on a World Scale*, combined volumes, New York: Monthly Review Press, 1974, pp. 139-40.
3. Karl Marx, *Grundrisse*, Lawrence and Wishart, 1969, p. 486.
4. Karl Marx to Vera Zasulich, 8 March 1881, in D. Riaznov (ed.), *Marx and Engels Archives*, 1926, p. 335. English trans. in Blackstone and Hoselitz (eds.) *The Russian Menace to Europe*, Glencoe: Free Press, Vol. III, 1952.
5. D.D. Kosambi, *An Introduction to the Study of Indian History*, Bombay: Popular, 1956.
6. Nihar Ranjan Ray, Presidential Address in K.S. Singh (ed.), *Tribal Situation in India*, Simla: IIAS, 1972, pp. 3-24.
7. See Arnold J. Toynbee, *A Study of History*, one volume edition, Oxford, Paperback Edition, 1972.
8. Suniti Kumar Chatterjee, op. cit., pp. 4-5.
9. D. Nath, 'Early Hinduisation of the Ruling Tribes of North East India', in *Proceedings of the North East India History Association*, Pashighat, 1986, pp. 253-8.
10. Cited in Suniti Kumar Chatterjee, *Kirata-Janakriti*, 2nd edn., Culcutta: Asiatic Society, 1974, p. 113.
11. Suhas Chatterjee, 'Early History of the Mizos', in *Proceedings of the North East India History Association*, Gauhati, 1988, pp. 101-5.
12. Ibid.
13. Laxmi Devi, *Ahom-Tribal Relationship*, Gauhati: Gauhati University, 1968, pp. 15-42.
14. Ibid.
15. N. Birchandra Singh, 'Muslim Institutions in Manipur', in *Proceedings of the North East India History Association*, Aizawal, 1984, pp. 89-92.
16. Ibid.
17. Suhas Chatterjee, *Mizoram Under British Rule*, Delhi: Mittal, 1985, p. 13.
18. Vumson, *Zo History*, Aizawl: Author, n.d., p. 109.
19. V. Ruata Rengsi, 'Pre-Colonial Technology of the Mizos', unpublished M.Phil. thesis, Shillong: North Eastern Hill University, 1988.
20. Alexander Mackenzie, *Memorandum on the North East Frontier of India*, Calcutta: Govt. of India, 1869.
21. Cited in Vumson, op. cit., p. 116.
22. As in note 17, p. 11.

23. The details in this section are based on H.K. Barpujari, *Problems of the Hill Tribes: North East Frontier,* Vol. I, Gauhati: Lawyers, 1970; Vol. II, Gauhati: United, 1976; Vol. III, Gauhati: Spectrum, 1981. Asoso Yonuo, op. cit., pp. 63-106, Suhas Chatterjee as in note 17.
24. Amalendu Guha, *Planter Raj to Swaraj: Freedom Struggle and Electoral Politics in Assam 1826-1947,* Delhi: ICHR, 1977, pp. 12-13.
25. Edward Gait, *A History of Assam,* Thacker Spink & Co., 1905, cited in Hokhishe Sema, *Emergence of Nagaland,* Delhi: Vikas, 1986, p. 63.
26. John McCosh, cited in ibid., p. 15.
27. Hokshishe Sema, op. cit.
28. Suhas Chatterjee, as in note 17, p. 52.
29. Ibid., n. 48, p. 55.
30. This section is based on the studies mentioned in note 23.
31. Based on the accounts of Bimal J. Dev and Dilip Lahiri, *Manipur: Culture and Politics,* Delhi: Mittal, 1987. Laldena, G. Kabui and Joykumar Singh, *History of Modern Manipur,* Imphal: Modern Book, 1991. V. Venkata Rao et al., *A Century of Government and Politics in North East India: Manipur,* Delhi: S. Chand & Co., 1991.
32. Suhas Chatterjee as in note 17, pp. 183-4.
33. Ibid., pp. 189-92.
34. Ibid.
35. Ibid., pp. 196-7.
36. Mizos described the white Britishers as 'Pale People'.
37. Asoso Yunuo, op. cit., p. 110.
38. Ibid.
39. Ibid., pp. 111-21.
40. N. Lokendra Singh, 'Socio-Economic Roots of Popular Movements in Manipur Valley', unpublished Ph.D. thesis, Imphal: Manipur University, 1990.
41. Ibid.
42. Laldena et al., *History,* op. cit., pp. 116-17.
43. This section is based on N. Lokendra Sing's op. cit. study as well as ibid.
44. Ibid.
45. Udayan Mishra, 'Naga Nationalisation and the Role of Middle Class', in B. Datta Ray, *Emergence and Role of Middle Classes in North East India,* Delhi: Uppal, 1983, pp. 151-69.
46. N.E. Parry, *The Lakhers,* London: Macmillan, 1932, pp. 12-14.

CHAPTER TWO

The Setting

The imminent 'tryst with destiny' did not quite seem to match the vision of freedom the Indian people had. Neither did it fit the image people had of free India because the Withdrawal Declaration of the British Labour Government was not the only withdrawal India faced on the eve of its independence. There was the prospective partition of India to meet the Muslim League demand for a separate Muslim homeland. The Sikhs had a scheme of Azad Punjab or Sikhisthan to counter non-Sikh hegemony over its people. In the east, there was a move to carve out an independent United Bengal to thwart its partition and a demand for an independent Gorkhasthan out of the Nepali speaking areas of Darjeeling and Kalimpong while in the west, there was a clamour for setting up a free Pakhtunisthan in the North-West Frontier Province. For many of the ambitious maharajas and dewans of the 560-odd Princely States, Britains departure from India provided an opportunity for reverting back to their pre British state of independence and monarchical autocracy. The territorially peripheral tribal communities in the Excluded Areas of north-east India wanted to remain independent of both India and Pakistan as they could not identify with either. Thus, British withdrawal was not the end of the tunnel for India. The future was still uncertain. Independence brought jubiliation as well as paranoia; hope as well as despair, promise alongside fear; sense of achievement as well as frustration at unforeseen developments. It was a foregone conclusion that free India would not be the India that the romantic nationalists had dreamt of.

DISINTEGRATION BEFORE INTEGRATION?

Inaugurating the Indian National Congress in 1885, its first president put forward the claim of Indian nationhood rather tentatively in the following words: '. . . if community of sentiments, community of feelings and community of wants enabled anyone to speak on behalf of others, than assuredly they (Indian National Congress) might justly claim to be the people of India.'[1]

By the time of the 1886 session the tentativeness had gone and a more pronounced, emphatic and clearer declaration was made wherein Rajendralal Mitra amidst cheers said:

> It is highly gratifying to me that we are here assembled together, delegates from the north, from the south, from the east and from the west—all anxious to join as members of one nation for the good of our country. . . . Diverse as we are in origin, in religion, in language, and in our manners and customs, but are not less than members of the same nation. We live in the same country, we are subject of the same Sovereign and our good and evil depend entirely on the state of government and the laws passed in the country. Whatever is beneficial to the Hindus is equally beneficial to the Mohammedans and whatever is injurious to the Hindus is equally injurious to the followers of Mohammed. Nations are not made of sects but of tribes bound together in one political bond. We are all bound by the same political bond and therefore we constitute one Nation.[2]

Barely two decades after the foundation of the Indian National Congress which professed to be the representative of all Indians irrespective of their religion, caste or language and to be 'national' in character, a counter organization was born in the form of the All India Muslim League (December 1906) as a representative body of the Indian Muslims. Soon after this the All India Hindu Mahasabha (1915) and the Akali Dal (1920) made their political appearance claiming to be the representative bodies of the Hindus and the Sikhs respectively thereby putting a damper on the claims of the Indian National Congress. All the more problematic was the fact that it posed a serious challenge to the concept of Indian nationhood as all the three communities in question—the Hindus, the Muslims and the Sikhs claimed to be separate nations. In other words, within five decades of the foundation of the Indian National Congress there was a triplication of Indian nationhood stratifying the Indian nationalist movement into three streams. It not only rejected Congress as the sole spokesman of the nation, but also weakened its bargaining power. Although the emergence of these organizations were initially brushed aside as 'insignificant events' they went on to become substantial movements as testified by the Lahore Resolution of the Muslim League (1940).

The forties of the twentieth century can indeed be described as the dangerous decades as a number of schemes put forward by different groups suggested Balkanization of India in order to safeguard the interests of the various dissenting communities. As early as 1933 Chaudhury Rahmat Ali formulated the Pakistan scheme. Muhammad Shah Nawaz Khan submitted a proposal in 1939 to divide India into five federal countries.[3] Subsequently the Punjab Muslim Student Association formed a plan that would establish a Pakistan Caliphate comprising the Muslim majority provinces of Punjab, parts of United Province, Central Provinces and Berar, the State of Hyderabad and the entire territory of Bengal and Assam. The head of such a State would be a spiritual dictator who would govern according to the injunction of the Koran and act as the 'shadow of God' on earth.[4] These plans culminated in the Lahore Resolution of the Muslim League (1940) which demanded the creation of Pakistan as a Muslim homeland and declared *inter alia* that 'the geographically contiguous units are demarcated into regions which should be constituted with such territorial readjustments as may be necessary; that the areas in which the Muslim are numerically in a majority, as in the North Western and Eastern zones of India should be grouped to constitute independent states in which the unity shall be autonomous and sovereign'. Commenting on this demand M.A. Jinnah had observed,

> such arrangement had become necessary because the Hindus and the Mussalmans belong to two different religious philosophies, social customs, literatures. They neither intermarry, nor interdine together and indeed they belong to two different civilizations which are based mainly on conflicting ideas and conceptions. Their aspects of life are different. It is quite clear that Hindus and Mussalmans derive their inspiration from different sources of history. They have different epics, their heroes are different and they have different episodes. Very often the hero of one nation is a foe of the other and likewise their victories and defeats overlap. To yoke together two such nations under a single state, one as a numerical minority must lead to growing discontent and final destruction of any fabric that may be so build up for the government of such a state.[5]

Jinnah not only demanded a Muslim homeland but also advocated the creation of similar homelands for other Indian 'nations' as well: 'If the British government are really earnest and sincere to secure peace and happiness of the people of their subcontinent the only course open to us all is to allow the major nations separate homelands by dividing India into autonomous national states.'[6]

Following this demand and the Simla Conference fiasco the Akali Dal in a memorandum to the Sapru Committee stated that though it favoured an United India, in the event of a prospective partition of India in favour of the League, they also would insist on the creation of a separate Sikh State. The executive committee of the Akali Dal officially adopted a resolution to this effect on 22 March 1946:

> Whereas the Sikhs being attached to the Punjab by intimate bonds of holy shrines, property, language, tradition and history, claim it as their homeland and holyland which the British took as a 'trust' from the last Sikh ruler during his minority and whereas the entity of the Sikhs is being threatened on account of the persistent demand of Pakistan by Muslims on the one hand and of danger of absorption by the Hindus on the other, the executive committee of the Siromoni Akali Dal demands for preservation and protection of the religious, cultural and economic and political rights of the Sikh nation, the creation of a Sikh state which would include a substantial majority of the Sikh population and their sacred shrines and historical Gurudwaras with provisions for the transfer and exchange of population and property.[7]

The Hindu Mahasabha on the one hand projected itself to be an apostle of Akhand Hindustan and on the other reinforced the claims of the League and the Akalis by talking in terms of Hindi-Hindu-Hindusthan and even countered the efforts of the Congress in creating a united India.[8] When it saw the creation of Pakistan an inevitability, a vigorous campaign was launched under the enthusiastic leadership of Syama Prasad Mookerjee for the partition of Bengal into two parts, with a view to establishing a Hindu majority West Bengal province in the Indian Union.[9] Amused by this development, F. Burrows, while reporting this Partition demand to Wavell, remarked 'Curzon must be chuckling in his grave'.[10] In fact there is nothing to show that the Mahasabha was against Partition and did not rejoice the prospect of a Hindu majority Hindustan. The Hindu Mahasabha movement supported by the leading capitalists of the region and the Congress decision in favour of such a division provoked sharp reactions from Premier Suhrawardy who described the demand put forward by the Mahasabha and endorsed by the Congress as 'short-sighted' and 'confession of defeatism'.[11] He mooted an idea of a United Bengal comprising both Hindu and Muslim Bengalees which would counter the designs of the communalists and help thwart the sinister plan to partition Bengal. He said that if the 'Noakhali carnage' was an example of hostility between the Bengalee Hindus and Muslims, there were many Bengalee villages, which were examples of their amity and unity.[12] In fact it was the outsiders, he pointed out, who had no roots in Bengal but were exploiters of its soil and did not want to see Bengal united. Therefore, instead of the partition of Bengal, which would be suicidal even from the point of view of the

Hindus, the Bengalees should work towards the formation of the United Bengal which 'will be a great country indeed, the richest and the most prosperous in India, capable of giving to its people a high standard of living, where a greater people will be able to rise to fullest height of their stature, a land that will truly be plentiful. It will be rich in agriculture, rich in industry and commerce and in course of time will be one of the most powerful and progressive states of the world.'[13] The idea was greeted enthusiastically in many quarters. Burrow not only gave his blessings to the principle of an independent Bengal but also became one of the virtual co-authors of the Bose-Roy-Suhrawardy Agreement. Unexpectedly even Jinnah was not averse to the idea. He said, 'I should be delighted. What is the use of Bengal without Calcutta? They had much better remain united. I am sure that they would be on friendly terms with us.'[14]

It was just a historical accident that Darjeeling came to be included under Bengal. Bought from Sikkim, this intended sanatorium was attached to Bengal by the British as they had initially done in the case of Assam and other parts of north-east India.[15] Assam was separated from Bengal in 1874 but Darjeeling continued to remain within Bengal. In 1914, the Hillmen Association of Darjeeling presented a memorandum to the Montagu-Chelmsford Commission seeking separation from Bengal. The same request was made to the Simon Commission in 1928. Both were however ignored. In 1934, the demand was more vociferously put before the British Government. In 1945, the All India Gorkha League was formed and the same demand was voiced through its mouthpiece *The Gorkha*. Weak and docile, this demand again failed to make any impact in the wake of the Pakistan and Sikhisthan resolutions.[16]

In the North-Western Frontier Province too there was a move for a Free Pathan State.[17] Betrayed by the Congress on whom it had relied upon and now at the mercy of the Muslim League the Khudai Khidmatgars under the leadership of Khan Abdul Gaffar Khan declared on 27 June 1947:

> We have decided to establish Pathanisthan, which will be an independent state of all Pathans. There will be no king and the land will be ruled by the entire Pathan nation jointly. For this independence of the Pathans we sided with the Congress and we fought our common enemy jointly. We were then called Hindus and Hindu agents but now when we refused to join Hindusthan we are forced to fight the referendum on the issue of Pakistan *versus* Hindusthan.[18]

The moment it became known that British withdrawal from India meant reversion to their original pre-British independent status, many of the ambitious rulers of the Princely States rejoiced the prospect. The rulers of Hyderabad, Bhopal and Travancore were more explicit in their aspirations. With 560-odd Princely States in British India such an eventuality could prove fatal and the end of the romantic nationalist dream of an independent united India. Among the Governor's Provinces, Assam had contemplated secession from India as early as 1937. Pushed to the wall by the hegemony of the Bengalee middle class and the grave threat of incessant immigration into Assam from the eastern Bengal districts reducing the Assamese into a minority in their own land, a section of the Assamese intelligentsia saw secession of Assam as the only way to 'save' the Assamese nationality. This feeling is clearly expressed in the following statement. 'We also want *swaraj* by all means. But it is also true that we do not want it at the cost of the extinction of our race.'[19]

A conservasionist movement grew out of these fears whose sole aim was to 'save' the Assamese identity from 'extinction'. Nilmoni Phukhan, Ambikagiri Roychoudhury and Gyannath Bora were protagonists of this movement which had the support of a large section of the Assamese people. The Ashomiya Samrakshini Sabha (1926) submitted a memorandum to Jawaharlal Nehru during his tour of Assam wherein it was stated:

> For years together we have been standing face to face with extinction as a people. . . . It is perhaps difficult for the outsiders to realise the true feeling of the outraged manhood of Assam. Desperation has taken possession of the minds of the people. And as a means of saving the Assamese race from extinction a considerable section of the intelligentsia has even expressed their minds in favour of secession of Assam from India. . . .[20]

The Asom Deka Dal, in a similar memorandum to Nehru stated: (if the existing trend continues) 'the temple of *swaraj* when it is built on the bank of Brahmaputra it will be on the grave of the Assamese nation . . . the only alternative . . . that we can think of is that we should get separated from India as Burma has done'.[21]

Gyannath Bora too, a leading member of the Assamese intelligentsia, in an article in a vernacular daily *Dainik Batori* advocated the secession of Assam as the only alternative open to the Assamese to save themselves.[22] Ambikagiri Roychoudhury even drafted an outline of a Constitution for an ideal Indian Confederation of Linguistic Nationalities where people could have dual citizenship, Indian as well as their own national state.[23]

With so many seeking withdrawal and secession, for a time it seemed that the colonial prediction that British departure would mark the disintegration of India[24] may prove prophetic.

BALKANIZE AND WITHDRAW

Although the demand for the partitioning India was vociferous from the Muslim League and the Akalis, it was still unbelievable that India could actually be broken up. The process was set in motion with Clement Attlee's announcement on 20 February 1947. Unless the Constituent Assembly became fully representative and formed a constitution by June 1947, His Majesty's Government would:

> have to consider to whom the powers of Central Government in British India should be handed over, on the due date whether as a whole to some form of Central Government for British India, or in some areas to the existing provincial Governments or in such other way as may seem most reasonable and in the best interests of Indian people.[25]

The Congress leaders welcomed this irrevocable decision to quit and assumed that in the absence of representatives from the non-Congress areas the Constituent Assembly would proceed to make a Constitution that would embrace all areas in India willing to accept it.[26] Nehru anticipated the continuation of the Cabinet Mission Scheme so that willing areas could form a Union of India.[27] The states would either enter the Assembly and help devise the arrangements for joining the federation, or reach 'particular arrangements' with the Union on a subordinate basis. Early in March 1947, the Congress Working Committee (CWC) passed resolutions that defined its policy in the aftermath of Attlee's statement. They called for the partition of Punjab between Muslim and non-Muslim areas. While they hoped for the entry of all provincial and state territories into the Constituent Assembly, they accepted that its work was 'essentially voluntary'. There must be no compulsion, and provinces and parts of provinces must be free to accept, by the choice of their own people whether to join the Union.[28]

On 8 April 1947 Nehru outlined the Congress approach to the transfer of power in an interview with Lord Mountbatten.[29] He emphasized that *a Constitution should not be imposed on any area against its will and that provinces and partitioned provinces should be free to join Hindustan-Pakistan or possibly even remain completely indpendent.*[30] On

1 May, CWC reiterated its acceptance of the principle of Partition by self-determination. For the sake of a final settlement of Muslim claims, the Congress accepted the cession by self-determination of the Muslim majority areas. Congress would lose to Pakistan the areas of Sind, Baluchistan, West Punjab, East Bengal and the NWFP but the possible loss of the whole of Bengal was averted and an assurance of Dominion Status for the rest of India within weeks was secured. Under the dual dominon deal there was to be a common governor-general for India and Pakistan and a joint defence council.

PRINCELY STATES

Policy and protest proceeded from the 'Memorandum on States' Treaties and Paramountcy that the Cabinet Mission released in May 1946.[31] It was the work of Sir Stafford Cripps supplemented by some suggestions from Sir Conrad Corfield, Political Advisor to the Crown Representative. It spoke of an interim period between the British Indian parties acceptance of a plan and final transfer of power. During the interim period the states could participate in the process of constitution making by joining the Constituent Assembly. The states were assured that the British Government would not and could not under any circumstances transfer paramountcy to an Indian Government. The rights surrendered by the states to the paramount power would return to the states. When British India became fully self governing, His Majesty's Government would cease to be able to exercise the powers of paramountcy, which must then lapse: 'Political arrangements between the States on the one side and the British crown and British India on the other will thus be brought to an end. The void will have to be filled either by States entering into a federal relationship with the successor Government or Government in British India or failing this, entering into a particular arrangement with it or them.'[32]

On 10 May, when Mountbatten showed the Cabinet's revised plan—Nehru alleged that it represented a Balkanization of India.[33] The states were practically encouraged to stand out of the Indian union, the larger ones to become allies of Britain, playing off Pakistan against the rest of India. This sparked off a political debate between the Congress and the governor-general's office. The Congress felt that after the transfer of power the paramountcy over the states should also be transferred to the Congress. Nehru condemned the proposed reservation of power to the princes and threatened to encourage rebellion in all states that stood out of the Assemblies. The cumulative result of the debate and Congress insistence was the creation of a States Department that would deal with concerned issues with V.P. Menon and Sardar Patel in charge of it. Thus, the policy of invitation for accession was formulated.[34] The Indian Union 'could never agree' to the states becoming independent 'which means having external relations and the power to declare war or peace and controlling its defence and communications. . . . The facts of geography cannot be ignored and the dominant power will necessarily exercise certain control over any state which does not choose to come into the Union.'[35] This provoked certain Princely States to favour outright independence. The more ambitious rulers or their dewans (of states like Hyderabad, Bhopal and Travancore) were dreaming of an independence which would keep them as autocartic as before. Such hopes received considerable encouragement from the Government of India's Political Department under Conrad Corfield till Mountbatten enforced a more rigid policy.[36] Even the Independence Act provided that the withdrawal of British meant the reversion to their original status as far as the Princely States were concerned.[37]

There was a hint of a rebellious mood among the people of the Princely States. A new upsurge of peoples' movement had begun in 1946-7 demanding political rights and elective representation in the Constituent Assembly.[38] Nehru presided over the Udaipur and Gwalior session of the All India States People's Conference (December 1945 and April 1947) and declared at Gwalior that states refusing to join the Constituent Assembly would be treated as hostile.[39] But verbal threats and speeches apart, the Congress leadership—or more precisely Sardar Patel, who took charge of the new States Department in July 1947 with V.P. Menon as the Secretary—tackled the situation in what had become the standard practise of the government: using popular movements as a lever to extort concessions from the princes while simultaneously restraining them. In other words, the incorporation of Indian states took place in two phases, with a skilful combination of baits and threats of mass pressure or both.

EXCLUDED AREAS

The hectic political activity over schemes and plans had also affected north-east India which consisted mostly of Excluded and Partially Excluded Areas. Assam was a Governor's Province but Tripura and Manipur were Princely States. The Khasi-Jaintia along with Garo

Hills were Partially Excluded but Naga Hills, the Mizo Hills and the hills of present Arunachal Pradesh, were under Excluded Areas. Though the 25 Khasi states under the administration of Syiems, Lyngdohs, Sirdar and Wahadadars were essentially Princely States, some of them were treated as Partially Excluded Areas. The Excluded Areas were under the executive control of the Assam governor. The Partially Excluded Areas were under the control of the governor and subject to ministerial administration, but the governor had an overriding power when it came to exercising his discretion. No act of Assam or Indian legislatures could apply to the Excluded Areas unless the governor in his discretion so directed. He was empowered to make regulations for these hills. The administration of these hills was his special responsibility. With no representatives in the Assam Assembly (the Partially Excluded Areas sent one legislator each) political activity above their village and local level could hardly have existed. The politics of the two larger parties of the Assam Legislature had minimal affect in the hills. The Naga tribal area of the Naga Hills district and the Tirap Frontier Tract were virtually outside British India as there was a statutory boundary between them and the adjoining districts of the province.[40] While the Government of India treated this area as tribal and unadministered, the Treaties of 1862 and 1874 with the tribes of these hills referred to them as foreign and a distinction was made between the boundary of the Queen and their country and the limits of the British territory was fixed at the foothills.[41]

During the period preceding independence that is being discussed presently, plans were mooted to remove the Naga and Mizo Hills from British India and to convert them into a British Crown Colony. As early as 1928 and 1930, John H. Hutton, the Deputy Commissioner of Naga Hills and N.C. Parry, the Superintendent of Lushai Hills had prepared plans for a separate province to be known as the North-Eastern Frontier Province with as many of the Backward Tracts it could possibly include in Assam as well as Burma.

John H. Hutton presenting the case of the Nagas to the Indian Statutory Commission had asserted that the tribals of north-east India were racially, linguistically, culturally, politically and economically distinct from the Indians. As such he was opposed to the inclusion of the hill districts in the reformed constitution. He believed that tribals of the hills district would not be served best by inclusion in the scheme of Constitutional Reforms. In fact, they would suffer by joining the people of an irreconcilable culture in an unnatural union which would ultimately harm them and the people of the plans too.[42]

N.C. Parry, Superintendent, Lushai Hills District also shared Hutton's opinion and argued for the exclusion of the Lushais from the proposed constitutional reforms.[43] In March 1928, N.C. Parry had placed before the government a plan for the future of the hill tribes. He had suggested the establishment of a North-Eastern Province comprising as many of the Backward Tracts it could conveniently include from Assam and Myanmar. The following were considered suitable for inclusion into such a province: the Garo Hills, Khasi Hills, Janitia Hills, Mikir Hills, Lushai Hills, North Cachar Hills, Naga Hills, Sadiya and Balipara Frontier Tracts, Chittagong Frontier Tracts, Pokaku and other Backward Hill Tracts in Burma. It was felt that Kohima would be a suitable headquarter as it connected with both Assam and Burma. There is no better exposition on the hill districts of the India-Bruma frontier—favouring their union under one administration— than that of Hutton's plan (1930). Hutton had that 16 districts in India and Burma be combined into an agency or commission. To Parry's plan Hutton added the Arakan Hill Tracts, the Chin Hills, parts of upper Chindwin districts, the Hukong Valley and the Shan states of Thangdut of Burma, Manipur, Tripura and Hakimpur Frontier Tracts. Without giving any reasons he wanted the Garo Hills, the Balipara and Sadiya Frontier Tracts to continue to remain under Assam. Such a province could support a cadre of its own without much difficulty for it would be extremely easy to recruit from Europe, which was not likely to be the case with any province in which service under a reformed local government was normal. It was felt that tribes would gain immensely by a consolidated treatment and sentiment. It would provide an opportunity for political advancement which could be converted into a pan-tribal sentiment covering a much wider area.[44]

However, the approach to this issue had to be changed in view of the constitutional developments between 1993 and 1935. As we have seen up until 1930, there were two plans to place these tribal areas under a single administration. The post-1935 period saw a new approach of separating these areas from India and Burma and to constitute a Crown Colony Protectorate under the direct rule of the British Crown. The most outspoken champion of this scheme was Sir Robert Reid, the then Governor of Assam (1937-42) who had assumed a paternalistic attitude towards the tribals of the north-east and argued that the British Government had a responsibility towards the future welfare of 'a set of very loyal primitive people who are habituated to look to us for protection' and who would not get it from any other source: 'It is up to us to see that they are given under our protection, a period of respite within which they will develop on their own lines and without outside influence but if the present opportunity to give them that chance is let slip, the danger is that it will never occur.'[45]

Reid based his argument on two premises: (i) the tribals of the north-east Indian hills were not Indian and (ii) in a fast changing political scenario, in the wake of the British departure from India, these tribals would not be cared for by the post-colonial Indian state. Convinced by Hutton and Parry's ideas Reid argued that 'They are not Indians in any sense of the word. Neither in origin nor in appearance, nor in habits nor in outlook and it is by historical accident that they are tagged to an Indian province.'[46] Therefore, 'We have no right to allow this great body of non-Indian animists and Christians to be drawn into the struggle between the Hindus and the Muslims which is now and will be in future with ever increasing intensity the dominating factor in India proper.'[47]

Reid found that on both sides of the so-called *watershed*, i.e. the frontier with Burma, there were a large number of tribes like the Nagas, Kukis, Lakhers, Chins, Khamtis and Kachins who have similarities in language, customs and social conditions. He was convinced that these tribes belonged to one broad group but had unfortunately been divided now between two administrations of India and Burma. It was, therefore, imperative that these divided people were united into one administration which would be ideal for their development because they had no future either in India or Burma. He reopened the issue of a separate province mooted originally by Hutton and Parry which he felt still could be implemented:

> Personally, I am in favour of Hutton's idea of North Eastern Frontier Province or Agency, embracing all the hill fringes from the Lushai land on the south right up to Balipara Frontier Tract on the north embracing on the way, the Chittagong Hill Tracts of Bengal and the Naga and the Chins of Burma and perhaps the Shan states too. I will put this under a Chief Commissioner and he in turn I imagine would have to be divorced, as Burma, from the control of the Government of India and put perhaps under some appropriate department of Whitehall.[48]

Gradually, Hutton and Parry's idea of the North-Eastern Frontier Province was replaced by Reid's own idea of a Crown Colony. Inspired by the Crown Colonies of Basutoland and Swaziland of South Africa, Reid set down to draft the Constitution of such a colony in north-east India comprising all the tribal majority districts of the then Assam and adjoining Burma, which would be independent of both India and Burma but under the direct rule of the Crown in Britain. He felt that this would enable the consolidation of this 'incredibly polygot area' into a uniform administrative unit with a common language. English could be the official language and its population for all practical purposes be regarded as a 'solid block of animists' and on the rapid process of becoming Christians. The form of polity visualized for it was to be on self-governing lines. Finance could be a problem as these areas had all along been deficit areas except the Jaintia Hills. Given their severance from India and Burma would mean the end of the present system of receiving finance from a ministry which had practically no responsibility and therefore no interest in their welfare. The only resort was to obtain finance from the Imperial sources. Reid also believed that a strong case could be made for contributions from both the Governments of India and Burma as well as the local government along whose territories this colony would exist. This contribution could be taken as matter of frontier insurance against incursions and protections. As far as manning the administration of the colony was concerned, the Burma Frontier Service could form the nucleus of a cadre under a chief commissioner.[49]

Reid found a supporter of this plan in his own state, Superintendent A.G. McCall of the Lushai Hills of Assam, who wrote:

> We have come to see very clearly that the Lushai is bound rather to the Mongolian than to the Aryan races. This begs the whole question as to whether it would not be better for the Lushai to seek shelter under the Colonial or Dominion Offices. While still remaining within the spheres of Mongolian influences, by a closer association with the hills of Burma, the Shan states, the Karens and others with whom the Lushai would find so much in common? The alternative is for Lushai to be handed over to the Aryan influences of India or Burma by a scarp of paper, in which they might possibly have no real understanding. . . .
>
> Logically, the case of such territories should rest in an international keeping, applying common standards and principles of financial aids. The succouring of all such people of similar material standard in any world of a new order would seem to constitute a common and proportionate responsibility of all major powers, united in any joint undertaking to preserve law and order through the world.[50]

The Secretary of State for India, L.S. Amery apparently favoured Reid's proposals.[51] When he was approached by Reginald Coupland for ideas on the backward tracts to be used for his third and final volume on the constitutional problem in India, Amery gave the professor a copy of Reid's note saying, 'I do this on a confidential basis on the understanding that they will not be quoted and do not represent the official view of Government concerned or his office. It would however, do no harm, I think, if the broad idea suggested by Reid were publicly ventilated if you feel it is attractive.'[52]

Coupland agreed with the idea and the amalgamation of the tribal areas of India and Burma and separate them in some way from their respective governments. In fact, Coupland echoed Reid's words when he stated, 'The inhabitants of both (Naga Hills and the Lushai Hills) are alike in race and culture. They are not Indians or Burmans but the Mongol stock. In no sense do they belong to the Indian or Burman nations.'[53]

In view of the common differences between these tribals and their advanced neighbours in the Indian plains or Burma Coupland advocated a separate administration for the tribals. The Coupland Plan caught the fancy of the Government of Burma operating from Shimla.[54] The issue of amalgamating the hills areas of Burma and India was discussed at a meeting of the Committee of Scheduled Areas between 5 and 11 December 1942.[55] One voice spoke for amalgamation and separation of tribal areas. Four others listened attentively for four days while C.W. North of the British Foreign Service argued in support of implementing the plan. A vote was taken whether the Scheduled Areas of Burma be amalgamated in whole or in part with similar areas outside Burma to form a North-East Frontier Agency. Four members voted against the amalgamation. North gave a dissenting opinion. The Chairman of the Commission of Scheduled Areas of Burma, H.J. Mitchell had earlier prepared a long confidential note on the subject which might have been read by these members and influenced their decision.[56] He had concluded his note saying that the proposal for amalgamating the scheduled areas of India and Burma into an agency administered from Whitehall should be dropped. Dorman Smith, the Governor of Burma was personally drawn to the scheme and wished to extend it to the hill areas under his charge, despite the decision of the Commission of Scheduled Areas. He was to admit later that he had gone wrong in flirting with Reid's plan and that it had resulted in a delay in his government's exploration of the reconstruction plans for the frontier people.[57] By August 1945, the proposition for a separate agency was dropped by Burma to prepare for other plans with the return of the government to Rangoon. However, in India, the Crown Colony continued to draw the attention of the last of the British administrators.

Impressed with Reids views, Amery borrowed them to make some special arrangements for other backward areas in India at large.[58] He suggested to the Viceroy, Lord Wavell that some extra constitutional arrangements for the protection of other backward tribes should be agreed to and included in a treaty between the 'new India' and the British Government, that except for the Assam-Burma tracts for which other arrangements might be made supervision over relations with the backward tribes might be vested in a British high commissioner. He also thought that it might just be possible that the reconstituted League of Nations might be induced to undertake certain responsibilities as regards these two areas on the lines of Mandates Commission.[59]

Reid's successor as Governor of Assam, Andrew Clow was disinclined to show much interest in the hill areas, though he did prepare in October 1945, a *Memorandum on the Future Government of the Assam Tribal People.* Put briefly his conclusions were that the transfer of responsibility to an external authority should be ruled out. Possible alternatives were a choice between linking the hills with the rest of Assam but subject to some separate provisions in respect of both legislature and executive functions, and a separate hill province sharing some of the administrative machinery including a common governor and capital with Assam.[60] Clow favoured the former alternative as it was not generally realized that the tribals were the most numerous and in the long run there was no future for the Assam hill tribes in separation from the plains. While recognizing the great contribution of anthropologists towards the hill people, he was not sympathetic to their outlook, which he felt was basically negative, one of preservation and exclusion. Had these advocates of presentation encouraged methods of progress suited to tribal needs, Clow said, or if they had developed the tribal system of government, the case would have been different. There had been, Clow said in opposition to Reid, no attempt to bring the tribes up to a level or to equip them to meet the changing world. Accounts 'generally somewhat imaginative' continued to circulate in early 1945 that government was holding on to a plan to create a Crown Colony.[61] In one such report, emanating from Calcutta, Wavell, was credited with taking home a plan for a province to be solely ruled by the British.[62] It also appears that the Indian Central Assembly had discussed these plans, but there was no official response as to whether there was any truth in allegations that schemes were under consideration for a Crown Colony and that no such scheme was being considered prior to the convening of the Constituent Assembly.[63]

J.P. Mills, advisor to the governor for the tribal areas, discussing the future of the hills of Assam in 1945[64] suggested three alternatives: inclusion of all the hills in Assam, the inclusion of some of the hills or the exclusion of all the hills of Assam from Reforms. He was personally in favour of the third alternative. He favoured the formation of a Union of states in the area. This Union should be under the control of either His Majesty's Government or the Government of India might be given the mandate. Sir Robert Reid also felt that it would be incorrect to say that land frontiers of India were impenetrable. The people living on either side met frequently. There was much interchange between the people on either side of the border. If a separate hill state was formed, all the hills areas could be integrated into one unit.

In case the scheme for a separate hill state was not acceptable, an undeterred Robert Reid suggested another alternative:

> A workable immediate arrangement might be found in the formation of the province of the Assam Valley only and in placing the Hills under it if they must be placed under a provincial Government without any of the safeguards that at present exists. There would be at least a chance that the old Assamese friendly method of dealing with the hillmen might be revived. But the accepted official view is that the Hills and plains of Assam would never co-exist as a single entity.[65]

In 1945, Andrew Clow considered all these schemes and thought of two possibilities; the merger of all the hill tribes of Assam, subject to the condition that the tribal customs and institutions were recognized and their outlook respected. If this was not practicable the alternative would be the constitution of a separate province for the hills with some link with regard to the administration of certain institutions. Clow felt, that

> On a long-term view, it is difficult to see any future for the hills as a separate province. While they are by no means without resources they seem too heterogeneous to form a satisfactory unit and too small even if fully united to sustain a healthy and progressive life of their own. The ultimate interest of both hills and plains lie in fusion. . . .
>
> Experience shows that it is much easier to divide states than to unite them and there is little doubt that the setting up of two provinces would create vested interests in both the areas which would oppose the union. Antagonisms tend to

arise, economic barrier grow and the people drift apart rather than together. The Hillmen whose future depends on healthy intercourse with the wider world and who have a good deal to contribute to it might well find themselves shut up in their fastness with a petty and impoverished administration. Indeed that stage might be reached when they would like to join and would be unwelcomed. Assam is never likely to be homogeneous as other provinces. The people of the plains are not so divided as those of the hills but they are far from being a single people such as can be found in equally larger areas in India. But the collection of the peoples in the hills and plains have been set out in a particular well demarcated corner of the world and their welfare will depend on this proving able to live together. . . .

There is no record of the Hill people ever combining as such under one political organisation at any period. Racially and linguistically, the Hill people of Assam belong to several ethnic groups like Monkhmer, Bodo-Kachari, Kuki, Chin, etc. with unknown sub-groups. Uniformity is no doubt observable in social organisation and even here there are innumerable differences in detail. The methods of organisations, customs, beliefs, and ways of life vary considerably from tirbe to tribe.[66]

On 6 May 1946, the Secretary of State for India, Sir Pethick Lawerence recorded in a minute, 'At the present stage of proceedings agreement had been reached by the Secretary of State and the Viceroy of the impracticability of transforming responsibility for the Backward tracts from the provinces to any outside authority whether that should be a British High Commission or a United Nation's Mandate.'[67]

This minute sealed the fate of not only the Crown Colony scheme for the hill areas of north-east India but the special arrangements that were on the anvil for other backward areas. With the convening of the Constituent Assembly all eyes were turned towards Delhi rather than London. It was already a foregone conclusion that the tribals of north-east India would have to live in India whether they wanted it or not. Manipur being one of the Princely States and the Naga and Mizo Hills being in the Excluded Areas, there fate was already being decided at the central level. The only hope was that their representatives might be invited to the Constituent Assembly. But with the change in Congress policy of not permitting withdrawal from the Indian union, the destiny of the north-east tribals seemed to have already been sealed as they were not allowed to aspire for a separate and sovereign nation of their own. Even before India had emerged as a post-colonial state the prospective position of its peripheral and numerically insignificant communities was already evident.

NOTES

1. W.C. Banerjee 'Presidential Address', Indian National Congress, 1885 Session in A.M. Zaidi and S. Zaidi (eds.), *Encyclopedia of Indian National Congress*, Vol. 1, Delhi: S. Chand & Co., 1976.
2. Rajendralal Mitra, 'Welcome Address', Indian National Congress, 1886 Session in ibid.
3. Cited in R. Coupland, *Indian Politics 1936-42*, London: OUP, 1944, p. 203.
4. M.A. Karnidkar, *Islam in India's Transition to Modernity*, Bombay: Asia Publishing House, 1969, p. 58.
5. Liaquat Ali Khan (Comp.), *Resolutions of the All India Muslim League, December 1939 to March 1940*, AIML, Central Office, Delhi, n.d., pp. 47-8.
6. M.A. Jinnah, 'Presidential Address', 27th Session, All India Muslim League, Lahore, 22-24 March 1940, in U. Kaura, *Muslims and Indian Nationalism*, Delhi: Manohar, 1977, App.V, pp. 193-4.
7. Baldev R. Nayar, *Minority Politics in the Punjab*, New Jersey: Princeton University Press, 1966, p. 89.
8. See Hindu-Mahasabha's role in the Round Table Conference in Uma Kaura, op. cit., pp. 53, 77.
9. Haroun or Rashid, *The Foreshadowing of Bangladesh: Bengal Muslim League and Muslim Politics 1936-47*, Asiatic Society of Bangladesh, Dhaka, 1987, p. 274.
10. Cited in ibid.
11. Cited in ibid., Suhrawardy's statement 27 April 1947, pp. 276-9.
12. Ibid.
13. Ibid.
14. Jinnah quoted in ibid., p. 290.
15. Sajal Nag, 'Phoenix Called Gorkhaland', *Shillong Times*, 6 May 1993.
16. Ibid.
17. Baren Ray, 'Pakhtun Nationalist Movement and Transfer of Power in India', in Amit Kumar Gupta (ed.), *Myth and Reality: The Struggle for Freedom in India, 1945-47*, Delhi: NMML and Manohar, 1987, pp. 225-6.
18. Ibid.
19. Memorandum to Nehru by Ashomiya Samrakshini Sabha, 1937, p. 4 (1), AICC, NMML.
20. Ibid.
21. Amalendu Guha, *Planter Raj to Swaraj: Freedom Struggle and Electoral Politics in Assam 1826-1947*, Delhi: ICHR, 1977, p. 316.
22. Ibid., p. 316.
23. Ibid.
24. R. Craddock, *The Dilemma of India*, London: Macmillan, 1929.
25. M. Gwyer and A. Appadorai (ed.), *Speeches and Documents on the Indian Constitution*, London, 1957, II, pp. 667-9, cited in R.J. Moore, *Endgames of Empire: Studies in Britain's Indian Problem*, Delhi: OUP, 1988, p. 75.
26. R.J. Moore, ibid.

27. Ibid.
28. Congress Working Committee Resolution, 6-8 March 1947, in M. Gwyer, op. cit., pp. 669-70 in ibid.
29. Ibid., p. 177.
30. Mountbatten Papers, Broadlands, Archives, 191, cited in ibid., p. 178.
31. Nicholas Mansergh (ed.), *Transfer of Power*, London: MSO, 1979, Vol. VII, p. 262, cited in ibid., p. 181.
32. Ibid., pp. 181-2
33. Ibid., pp. 185-6
34. Ibid., p. 189.
35. Nehru to Ismay, 19 June 1947, Mountabatten Papers, 210, quoted in ibid., p. 191.
36. Sumit Sarkar, *Modern India*, Delhi: Macmillan, 1983, p. 480.
37. Ibid.
38. Ibid.
39. Ibid. The following lines are also from the same source.
40. India Office Library Records, L/PS/12/3115A, No. 22, File 6, Memorandum on the Tribal and Excluded Areas of North Eastern Frontier, para 4, cited in D.R. Syiemlieh, 'Response of the North Eastern Hill Tribes of India towards Partition and Independence, *Indo-British Review: A Journal of History*, Vol. XVII, Nos. 1 and 2, September-December 1989, p. 27.
41. CSAA, 'Pawsey Papers, Clow to Pawsey, 24 April 1947', cited in ibid.
42. Deputy Commissioner, Naga Hills District, Hutton to the Indian Statutory Commission Memorandum of the Government of Assam, Indian Statutory Commission, Vol. XIV, London, 1930, pp. 111-18.
43. Superintendent, Lushai Hills, ibid., pp. 118-22.
44. As in note 42.
45. Robert Reid Collection, MSS, EUR E278/19. 'Assam and the North East Frontier of India', pp. 19-20, cited in D.R. Syiemlieh op. cit. Also Robert Reid, 'Assam', *Journal of the Royal Society of Art*, Vol. XCII, p. 247; Robert Reid, 'India's North East Frontier', *Journal of Royal Central Asian Society*, Vol. 31, Part I, January 1944, pp. 165-74. Also D.R. Syiemlieh, 'The Crown Colony Scheme for North East India 1928-1947', in Proceedings of the North East India History Associations, 2nd Session, Dibrugarh, 1981, pp. 172-8.
46. Ibid.
47. Ibid.
48. Ibid.
49. Ibid.
50. A.G. McCall, *Lushai Chrysallis*, London, Luza & Co., 1949, pp. 241-2.
51. D.R. Syiemlieh, *British Administration in Meghalaya: Policy and Pattern*, Delhi: Heritage, 1989, p. 191.
52. Ibid.
53. Reginald Coupland, *The Future of India*, London: OUP, 1943, p. 164.
54. D.R. Syiemlieh, as in note 45, pp. 28-9.

55. Ibid.
56. Ibid.
57. Ibid.
58. Ibid.
59. Ibid.
60. Andrew Clow, *Memorandum on the Future Government of the Assam Tribal People*, Shillong, 1945.
61. Ibid.
62. D.R. Syiemlieh as in note 51, p. 191.
63. Ibid.
64. Ibid.
65. Ibid.
66. Andrew Clow, op. cit.
67. D.R. Syiemlieh as in note 45.

CHAPTER THREE

The Crisis

The tribals of north-east India were caught unawares in the whirlpool of developments in the subcontintent. The sudden rush of events were confusing for them. The British decision to withdraw was so sudden and abrupt for the tribals (although it was not so for the rest of India) that they faced a huge epistemological crisis. British colonialism had opened up their tribal exclusivity and insularity, exposed them to the so-called civilized world, put an end to their traditional lifestyle and at the same time confined them to their own areas through devices like Inner Line Regulations and Excluded Area, etc. These tribes were subdued and subordinated but not considered important enough to be integrated into the socio-economic and political life of the rest of the British Empire in India. While colonialism kept them outside the socio-political boundary of the country, within the confines of their own world a rapid social revolution was taking place through the spread of Christianity which had begun to transform the life and values of these animist tribes. With the coming of the reforms a new culture of education and politics percolated down to the hill areas as well, and as spill-over effects resulted in gradual politicization of these essentially apolitical people. In the words of a Naga elder, these tribes were stopped in the middle of their history and submerged by a plethora of exogenous forces that were let loose on them which they could not resist. The educated among them found it offensive that though they were in the throes of modernization, there were still referred to as tribals and primitives.[1] Their society had lost its pristine quality but was still at a level unacceptable to the apostles of modern civilizations.[2] They could not revert back to their history but were not allowed to move on their own. The non-tribals and the Christian missionaries insisted on their retaining the 'tribal look' and treated them as museum pieces[3] but their own society had lost touch with its traditions.[4] They were told that they were peace-loving hillmen when they were proud of their violent past and history of head hunting. They were unable to understand the reason why they were described as uncivilized even when they had terrorized the plains people through their might. They were said to have maintained splendid isolation from the rest of India when they had constant interaction with the Indian plains even before such nomenclatural demarcation had been made. So far, the distinction, if at all, had been between the hills and the plains, but now it was going to be between India and non-India. And all this happened at a time when a kind of homogenization had emerged between the people of the plains and the hills at least at the middle class level. This was a dilemma, and a major crisis for the tribals.

MIDDLE CLASS ACTIVATED

Although the Naga-Mizo tribes and the Meitheis were apolitical in the sense that they were recent entrants in bourgeois politics, the newly emerged middle classes were not so. They were fully equipped with the nuances of such political processes and were even aware of the weaknesses of their communities vis-à-vis their participation in such politics. Significantly, they had learnt the nationalist discourse and the power it held over any other discourse. These middle classes were the pioneers of momentous changes that these areas witnessed during the next few decades. The British in successive Census Reports had enumerated the hill population and showed that various tribes in the Naga Hills were sub-tribes of one generic tribe—the Nagas or Mizos, which was a revelation to the respective tribes themselves. So far they had only thought in terms of these so-called sub-tribes and formed political associations accordingly, e.g. Ao Students Association, Angami Students Association, Lushai Student Association, Paite Student Association and so on. Now the middle class leadership took initiative to form associations which would represent themselves as one tribe and not as numerous sub-tribes. This was a result of the consciousness that in bourgeois politics numerical power of communities reflected competitive strength and *vice versa*. The Christian missionaries had introduced Roman script for the yet-unwritten tribal languages. The detribalization effort of the missionaries had also reduced the inter-tribal feuds and head-hunting substantially and brought closer interaction between various tribes of the Naga and Lushai Hills. The middle classes of these respective areas, now well-versed with the nationalist discourses found it appropriate to present themselves as a nationality or nation. The integrationists presented themselves as a subnationality of the prospective Indian Union while the secessionists presented the claim of separate nationhood. Such construction was irrespective of the historical evolution of the respective groups and was based purely on the power of such discourse and the kind of polity the middle classes foresaw for their people vis-à-vis their own aspirations in that set up. Thus, there was widespread use of concepts like nation, nationality, ethnicity, sovereignty, independence, colonialism and expansionism. A section of the Naga, Mizo and Meithei middle classes were now ready to accept the hegemony of the middle classes of the rest of India while the other section sought to challenge it and take them head no. As far as the Indian middle classes were concerned they welcomed this weak and recently evolved hill leadership under their hegemony but not their challenge. As a result of this confrontational attitude a crisis situation was inevitable in India's north-east.

RESPONSE TO BRITISH WITHDRAWAL

The tribals with their laid-back lifestyle had by now accepted the fact of British colonialism—in the guise of a paternal government—after prolonged years of mutual hostility. Responding to the tribal fears and apprehensions, the British administration had decided not to impose constitutional reforms on them.[5] But there were no well meaning gestures from the Indian leadership. In fact, if at all, it was the Indian National Congress which in its Faizpur session (1936) condemned the colonial devices like Excluded Areas and Partially Excluded Areas which it felt was

> another attempt to divide the people of India into different groups with unjustifiable and discriminatory treatment and to obstruct the growth of uniform democratic institutions in the country . . . the separation of the these Excluded Areas and Partially Excluded Areas is intended to leave a larger control of disposition of exploitation of the mineral and forest wealth in those and keep the inhabitants of those areas apart from the rest of India for their easier exploitation and suppression.[6]

Under the British the tribals had felt that they had the freedom to follow their own customs and way of life, and function in their kind of political and economic environment. But the end of the Second World War brought in drastic changes, which the tribals had not anticipated. The British declaration of withdrawal by June 1948 came as a bolt from the blue. Suddenly there was talk of independence, partition, secession of Princely States, Crown Colony, etc. A prominent Naga leader, who had lived through those changing times, summed up the situation as follows:

> The Nagas made a leap, as it were, from a distant past into the glare of the present century . . . found the world greatly changed. They looked about with uncertainty and pinched themselves to be assured that all that was true. . . . People became suddenly restive with the existing state of affairs. There was social unrest, economic unrest, political unrest. Everywhere there were cry for better, bigger, nobler things. The era brought a new impetus to all fields of human endeavour.[7]

The weak middle class that had emerged among the tribals could not but respond to the changing times. The tribals were bewildered, apprehensive and panicky because no one really talked about them. It seemed they did not have any say in matters concerning their own lives and future, and that other people were going to decide it for them and they had to live with it whether they liked it or not. The dilemma and confusion of the tribals of north-east India was very aptly and representatively recorded in the memoir of a Naga leader:

> The political wave over India was rising rapidly and by March 1945, the elders of the community had set up the Naga Tribal Association and posed some tough questions:
>
> (*a*) What are the Nagas going to do?
> (*b*) What is the future of the Nagas?
> (*c*) Are we Indians?
> (*d*) Are we not a part of India?
> (*e*) What will be our future provisions?
> (*f*) What are our safeguards?
> (*g*) Where do we stand in future?
>
> The questions were many but answers none.[8]

The Mizos too had a similar dilemma. Ethnically they were closer to Burma. In fact, half of the Mizo tribe lived on the other side of the frontier which had been artificially created between the two: India and Burma. Indeed, few other people had suffered more than these tribes who had been subjected to two successive partitions: one in 1937, when Burma was separated from India and another in 1947, when East Bengal was separated from India. Both events had affected the Naga, Mizo, Arunchali, Khasi, Jaintia, Garo and Tripuri tribals severely though no one focused on the trauma borne by these people. The Mizos, except for their educated offsprings, had no concept of an Indian nation. Their village, their people were their *hnam* (Mizo equivalent of nation). Those who lived close to the Burmese border felt that after the British withdrawal they would automatically be a part of Burma and would live with their brethern.[9] The Meitheis had a more serious problem. Although they were proud Hindus and were connected with India in many ways, they were being reportedly thrust into an union with Burma.[10] The Burmese Minister of Information, U Ba Choe claimed that Manipur had been a part of Burma, which seceded from it only about a 100 years ago.[11] And argued that since Manipur had refused to join Muslim Bengal as envisaged in the partition scheme, it should be given back to Burma.[12] Amidst panic, another news item appeared in the national newspapers that Burmese Premier Aung San was invited to Manipur ostensively to finalize Manipur's incorporation into Burma.[13] The resentful Meitheis had a meeting on 18 May 1947, sponsored by the Manipur State Congress, to protest such reported move.[14] Some insinuated it to be a Communist design dragging the Manipuri Communist leader Irabot Singh's into it.

The immediate reaction of the tribals was to look up to the British since no support was offered by the Indian nationalist leadership. While on the other side of the border, the Burmese leader Aung San grasped the predicament and dilemma of the Chin tribes living on the Indo-Burmese frontier, the Assamese leaders had no understanding of the problem. They knew next to nothing about the Mizos, leave alone being able to grasp the intricacies of the Mizo situation. The same was true of the central leadership in India. As far as Meithei community was concerned, the State Congress unit of Manipur was campaigning for its incorporation into India, as will be seen later, without trying to understand the crisis their people were undergoing or allowing them enough time. From the British too, what they received were plans to retain them under colonial rule instead of promises to grant them independence and self-rule outside India. These plans were variously named North-Eastern Frontier Province Plan, Crown Colony Plan, etc. There were mixed reactions to these plans:

> Most of our people were not at all aware of what was coming into the political arena of India; they just had no idea of the rapid developments that were taking place in the rest of the country. (But I had certain knowledge of what was likely

to happen in India soon and which would surely affect the whole of Nagaland). I was a very worried youngman.[15]

While Rev L. Gatpoh who represented the Jaintia Hills in the Assam Legislature hoped that these hills would either become a colony or protectorate,[16] his friend, colleague and minister in Assam Government. Rev J.J.M. Nichols Roy who was returned on a Congress ticket from the Shillong Constituency took the opposite stand.[17] He informed the British Cabinet Mission that 'The people of the hills who are educated and who have had experience in this political rule are greatly against such a rule.' He did not think that a protectorate would be economically viable.'When the whole of India will get independence,' he told the Mission, 'the hill people of Assam should also get their own share of independence and they should be connected with the Province of Assam.'[18] Three Garos representing their people were 'filled with dismay to hear the rumours that there is a plan of some British officials in Assam to exclude our districts from Assam and India'.[19] They opposed the plan as undesirable and demanded that their hills be merged with Assam and India. Nagas met in Kohima early in 1945 and agreed to remain in the Crown Colony provided they have their own Legislative Council.[20] Although A.Z. Phizo claimed that 'the best brains of the Nagas were whole heartedly with the British in the Scheme for that was a part of their spontaneous loyalty',[21] according to a more reliable information, the Nagas 'opposed it vehemently since they had no affection for any kind of British imperialism and colonialism in their land'.[22] The Mizos of Lushai Hills voiced their disapproval and turned down the proposal through the Mizo Union as they resented the British patronization of the rule of chiefs over the Mizo people.

The other option for the tribals was to look up to India, which after a long struggle against colonialism was soon going to emerge as a triumphant major nation. The Cabinet Mission had suggested the setting up of an Advisory Committee on the Rights of the Citizens, Minorities, Tribals and Excluded Areas. Accordingly the Constituent Assembly was to meet and formulate constitute such a Advisory Committee where tribal representatives would be invited to participate. But it would mean joining India, which had a new image now in the tribal minds. This changed image also ensued a corresponding fear and apprehension about Indian rule over the tribals.

In fact, they had never anticipated that a day would come when the British would leave and they would have to decide their own future. It was even worse that the Britishers were going to be succeeded by plainsmen about whom they knew very little. What made them suspicious about the plainsmen was that though they never had much to do with the tribals so far were now suddenly asking them to join the Indian Union. India, for them, under the changed circumstances was a world they were hardly familiar with and Indians—a people they hardly could identify with. The India and the Indians that they were familiar with were only the foothills and border tracts, and its inhabitants. That too was only during pre-British times. The colonial masters had prevented them from continuing such interaction as a result of which the two communities had become alien to each other. By now momentous changes had taken place both in the plains and hills. Even the image of the plainsmen that the tribals had, had undergone substantial change. The weak and meek plainsmen who were terrorized by the raiders from the hills were now threatening to be their new masters. And it was something which the hillmen strongly resented. The Nagas felt that they were a people with 'their own culture' and hence should be left alone to manage their affairs.[23] Indian administration to them meant the rule of *babus*, a category of people they mortally detested. They did not want to be left at the mercy of these Indian *babus* as they had found the plains people to be arrogant who looked down upon the Nagas as a naked and primitive people. And also the fact that they frowned upon their sexual uninhibitedness and passion for carousing hurt the educated Nagas.[24]

CHANGING IMAGES

The hillmen, both the Nagas and the Mizos had a relationship of interdependence with the plains people of the Ahom and Cachar states respectively. If the Nagas and the Mizos were dependent on the plains as an outlet where they bartered their products and most importantly for the perpetration of raids and head-hunting, the plainsmen of the Brahmaputra, Barak and Suma Valley too were dependent on the Nagas for salt, herbs and medicines, elephant tusks, rhino horns, rubber and other such forest products.[25] The tribals had an image of the plainsmen as being a friendly lot. Moreover, these people were also easy prey to tribal raids, kidnapping and head-huntings, and were terrified of the tribals who would suddenly descend from the hills and carry away their dear ones as slaves or prisoners, destroy the standing crops and hutments and behead people to carry their heads as trophies. In general, the tribals didn't have a high regard for these plainsmen and viewed themselves as 'superior' and 'mighty'. The tribal chiefs considered the frequently raided area as their sphere of influence and the inhabitants as their subjugated subjects even though the area did not really fall under their suzerainty and they had not formally conquered it; they only raided and perpetrated kidnapping and head-hunting in the area frequently. As a matter of fact the maharaja of Manipur, Tripura and Cachar claimed suzerainty over the Naga and Mizo hills respectively but they had no control over these areas or the tribals who considered themselves sovereign and free. It is interesting to note that on the one hand the plainsmen considered these hillmen as savage and barbaric on account of the raids and murders and on the other the Naga and the Mizo too looked down on these plainsmen as lacking the courage to fight. They found them to be ridiculously weak and inferior, incapable of defending themselves and their women and children from the tribal raids. Their warfare and weaponry was too backward to fight and thwart the warlike hillmen descending upon them suddenly. In fact, the inhabitants of the foothills lived at the mercy of the tribals which made the Nagas and the Mizos feel powerful mighty and a symbol of terror for the plainsmen of Assam, Cachar and Sylhet. The memorandum submitted to the Indian Statutory Commission (1929) by the Naga delegates had made a reference to this.[26] The tribals therefore, had no occasion to view these 'weaklings' as any kind of threat because in the relationship between the tribals and non-tribals it was the hillmen who were supreme and had arbitrary powers.

By the forties of the twentieth century there was a metamorphosis in terms of their image as well as reality. The tribals realized and resented the fact that not only were the British leaving but it was the plainsmen who were going to replace them as 'rulers'. A century of colonial rule, detribalization, Christianization and exclusion had changed the tribals too. They had mellowed down, their ideas, and images of others had changed and now they had a Western-educated middle class leadership to lead them. They had not fought a war since the last one against the British invaders. Head-hunting and raiding on the plains had been stopped.[27] The missionaries and the British administrators had made them aware that it was not the plainsmen but the tribals themselves who were backward and savage. The constant reference to them as 'tribals' and their 'primitive ways' made them conscious of this. The introduction of modern hygiene, medicines, dresses, haircut, schools, churches and so on by the missionaries[28] and their effectiveness in modernizing the hill people were an eye-opener. But being conscious of their primitiveness made the tribals insular. The hitherto confident tribes who had considered themselves 'mighty and superior' vis-à-vis the plainsmen now became different about dealing with them. Another cause of their diffidence was that the missionaries and colonial administrators constantly referred to the plainsmen as 'hostile people'.[29] The presentation of the plainsmen as different from everything that the tribals were—from their looks to food habits—had a devastating impact. The tribals could not visualize themselves as 'equals' or 'being able to adjust in mainstream Indian society and polity'.[30] Their personal interaction with the plainsmen also showed that they were treated as 'untouchables' in a largely divisive Indian society. Now that they were Christian they were more unwelcome in the complex Indian social structure. Their Mongoloid looks, their Tibeto-Burmese languages and their culture had little in common with that of the dominant Indians. In fact, they realized that they had nothing in common with the Indo-Aryan socio-cultural fabric: 'our languages are quite different from those of the plains and we have no social affinities with either the Hindus or Muslims. We are looked down upon by one for our beef and by the other for our pork and by both for our education, which is not due to any fault of ours.'[31]

The separatist demands put forward by the Muslim League, the Akali Dal, and the communal aggressiveness of the Hindu Mahasabha had only reinforced the apprehensions and fears of the tribals about their participation in the post-colonial Indian State. It was argued that if the Muslims, Sikhs or the depressed classes who were part of the Hindu fold and had cohabited with the Hindus for centuries could not live together any longer and demanded security and protection in the form of homelands like Pakistan, Sikhistan and so on, the Nagas or the Mizos would be totally unequipped to withstand the hegemony of the Hindus.[32] The tribals who were political novices and socio-culturally 'alien', and numerically weak only constitute a fraction of the massive Indo-Aryan society and polity, would be in no time absorbed within the majority and their identity would be lost forever. The proud and freedom loving tribals did not want to lose their identity, they still wanted to make decisions as far as their lives and future was concerned and refused to surrender as subjects to a people whom they had once considered inferior. The rhetoric of the British administrators like J.H. Hutton, N.C. Parry, A.G. McCall and Robert Reid[33] provided the necessary stimulus in reinforcing the image the tribals had built of post-colonial India in their minds. Reid in fact did not want the Christian tribals to be sandwitched between the two warring groups: the Hindus and the Muslims.[34]

The gullible tribals considered the patronizing attitude of the British administrators as being sympathetic. In fact, it was also said that Adams, advisor to the Governor of Assam on the eve of British withdrawal from India reportedly advised the Naga leaders to accept whatever terms the Indians offered to them for the time being as India was anyway going to disintegrate within the next five years subsequent to which they could also have their own nation-state.[35] Such rumours that were floating around were not contradicted and were gradually turning into beliefs nor was there any counter rhetoric from the Indian nationalists to allay the fears and misgivings of the tribals.[36] It was a straight case of the tribals being taken for granted and their simplicity and political naivette exploited as we shall see subsequently.[37] The hesitation of the tribals was construed as reluctance to join the union by the disintegrationist political environment of the nascent nation-state. The innumerable withdrawal announcements encouraged the Nagas and the Mizos too to think it terms of separation and withdrawal. The precedents and examples were already there, and also the leadership. They just had to decide about their withdrawal. In a political climate where secessionist and separationist ideas seemed to thrive, the tribal leadership found it easier to contemplate withdrawal rather than merger. But there was a stream of thinking which was not in favour of outright severance of ties with India.[38] There was thus a difficult situation in which the tribals had to choose between two courses of action.

THE FEAR

The Nagas were not the same people in the forties of the twentieth century whom the British had conquered in the later half of the nineteenth century. Great changes had taken place since then. The First World War blew strong winds across Nagaland in terms of ideas and images. Then there was the battle of Kohima against the Japanese in the Second World War. The Nagas not only saw the war but experienced its ravages. They worked as helpers and porters in the British Army. The head-hunting Nagas accustomed to tribal warfares actually witnessed a modern warfare. Then there were the Naga soldiers who formed part of the British Army returning home from overseas after the war. There were refugees trekking from Burma to

India through Nagaland. Close on the heels came the announcement of British withdrawal, separatist claims of the Muslims and Sikhs and the prospective partition of India. There were questions regarding the future of the Princely States and tribal areas. The Nagas were, to quote secretary of the Naga National Council, T. Aliba Imti's words, 'at the most critical time of their history. They were neither sure of their identity nor their future.'[39] There was a serious debate going on among the educated Nagas over their identity—whether they were Indians or not, and they form a part of India or not.[40] The long years of protective exclusion from India and Indians had inhibited them from identifying with India. But at the same time they formed a part of British India. But they know that though India consisted of a heterogeneous people, they were distinctly different from the Nagas in social and cultural terms. The backward Nagas were no political match to them. So there was every possibility that 'thrown among forty crores of Indians' the one million Nagas with their 'unique system of life will be wiped out'.[41] This 'unique system of life' was precious to the Nagas and they desired its perpetuation. While this desire formed the core of the Naga popular perception of 'independence', 'sovereignty' to them meant to be 'left alone' to live life in the inherited and customary was—however crude and uncivilized it might seem to others. Whereas joining India might mean a 'threat to their old way of life, their freedom, their valued traditions, their customary laws, their land (and mystic mountain homes)'.[42] They were apprehensive that becoming part India would mean interference in their socio-economic life, an alien administrative setup, imposition of taxes and inability to develop according to their own free will. Essentially they feared the rule of people 'who had no knowledge about the Nagas'. They had conveyed these fears to the British Government as well as Indian leadership repeatedly in the memorandum submitted to the Statutory Commission in 1929 and to the Constituent Assembly. But at the same time they were not in favour of instant severance of all ties with India. T. Aliba Imti felt that it would be 'unwise' for the Nagas to cut themselves off from India at that stage.[43] The Nagas could press for 'protection' against the fears and apprehension and secure 'Home-rule' under Indian administration. Since the debate over the identity and future of the Nagas was still continuing and the fear of alien rule still persisted, the Naga elite wanted time to resolve these issues themselves. They wanted a ten-year interim arrangement at the end of which the Naga's could decide if they wanted to merge with India or otherwise. Up until then they wanted a political state conducive to the perpetuation of 'Nagaism'—the Naga way of life. But despite initial agreement, the Government of India backed out and refused the ten-year term option.

An example of the Naga view of independence is provided by T. Sakhrie, the NNC secretary wherein he clearly stated the life this community feared it would lose if it became part of India.

> In the life of the village the family is a permanent living institution, a conscious unit in the national polity. Every family is proud of its own and no family has ever been left by their fellowmen to the mercy of circumstances. Possessing his own house, built on his own land, no family ever pays tax. Forest, woodlands and rivers belong to the people for their exploitation without paying taxes. We cultivate as much land as we need and there is no one to question our rights. We have food to eat and drinks to drink exceedingly above our needs. Truly God has been good to us. Three square meals a day and Zu (rice beer) without measure. We have no beggars. . . . It has no landlords to harass it and no revenue collectors to knock on its doors. For the family is the master of its own affairs and wonder of wonders we have no jail. We do not arrest nor ever imprison anyone. Our civil authority is God in the matter of life and death. We fear nobody, individually and collectively. We are a healthy people and fear corrupts the health of men. What peace we have. No police no CID, we have no locks. Our granaries are kept outside the village and no guard is needed for there is no one to steal from them. We travel as we like and it costs us nothing. If by ill-fortune a man falls sick or dies, he is brought home to his family without counting the costs. We talk freely, live freely and often fight freely too. There is order in this chaos; if I were to choose a country, it would be Nagaland, my fair Nagaland again and again.[44]

The Nagas had a 'shrewd suspicion' that there was a conspiracy to take away this—freedom of 'living freely, taking freely and fighting freely'. Becoming a part of India to them was an 'imposition of an alien culture and administration' which would mean a loss of their land and freedom. It is said that the 'Naga love for his ancestral home and fields is so great that the slightest suspicion regarding its safety drove him to destruction.' During the pre-accession period, the fear of loss of land and freedom, and Indianization were harped on continuously so effectively that it became a part of their psyche.

> The tillers of soil who had grown and lived on the land, know the precious value of the land to which they are affectionately attached. Living their lives in the mystic mountain houses, the villagers felt a threat to their old way of life, their freedom, their valued traditions, their customary laws, their land, and everything that was theirs but begin to wonder if in the changing context of things, it would be possible anymore.[45]

While discussing the Simon Commission proposals for the Naga Hills Mr Cadogan a member of the House of Commons (May 1935) who had talked with the people of the Naga Hills, told the House that these hillmen 'resent' even the 'slightest suspicion that something is being done to take away from them their immemorial rights and customs'.[46] There was also a stronger lurking apprehension in the tribal minds that the teeming masses of Indian plainsmen would over crowd their habitat, disrupting their traditional way of life and depriving them of their most precious possession—their lands. The tribals did not possess anything in terms of material assets and were therefore all the more fanatically attached to their land which provided them and their families the essential sources of sustenance year after year. Therefore, if the British were leaving, the Nagas were not ready to let anyone else into their land to rule over them.[47] The Naga perception of freedom has to be understood within this context.

THE HOPE: FREEDOM FROM FEUDAL OPPRESSION

Unlike the Nagas, the Mizos (Lushais) were not direct participants in the Second World War. But on the other side of the border, in Burma, their brethren did go through the war. Tiddim, one of the main towns of Burma inhabited by the Chins to which the Lushais belonged, was occupied by the combined Japanese-INA Army. Although one of the Mizos joined the Japanese Army despite invocations, the Chins referred to the Japanese as *to thak* or the new masters.[48] Thus, they too felt the winds of change. The closeness of the Japanese troops and the political enslavement of the Mizo people at the hands of the British superintendent and their own Mizo chiefs' fostered political consciousness in these hills. News of the nationalist struggle for independence being waged in the plains under the leadership of Mahatma Gandhi on the Indian side of the frontier and Aung San on the other kept filtering through the sieves of British censorship. The erstwhile apolitical tribals now were beginning to be apprehensive about their future. Those living close to Burma felt that they would prefer to be part of that country while those who lived in Assam wished that they would be left alone.[49] They had no idea of the emergence of modern Indian or Burmese nation. And merely wanted to live with their own people, and their ethnic tradition, international demarcation of borders at the point meant nothing to them. But the educated among them knew it was time to make decisions. Education had already opened the windows of the world to the few educated Mizos. The ex-servicemen coming back home after the war also related new idea and experiences. The new outlook influenced the Mizo perception of independence which was in turn determined by an immediate problem the Mizo populace was facing—the oppressive rule of the chiefs. From the time the Sailos assumed chieftainship Mizos have been reeling under their oppressive rule. The theoretically egalitarian society was virtually polarized into two loose classes of people, the chiefs, the *upas* (close advisors) and their favourites on the one hand and the commoners on the other. The chiefs generally functioned like autocratic rulers treating common people 'as personal servants and even salves'. Entitled to a number of customary taxes, the chiefs paid *fathang* or taxes in kind out of the total individual share of paddy, *Sachchiah* or the best portions of meat of animals, animals killed, in a hunt and *Kmaichchiah* or part of the best honey obtained. Besides these, people had to pool their labour to construct the chiefs house whenever summoned to do so. The situation was amply recorded in the Mizo folk song:[50]

Bai thak arva
artui khawn leh lal hnungvi rengkaning tawh
kawltu chawi lal daltu an ni sazai hian pui an ni

(We have had enough of Chief's rule. He orders us to do all his work which we have to do. He demands eggs and chickens frequently from us which we cannot refuse. We always have to carry out his orders and in the process get late for our own work. Alas! this is indeed a severe punishment.)

There are many such folksongs which express similar grievances against the oppressive rule of the chiefs. Suffice it to say that the chiefs' office had ample opportunities to practise corruption and indeed they did. They took bribes (*ramhual*) from villagers who wanted to be allotted best of land. The chiefs had their own favourites who were granted special favours at the cost of the commoners. The Lushais has risen in a massive widespread but unsuccessful revolt against the chiefs just before the advent of the English (*c.* 1800).[51] The British recognition of the office of chieftainship not only perpetuated their rule, but strengthened it. Under the colonial protection the chiefs began to abuse their power and authority. The immediate issue before the Mizos was to get rid of the chiefs. The situation was complicated by the emergence of a small educated Mizo intelligentsia which sought recognition as the Mizo elite. This was resented by the chiefs who were not only the traditional elite but were also recognized as such by the British.

The imminent withdrawal of the British from India provided an opportunity to secure the abolition of chieftainship. The Mizo commoners were optimistic that they could secure an assurance to this effect from the Indian National Congress and merger with India on this condition. For the Mizos the fear was the continuation of chieftainship which they wanted to halt even at the cost of losing their sovereignty.

APPREHENSION

The Meitheis, even though a Mongoloid race and Tibeto-Burmese speaking, were different from the Nagas and Mizos. Hinduism was a state religion in Manipur from the eighteenth century. Even though imposed from above, Hinduism soon established a stronghold. Within a century, there was a rudimentary caste system in operation, dominance of Brahmins and social exclusion of the tribals from the Hindu society. At the same time, it blended well with the pre-Hindu semi-tribal structure producing a synthesized Hinduism. The Metheis, specially the dominant Kshatriyas and the Brahmins who were surprisingly sizeable section of the population took pride in being Hindus and a constituent of the Indian civilization.

Manipur also has a rich history of social and political movements. Colonial rule and the consequent socio-economic transformation of Manipur destabilized the closed society and created quite a few tensions in its feudal structure. The anti-colonial resistance movement led by Tikendrajit Singh did not end with his execution. It had filtered down to the masses. This popular unrest against the British entry into Manipur and its colonial regime continued till the 1940s. The Kuki Rebellion (1917-20) and the movement under Jadonang and Gaidinliu (1930-49) were part of this unrest and attempts to shake off the oppressive regime. Then there was a movement against the abolition of slavery and *lallup* (1892) followed by Bazar Boycott Agitation (1920) and Anti-Pothang Agitation (1909-11). This was followed by the Nupilan Movement (first phast—1904, second phase—1939-40), Sanamahi Movement (1930), State People's Movement for Responsible Government (1946-8) and the Communist Movement (1948-50) attempting a Telengana-like uprising. Among these, the Bazaar Boycott Agitation, the Sanamahi Movement and the Nupilan Movement though results of local conditions, had serious implications as far as the shaping of the anti-Indian attitude was concerned.

Along with the British, it was the Marwaris, and the Sikh merchants-cum-moneylenders who entered Manipur and monopolized the trade the mercantile practice. Often they would buy up the

Imphal valleys entire rice production for export. This often created severe shortages in the local market. The war time export during both the wars by the Marwari (called Mayangs by the Meithies) traders succeeded in creating a severe crisis and famine conditions in Manipur. The sheer severity of the situation prompted the women folk of Manipur to organize and lead an all-womens' movement known as the Nupilan Movement (1939-40) protesting against the export of local rice by outside traders. This successful movement created a negative image of Indian businessmen and traders as 'unscrupulous people'. The continuation of such practice by the Marwari traders despite protest movement and social exclusion only reinforced the negative image of Indians in the Meithei mind.

Another significant development took place in the 1930s in Cachar where a sizeable Meithei population lived. The rejection, socio-religious ostracization, and disapproval of the Meithei Hindus by the Bangali caste-Hindus made the Meithei community reject Hinduism and revert to their former animist religion known as Sanamahi. Thus, the Sanamahi Movement was an effort to reject Hinduism and go back to the Sanamahi cult. Though the movement was not successful then (it was a huge success in the 1970s) it made people aware of their pre-Hindu roots as well as the possibility of being rejected as Hindus by the vanguards of mainstream Hinduism. Thus, an image of Indian as a hostile cultural, economic and political system and Indians as part of that system was slowly being built in the popular mind. The Meithei mind had slowly begun to have misgivings and apprehensions about India. The image of the exploitative Marwari businessmen loomed large in his vision whenever he thought of India and Indians about whom he had very little idea.

Manipur was one of the first states to launch a State People's Movement against princely autocracy favouring a popular government. Prolonged struggle under the leadership of Hizam Irabot had succeeded in installing an elected state Assembly. The release from a claustrophobic autocracy and peoples' victory was celebrated with festivity but it was short lived.

NOTES

1. More than the Indian plainsmen, who anyway had virtually no interaction with the hill people after the British had taken over the hills, it was the British administrators and the Christian missionaries themselves who made such references in their words and actions.

   See, Frederick Downs, 'Study of Christianity in North East India', *NEHU*

Journal of Social Sciences and Humanities, Vol. IX, 3, July-September 1991, pp. 1-26.

P.T. Phillip, *The Growth of Baptist Churches in Nagaland*, Guwahati: CLC, 1976.

A.Y. Konyak, *From Headhunting to Soulhunting*, Aizawl: Synod Publication, 1981.

Rev. Zairema, *God's Miracle in Mizoram*, Aizawl: Synod Publication, 1978.

J.H. Morris, *The Story of Our Foreign Mission*, Aizawl: Synod Publication, 1930.

J.M. Lloyd, *On Every High Hill*, Aizawl: Synod Publication, 1984.

L. Pulamte, *An Examination of Factors that Led to the Conversion of the Hmar People: A Historical Consideration*, Bangalore: South Asia Institute of Advanced Christian Studies, 1985.

Asoso Yonou, *The Rising Nagas: A Political and Historical Study*, Delhi: Vivek, 1974, pp. 107-59.

2. In fact even the official Simon Commission referred to some of the tribes as 'backward'. Interestingly, reacting to this description, Cadogan, one of members, said in the House of Commons, in May 1935 that 'It is true that some of these tribesman eat food which, if you or I eat, would give us ptomaine poisoning at once, but you and I have no right to say that because a third person can digest food which we cannot digest, that person is therefore backward. It might be that his inside had reached a more advanced state of evolution than yours or mine, but it is a mistake to imagine and, I am speaking seriously that because their customs are different from ours, they are backward in every sense . . . these little tribesmen are more sophisticated in their own way then perhaps the committee may imagine.' See Asoso Yonou, op. cit., pp. 133-4.

3. Aliba Imti in his memoir reports that in the Naga Hills there was a unwritten regulation ordered by the deputy commissioner that 'no (tribal) student could dress in the western way and to have his hair cut in the western mode. They were to dress in loin cloth as that was the dress of the tribals and to have their hair cut in the tribal way, round the head and anyone not found in this tribal attire and hair cut was to be fined a sum of Rs. 2—a big sum in those days.' See T. Aliba Imti, *Reminiscences: From Impur to Naga National Council*, Mokokchung: Author, 1988, pp. 35-6.

   Frederick Downs, op. cit., also reports about such restrictions on the tribals by Christian missionaries. Also see, Asoso Yonou, op. cit., for corroboration. What is striking was that both the missionaries and colonial administrators wanted the tribals to retain their 'tribal looks' but effected changes in all their practices and customs and imbued them with victorian values and morals superseding their own.

4. S. Lokendrajit, 'Identity and Crisis of Identity', *North East India History Association Proceedings*, Pashighat, 1986; Hector D'Souza, 'The Emergence Self of Nagaland', in Subhadra Mitra-Channa (ed.), *Nagaland: A Contemporary Ethnography*, Delhi: Cosmo, 1992, pp. 275-90.

5. The Simon Commission declared both the Naga and Mizo Hills as 'Excluded' from the purview of Reforms.
6. A.M. Zaidi and S.G. Saidi, *Encyclopaedia of India National Congress*, Vol. II, (1936-8), New Delhi: S. Chand and Co., 1980, pp. 262-3.
7. T. Sakhrie quoted in Verrier Elwin, *Nagaland*, Shillong: Govt. of Assam, 1963, pp. 71-2.
8. T. Aliba Imti, op. cit.
9. Nirmal Nibedon, *Mizoram: The Dagger Brigade*, Delhi: Lancer, 1980, p. 26.
10. *Hindusthan Standard*, 14 May 1947, cited in K.M. Singh, *Hijam Irabot Singh and Political Movements in Manipur*, Delhi: B.R. Publishing, 1989, p. 203.
11. *Hindusthan Standard*, 14 May 1947, cited in ibid.
12. Ibid.
13. K.M. Singh, op. cit.
14. Ibid.
15. T. Aliba Imti, op. cit., p. 48.
16. D.R. Syiemlieh, 'Response of the North Eastern Hill Tribe's of India Towards Partition', in *Indo-British Review: A Journal of History*, Vol. XVII, Nos. 1 and 2, September-December 1989, pp. 27-35.
17. Ibid.
18. Ibid.
19. D.R. Syiemlieh, 'The Crown Colony Protectorate for North East India: The Tribal Response', in *North East India History Association Proceedings*, 1990 Session, Imphal, pp. 206-11.
20. Ibid.
21. A.Z. Phizo to C. Rajagopalachari, 22 November 1948.
22. Asoso Yonou, op. cit.
23. Nari Rustomji, *Imperilled Frontiers*, Delhi: OUP, 1989, p. 29.
24. Ibid.
25. Details given in Appendix I.
26. Memorandum to the Indian Statutory Commission from the Naga Club, *Indian Statutory Commission Report*, Vol. XIV, London, 1930, pp. 109-10.
27. J.P. Mills Report on Naga Hills, Census of India, 1931.
28. Fredrick Downs, 'Study of Christianity in North East India', *NEHU Journal of Special Sciences and Humanities*, July-September 1991, pp. 1-76.
29. Asoso Yonou, op. cit., p. 134.
30. It was clearly evident in the Naga Club Memorandum to Indian Statutory Commission and early NNC Memorandum to the Government of India. See note 26.
31. As in note 26.
32. D. Ronghaka, *Zoram Independent*, Aizawl, 5 May 1947, pamphlet distributed in Aizawl.
33. Loc. cit., see chapters, 'The Setting' and 'The Legitimization'.
34. Robert Reid, 'Assam', *Journal of Royal Asiatic Society of Arts*, Vol. XCII, April 1944, p. 247.

35. A.Z. Phizo to C. Rajagopalachari, 22 November 1948.
36. The only exception was Nehru who wrote a letter to the secretary, NNC.
37. Details on how the Assam Premier called the Naga and Mizo representatives to participate in the Constituent Assembly and opt for India is given in the subsequent chapters.
38. A. Aliba Imti and T. Sakhrie were leaders of this stream.
39. T. Aliba Imti, pp. 27-8.
40. Ibid.
41. Naga National Council Memorandum to His Majesty's Government and the Government of India, 20 February 1947.
42. Ibid.
43. T. Aliba Imti, secretary, Naga National Council, Public Address, Kohima, 6 December 1946.
44. T. Sakhrie, cited in Verrier Elwin, *Nagaland*, Shillong: Govt. of Assam, 1963, pp. 73-5
45. Same as note 41.
46. Verrier Elwin, op. cit., pp. 36-7.
47. Nari Rustomji, op. cit.
48. Nirmal Nibedan, op. cit.
49. Ibid.
50. Thanpuii Pa Mizo Hla (Mizo Songs) in R. Sena Samuelson, *Love Mizoram*, Imphal: Goodwill Press, 1985, p. 54.
51. Sankhima, 'A Mizo Uprising', *Proceedings of the North East History Association*, 1989 Session, pp. 200-5.

CHAPTER FOUR

The Defence

An immediate response of the tribals at the rush of events and the insecurity and fears it generated in their minds was to politically activate themselves. They realized that to safeguard their interests and aspirations it was essential to come out of their insularity and participate in the political process. Such participation in the bourgeois political process required solidarity and unification of the tribes to equip themselves to combat the hegemony and dominance of the prospective post-colonial state of India and more importantly, to resist being taken for granted and be able to assert their right to decide the future course of action.

This Unification and Solidarity Movement developed at three levels. First, at the level of all the tribes of the north-east, second, at the level of each sub-tribe and the third, at the level of each generic tribe.

At the first level, leaders of the various tribes realized the necessity of unification of all the hill people in a single but federal unit and to articulate their political aspirations. Initially they formed the Hill Leaders Union (1945) in Shillong, which worked for the welfare of the hill areas of Assam. Prominent among its founders were Capt Lyngdoh, Rai Bahadur Rupmei, McDonald Kharkongor, Rev J.J.M. Nichols Roy and J. Marak. There was also a move to unify the tribals of the hills and the plans, which resulted in the formation of the Plains and Hills Tribals and Races Association (1945). But both the organizations petered out within few years.[1] Then in 1946, same of the tribal students studying in Calcutta formed an organization called the Indo-Burma Movement whose aim was:

> to unite into one unit all parts of the land lying along the border of India and Burma and other adjacent areas which are inhabited by a similar kind of people and which can be conveniently demarcated into a unit; the unit thus formed be designed [*sic*] as 'Indo-Burma' and the people dwelling in it be called collectively Indo-Burmans whilst retaining their tribal names separately (Indo-Burma and

Indo-Burman may be changed if better names can be found). The future status of Indo-Burma thus formed (whether it will be an absolutely independent unit; an autonomous unit in free India, a part of Burma or Assam, etc.) will be decided by the representative body of the people.[2]

At the level of sub-tribes there were already organizations like the Ao Students Association, the Angami Student Association, Paite Association, etc.

At the third level there were moves to organize all the sub-tribes into one generic unit under one organization. Here too the initiative had come from the students who emerged as the natural leaders of their people.

We did not have many leaders just a handful of them and all of them were Government Servants. So even before I appeared (for) my final B.A. examination our leaders wrote to me that I should come and join the Naga People in their search for answers to so many questions . . . events took place so fast especially after Mountbatten took over as Governor General and Viceroy, that I had (to) open the Naga National Council office at Kohima on the 1st of November 1946.[3]

Prior to the formation of the Naga National Council there was the Naga Club which was the main centre of social and political meetings. Charles Pawsey, a long serving civil servant working in the Naga Hills established the Naga Hills District Tribal Council which united all the Nagas and merged all the Naga Tribal Councils. But the fast changing political scenario in the subcontinent threw Pawsey's plan in a quandary and his incipient Tribal Council had to be turned into the Naga National Council at a meeting held by the representatives of different tribes in Wokha, the centre of Lotha Nagas in February 1946. It primarily aimed at representing Naga interests and mobilizing support to the British officers working for its social, economic, political and cultural development. Originally, it consisted of 29 members, representing various tribes and published a monthly newspaper entitled *Naga Nation*. It marked a momentous event for the Naga people:

Our people were yearning for a change in our way of life because we were aware of the changes that were taking place near and around us but we were still chained to the old way of life and this was the reason why the whole Naga people welcomed the starting of the Naga National Council and freely exchanged our individual views and problems. Public opinion till that period was very much restrained because of the policy adopted by the British power but when the common people saw that the Naga National Council could be their mouthpiece, the spontaneous response was most encouraging.[4]

At a time when the Cabinet Mission Plan for a federal India was being discussed and debated throughout the country, the Naga National Council held a meeting at Wokha on 19 June 1946 and passed a resolution that it stands for the solidarity of the Naga Tribes including those of the unadministered areas. It strongly protested against the grouping of Assam and Bengal and urged that the Naga Hills should be retained in an autonomous Assam in free India with local autonomy. It demanded a separate electorate and due safeguards for the Nagas. The Assam Premier Gopinath Bordoloi visited Naga Hills in the same month to enlist Naga support for the Assamese cause. While doing so he assured sympathy to the Naga cause.[5] In October 1946, fearing the entry of Indian political parties, the Nagas passed a resolution that no member of any political party (other than NNC) would be allowed to enter into the Naga Hills without its permission apart from what was stipulated in the Inner Line Regulations. In December 1946, the draft constitution of the NNC was prepared. It talked about preserving the customs and traditions of the Naga people and to work for the growth of democratic self-government and material welfare of the people, and was subsequently adopted in 1947. But things were changing rapidly. There were unification moves all around responding to the demand of the changing times. The Garos formed the Garo National Council, the diverse Lushai tribes integrated themselves into the Mizo Union and the Khasis formed the Khasi State People's Association in north-east India. T. Aliba Imti, assuming the secretaryship of NNC, addressed a public meeting in Kohima on 6 December 1946, wherein he emphasized the need of the hour:

The NNC stands for the unification of all the Naga tribes and their freedom ... and *cannot accept anything* dishonourable at the time of deliberations for our country. I know that the Nagas are a distinctive community with sufficient technical characteristics. Today *we are in the most critical time of our history*. Everything around us in moving and the time has come for us to move rightly. *We cannot sit idle waiting to receive only what others assign us*. We must take initiative and make history of our own choice. Our destiny rests upon our shoulders ... you are looking beyond the ocean for help. Cutting it short I declare to you that Great Britain will never endanger her foreign policy for the sake of you. Lastly, never forget that you have been *excluded from every angle of life*. Who is responsible for it? I have but one word to say. *Our country is connected with India connected in many ways. We should continue that connection.* I do not mind whether future India be a Congress Government or a League Government. But as a distinctive community as I stated before, we must also develop according to our genius and taste. Hence, protection becomes inevitable. We shall enjoy home rule in our country, but on broader issues be connected with India. We must fight for it. We must get it. Keep on watching.[6]

The turbulent forties and uneven political developments affected Mizoram too. Apprehensive of their future and the uncertain present the Mizo intellectuals and elite felt that the first necessary step to determine the course of their future was to have a political party of their own.

EMERGENCE OF THE MIZO UNION PARTY

The advent of British rule had somewhat altered the socio-economic structure of the Lushai Hills. The British sought to detribalize the Lushais through the introduction of Christianity, Western education, modern hygiene and medicine. The result of these changes was the emergence of a middle class which became the natural leaders of the Lushai's. The extension of administration integrated all the sub-tribes by halting the migrating process and inter-tribal feuds. As a result the disintegrated groups gradually started loosing their sub-ethnic identities to the extent that in the late British period the Census Reports began classifying them as Lushai, Kuki, Pawi, Lakher, Hmar, etc.[7] Almost the entire population in and around the major administrative centre of Aizawl and Lunglei were known as Lushai, their immediate neighbours on the south as Pawi and inhabitants of the south-east corner of the district as Lakher.[8] Stray groups of population on the northern side were called Hmar and the inhabitants of the southern hills of Manipur were given the name of Kuki. Benefits of administration and Church education went to the people of northern and central parts. Thus, the Lushais emerged as the most advanced group followed by the Hmar. It was from these two sections that the early leadership of the Mizos emerged.[9]

Under the initiative of the Church and the administration the Mizos gained experience in organizing their community and set up the Young Lushai Association (YLA) in 1930. It was a socio-religious organization dominated by church leaders and prominent citizens who collectively worked for the social welfare of the people. The main objectives of the YLA were: (1) to utilize leisure constructively,

(2) work towards the improvement of Zoram, and (3) advocate the Christian way of living. The YLA soon realized that the term 'Lushai' included only one ZO tribe. Thus, the term was replaced by 'Mizo' to include all the sub-tribes. R. Vanlawma, the first matriculate among the Mizo's was its general secretary.[10]

The Mizos were generally complacent under British rule. After a long period of violence and hard struggle for subsistence, they had settled down to a peaceful life. But the stupor was broken by the abrupt British decision to withdraw from India, and left the Mizos uncertain about their political future. They first had to mobilize themselves under a single political organization. But the Mizos had another problem to confront: *autocracy* of the chiefs. The Mizo tribals had evolved a strong patriarchal system where the chiefs had supreme power over the rest of the society.[11] This development was the result of a long evolution of its political system, during which the Salio chiefs emerged as the most prestigious clan among the Mizos.[12]

The rule of these Salio chiefs in course of time became autocratic and oppressive. Each chief ruled his own territory (*ram*). The chief would take the best plot of land and the next best was taken by the *ramhuals*. The chiefs allowed people to cultivate their land and in return took tributes in kind (*fathang*) which consisted of six kerosene tins of paddy and animals killed in the hunt called *sachiah*. He was entitled to a share of the best honey collected by the people called *khuaichiah*. As an arbiter in settling disputes he also received fines in kind in the shape of the *mithun* (wild bison). The chiefs could expel anybody from the village or his territory.[13] The people had to pool their labour to construct the chief's house and cultivate his land occasionally. The chief could also summon the people to work for his favourite councillors (*upas*). This left the commoners with no time for their own work. Quite often there was forceful confiscation of the commoner's property. Some of the chiefs were so dominant that British officers who came in contact with the Mizos suggested a policy of reconcilation.[14] These officers administered a district through the chiefs and conferred on them even greater powers than they enjoyed traditionally.[15] The British officers held discussions with the chief's council which had 22 elected chiefs. The council was taken to be the representative of the people, thus, the Mizo society was divided into two groups, a small minority of chiefs who ruled over a majority of commoners. The commoners were not only victims of this oppression, even for approaching the government for redressal of their grievances they had to go through their chiefs.

The British administration had always used the institution of chieftains to rule and influence people.[16] During the Second World War the chiefs were made to take an oath that they would fight against the Japanese as their enemy.[17] But, by the end of the Second World War, the British administration realized that not only were the people agitated over the continuation of the oppressive rule of the chiefs but were no longer isolated from the political developments in the rest of the India. The secret meeting of the Mizo youths with Rev J.J.M. Nichols Roy, was a proof of this. Something urgent had to be done to counter this tendency. The opportunity was offered by the election of circle representatives. The administration of the Lushai Hills was based on the division of the hills into circles, and people from these areas elected representatives to form a District Conference to assist the administration. The District Superintendent Mcdonald called for the election of circle representatives which was held on 16 January 1946.[18] The subsequent District Conference of the representatives showed that the commoners had 23 representatives while the chiefs had 20 representatives. The District Conference which was represented by circle representatives of the commoners was supposed to be elected by households. The common people felt that since they were in a majority they should have more representatives than the chiefs.[19]

But the president of the conference, Superintendent Mcdonald rejected the demand. The ill-conceived plans of the administration to use the chiefs as tools was exposed. The enraged commoners boycotted the conference and arranged for a separate conference of the commoners.

To pursue any political activity it was mandatory for the Mizos to obtain the permission of the administration. R. Vanlawma, the general secretary of the Young Lushai Association (later renamed as Young Mizo Association) and had experience in running organizations, sought permission and was allowed to hold to commoners conference. On 9 April 1946, the conference was held in Aizawl where a resolution was passed in favour of the formation of a political party, was taken to the superintendent who approved the proposal.[20] Thus, on 9 April 1946 the first political party of Mizoram, the Mizo Commoners Union was formed. The shrewd Vanlawma insisted on using the word Mizo in place of Lushai as the former was a generic ethnic term, which would include all the Mizo tribes rather than the Lushai which was the name of just one sub-tribe.[21] His idea was to integrate all the sub-tribes of Mizo's under one umbrella organization.

At the same time the word 'commoners' implied the strong anti-chief character of the party. But since the anti-chief character of the party was dividing the Mizos between the chiefs and commoners and thereby weakening their strength, Vanlawma had it deleted and the party came to the known as the Mizo Union.[22]

The constitution approved the name 'Mizo Union' and declared the organization to be only for the Mizos, even those living in and outside the Lushai Hills (e.g. Manipur, Tripura, Assam) were eligible to become a member of the party.[23] It listed the Mizo tribes and sub-tribes which could join the party: Lushai, Hmar, Ralte, Paite, Dawland, Kwan, Thadou Chiru, Aimual, Khawl, Tarau, Anal, Purum, Tikhup Vaiphei, Lakher, Kaihpen, Pangkhua, Tlanglau, Baite, Hrang-khawl, Bawmzo, Miria, Dawn, Kumi, Khiang, Anan, Khiante, Rangte, Khawlhring, Chawngtu, Vanchiu, Chwte, Ngente, Tiau Renthlel, Hnamte, Pautu, Rawithe, Vangchia, Zawngte and Fanai.[24]

The following were the aims and objectives of the party:

1. To unify and integrate all the members of the Mizo people and evolve means to the best way of governing themselves and their land and ultimately to the formation of an independent Mizoram.
2. To normalize the relation between the chief and ministers with those of the commoners.
3. To ensure better understanding between the Mizos of the all places.
4. To better the standard of living of all Mizos and to improve the low status of the Mizo women.
5. To act as the representative of the Mizo people.
6. To popularize the Mizo language so that the Mizo culture is better appreciated.
7. To reform laws made by the forefathers which had become irrelevant in the present context and uphold those which continue to be good for the Mizo people.[25]

The conference elected Pachunga, a rich Hmar businessman as the party's founder president and R. Vanlawma, an influential intellectual belonging to the Ralte sub-tribe, as the general secretary of the Union. Lalhema was elected as the vice-president, Lalbuaia as the assistant secretary, Lalminthanga as the secretary of finance and Thanga as the treasurer.

In his inaugural speech Pachunga made the following observations on this momentous occasion:

For a long time we have been striving for the unification of the Mizo people and have a forum where the progress of the Mizo people could be discussed. Those of us who are aware of the developments in the outside world were convinced that we need to do something ourselves.

We, therefore, after some deep contemplation, decided to form the Mizo Union and had a talk with the Superintendent of the Lushai Hills in this regard. He appreciated the problems that we Mizos confronted and thus permitted us to go ahead with the plans.

Thus, we formed the Mizo Union on 9th April 1946, which is a result of our long aspiration.

Thus, from the 19th of April 1946, the Mizo Union came into being as the first political party of Lushai hills. It is my belief that all of us wish it a success. It is also my belief that this Union will elevate, the conditions of the Mizo people and it will become a leading body in the future too.

The adopted constitution of the party has several clauses and objectives. Please study them diligently to know how we are going to work. If there is anything you do not understand please ask our leaders living in Aizawl to explain to you.

I have been elected the first President of the Mizo Union in this first conference held on 25th and 26th April 1946. I am happy but I appeal to you all to kindly help me carry out such a huge responsibility that is bestowed on me. At the same time please be patient with me in my inefficiencies and help me to make the party function effectively.[26]

Thus, a sparsely populated loose conglomerate of sub-tribes who were not even aware of their generic tribal identity had been integrated and unified. The migratory process of groups of clans and sub-tribes were halted and suppressed by the British conquest. Placing the tribes under a modern administration stopped their mutual feuds and inter-tribal violence. Christianity brought them under a single religion thereby, reducing their adversities. Closer contact and the necessity to communicate with each other necessitated the use of a single language. Since, the Lushai sub-tribe was preponderant in Aizawl where the administrative headquarters was, the language of the Lushais emerged to be the *lingua franca*. The decadal census enumeration and the administrative necessities provided them with an identity. Besides their village identity they became aware of their sub-tribal and generic identity. They began to use both their sub-tribal identity like Hmar, Pawi, Lakher, etc., along with the generic term ‘Mizo’. Thus, the Young Lushai Association formed in 1930 was changed to Young Mizo Association in the early 1940s.

For the Mizos the sudden British declaration to withdraw from India was a bolt from the blue. They were left with no time to discuss their future vis-à-vis the British withdrawal from India which included the Lushai Hills.

The Mizos had just acquired an identity for themselves. The British administration had kept them away from the reform schemes and also away from information regarding the freedom struggle in the mainland. They were still a disintegrated lot. The most important fact was that they were reeling under the oppression and dominance of the chiefs. The British administrator's conciliatory policy towards the chiefs had aggravated the situation. Hence in 1946, the Mizos were confronted with a huge crisis: one resulting from the evacuation of the British and the other the oppressive rule of the chiefs. Ironically the political party which was founded to counter the perpetuation of the rule of the chiefs also served as the Mizo representative in deciding its political future. With the setting up of the Mizo Union, the Mizos now were ready to confront the crisis that faced them.

The formation of the Mizo Union was significant to the Mizos in three major respects. Firstly, it unified most of the large and small sub-tribes and clans under one generic category called the Mizos. Secondly, it integrated the stratified Mizo society into one whole, e.g. the division between the chiefs, his favourites and the commoners was now sought to be removed and all of them were to be placed on an equal footing. Thirdly, the Mizos were now provided with a platform of their own through which they could meet the impending crisis. The Mizo Union thus emerged as a representative organization of all the Mizos irrespective of their sub-tribal affiliations, social status and even regional barrier. This is evident from the fact that many Mizos who were not residents of the Mizo Hills but from the neighbouring states of Tripura, Manipúr, Cachar and even Burma joined the Mizo Union. The endeavour bore fruits immediately in the sense that it brought prompt recognition to the Mizos as a separate community.

RECOGNITION TO THE MIZOS

The Mizos are a large group of conglomerate sub-tribes dispersed over a vast tract known as the Chin Hills spread over the Indo-Myanmar frontier. About half of their people live on the other side in Myanmar while the rest has spilled over this side of the Indian frontier. They inhabited an area that was mostly unadministered and therefore was not demarcated by any political boundary, and moved freely in the area. It was the British conquest which bound them within the frontiers of British India but even then there were no restrictions on their movements in the Burmese tracts as Burma was a part of the British Empire. Since the border areas between India and Burma were unadministered areas it did not disturb the free movement of the Zo tribes between the two. The first blow came when Burma was separated from India in 1937 which divided the people between two countries and even blocked their economic and social exchanges. The final crisis came when the British declared their intention to leave India. Although the Mizos were a part of India, few nationalist leaders sympathized with their plight. It was reported that the Indians were going to take over from the British the administration of the Mizo Hills without consulting any of them. The Mizos were fearful of this prospect but neither Indian leaders visited them to dispel their misgiving nor were their opinions invited.

The situation started changing after the formation of the Mizo Union. It began to attract attention from the neighbouring areas like the Naga Hills, Khasi-Jaintia Hills and Tripura. T. Sakhrie, the general secretary of the Naga National Council, participated[27] in the First General Assembly of the Mizo Union held in September 1946. The Khasi leader Rev J.J. Nichols Roy, who was also a minister in the Gopinath Bordoloi Cabinet, invited Vanlawma to Shillong, the capital of Assam for discussion. His visit to Shillong was given wide coverage in the Shillong newspapers, and was interviewed by S.B. Choudhury, the editor of *Shillong Times*. Vanlawma observes in his memoir that the question addressed to him made him realize that even the neighbours in Shillong knew almost nothing about the Mizos.[28]

CABINET MISSION: BEGINNING OF THE DILEMMA

The advent of the Labour Party to power in Britain hastened the process of transfer of power to India. But the unresolved communal tangle involving the demand for a sovereign Muslim homeland to be carved out of India led British Prime Minister Clement Attlee to send a Cabinet Mission to India, which included Pethic Lawrence, Stafford Cripps and Alexander, the last two being members of the British Cabinet. The Cabinet toured India from March to June 1946, during which it consulted Indian leaders on the issue of interim government and principles and procedures of framing a constitution that would give independence to India.[29] Andrew Clow the Governor of Assam appeared before the mission on 23 March to apprise them of the situation in Assam. He stated that Assam has always had a distinct identity and this must be preserved in the future constitution of India in the form of a separate state.[30] Saadulla, the Muslim League leader and former Chief Minister of Assam met the mission the very next day and tried to convince it that Assam was a Muslim majority province and therefore it should be incorporated in the proposed State of Pakistan.[31] Failing to arrive at a scheme acceptable to all parties, the mission suggested a three-tier federal system wherein areas such as defence, foreign affairs, communication were to be vested in the Centre. All other residuary powers were to be vested in the provinces which were to be grouped into three zones or sections. Section A was allotted to the Hindu majority provinces, B and C for the Muslim majority provinces in the north-west and the north-east. Since a full-fledged Pakistan seemed impossible, this scheme provided Mohammad Ali Jinnah with a choice of opting for a united country where the Muslims would have a majority in both north-west and north-east.

The schemes spelt doom for Assam. In case of partition, Assam had the danger of being transferred to Pakistan. Even in the alternative scheme it was not only clubbed with the Muslim majority provinces but was also with Bengal which it dreaded. The Assamese had been fighting a two-pronged battle for a long time; one, to resist the growing strength of the Muslims in Assam and two, to counter the hegemony of the Bengalees in their province.[32] Confronted by this twin threat, the Assamese leadership started a sustained campaign against both the schemes. In this endeavour they sought to enlist the support of the tribals to strengthen their case.

Gopinath Bordoloi, the Assam Premier invited the Khasi, Naga, Garo and Mizo tribals, who were part of the Assam province, to apprise them of the situation and seek their support to thwart the schemes. Vanlawma, the general secretary of the Mizo Union was invited telegraphically. When Vanlawma met Bordoloi in Shillong, the latter apprised him of the crisis and convinced him that the future of the province of Assam was in the hands of the tribals. If the tribals promise to opt for India after independence Assam could be retained in India. Together with the tribals, the Hindus would outnumber the Muslims thereby thwarting the Muslim claim that Assam was a Muslim majority province. And it was only in a secular and federal India that the future of the tribals was secure. Vanlawma was caught in a very difficult situation. Although the Mizos were aware of the impending crisis out of Britain's departure from India and their uncertain future, he was not in a position to take such an important decision on his own, especially such a serious one of promising to opt for India, and added that,

> It was very difficult to take a decision myself, without consulting colleagues, as we had not made any decisions beforehand. Most of us would want to become independent after the British quit, but the chiefs refused to follow the decision taken by the Mizo Union. So it was not possible to take steps for independence, but we were not in a position to opt for India either. But decision had to be taken. If I refused to help India, India or Pakistan might impose a status, which we might not be able to object. So I was of the opinion that it would be better to bargain for the best status that India could offer.[33]

Vanlawma thus expressed his misgivings and apprehensions about opting for India and demanded safeguards. Vanlawma cited the example of Shillong, the then capital of Assam, and said that even though it was a tribal area, its business and politics was wholly dominated by non-tribals. He would not like the Mizo Hills to become another Shillong by allowing free access to non-tribals. He emphasized that the tribals were vulnerable to economic exploitation by non-tribals who were expert businessmen, the tribals were no match for them. Moreover, even before the British departure the Indian newspapers were demanding the repeal of acts and regulations like Excluded Areas and Inner Line Regulations, which the British had evolved to protect the tribes from the non-tribals.

Vanlawma therefore extracted a promise from Bordoloi that these regulations meant to protect the tribals would not be rescinded once they join India. He vigorously bargained for his people and said:

> We are a Mongoloid people and coming from the east we are ethnologically [*sic*] different from you who come from the west. We are now Christians but even before we converted to Christianity our religion differed quite substantially from yours and it will not be possible to live with Indians under similar Law and Regulations. You are requesting us to opt for India and as a matter of fact we have the right to opt for Pakistan as well or go for independence. At the same time we are financially weak and lag behind in civilisation. We are a small nation and we need a great nation to depend upon. If we are going to help you, will you as an Indian leader, come forward to help us in obtaining our own legislature and administration? Will you help us to manage our affairs alone so that we can survive among other nations?[34]

Bordoloi reportedly assured Vanlawma of retaining the protective regulations and promised adequate representation in the Assam legislature as well as in the Indian Parliament.[35] But Vanlawma was shrewd enough to know that a small tribe like the Mizos might be given a mere two or three seats in a legislature of hundreds. Hence, he demanded a promise of full autonomy or separate administration for the Mizos:

I know in the legislature matters are decided by the majority. How can a microscopic minority like us be heard? In the Indian Parliament we would not have representation unless special arrangement(s) are made for us in the legislature or Parliament. If you insist on having the same laws and regulation (which operate in other parts of India) in the Lushai Hills too, our discussion should end here itself. If you want us to help you keep this area from becoming a part of proposed Pakistan, it will be your turn to safeguard our existence.[36]

Premier Bordoloi it is believed did promise to try and ensure substantial autonomy to the Mizos. It was felt that 'If Nehru introduced such an autonomy bill it would was likely to be passed because Lord Mountbatten was a friend of Nehru's and would support the proposal.'[37] He also seriously assured Vanlawma that no law, which might aggravate the survival of the Mizos, would be imposed on the Lushais. Both of them agreed on the question of autonomy for the Lushais, with matters relating to finance, defence and communication remaining with the centre. Thereafter, 'Vanlawma and Bordoloi concluded their negotiations with a Gentleman's Agreement whereby, Vanlawma as representative of the Mizo Union would opt to join India and Bordoloi as Chief Minister of Assam would obtain autonomous status for the Lushai Hills District.'[38] Bordoloi also offered the membership of the Sub-Advisory Committee of Tribal Affairs which was to be formed by the Constituent Assembly under his chairmanship.[39] Vanlawma accepted the proposal.

ANTI-CHIEF MOVEMENT

As pointed out earlier the formation of the Mizo Union was necessitated by the political contingency of the time, and its emergence was hastened by the continuing hegemony and autocracy of the chiefs. This was acknowledged in a subsequent memorandum to the Government of India by another political party born out of the Mizo Union.

When the Second World War came to an end, there dawned a possibility of the British quitting their Indian Empire including the Lushai Hills (or Mizoram), a political party called the Mizo Union was formed in the 9th April, 1946. People of all ranks and files were drawn to this movement because they were tired of the Chiefs rather than their eagerness to ensure their future political welfare.[40]

In the First General Assembly of the Mizo Union, this resentment became more pronounced. The assembly was held on 24 September 1946, wherein 700 representatives (two from each sector) participated. In the assembly a pamphlet was circulated by the party, which proposed to abolish *ramhual*, a privilege enjoyed by the chiefs.[41] This alarmed the district superintendent as he was afraid that the chiefs authority was being challenged and eroded by the Mizos which might lead to violent confrontation between the chiefs and the commoners. To pacify the angry chiefs, he ordered the Mizo Union to shift their meeting place from the Middle English Boys School to the Zawlbuk (Mizo Bachelors Dormitory) in the Thakthing area.

Sensing the growth of the Mizo Union, Superintendent Mcdonald became careful. He was not in favour of the Mizos joining India and suspected that the Union had connections with the Indian National Congress.[42] He organized a District conference on 7 and 8 November where all prominent Mizo leaders were invited to discuss the political future of their community. It was proposed that the Mizos be taught about democratic institutions and a constitution for future Mizoram (Vanthlang Rorel Khawl) be drawn up so that the Mizos could function on their own after the British left. 'I am afraid that Mizoram is going to vanish unless the Mizos learn the democratic system while the British are here. Therefore the British must teach the democratic system to the Mizo leaders.'[43] The proposals that were to be approved in the meeting had a clear pro-chief bias, as can be seen.

1. To confirm the existing established method of the Mizo chiefs inheritance and maintain it unless 4 out of 5 blocks (Mizoram was divided into 5 blocks) agreed to change the method.
2. The highest Mizo political office must be held by Mizo chiefs not by commoners or any Mizo Union Party leader.
3. The number of representatives from the Mizo common people and chiefs must be equal.
4. To divide Mizoram into 15 sections and draw one representative each from the common people and the chiefs for a total of 30. In addition two representatives are to come from Aizawl and one from Lunglei.[44]

This was to be the framework of a future independent Mizoram. The Mizo Union Party could not have endorsed the constitution as it stood for total abolishment of the office of chieftainship. Saprawnga, on behalf of the Mizo Union, wrote to Mcdonald that 'unless you allow the commoners to have twice as many representatives as the chiefs, we feel inadequate in representing the Mizos. Therefore, we will not attend the meeting.'[45] Mcdonald rejected the proposal and instead accused the Mizo Union leaders to be more concerned about their personal welfare than the future of Mizoram.[46] He invoked the common Mizos to come and voice their opinion against their leaders who were not concerned about the future of Mizoram.[47] The meeting was boycotted by the Mizo Union leaders which resulted in very thin attendance. An important issue like the constitution of a future Mizoram could not be discussed or approved in such a poorly attended meeting. The abstention of the Mizo Union, which was the only political party of Mizoram, rendered it meaningless. Hence the proposals were abandoned.

Thus, the British administration's attempt to promote the idea of an independent Mizo state failed due to their policy of perpetuating the autocracy of chiefs.[48] Mcdonald formulated the proposals, but the commoners led by the Mizo Union leaders could see through the motive of the British administration. Even though they idolized the British, they refused to accept the colonial administration's proposal which aimed at perpetuating chieftainship. From then on, the anti-chief character of the Mizo Union Party became more pronounced. This became stronger when the Mizo Union Party was revamped with a new executive body in November 1946.

THE NEW LOOK MIZO UNION

In the assembly of 24 September 1946, an unusual event took place. Questions were raised regarding the credentials of Pachunga to function as the president of the Mizo Union. It was felt that he was not educated enough to hold the high post of the party president. On hearing this comment Pachunga insisted on resigning but was persuaded to continue.[49]

At a meeting of the Mizo Union block level office bearers which was held at the Zawlbuk of the Thakthing area in Aizawl on 6 November 1946, there was severe criticism of president Pachunga who was suspected to be a supporter of the chiefs and British administration.[50] And as mentioned earlier since he lacked college education he was considered unfit for the prestigious post of the president of the Mizo Union. Amidst chaos the Mizo Union leader from Lunglei, Saprawnga unexpectedly moved a no-confidence motion against all the office bearers of the Mizo Union.[51] He sought the dismissal of the existing executive body and demanded fresh election. Vanlawma the general secretary of the party tried to explain to the leaders that since it was only a block level office bearers meeting a 'no-confidence motion' could not be moved. According to the Mizo Union Constitution there has no provision for election at this level and was only possible in a general assembly meeting. But no one paid any attention to his request. An impromptu election was held amidst chaos in which Khawtinkhuma—a Mizo from Tripura with a masters in History—was elected as the new president of the party. Lalbiakthanga who also had a college degree was elected vice-president. Vanlawma, the architect of the Mizo Union, sensing the turmoil, tried to withdraw from the contest against the candidature of Vanthuama the candidate proposed by Saprawnga. But the election resulted in a tie, and was broken by the chairman of the meeting Lalheima who cast this vote in favour of Vanthuama. Thus, the party unexpectedly, in mid-session, had a new executive body which entirely now consisted of educated office bearers.

But the crisis was not over yet. The election was in contravention of the Mizo Union Constitution and therefore the defeated members refused to step down. This resulted in two sets of office bearers. At the request of Lalheima, Mcdonald intervened by confiscating files and a Union's fund of Rs.15,000. The quarrel eventually ended with the party splitting into two by early 1947. The Right wing of the Union was called the Mizo Union Council.[52] It was led by Pachunga and supported by Lalmawia, Rev Zairema and Lalbiakthanga. The Left wing or the Mizo Union was led by Dengthuama, Khawtin Khuma, Saprawnga, Bawichuaka and Vanthuama.[53] While the former was anti-India, pro-chief and pro-British, the new Mizo Union tended to be militant, anti-chief and an integrationist organization.[54] It is also noteworthy that most of the new office bearers of the Mizo Union were from outside Mizo Hills and strongly advocated the integration of the districts with India.[55]

The remaining part of the year witnessed continued conflict between the two groups. There were also few changes in the executive body.[56] However, gradually the Left wing Mizo Union Party consolidated itself as the true representative of the Mizo people. There was initial suspicion about the educated leaders, but the party through its radical anti-chief policy was able to win over the people. But still a section of Mizos supported the right wingers, not on the strength of its policies but largely due to the presence of individual leaders like Vanlawma. Thus, the Mizo society was polarized between the Right and the Left wings of the Mizo Union Party. Besides the political situation of the subcontinent was also becoming clearer. It was apparent that the British were about to withdraw from India leaving it independent. It was also evident that there would be a partition of the country into India and Pakistan. The Left wing of the Mizo Union was in favour of integration with India and had not yet contemplated any other option. But there were occasional outbursts, mainly from the Right wing about an independent Mizoram after the British withdrawal. These conflicting views were debated when the Bordoloi Committee sent its invitation to the Mizo Union to select nominees to co-opted members of the above committee.[57] It started the first serious debate on the issue whether the Mizos should join India or remain independent.

MANIPUR

After the fiasco of the accession of Manipur to the federation proposed in the Government of India Act of 1935,[58] it went through one crisis after another which though local in character reflected the essential tensions of a transforming structure under the influence of global changes.

In fact, the period between 1900 and 1950s has been aptly described as a 'period of social movements' in Manipur. The long popular protest movement against the prevailing system of slavery (*Minai channaba* and *Minai Asanba*) and *lallup* (compulsory service to the state) eventually resulted in the abolition of both (1882). This was followed by a reactionary movement against the above abolition organized by the princes, who were the beneficiaries of both these forms of slavery. Then there was other movements such as the Bazaar Boycott Agitation (1920), Anti-*Pathang* Agitation (1909-11) an incendiary and popular protest (1904).[59] The Kuki rebellion burst out during 1917-20 against the British Raj which was ruthlessly suppressed. But it was revived by Jadonang followed by Gaidinliu in (1930-49).

The educated middle class of Manipur had started to assert themselves and react against the various oppressive socio-religious policies of the king and the Brahmins. In very broad terms these can be divided into two main trends. The first trend, usually known as the Sanamahi Movement had a semi-revivalistic character and was led by Naorem Phullo from Cachar. Naorem Phullo Singh a Meithei, faced the hardships of a minority community in Cachar. The severe economic problems of the Meithei peasantry, along with the religious and cultural arrogance of the Bengalee high-caste Hindus in Cachar had made the life of the Meitheis difficult. Phullo[60] who was working as an assistant sub-inspector in the Railway Police, resigned from his job and immersed himself in the task of investigating into the causes responsible for the pathetic conditions of the Meithei peasantry in Cachar. In the process Phullo launched a programme of socio-economic regeneration of the Meitheis and founded the Apokpa Marup in Cachar (1930). The Marup tried to revive the traditional religion of the Meitheis known as Sanamahi and its gods like Pakhangba, Sanamahi Leimaren and emphasized their relevance for the moral, social and economic regeneration of the community. It also made efforts to recover the ancient Meithei manuscripts known as *puya*, popularize the Meithei script and de-Sanskritize the history of Manipur. Its protagonists dismissed their the *Mahabharata* connection with the Meitheis as a myth and also exploded the myth of Aryan origin. In his collection of essays entitled *Meitheigi shel Chatnaba Hambi* (The Cause of Meithei Poverty) Phullo strongly argued that as the Hinduism followed by the Metheis involved numerous ceremonies, rites and rituals it drained the resources of the people. He also exposed the exploitative character of Brahmanism and the Brahmanic clergy of Manipur. Although the Sanamahi movement did not have much of an impact at that time, the aspect of *Apokpa Marup* appealed to the problem-ridden people of Manipur. The educated Meithei middle class took a different course of action. On the one hand, they wanted to reform the society and on the other, they wanted to preserve Hinduism and its affiliated streams of culture. They were more interested in removing the ills of Hinduism that had crept into it over the years in Manipur rather than removing Hinduism itself.[61] Pandit Atombapu Singh (1889-1963),[62] one of the pioneers of this school of thought took up the task of translating into Manipuri the original Hindu texts like the *Bhagavat Gita*, *Rigveda*, *Gita Govinda* and other such classical texts of Gaudiya Vaishnavism. The purpose of such a move was to instil a new spirit in the dying Hinduism of Manipur. In an article 'Matam Asida Maipurgi Wakhal' (Social Thinking in Present Manipur),[63] the author Gokul Chandra Singh made a scathing attack on the Meithei Brahmins whom he described as a degenerated lot, a community that was not adjusting to the changing times. The same line of argument was put forward in an essay in *Yakairol* which pointed out that while the Meitheis were struggling for higher education, the Brahmins did not bother to study beyond the scriptures.[64] In a hand written pamphlet 'Houjikki Amang Aseng Amasung Madudagi Kannanaba Upai' (The problem of Amang Aseng and the Way to Solve it) Irabat Singh argued that the legitimacy given by the religious authority to the civil system of Mangba-Sengba was due to an incorrect understanding of Hinduism.[65] And such evils could be rooted out by reforming Hinduism. At the same time this new middle class had progressive ideas and encouraged female education and advancement of overall education for Meithei youths.[66] This group of people had not only seen the contradictions of colonial rule but also the evils of monarchy. And as the emerging middle class this group advocated the establishment of a responsible government.

The demand for the establishment of a responsible government in Manipur is closely related with the birth of the Nikhil Hindu Manipuri Mahasabha, a socio-religious organization which was established under the patronage of the maharaja of Manipur in 1934. All the leading personalities of Manipur were members of this Mahasabha. The political developments in the Indian mainland and the nationalist movement inspired this elite group to seek a change in the nature of the colonial rule and monarchical autocracy. With this objective in view the Nikhil Hindu Manipuri Mahasabha was converted into a political organization called the Nikhil Manipuri Mahasabha. This change come about during the fourth session of a conference held in Imphal on 30 December 1938 of the erstwhile socio-religious organization.

The composition and the political affiliation of the members of the Mahasabha clearly revealed that it was constituted by two groups of people having two different sets of political objectives. One group was in favour of integration with India after British withdrawal while the other was against it. These differences surfaced in their political decisions at a later date. But this did not create any major hurdle in the functioning of the organization because of their hostility towards colonial rule and monarchical autocracy.

On the eve of the outbreak of the Second World War another crisis hit Manipur. To meet wartime food requirements, the government was purchasing large quantities of rice. Taking advantage of the situation the unscrupulous Marwari traders who had by now established a firm grip over the Manipuri economy, bought up its entire rice production and exported it for huge profits. As a cumulative result the subsistence economy of Manipur faced a huge food crisis. As there was no rice available in the local market it led to an artificial famine-like situation. Tension was high specially because the unscrupulous traders were Marwaris from the Indian plains (Mayangs). The Manipuri women launched a massive agitation against the export of rice and demanded official intervention. This movement came to be known as Nupilan (1939-40) and immediately spread like wildfire and though led by womenfolk, drew support from all sections of the society.

The Nikhil Manipur Mahasabha split into two over the question of support to this movement. One section led by Irabat Singh wanted to offer whole hearted support to it, whereas the other opposed such support. As a result of the split the faction led by Irabat Singh formed a new party called the Praja Sammelan whose avowed objectives were the abolition of colonial as well as feudal rule and the establishment of a responsible government.

In the meanwhile, the Second World War hit the world and along with it came the Indian National Army (INA) offensive in Manipur.[67] The campaign was ill-timed as it coincided with the weakening of the Axis Power.[68] Moreover, the INA contrary to their expectations failed to enlist the support of the nationalist leaders in India. They also failed to gain sympathy from the people of Manipur and Nagaland.[69] It appears that Subhas Bose, the INA leader had not established any contact with Manipuris up until 7 March 1944, when his handbill—containing documents and Gandhi's photo—was distributed to them.[70] Even after this only a small number of Manipuris joined the INA.[71] On the other hand, the British were able to obtain supplies and manual help from the Nagas and Manipuris when the Imphal-Kohima road was blocked.[72] Hijam Irabot was the only known leader to have supported Bose, but he was arrested under the Defence of India Rules in 1944 and was in the Silchar Jail for eight months.[73]

The post-War period saw Irabat Singh as a confirmed revolutionary with a Leftist ideology. His stint at the Sylhet Jail following high involvement in the Nupilan Movement had proved for him a training ground in Marxian ideology.[74] The failure of the INA was also a disappointment. He along with his Manipur Krishak Sabha intensified its socio-political reform movements. Irabot's slogan, 'land to the tiller' caught the fancy of the peasants. The demand for 'full responsible government', through 'adult franchise' way again adopted and passed at the second conference of the Manipur Krishak Sabha held in Nambol on 16 May 1946.[75] In response to the Cabinet Mission proposals, the Manipur State Praja Sammelan also reiterated the need for a Legislative Assembly in Manipur. In its resolution, it said,[76]

> that the Cabinet Mission and the Chambers of Princes have made a public proclamation as regards the introduction of the Legislative Assembly into those native states where the legislature has not yet been formed. The necessity of the existence of a legislature is a keenly long felt want and people have so long been enthusiastically demanding it. It takes air that the said assembly be soon introduced into Manipur. If it is a fact the Sammelan hopes that your highness the Maharaja of Manipur would graciously fulfil the long cherished hope of the Praja with a royal proclamation.

On 16 May 1946, the Manipur Krishi Sammelan too converted itself into a political party. This was followed by the establishment of the Manipur State Congress Party on 4 October 1946. Subsequently, it became a unit of the Indian National Congress. All members of the Nikhil Manipuri Mahasabha joined the Congress. Like other parties the Congress too demanded the abolition of the monarchy and establishment of a responsible government based on the principles of democracy and adult franchise.[77]

The imminence of British withdrawal made the people as well as the maharaja restive. While the movement for responsible government was intensified, the autocratic monarch dreamt of retaining the sovereignty and rule but sensing the peoples' mood for responsible government he relented and was willing to concede at this crucial juncture. He requested the British Residency in Manipur to allow him to make a royal proclamation regarding the setting up of a new administration. The British Political Agent, Gimson asked the maharaja for a copy of the draft.[78] In course of his letter dated 30 October 1946, Maharaja Budhchandra expressed a desire to establish a democratic system of administration with an elected Advisory Assembly constituted by representatives of both the hills and plains. But in real terms the maharaja had prepared only a new set of Administrative Rules. Agitated, the State Congress Party submitted a memorandum on 1 November 1946 for the establishment of a proper Legislative Assembly.[79] The maharaja sensed the belligerent mood of the people in the changed circumstances and issued a formal order (12 December) to constitute a constitution making committee to prepare a new constitution for the state. On 27 July 1947, the committee submitted its constitution to the maharaja. However, the maharaja was not fully prepared to implement the demands of the political parties.[80] Instead he formed an interim government in Manipur on 1 July 1947. The Manipur State Durbar was abolished and renamed as the Manipur State Council.[81] On 15 July 1947, Pearson, the President of Manipur State Durbar became the Chief Minister of Manipur. But soon he was replaced by Priyabrata Singh the younger brother of the maharaja.[82] Amidst such developments, the British withdrew and on 15 August when India was declared independent. Manipur reverted back to its old status—an independent sovereign monarchy.

EMERGENCE OF THE CONCEPT OF INDEPENDENCE

The Naga move bore fruit immediately. Nehru wrote to T. Sakhrie, secretary of the newly formed Naga National Council on 1 August 1946 assuring him of safeguarding the Naga interests and political aspirations.[83]

> It is obvious that the Naga territory in eastern Assam is much too small to stand by itself, politically or economically. It lies between two huge countries, India and China, and part of it consists of rather backward people who require considerable help. When India is independent, as it is bound to be soon, it will not be possible for the British government to hold on the Naga territory or any part of it. They would be isolated there between India and China. Inevitably, therefore, this Naga territory must form part of India and of Assam with which it has developed much close associations. At the same time it is our policy that Tribal areas should have as much freedom and autonomy as possible so that they can live their own lives, according to their own customs and desires. Thus, the solution would be that the Naga territory should be an internal part of Assam province and yet should have a certain measure of autonomy for its own purposes. How this should be worked out is a matter of further consideration between the peoples concerned. So far as I can see, there is no reason why there should be any excluded area apart from the rest. The whole Naga territory should go together and should be controlled in a large measure by an elected Naga National Council. At the same time the Nagas should have representatives in the Assam provincial assembly and should participate fully in the life of the province. I am glad that the Naga National Council stands for the solidarity of all the Naga tribes including those who live in the so-called unadministered territory. I agree entirely with your decision that the Naga Hills should constitutionally be included in an autonomous Assam in a free India with local autonomy and due safeguards for the interests of the Nagas.
>
> As for separate electorates for the Nagas, I am not clear in my mind as to how this will work. Generally speaking, we are against separate electorates as these limit and injure the small group by keeping it separated from the rest of the

nation. But if the Naga territory is given a measure of autonomy, some arrangement will have to be made for their proper representation.

As you know the Congress is opposed to any forcible grouping of Assam with Bengal. We are of the opinion that this is a matter for each province to decide. Assam has already expressed its opinion on the subject. What the future will be, I cannot say, But I cannot conceive of Assam being compelled against its will to form a group with Bengal.

As Advisory Committee will be elected by the Constituent Assembly it should have representatives of the Tribal areas and I hope the Tribal territories of Assam will be directly represented on it. The findings and decisions of the Advisory Committee will probably not be finally binding upon the Constituent Assembly but they are bound to carry great weight. I imagine the findings will be accepted almost in their entirety unless they go against some direct provision in the Constitution.

As I have said above the Excluded areas should be incorporated with other areas. It may be that certain special provisions for their protection and development will be made. I should like them to be treated as part of the entire Naga territory.

I see no reason whatever why an extraneous judicial system should be enforced upon the Naga Hills. They should have perfect freedom to continue their village panchayats, tribal courts, etc., according to their own wishes. Indeed it is our wish that the judicial system of India should be revised, giving a great deal of power to village panchayats.

About the unadministered territory which still contains, according to you, a number of head-hunters, I cannot definitely say how soon and in what manner it should be brought into the province. This is to be devised in consultation with the people concerned. Naturally some special provisions will have to be made to develop these people.

The question of common language must also be finally decided by the Naga themselves. The only two possible languages which would be helpful to them are Assamese or Hindustani. Most of them know some Assamese already. I think it would be desirable to encourage Hindustani as this will bring them in touch with the various changes and developments taking place in India.

Assam is still largely undeveloped and there is plenty of room for agricultural, horticultural and industrial development. This development should be so organised as to benefit the people of the soil. Certainly the people of the Naga Hills should not be exploited by others, and their right to own and work on the soil should remain with them. We should be entirely against the development of large estates owned by outsiders there. What form land ownership should take, whether it should be communal, co-operative or kind of peasant proprietorship, should be determined in consultation with the people concerned.

I might add that I am specially interested in these Tribal areas not only in the north-east of India but in the north-west as well as the Centre. They present different problems. I hope that in an independent India there will be special department(s), both in the Centre and in the provinces concerned, for the protection and advancement of Tribal areas. I do not want them to be swamped by people from other parts of the country who might go there to exploit them to their own advantage.

As far as the Mizo Hills were concerned on his return from Shillong after meeting Bordoloi, Vanlawma found T. Sakhrie and A.Z. Phizo, the Naga National Council leaders in Aizawl seeking the support of the Mizos in their struggle for 'independence'.[84] They asked Vanlawma to declare Lushai Hills independent and even offered to merge the Naga Hills with it to form one independent country whose official language could be the Mizo language.[85] Vanlawma in view of his commitment to Bordoloi promptly turned down the offer.[86] But when the Sub-Advisory Committee of the Constituent Assembly on Tribal Affairs under the chairmanship of Bordoloi was formed, Vanlawma had already been toppled from his secretaryship of the MU. The new president of the party Khawtinkhuma and Saprawnga were offered co-opted membership in the Sub-Advisory Committee. Vanlawma advised the two members not to accept co-opted membership and demand full-fledged membership which had been given to the Nagas, Khasis and Jaintias.[87] It was also considered a violation of the 'Gentleman's Agreement' that Vanlawma had with Bordoloi.[88] In such a situation the two MU office bearer's acceptance of co-opted membership was viewed as 'unnationalistic' and 'yielding to the wishes of the Indians'.[89] District Superintendent McDonald was also alarmed by the situation and attempted unsuccessfully to block the membership of Khawtinkhuma.[90]

The decision of the two members to participate in the Bordoloi Committee raised a hue-and-cry from the opposition. Reviewing the situation at a public meeting in Aizawl, Vanlawma expressed his bitterness over the violation of his agreement with Bordoloi and demanded that, on the ground of breach of trust, the Mizos should refuse to be a part of India and declare complete independence. 'In the ancient past Mizoram was not under anybody's governance. Now that the British who controlled us are about to leave the Asian subcontinent we should resume the status we held before the arrival of the British. We should demand total independence. . . .'[91]

The Mizos attending the meeting were greatly agitated. Some were for independence and others were fearful of its consequences, and this led to a public debate on the issue. Responding to the question as to why the MU had not favoured independence right from its inception but was raising it at this stage, Vanlawma said,[92]

When we formed Mizo Union party the British administration was not clear as to when and how they were going to leave India. Under them the country was taken care of nicely and if we had mentioned independence when we started Mizo Union party, the British would not have let us start it at all. But now that India is going to obtain independence, we feel that they will be ruling our country and not considering our own interests. However, the attitude of the Indian people is becoming clearer. They failed to carry out their promise to us: that we would have full membership on the planning board and have asked us to be co-opted members only and might intend to give us still less than self-determination in the future. Now that we know that they are not going to carry out their promises our future looks very uncertain. Therefore, we must govern ourselves. At the moment we have enough supplies and if we lack supplies we will still find some other country to help us. And if we look at our natural resources and increase our produce by improving our farming system we will be able to produce a sufficiency of things. Now is the time to fight for our independence.

The defendant, Vanthuama, general secretary of the MU stood up at the public meeting and replied:

It is impossible for us to fight for our independence now. If we look around us, we see the Darwin theory—the more powerful swallowing up the less powerful. If and when we are truly more powerful, we will swallow the Indians and if they are more powerful than us, then they will swallow us. Besides if we are independent where will we get salt and iron ore to make our farming equipment and how are we going to make money.[93]

There were sharp differences between the two sections of the public. The meeting took the form of a debate between Vanlawma and Vanthuama representing two schools of thought. Vanlawma responded to Vanthuama's argument by saying:[94]

Pu (Mr.) Vanlawma's statement on Darwin's theory seems to me to be an attempt to escape reality. We all know for sure that we the Mizos are much smaller and less powerful than the Indians. For that very reason we created the Mizo Union Party. . . .

Concerning salt and iron ore our ancestors, though less advanced than we, were self-sufficient and even made their own guns. If our ancestors knew how to trade with their neighbours we certainly ought to be able to take care of our own affairs. Concerning money we can use it as the rest of the world does. If we have enough food there is no need in fact to be unduly alarmed about our future.

Thus, the meeting even divided the residents of the Aizawl town into two. The southern localities of Aizawl were in agreement with

Pu Vanthuama and against independence and the northern localities of Aizawl were in agreement with Vanlawma, supporting independence.[95] This meeting marked the emergence of a new concept, that of total independence.

By the beginning of 1947, conditions in the Indian subcontinent were changing very fast. The imminent independence of India, its partition, withdrawal attempts by the Princely States, creation of an independent United Bengal and Sikh homeland were the dominant issues of the times. The process of decolonization, the withdrawal of colonial powers and freedom of the colonised countries were taking place the world over. 'Nagas too fell in the same curious chain of processes.'[96] The Nagas were sure that they needed self-rule to safeguard themselves. They were encouraged by the Muslim League victory and the colonial schemes to create a separate area for the tribals. Against this background the political stand of the NNC also underwent change and wanted to secure a dominant political position for the Nagas. Soon they started thinking in terms of complete independence from India rather than an autonomous unit within the Assam province.[97] By 1945, the principle of self-determination had become a potent weapon for struggling nationalities as was evident from the situation in Indo-China, the Philippines, India, Burma and Palestine. At least the developments in Burma directly influenced the developments in north-east India. Under the Constitution of 1947, the Union of Burma with the exception of Kachins and Karens were empowered with the right to secede after a period of ten years from the time of implementation of the Constitution. This encouraged the Nagas of India to demand similar rights. In fact, the Nagas of Burma had already organized themselves under the Naga National Council of Burma. 'At last, they filled with patriotic enthusiasm, voiced out from a moderate demand for same sort of regional autonomy in Assam to outright sovereign independent Nagaland without giving due consideration to the concept of Crown Colony or a Trust Territory under the United Nation (UN) charter as they were feeling a shiver of apprehension of losing their identity with the disappearance of British rule in the midst of Hindu rule'.[98] But it also tried to balance this demand by accommodating the idea of a section of the leadership that it was not advisable to completely severe all ties with India. Hence it was considered that a ten year interim period within India would be useful. A resolution was adopted to this effect by the NNC on 20 February 1947 and submitted to His Majesty's Government and the Government of India. The memorandum stated,[99]

The Naga people were independent and their country was not subjugated by the Ahom Kings of the Assam Valley, who ruled over for seven hundred years. They never formed part of Assam or India at any time before the advent of the British. Little was known of Nagaland when the British obtained suzerainty over the Assam Valley by the treaty of Yandaboo. The British first attacked the Naga people in 1829, but the fight went on for fifty years till the Ao country was taken over in 1869. Since then the Naga people have remained loyal, friendly and peaceful. In the first World War, thousands served in distant France to help the British and the allied cause. In the recent Second World War, when the Japanese army attempted to invade India through Nagaland, it was the co-operation of the Nagas both in intelligence and jungle warfare which enabled the British forces to halt the invasion at Kohima, the headquarters of the district, thus saving Assam and the rest of India from the devastations of war. These freedom-loving Nagas look up to HMG and the Government of India to do the just and proper thing and grant them their just demand for setting up an interim Government of Naga People. As the Modern World recognises the importance of psychological implications dealing with nations to have peace within (and) without, it is necessary to know the tradition and national aspirations of people and to respect them. The attitude of a people has a great bearing in the formation of national policy. In framing the constitution of India certain thought provoking factors must not be ignored: (i) Ethnically Nagas are from a distinct stock. (ii) They have a distinct social life, manner of living, laws and custom and even their method of governance of the people is quite different. (iii) In religion, the great majority of the Nagas are animists but Christianity which was introduced by the American Baptists long before the advent of the British rule is now speedily spreading. Such factors as the above make it imperative that the Nagas should have a separate form of Government. The Nagas have an efficient system of administration. Most of the tribes retain to a considerable degree their ancient laws and customs and village organisation which have lasted through centuries, and these form an integral part of their life and once destroyed or allowed to decay, can never be replaced by a system so suitable to them. Democracy in its purest form exists among the Nagas. The basis of the Naga system is the village organisation. Every village is a sovereign independent unit in the tribes. Village is managed by a council of elders and men of influence elected by the people. Such a polity, such a state of society and democratic life cannot be found in any other part of India. In the 1935, constitution for India and Assam, the areas inhabited by the Nagas were kept outside the jurisdiction of the provincial and central popular governments and were formed into 'Excluded Areas', where the legislatures had no way and the Nagas were kept under the special responsibility of the Governor of the Province in his capacity as the Crown Representative. In other words, the Naga people have had no connection with the policies and politics of different groups of Indian politicians. Ought the British Government or the Government of India throw this society into heterogeneous mixture of other Indian races? A constitution drawn by the people who had no knowledge of Nagaland and the

> Naga people will be quite unsuitable and unacceptable to the Naga people. Thrown among forty crores of Indians the one million Nagas with their unique system of life, will be wiped out of existence. Hence this earliest plea of the Nagas for a separate form of interim Government to enable them to grow to a fuller stature should be acceded. In the light of the facts stated in the foregoing paragraph and in view of the isolated geographical position of Nagaland and taking consideration of the Naga polity and the compact block of Nagaland, this Memorandum is placed with the authorities for setting up of an interim Government of the people with financial provisions for a period of ten years, at the end of which the Naga people will be left to choose any form of Government under which they choose to live.

It is said that the former Assam Premier and Muslim League leader Saadulla helped in drafting this memorandum but when Pakistan was conceded and not Nagaland, Saadulla advised Phizo and Kevichusa to make the best of the situation within India.

This resolution adopted by the NNC which was subsequently submitted to His Majesty's Government and the Government of India as a memorandum was a momentous event in the history of the Naga people for, this was the first time they had demanded complete independence and severance of all ties with India. And this was to dominate the political life of the Nagas in the subsequent period. The ten-year interim government was only to enable themselves to be trained in modern governance and achieve economic viability. This period could prove to be the acid test for the Nagas. If it failed they could always opt for India at the end of ten years. But the changing course of events proved that it was not to be. It is interesting to note that just before this resolution was adopted, Sir Andrew Clow, Governor of Assam visited Mokokchung in January 1947, where he met the leaders of all the northern Naga tribes and had correctly sensed the new mood of the Nagas. He, therefore, made it a point to explain to them that,

> The British raj was being withdrawn shortly and the future Government of India including Assam and its Hills will be a matter for the people of the land to decide. The Constituent Assembly, which is charged with working out the plans for the future has already started work in Delhi and it will have to consider, in due course the position of the hill peoples. They should, therefore, themselves be thinking over the question and form their own conclusions regarding what they want. It is not practicable for the Naga tribes or even the Nagas as a whole to set themselves in a separate state or states (as some of them want) or even as a (separate) province of India. If they did they would always remain poor and

backward and could not supply even the inadequate services they already enjoy. They would therefore be well advised to seek to form part of the province, but to retain matters of local concern in their own hands.

Even in the plains many matters of local concern are run by the people of the district concerned, and it here, where their customs and culture differ so much from those of the plains, they could reasonably claim a larger sphere for local authority, including control of their own land and conservation of such authority such as is traditionally theirs.[100]

NOTES

1. Information regarding the formation of both these organizations were provided by T. Aliba Imti, *Reminiscence: Impur to Naga National Council*, Mokokchung: Author, 1988, pp. 11-12.
2. Resolution of 'Indo-Burma Movement' of December 1946, cited in Asoso Yonuo, *The Rising Nagas: A Historical and Political Study*, Delhi: Vivek, 1974, p. 165.
3. T. Aliba Imti, op. cit., p. 28. This was the Kohima office. The Naga National Council had already been established in February 1946 at Wokha.
4. Ibid., p. vi.
5. The draft Constitution is available in ibid., pp. 163-4.
6. Ibid., pp. 164-5. Also see T. Aliba Imti, op. cit.
7. S.K. Chaube, *Hill Politics in North East India*, Delhi: Orient Longman, 1973, p. 161.
8. Ibid.
9. Ibid.
10. R. Vanlawma, *Ka Ram Le Kei* (My Country and I): *Political History of Modern Mizoram*, Aizawl: Zoram Printing Press, 1972.
11. Suhas Chatterjee, *Mizo Chiefs and Chiefdom*, Delhi: MD Publication, 1995.
12. B.B. Goswami, 'The Mizo's in the context of State Formation', in Surajit Sinha, *Tribal Politics and State System in Eastern and North-Eastern India*, Calcutta: K.P. Bagchi, 1984.
13. Vumson, *Zo History*, Aizawl: Author, n.d., p. 244; S. Chatterjee, op. cit.
14. Surajit Sinha, op. cit., p. 32.
15. R.N. Prasad, *Government and Politics in Mizoram*, Delhi: Northern Book Centre, 1987, p. 75.
16. Ch. Saprawaga, 'Factors Contributing to the Mizo Problems', *Tribal Mirror*, 1967, Vol. 3, cited in S.K. Chaube, op. cit., p. 161.
17. L.B. Thanga, 'Basis of Autonomy Movements in Mizoram: Historical Background', in R.N. Prasad, *Autonomy Movements in Mizoram*, Delhi: Northern Book Centre, 1994, pp. 72-4.
18. *Report of the sub-committee on the tribal and excluded areas of North East Frontier Evidence Part-I*, cited in S.K. Chaube, op. cit., p. 170 and B.B. Goswami, op. cit., p. 131.

19. B.B. Goswami, op. cit., p. 131.
20. R. Vanlawma, op. cit., p. 88.
21. Ibid.
22. Ibid.
23. *The Mizo Union Party Constitution* (in Mizo), Aizawl, 1946.
24. Ibid.
25. Ibid.
26. Mizo Union File, *Mizoram State Archives*, translation from English.
27. C. Pahlira, 'Mizo Hills in the Indian Union', *Tribal Mirror*, Vol. IV, 1970.
28. Vanlawma, op. cit., p. 97.
29. Sumit Sarkar, *Modern India, 1885-1947*, Delhi: Macmillan, 1983, p. 428.
30. Sajal Nag, *Roots of Ethnic Conflict: Nationality Questions in North East India*, Delhi: Manohar, 1990, p. 152.
31. Ibid.
32. Ibid. for detail.
33. Vanlawma, op. cit., p. 119.
    This was substantiated by Pahlira, op. cit., and Amit Nag, *The Mizo Dilemma*, Silchar: Tribal Minor Publication, 1984, p. 21.
34. Ibid.
35. Ibid.
36. Ibid.
37. Ibid.
38. Ibid., also Vumson, op. cit., p. 249.
39. Vanlawma, ibid.
40. Memorandum to the Government of India by Mizo National Council, Aizawl, 1965.
41. Vanlawma, op. cit., p. 108.
42. Ch. Saprawnga, *Ka Zin Khawng*, Aizawl, p. 125.
43. Memo No. 10772-1873 G. of 13.11.1946 in *Vantlang Hnena Hriatirna*, Aizawl, 1946, p. 2.
44. Khawtinkhuma and Vanthuama, *Mizo Union Mite Hnena Thuchan*, Aizawl, 1947, p. 2.
45. Cited in *Vantlang Hnena Hriatirna*, op. cit., p. 4.
46. Memo No. 10772-1873 G. of 13.11.1946 in *Vantlang Hnena Hriatirna*, Aizawl, 1946, p. 2.
47. Ibid., p. 3.
48. In fact Saprawnga accused the British of treating the Mizos as Slaves. In reply Mcdonald called him an 'energetic fool'. Saprawnga, op. cit., pp. 109-11.
49. Vanlawma, op. cit., p. 108.
50. This was proved later on when after the split of Mizo Union, Pachunga supported the constitution framed by Mcdonald.
51. The details of the event are given in Vanlawma, op. cit., pp. iii, 112, Saprawnga, op. cit.

52. Mizo National Council, Memorandum to Government of India, 1965.
53. R.N. Prasad, op. cit., p. 79.
54. S.K. Chaube, op. cit., p. 162.
55. Ibid., p. 161
56. R.N. Prasad, op. cit., pp. 249-50.
57. Vanlawma, op. cit., p. 119.
58. Bimal J. Dev and Dilip K. Lahiri, *Manipur Culture and Politics*, Delhi: Mittal, 1987, pp. 100-1.
59. See N. Lokendra Singh, 'Socio-Economic Roots of Popular Movements in Manipur Valley, Ph.D. thesis, Manipur University, 1990. Also N. Joykumar Singh, *Social Movements in Manipur*, Delhi: Mittal, 1992.
60. Ibid.
61. Ibid., pp. 236-42.
62. Ibid.
63. Ibid.
64. Ibid.
65. Ibid.
66. Ibid., pp. 242-3.
67. Laldena, 'The INA Movement', in Laldena, G. Kabui and Joykumar Singh, *History of Modern Manipur*, Imphal: Modern Book, 1991, pp. 174-82.
68. Ibid.
69. Ibid.
70. Ibid.
71. Ibid.
72. Ibid.
73. Joykumar Singh, 'Movement for Responsible Government in Manipur (1938-48)', *Proceedings of the North East India History Association*, Barapani Session, 1983, pp. 202-9. See also his *Social Movements in Manipur*, Delhi: Mittal, 1992.
74. Ibid.
75. Ibid.
76. Ibid.
77. Ibid.
78. Ibid.
79. Ibid.
80. Ibid.
81. Ibid.
82. Ibid.
83. Nehru to T. Sakhrie cited in the *National Herald*, 6 August 1946.
84. Vumson, op. cit.
85. Ibid.
86. Ibid., pp. 136, 252. Also, B.B. Goswami, op. cit., p. 138.
87. Ibid.
88. Ibid.

89. Vanlawma, *Ka Ram* . . . , op. cit., p. 119.
90. Ibid.
91. Ibid.
92. Ibid.
93. Ibid., p. 122.
94. Ibid.
95. Ibid., p. 124.
96. Asoso Yonuo, op. cit., p. 166.
97. Ibid.
98. Ibid.
99. *Naga Nation*, February 1987.
100. Cited in Asoso Yonou, op. cit., p. 169. Also see V. Venkata Rao et al., *Century of Government and Politics in North-East India*, Vol. III, Mizoram, Delhi: S. Chand & Co., 1987, pp. 38-9.

CHAPTER FIVE

The Legitimization

Withdrawal from a political union required justification, which could be provided only by claims of a separate nationhood. The Muslim League and the Akalis had followed this pattern. Their withdrawal declarations were preceded by claims of separate nationhood. Even the Hindu Mahasabha's stance on 'Akhand Hindustan' was altered on a similar premise. But such a claim was not easy for the Nagas or the Mizos to make. If a community claimed a separate identity, it would have to present a 'national' entity, assert the right to conserve that entity, depict the existing or emerging conditions as uncongenial for conservation and perpetuation of that identity and then assert self-rule as the only means to sustain and perpetuate that national identity. These terms and concepts were entirely new to the tribal society. The ideas and history of nations had indirectly influenced them but in the sense of modern bourgeois politics they were still a apolitical people. The British efforts at keeping the tribals in isolation had prevented them from active participation in the nationalist politics of India. On the eve of Indian independence they discovered that they were not even one tribe, not to speak of one nation which implied that by the Western, nineteenth century, liberal-rationalist parameters they failed to qualify as independent nations. Therefore, a national identity had to be constructed to present the Naga or Mizo national question vis-à-vis the Indian nation-state. For such a construction, the materials available to them were from the precedents and inspiration provided by contemporary Indian history, ideas provided by the colonial administrators and the Christian missionaries, and the leadership came from a middle class with Western education and values. During the colonial regime the tribals had become modern enough to be conscious of their identity. The massive detribalization coupled with monetization and commercialization of agriculture and Westernization in other spheres of life had laid the basis of that process. We shall first study that process upon which the construction of national identity was based.

EMERGENCE OF MODERN IDENTITY CONSCIOUSNESS[1]

The kind of identity that had to be constructed for natural consciousness was not indigenous but Western in character. This identity consciousness which we shall call modern identity—intrinsically Western—had already emerged with the advent of colonial rule and under the initiative of the Christian missionaries—the agents of Westernization in these hills of north-east India. This changed orientation towards identity both in terms of notion and reality, formed the basis of the formulation of 'national identity' of the Nagas, Mizos and Meitheis by their respective leadership. Prior to the advent of British rule, the primary units of identity were clan, family and village or a small grouping of villages as in the Khasi states. Most of the village communities of the Nagas and Mizos were regularly at war with each other and in several cases had developed dialects that were so different that communication among them was difficult if not impossible. Each village community had its own culture and offer its own religion and dialects. One would be hardpressed to look for commonalities to identify them as members of single a tribe or what constituted a tribal level as distinct from a village level community. 'In the pre-British period most of the tribes were not conscious of their ethno-tribal identities and their world was confined to their family, clan, "khel" and village. Terms like Naga, Kuki, Abor, Lushai, Garo, Chulikata and Kapur-shor were given to them by non-tribal plains people . . . even the major tribal groups in Nagaland, such as Ao, Angami, Lotha and Konyak—got their names from other tribes.'[2]

There was a general awareness that a group of villages living in a particular geographical area were somehow related to each other as groups in a way that they were not related to each other. There were similarities in terms of myths, religion and social custom and language—but the differences in these areas were even greater. T.C. Hodson wrote, 'In most respects the idea of a tribal solidarity meets with no recognition'.[3] He found that a Kabui Naga, for instance, was not 'acquainted with the general legend that all Kabuis are descended from one of the three brothers, but probably regards it as far-off events devoid of any real importance'.[4] Writing a decade after Hodson, J.P. Mills described the individual Lotha/Kyong village as essentially independent of each other but pointed out that the Lothas like Angamis have traditions about the common origins of the various clans of the tribe.[5] Thus, there was a rudimentary sense of identity but it was strictly non-functional except in matters of marriage, which had to take place outside the clan but within the tribe. In his book on the Ao Nagas, W.C. Smith attempted to determine the constituents of Ao tribal identity. He found that 'it is difficult to find any one unifying principle on which the tribe might be said to depend'.[6] With some extra effort he detected that the Aos lived within clearly defined geographical boundaries and that their physical appearance was 'distinctive'. Further they were the only people who use the Ao language even though the main dialects of that language were very dissimilar from each other. Again 'in matter of traditions and beliefs, with their attendant rites and ceremonies, there is found the greatest unity',[7] even though there were many variations. Perhaps the most important factor, which Smith found, was their belief in a common origin and hence kinship.

Language has been one of the most obvious means of determining the tribe to which people belong. In the north-east each tribe has its own language or rather a dialect. Still language was a weak unifying factor due to the differences in dialects. Hodson noted that the linguistic link was weak among the Tangkhuls due to this reason. He found that the language of the Tangkhuls from the extreme south was totally incomprehensible to those living in the far north. The dialect of each village functioned as a full-fledged language.[8] In 1925, Smith observed that the two Ao dialects were virtually different from each other. In a more scientific study of the Aos, first published two years after Smith's, Mills provided a detailed description of the linguistic diversity that existed and to some extent still exists.[9] Writing on the subject Milton Sangma observed that 'originally there were eleven groups among the Garos, each inhabiting a distinct part of the Garo hills districts. Each group lived in splendid isolation and thereby evolved a distinct culture and dialects of their own.'[10]

Though during the pre-British period tribe was not a primary reference point for identity among the hill people of the north-east, in the British and post-British periods it became increasingly so. British bureaucrats needed to classify and name the peoples they governed. There were compilations for the Census Reports and other official enumerative documents. In the process, it was these bureaucrats who first systematically assigned names to tribes often using names given to them by their neighbours or names apparently arising out of understanding or even misunderstanding of the informants. Indirectly the administrative procedures had contributed in creating a sense of identity among the tribals as they started responding to the description given by the rulers in the Census Reports and other records. This was followed by the efforts of Christian missionaries who strengthened the identity formation process in various ways.[11] The first important contribution of the missionaries towards the formation of identity consciousness among tribals was the standardization of their languages. For their proselytizing activities the missionaries needed a language to communicate with the tribals. And in order to do so they gave the tribal languages its written form for which they chose one of the dialects and in the absence of a script made use of the Bengalee or Roman alphabets, and endowed it with a written form. The written form of the language was then recognized by the government, thus becoming not only the language of education throughout the area inhabited by a tribe but also the language of administration. With the spread of education and administration the standard language gradually displaced the other dialects, especially among the literates.

Closely related to the creation of a standard language was the mission and church controlled educational system that promulgated it and the incipient literature that was being created. While there were some government schools at major centres of the Naga and Lushai Hills, Manipur and Khasi-Jaintia Hills, the government entrusted the responsibility for education to the missions, especially the Baptist and Presbyterian Missions. These schools spread knowledge of the standard language, thus making meaningful communication possible among the various dialect groups. They also established an educational network based on the village primary schools, from which the best students went to a middle school located in the mission centre. The able students thus for the first time came into contact with members of their tribe from areas with which they had no previous association. These schools also created the tribal elites who were to become the leaders of the solidarity movements.

Equally important has been the ideological and organizational contributions of the Christian Church to the tribal identity. It offered an attractive ideological alternative to the previously held weak belief system.[12] At the same time it is also true that to a great extent the people modified and indigenized the Gospel proclaimed by the missionaries, there were nevertheless certain features of the received forms of the new faith that brought about changes in their world view and in doing so contributed to the development of tribal identity. The most important element of the new faith was perhaps its comprehensive nature. Whereas the traditional tribal religions had generally been perceived to be relevant mainly to the village or group of villages, Christianity was proclaimed as relevant to the whole tribe. This comprehensiveness or universalism was reinforced by an emphasis on evangelism and service to all people including those with whom traditional relationship had been hostile. The Christian evangatlists were the first to establish significant positive contact among villages traditionally hostile to each other. Some were employed by the mission, some by the churches, and a great majority were volunteers. They were in a very real sense, the first agents of tribal solidarity. As the number of Christians from all sections of the tribe increased, a sense of distinctive tribal identity began to emerge.

Another important way in which Christianity contributed to the development of a tribal identity was the creation of ecclesiastical structures. When members of a tribe converted to Christianity they were organized into local churches. These local churches were the first to bring together whole tribe in single platform which went a long way to strengthen the tribal identity. Church organizations brought together thousands of individuals from the entire tribal region for annual meetings at which they carried out common business as well as 'sought inspiration and fellowship'. Long before politically oriented organizations promoting tribal solidarity appeared on the scene, the tribal level churches provided an enduring and comprehensive experience of tribal unity.

COLONIAL CONSTRUCTION

While presenting the Naga case to the Indian Statutory Commission (1929), John H. Hutton, the then Deputy Commissioner of the Naga Hills, argued that the tribals of north-east India, particularly the Nagas and the Mizos, were not Indians in any sense of the term.[13] The Mizos (then Lushais), for example, belonged to the Mongoloid race and were akin to the Chins of western Burma. Similarly, the Nagas belonged to the Indonesian stock of Mongoloids and were closely connected with the Pagans of Malay, Borneo and the Philippine islands. Although they lived in contiguous areas, they became a part of the Indian subcontinent only after the British conquest of the tribes. Prior to this they were free and sovereign. The neighbouring Assamese and the Bengalees had never been able to conquer them at any point of time. As such they had never been able to accept the Indo-Aryan Indians due to their distinct racio-ethnic attributes and strong cultural dissimilarities. The tribals practised animism while the Indians were either Hindus or Muslims. While the animists were tolerant, the Hindus and Muslims of India ostracized them for eating beef and pork. The tribal society did not observe the caste system and if they joined the Indians they would be relegated to the lowest stratum of the hierarchical structure. Unlike the plains, the Nagas and Mizos did not have social ills such as child marriages, restrictions on widows or evils like prostitution. The tribals spoke languages that could be categorized as Tibeto-Burmese while the Indians largely spoke Indo-Aryan languages.

Hutton went on to argue that not only was there anything in common between the Indians and these hill tribes, on the contrary there existed a 'deep-rooted antipathy' between the two. Therefore, they should not be clubbed together by the reform schemes. And also that tribals should be kept out of all such reforms as they lack education and political experience, and were yet unequipped to participate in self-government processes. The echo of the same arguments can be found in the memorandum submitted to the Simon Commission by the Naga delegates which was not coincidental. It borrowed heavily in terms of ideas and language from Hutton and it is even likely that he had lent a hand in drafting the memorandum. A look at the memorandum would reveal this:

> We, the undersigned Nagas of the Naga Club of Kohima, who are the only persons at present to voice for our people, have heard with great regret that our Naga hills were included within the Reformed Scheme of India without our knowledge. But as the administration of our hills continued to be in the hands of British officers we did not consider it necessary to raise any protest in the past. We now learn that you have come to India as representative of the British Government to enquire into the working of the system of government and the growth of education and we beg to submit below our views with the prayer that our hills may be withdrawn from the Reform Scheme and placed outside the Reforms but directly under the British Government. We never asked for any reforms and we do not wish for any reforms.
>
> Before the British Government conquered our country in 1879-1880, we were living in a state of intermittent warfare with the Assamese of the Assam Valley to the north-west and the Manipuris to the south of our country. They never conquered us, nor were we ever subjected to their rule. On the other hand, we were always a terror to these plains people.
>
> . . . Our country within the administered area consist of more than eight tribes, *quite different from one another with quite different languages which cannot be understood by each other and there were tribes which are not known at present. We have no unity among us and it is only the British government that is holding us together now.*
>
> Our education at present is poor. . . . *We have not got one yet who is able to represent all our different tribes* or master our languages much less one to represent us in any council of a population. However, our population . . . is very small in comparison with the population of the plains district in the province, and *in any*

representation that may be allotted to us in the council will be negligible and will have no weight whatsoever. . . .

Our country is poor, it does not pay (for) its administration. *Therefore we are afraid that new heavy taxes will have to be sold* [*sic*, imposed (?)] and in the long run we shall have no claim in the land of our birth and life will not be worth living then. Though our land at present is within the British territory, government have always recognised our private rights in it, but if we are forced to enter the council the majority of whose members is sure to belong to other districts, *we also much fear the introduction of foreign laws and customs to supersede our own customary laws which we now enjoy*. For the above reasons, we pray that the British government will continue to safeguard our rights against all encroachment from other people who are more advanced than us by withdrawing our country from the Reformed Scheme and placing it directly under its protection. If the British government, however wants us to throw away, we pray that we should not be thrust to the mercy of the people who could have never conquered us themselves, and to whom we are never subjected, but to leave us alone to determine for ourselves as in ancient times.[14]

N.E. Parry, the Superintendent of the Lushai Hills also advocated the exclusion of the Lushai Hills from the reform proposals on the same grounds.[15] He argued that unlike the Indo-Aryan plainsmen of India the Lushai tribals belonged to the Mongoloid race and were affiliated to the Kuki-Chin clan of Burma. They were not only distinct from the Indians from a socio-cultural point of view, there was mutual distrust between the two. The Lushais were educationally and politically quite backward which made the proposed reforms unsuitable for them. He felt that under the circumstances the 'union' between the two communities would be 'unnatural' and in the long run only load to a feeling of resentment towards one another.

The Government of Assam itself supported such views[16] when it observed that 'there is no sympathy on either side and any union (between the hills and plains people) is an artificial one resented by both the parties'. There was an inherent ambivalence in the government stand because it simultaneously stated that 'our aim should be not to retain the aboriginal areas as picturesque survival but to secure their development by absorbing them with the rest of the (Indian) community. The process of assimilation has been going on and to put an obstacle in its way would be a retrograde step.'[17]

On the eve of British departure from India the Crown-Colony Plan was mooted which soon caught the fancy of quite a number of British administrators and constitutional experts. In this context Robert Reid, the Governor of Assam put forward the oft-repeated arguments of the last two decades once again, which was a clear indication that during this long period of time the British thinking had not moved any further on the subject. Reid had already tried to establish the tribals—were not Indians (as already shown in Chapter 2) and they were in Indian territory by an accident of history.[18] Adopting a self-imposed paternalism towards the tribals, whom the subsequent colonial invasions had almost depopulated, Reid took it upon himself to protect these 'set of very loyal, primitive people who are habituated to look to us for protection'.[19] Reid felt that British had no right to place the tribals between the squabbling Hindus and Muslims in India[20] but should be separated to constitute a Crown-Colony.[21] A.G. McCall, Superintendent of Lushai Hills (1931-43) also shared Reids come to see concern about the tribals.[22] The views of the British administrators, and Reginald Coupland, a constitutional expert, who supported the Crown-Colony Plan of Reid had a direct impact on the tribals on the eve of Indian independence when they were struggling to visualize nationhood on the basis of a structured separate identity for themselves. Besides this the century long colonial rule, which excluded them from the age-old interaction with the plainsmen through institutionalized practises, had its impact on the tribal mind. The Christian missionaries also perpetuated these colonial ideas not only through discourses but very many active processes.[23] Traditionally life for the Naga and Mizo tribals had been one of constant interaction with the plainsmen and under British rule had become institutionalized and legalized seclusion.[24] It was therefore, easy for the vulnerable tribal minds to easily internalize these ideas by ignoring the past which they had shared with non-tribals. Therefore, when the tribal middle class in the late 1940s set out to work on their national question, they were merely borrowing from the colonialists and putting together a consciously evolved identity.

NATIONALIST CONSTRUCTION

The tribal middle classes found the colonial theories very handy. And drew inspiration and ideas for the construction of a national identity for the Nagas and Mizos respectively from these sources. But construction of an identity by itself was not sufficient. There was a coeval necessity to work towards making such an identity a reality. In other words, the tribal middle classes not only had to speak of their tribes as a unified national entity but also to work for such unity among the diverse and warring sub-tribes. It also had the task of giving these national entities an enumerable past and an ancestry, which would legitimize their claims to separate nationhood. The job was all the more difficult because it had to provide the 20 odd Naga tribes—who not only were unaware of being Nagas but had a history of perpetual inter-tribal warfare and head-hunting—a common history and a heritage of unity and integrity. Similar was the case with the Mizo leadership. The colonial administrators who sympathized with the tribals in their effort to maintain a separate identity also viewed these internal problems with concern and emphasized the need for unification. At the opening of the hall of the Central Tribal Council of 27 November 1946, Adams, the then Deputy Commissioner of the Naga Hills said, 'Last of all, I should request you to stop the use of hot words amongst yourselves. Perhaps some use too many hot words but you must remember that these words always delay the unity of your people. Try to settle all affairs and misunderstanding amicably. By doing this you will make yourselves a nation.' Despite the simplified shortcut to nationhood provided in the above invocation, the message for the need of unification was sent across. Since unification was a long-drawn historical process, which required time, the alternative open to them was to present the tribes as an already united entity. With this objective the Naga Hills District Council (1945) was immediately changed to the Naga 'National' Council (1946), and began its monthly publication *The Naga Nation*. The new Council had a studied representation from all the 29 Naga tribes to make it representative and 'national' in character. It proclaimed that it stood for the 'solidarity'[25] and 'the unification of all Naga tribes and their freedom'.[26] To demonstrate its numerical strength it included even the tribes of the then North-Eastern Frontier Agency within its purview claiming them to be Nagas as well. Thus, formed the Naga National Council (NNC) as the representative of its people set out to construct a national identity for the Nagas:

> In framing the Constitution of India few thought provoking factors must not be ignored: (1) Ethnically Nagas are from a distinct stock. (2) They have a distinct social life, manner of living, laws and customs and even their method of governance of the people was quite different. (3) In religion the great majority of the Nagas are animists but Christianity which was introduced by the American Baptists long before the advent of the British rule is now speedily spreading.[27]

It also attempted to provide the Nagas a past, which was not an ordinary past but with a nationalist content:

The Naga people were independent and their country was not subjugated by the Ahom Kings of the Assam valley who ruled over for seven hundred years. The never formed part of Assam or India at any time before the advent of the British. Little was known of Nagaland when the British obtained suzerainty over the Assam valley by the treaty of Yandaboo. The British first attacked the Naga people in 1829, but the fight went on for fifty years till the Ao country was taken over in 1869. Since then the Naga people have remained loyal friendly and peaceful. In the First World War, thousands (of Nagas) served in distant France to help the British and the allied cause. In recent Second World War when the Japanese army attempted to invade India through Nagaland, it was the co-operation of the Nagas both in intelligence and jungle warfare which enabled the British forces to halt the invasion at Kohima, the headquarters of the District, thus saving Assam and the rest of India from devastations of war.[28]

The appropriation of the colonial construction of Naga identity and the appeal to British Government for patronage against the services rendered to the empire during crises, was too obvious in the above memorandum. The other significant aspect of the Naga nationalist construction was its painstaking effort at contrasting the Nagas against the so-called Indians. It is interesting to note that the Naga intelligentsia was conscious that there was very little material to present their community as a unified entity but it was easier to show the differences that existed between the plainsmen and the Nagas. Therefore, these differences were handpicked to depict the separateness of the Nagas. The results of such 'compare and contrast jobs' were also used to prove that Naga society was still pure and perfect, free from the evils which the Indian society suffered from. As such it was an ideal society which they did not want to lose to India. 'Truly we are a peculiar people. We are all equals. Men women have equal status. No high or low class of people. There is no communal feeling. Neither are there religious differences to disturb our harmony with our conditions. There are no minority problems . . . we have no beggars. It has no landlords to harass it. . . . And murder is very rare.'[29]

Borrowing heavily from his comrade Sakharie, Phizo when he took over the leadership of the NNC continued to base his construction on the same ideas despite his extremist ideology because it suited the Naga demand for independence. His original contribution was his allusion to Mahatma Gandhi and his concept of *Ram Rajya*, which he felt, fitted perfectly the Naga way of life:

Nagaland is a wonderful country and the people are a peculiar people who are happy and contented. It is a country in this twentieth century where there is no political party, no class distinction, no class feeling or caste system, no complaint of economic maladjustment, no pauper, no (family without) property, no liquor ban, no opium den, no dancing hall, no brothels, no law for death penalty, no law to imprison a person, no land tax of any kind. It is purely a country of people owned by the people, managed by the people for the common interest of the people. Every village is a small republic and has its own council and assemblies established from time immemorial and it is dynamically alive, Nagaland is a country of Mahatma Gandhi's dreams.[30]

Having constructed the separateness of the Nagas as a 'people' Phizo then tactically went on to appeal to the conscience of India as a newly born but mighty nation to let live smaller 'nations' like the Nagas.

There will be no honour to deceive or cheat a small people like the Nagas. India must consider the position of the Nagas and compare her own position of the past. If India once felt the weight of domination of people who were four thousand miles away, whose population was seven times smaller than her own population, from a country twenty times smaller than India itself, the Nagas will feel the weight of the connections with India like the rat under the foot of the elephant. Some other people on the border joining Indian Union voluntarily must not form the basis of consideration . . . there is another cause which eats up the confidence of men and sows seeds of discontent of one people against another: that is fear, the greatest cause of all the worries and troubles of mankind. Fear of invasion, fear of starvation by blockade, fear of economic disadvantages and exploitation. Fortunately the Naga people do not entertain the sense of fear whether of invasion or of blockade. Standing as a nation, we are not afraid for that. Definitely there is distrust of economic exploitation in the fair name of development and industrialisation.[31]

Phizo continued his crusade in the same manner even after he was arrested by the Government of India on charges of sedition and inciting secessionism. His tactic continued to be the same too: appealing to the conscience of the bigger nation and at the same time warning it against the continued occupation of the Naga Hills:

Since we endured a life together as the British conquered subjects along with the Indians, we sincerely believed India not to interfere with our liberty and freedom. Now the British has left and India is politically free. But the possibility of India's annexation of Nagaland and domination over the unwilling Nagas have become more a fearful problem than the British imperialism whose home country was at least several thousand miles away. Day by day this appears to be nearer to the fact than a mere possibility. We give all the praises and glory to

India and particularly to Indian National Congress for compelling the British to quit sooner than expected. But I hope India shall not become selfish and naughty in her interest as people do not know how to meet and besides, we two are strangers to one another [*sic*]. Still now I refuse to believe that the old urge for domination and exploitation in the name of safeguards, protection and development of the country has already gripped the heart of India and within so short a time of attaining her freedom.

I do not think India has assumed that she has inherited the *whitemens' burden* to look after the welfare of the underdeveloped people of the coloured races against their will, but rather she has taken the lead to champion the cause of human rights.[32]

As part of the construction of the Naga national question, Phizo then adopted a national flag for the Nagas and asked his creative comrades to compose a national anthem for the Naga nation. Here again the Naga leadership relied on the British. The national anthem that they adopted was only an adaptation of the American national anthem.

God bless my Nagaland land that I love
stand beside her and guide her
through the night with the light from above
from the mountains and the valleys
and the hill tops where I roam
God bless my Nagaland
My home sweet home.

In the Mizo Hills there had been early efforts at unification of the diverse Mizo tribes. In 1940, the Young Lushai Association (1930), a socio-religious organization set up on the lines of the Young Mens Christian Association of England, was changed to the Young Mizo Association as the name 'Lushai' denoted only one of the many Mezo tribes. Therefore, a generic term 'Mizo' was consciously adopted to replace the term 'Lushai', so that all the diverse Mizo tribes could be brought under one single political organization which would eventually unify these multiple tribes and sub-tribes as one Mizo community.[33] Even when a political party was set up in Mizoram in 1946 to deal with the crisis situation that arose out of the sudden British withdrawal from India and the dilemma over the merger with India, there was a deliberate and conscious decision to name it after the entire tribe, e.g. the generic Mizo rather than the particular Lushai by which they were still known to the outside world and specially the British. Thus, the Mizo Union had come into existence.

During negotiations on the eve of India's independence between Gopinath Bordoloi, the Premier of Assam and Vanlawma, when asked to opt for India, the Mizo leader stressed upon the separate identity of the Mizos vis-à-vis the Indians:

> We are a Mongoloid people and coming from the East we are ethnologically different from you who came from the West. We are now Christians and even before we converted to Christianity our own religion was different quite substantially from yours and it will not be possible to live with Indians under the same laws and regulations . . . we are a small nation and need a great nation to depend upon . . . will you leave us alone to manage our affairs so that we can survive among other nations?[34]

Pachunga, another Mizo leader of the secessionist faction within the Mizo Union repeated the same thesis to declare that 'we Mizos have nothing in common with the *vais*' and 'Mizoram is for the Mizo people'.[35]

Around this time (5 May 1947), a pamphlet entitled *Zoram Independent* written by D. Ronghaka was published and distributed in Aizawl. The pamphlet advocated that Mizo Hills should declare itself independent. The English translation of the Mizo pamphlet read.

> Every nation in the world strives for independence. India has struggled long to secure their independence. So have the Muslims of India for their independence. If the Mizo does not fight for their independence, they will remain slaves (Tuk Luh Bawi) which practise has been abolished long ago. We should fight for independence to avoid becoming slaves again. The fact that we speak one language (which proves that we are one people) is reason enough for us to strive for independence. . . . If we are independent, all of us will be happy because then we will be working for our own future. It might be difficult at the initial period but it would be a worthwhile struggle. . . . Because of our religion alone we should be away from the Indians. All around us, different religious groups seem to form their own countries. The Burmese are Buddhists. The Indian are Hindus and the Pakistanis Muslims. Why should not we Mizos who are Christians have our own sovereign country.[36]

Unlike the Nagas or the Mizos, the Meitheis were neither tribals nor disunited. In fact, they were like the plainsmen in many ways and this posed a problem in structuring the Meithei national question. In the eighteenth century, Hinduism was imported to Manipur as a state religion to legitimize the rule of a particular dynasty. Soon as the state religion it overwhelmed the existing Sanamahi cult. With the advent of Hinduism Sanskritization and Brahmanic culture made its appearance in the Meithei land. There emerged a synthesis between the superimposed Hindu religion and culture and the pre-Hindu animist culture, which gave rise to a composite culture. During the colonial period the Meitheis consolidated themselves as an ethnic entity and by the time of British withdrawal they had a kind of national entity in the subcontinent. As such the Meithei dilemma was different: they were not certain as to whether the Indian nation recognized their national status or for that matter their *Hindutva*.

There were even misgivings about whether the Indian Hindus at all considered them (Meithei Hindus) as 'Hindus'. The circumstances that led to the emergence of rebel leader Naorem Phullo proved that the caste-Hindus of Indian plains did not. Added to this was the Meithei experience of the Indian plainsmen as merchants and businessmen who had literally impoverished Manipur and created artificial food shortage and famine conditions by exporting its crops and agricultural products. Merger with India could mean entry of many more of such elements with devastating consequences. These prospects and made the Meitheis wary of Indian rule and a faction had emerged which advocated retention of Manipur as an independent and sovereign entity. But a larger faction wanted to merge with India which as a new born nation it was felt would recognize the nationality rights and aspirations of the Meitheis. As Hindus and a small nation which had close ties with India it wanted to retain its cultural and political links but the reality of merchant capitalism and the manner in which Manipur's Merger with India was secured made them wary of Indian rule.

Therefore, while structuring the national question of the Meitheis[37] the rebel faction stressed those aspects of Meithei identity which distinguished them from the Indians and denounced Hinduism as a foreign religion which had a bad influence on the life and ways of its people. They projected the Meitheis as a small nation oppressed by a dominating Indian nation and depicted the Indian State as a colonial state. The earlier insurgent organization, United National Liberation Front (UNLF, *c.* 1965), had the avowed objective of secession from India and to step up an independent state of Manipur based on the racio-ethnic identity of the Meitheis.[38] The separateness of the Meitheis was constructed by isolating the Mongoloid features, the Tibeto-Burmese language, which had almost been lost by then and the Bengalee script was being used, and upheld Sanamahism as the original religion of the Meitheis. It identified with and ideologically supported the Naga and Mizo movements and even conceived of an ambitious Pan-Mongoloid Movement in north-east India. But subsequently it gave up this approach and even declared movements based on race and ethnicity like those of the Nagas and Mizos as 'narrow nationalism' and talked about ushering an 'armed revolution' against the Indian State by unifying all the oppressed ethnic groups of north-east India. It felt there was a growth of 'militant nationalism' among the many aggrieved groups who were fighting their 'private revolutions'. And that each militancy could be brought under a 'common revolutionary banner' to bring about a larger revolution. To achieve such an objective following the principles of unity, democracy, nationalism and independence through which 'bondage and alien rule' could be fought against. It rejected ideologies of the Left like Marxism, Maoism, Leninism, describing them as 'foreign ideals' and 'imported social outlook', unsuitable for Manipuri conditions. Instead it draw inspiration from Manipur's own ethos. The UNLF postponed fighting for such a revolution as it felt it was not yet physically ready to fight the mighty Indian State and would rather prepare grounds for the revolution: 'to grow from within' and maintain 'diplomatic contacts with foreign sovereign countries of the world, and neighbouring Asian power' so that it can earn immediate recognition in the event of victory. The Revolutionary Government of Manipur (RGM) had no pretension of addressing itself to the common ethnicity of the region though it was not against the idea of a 'joint struggle'.[39] It too held the 'Meithei way of life and Meithei philosophy' as its ideal and sought to revive them. It blamed the advent of Hinduism for mellowing down the martial spirits of the Meitheis, an erstwhile martial people. It therefore launched a massive de-Hinduization and de-Sanskritization movement along with the revival of the Sanamahi religion. The RGM was not only successful in activating such a movement in Manipur but even created a strong identity consciousness in the state. It also campaigned against the plainsmen who lived in Manipur either temporarily or permanently which resulted in anti-outsider riots in the valley. It spread the view that outsiders were going to reduce the indigenous Meitheis into a minority in their own land. Outsiders were described as exploiters and drainers of Manipuri wealth. Its sister organization, the Pan Manipur Youth League (PANMYL) and its mouthpiece, *Resistance*, carried out a sustained campaign on these issues and even pioneered physical mobilizations.

From the preceding analysis we find that all the three groups in question, the Nagas, the Mizos and the Meitheis, had first attempted to isolate certain common features either racial, cultural, social or otherwise and then projected themselves collectively in their respective groups. It is true that except perhaps the Meitheis, the other two groups lacked the accepted theoretical features of an ethnic group or nationality or even the semblance of a national entity, such as a unified, stable community of people, a common language, a common economic life or mental make-up. Worse still, they even lacked the consciousness of belonging to one group. Therefore, to project their common identity it was essential to isolate commonalities among the groups belief in like the Mongoloid features, Christianity, Tibeto-Burmese languages, etc. But significantly they emphasized on aspects that differentiated them from the 'Indians', who were non-Mongoloid, either Hindus or Muslims generally and spoke Indo-Aryan languages.

It also attempted to create myths and history of their ancient origin and heritage. All the three groups asserted that they had been independent from time immemorial whereas the written history of the Nagas and Mizos hardly goes beyond the seventeenth century. The Meitheis of course had a longer history and were proud of it, which they asserted was as rich if not richer than Indian history. We find that there were conspicuous attempts at separating itself from the Indian national history and giving itself an independent past—unique and not connected in any was to the Indian ancestry. It then strived to provide the Meitheis with an ancestry, which was older than that of India's and far more advanced than other nations of the region.[40] There was a conscious effort to delink it from the Aryan connection, a theory which had been developed after the adoption of Hinduism. The most significant contribution of this construction was the rejection of *Mahabharata* connection of the Meitheis—the famous Arjun-Chitrangada-Vabhruvahan episode—saying that the present Manipur was not the one alluded to in the epic. Manipur history was then traced back to AD 33.[41] It as proudly claimed that Manipur had a written system of law as early as AD 4. Manipur was proudly cited by them as a 'Asiatic Sovereign' and 'one of the great Mongolian civilizations which spread from the central part of the former USSR to the far-east of Japan and one that was comparable to the civilized empire of China and Burma of ancient times'.[42] Although colonial theories regarding the past and present of Manipur were rejected, a colonial anthropologist's view was adapted to depict that Manipur was 'a singular oasis of comparative civilization and organised society set in the midst of congeries of barbarous peoples over whom its rulers exercised authority'.[43] It also appropriated other advantageous aspects of the traditionally held theories of Meitheis being a 'highly civilized' people, the 'most advanced section of the Kuki-chin people' and that they were not Aryans in any respect.[44] Similarly, the Mizos too declared themselves as a part of the great Zo tribe of South-East Asia who were spread all over India, Burma and Japan. The Nagas proclaimed themselves to be a part of the great Indo-Chinese tribes who had hegemony over the tribes of present Arunachal Pradesh. The three groups were also proud of the fact that no so-called Indian ruler could conquer them until the British did. The Nagas and Mizos took pride in the fact that even the British kept them unadministered. The Meitheis eulogized their battle against the English and the retention of their status as a Princely State while the rest of India was under British rule. While the Nagas and Mizos were proud that they had not been influenced by Hinduism or Islam, the Meitheis took pride in their own religion and even wanted to revert back to their pre-Hindu animist status.

NOTES

1. This section is based on the study by Frederick Downs, *Study of Christianity in North East India*, Lecture series, 19-20 April 1991, Shillong: Department of History, North Eastern Hill University.
2. S.M. Dubey, 'Inter-Ethnic Alliance, Tribal Movements and Integration in North East India', in K.S. Singh (ed.), *Tribal Movements in India*, Delhi: Manohar, 1982.
3. T. Hodson, *The Naga Tribes of Manipur*, London: OUP, 1911, p. 81.
4. Ibid.
5. J.P. Mills, *The Lotha Nagas*, London: OUP, 1922, pp. 96-7.
6. W.C. Smith, *The Ao Naga Tribe of Assam*, London: OUP, 1925, p. 52.
7. Ibid.
8. Ibid., p. 81.
9. Ibid., p. 322.
10. Milton Sangma, *History and Culture of the Garos*, Delhi: Oriental Pub., 1981, p. 134.
11. Frederick Downs as in note 1 above subsequently published in *NEHU Journal of Social Sciences and Humanities*, July-September 1991, pp. 1-76.
12. D.N. Majumdar, 'Garo National Council', in K.S. Singh (ed.), op. cit., pp. 203-14.
13. Note by J.H. Hutton, DC, Naga Hills, *in Indian Statutory Commission Report*, Vol. XIV, London, 1930, pp. 111-17.

14. *Memorandum to the Indian Statutory Commission from the Naga Club*, Kohima, January 1929, in ibid.
15. Note by N.E. Parry, DC, in *Indian Statutory Commission Report*, op. cit., pp. 118-22.
16. Memorandum of the Government of Assam, in ibid., Vol. XIV, London, 1930, pp. 111-18.
17. Ibid.
18. Robert Reid, 'Assam', *Journal of Royal Asiatic Society of Arts*, Vol. XCII, April 1944, p. 247.
19. Ibid.
20. Ibid.
21. Reginald Coupland, *The Future of India,* London: OUP, 1943, p. 164.
22. A.G. McCall, *Lushai Chrysalis*, London: Luzac & Co., 1949, pp. 241-2.
23. Cf. Nihar Ranjan Ray. Inaugural Address, in K.S. Singh (ed.), *Tribal Situation in India*, Simla: IIAS, 1972, p. 20.
24. The colonial state and the Christian missionaries not only strived to keep the tribals away from the plainsmen but even laws like the Inner Line Regulations were enacted for such purposes.
25. Naga National Council, *Resolution Passed on 19 June 1946, at Wokha, Naga Hills.*
26. T. Aliba Imti, secretary, Naga National Council, Public Address in Kohima, 6 December 1946.
27. *Memorandum of His Majesty' Government and the Government of India from the Naga National Council*, 20 February 1947.
28. Ibid.
29. T. Sakhrie, secretary, Naga National Council, cited in Verier Elwin, *Nagaland*, Shillong, 1961, pp. 73-5.
30. A.Z. Phizo, *Letter to C. Rajagopalachari, Governor General of Free India*, from Presidency Jail, Calcutta, 22 November 1948.
31. A.Z. Phizo, *Nagaland: A Strange Country in Asia,* Kohima: NNC, 1950, p. 4.
32. Ibid.
33. B.B. Goswami, *The Mizo Unrest: A Study of Politicisation of Culture*, Jaipur: Alckh, 1979, pp. 120-31.
34. Vanlawma, *Ka Ram Le Kei*, Aizawl, 1972, cited in Vumson, *Zo History*, Aizawl: Author, n.d., p. 250.
35. Cited in ibid.
36. Pachunga in a recorded public address, Aizawl, 21 February 1947, cited in R.S. Samuelson, 'The Mizo Independence Movement', M.A. thesis, Humbolt University, USA, 1976. Subsequently published as *Love Mizoram*, Imphal: Goodwill Press, 1985, pp. 41-2.
37. We are dealing with the initial spurt of secessionist activities and the consequent construction of national question here. But in Manipur this initial spurt began in the 1960s. So the period for Manipur would be between 1965 (the birth of UNLF) and the emergence of PLA.

38. Kshetri Rajendra Singh, 'Social Movements in Manipur: A Study of Two Movements', unpublished Ph.D. thesis, Centre for Social Studies, Surat, 1987, pp. 151, 233; M. Bharati, 'Insurgency in Manipur', unpublished M.A. thesis, M.S. University of Baroda, 1993.
39. Consocom: *Revolutionary Government of Manipur: A Review Pamphlet*, Imphal, n.d.
40. The task was systematically carried out primary by *The Resistance,* a UNLF daily.

    Interestingly, before the advent of Insurgency the same theory found unqualified support and reinforcement from Meithei scholars like Pt. Atompapu Sharma, W. Yumjao, Hijam Bijoy, Mutum Jhulon, Nandalal Sharma, N. Tombi and even the Manipuri Shahitya Parishad.

    For the opposite theory see Kangjiya Gopal, *Adungeige Kangleipak Natte,* Imphal, 1979.
41. N. Kellachandra and L. Ibungonal Singh (ed.), *Cheitharol Kumbaba* (Manipuri Royal Chronicle), cited in N. Sanjaoba, 'Genesis of Insurgency' in his (ed.), *Manipur: Past and Present,* Delhi: Mittal, 1989, pp. 245-90.
42. M.M. Ghose *Manipur: Did Manipur Princes Obtain a Fair Trial,* London, 1891; J. Roy, *History of Manipur*, Calcutta: Firma KLM, 1973.
43. J. Lyall cited in N. Sanajaoba, op. cit.
44. Kshetri Rajendra Singh, op. cit. citing S. Chatterjee, *Kirata Janakriti*, Calcutta: Asiatic Society, 1957.

CHAPTER SIX

The Accession

The impending freedom of India with Partition also signaled the demise of the Indian Princely States. For the 562 states occupying almost two-fifth of the subcontinent the rush of events that precipitated the dissolution of the Raj was abrupt. For almost a century, the princes had been encouraged to regard themselves as a bulwark of stability in India and various strategies had been devised by the Raj to strengthen their position in the face of the corrosive impact of nationalism.[1] However, when the moment came for the British Raj to bow out of the Indian stage, it failed to ensure the continued survival of the Princely States.[2] The Cabinet Mission had laid down that with India's independence the doctrine of paramountcy would lapse and that the states could negotiate terms with the successor government in constituting a power block alongside the Hindu and Muslim group of provinces. Many states welcomed the idea; some even set up a committee to negotiate the terms with the Indian parties.[3] However, discords between the Congress and the League and the hostility of the Congress towards the pretension of the princes prevented any progress in that direction.[4] What precipitated matters was the Partition Plan of 3 June.[5] While the plan affirmed that paramountcy would lapse, it frankly discounted the rights of states to declare their independence through a federation of states or becoming dominions on an individuals basis. With the concurrence of the Congress and the League, Mountbatten set up two States Department to resolve the problem of the accession of states.[6] At the suggestion of Sardar Patel the Congress devised a formula which required the states to accede to India by ceding certain subjects in which the common interest of the country were involved.[7] In other matters, pledged Patel, 'We would scrupulously respect their continuous existence'.[8] Some of the princes knew that the die had been cast and had resigned to their respective fates while in other Princely States peoples' movement for responsible government had indicated their preferences.[9] The more ambitious rulers or *dewans* of states like

Hyderabad, Bhopal and Travancore were dreaming of an independence which would keep them as autocratic as before and such hopes received considerable encouragement from the Government of India's Political Department under Conrad Corfield until Viceroy Lord Mountbatten enforced a more strict policy.[10] The imminent declaration of independence by Hyderabad, Bhopal and Travancore would unleash yet another serious crisis setting examples to other states. Mountbatten could clearly see this prospect.[11] Hence, he hastily summoned a conference of princes in late July, where he used his persuasion to get the princes to sign the Instrument of Accession highlighting the advantages that these terms gave to princes and warning that failing to do so before 15 August would leave the princes without an outside mediator to argue on their behalf.[12] Whatever resistance there was among the princes seemed to have crumbled at this point and by 15 August almost all had signed the Instrument of Accession except for Hyderabad, Kashmir, Junagadh and Manipur.[13] In doing so some of these princes were influenced by the political developments in their respective states because meanwhile a new upsurge of state peoples' movement for responsible government had erupted in those states. These movement were anti-monarchial, anti-feudal and pan-Indian in character.

The non-Malayalee citizens of south Travancore were disgusted with the oppressive rule of the Malayalee king of Travancore and directed their anger against the Malayalee community.[14] Based on such a situation the ambitious dewan of this Princely State launched a move for an independent Travancore and Cochin Movement and declared its intention of not joining the India Union. It came up with an American model of constitution for itself. The Communist activists, who had built a very powerful base among the coir factory workers, fishermen, toddy-tappers and agricultural labourers employed by the *jemmi* landlords, launched a massive campaign against this conspiracy. The police repression was followed by the rebels acquiring military training for self-defence. There was a violent confrontation between the state and the rebels in Punnapra and Valayar in which at least 800 people were massacred by the police. This event coincided with the ongoing *Aikya* Kerala Movement, which had been working for the formation of a multilingual Kerala state, that would include Travancore and Cochin.[15] The movement was a joint venture of the Kerala Pradesh Congress Committee, Travancore State Congress and Cochin Praja Mandalam, which had the support of the maharaja of Cochin too. The hostility against the

Travancore royalty consequent to the brutal suppression of the Punnapra-Valayar Movement strengthened the anti-monarchial stand of the movement and attracted mass support for the unification of Kerala and its integration with the Indian Union. Even though the royalty tried to back out and retain in autocracy, the Punnapra-Valayar and *Aikya* Kerala Movement prevented a possible secession from India and facilitated the merger of Travancore-Cochin with the Union.[16]

July 1946 to October 1951, saw the rise of another massive Communist led peasant insurgency in the Telengana region of Hyderabad state, where a small Urdu speaking Muslim elite had a religio-linguistic hegemony over the majority of Telegu speaking people.[17] There was a total violation of political and civil liberties and the grossest form of feudal exploitation was perpetrated by Muslims and high-caste Hindu *deshmukh* landlords and jagirdars who extorted *vetti* (forced labour) from the peasants and retained bonded labourers through a debt-trap. While the ambitious Nizam was conspiring to set up an independent state and not join the Indian Union the peasants broke out in revolt. The bloody guerilla warfare of the peasants against the ruthless *razakar* army of the Nizam lasted a long time and succeeded in establishing several independent pockets in the region. This anti-Nizam movement brought about the collapse of the autocratic regime of India's biggest Princely State when the Indian Army entered the scene and paved the way for the integration of Hyderabad with the Indian Union. The movement of the Andhra Mahasabha for separation from Madras and the formation of a separate Telengana province also had contributed immensely to the integration. The pan-Indian character of the Telengana uprising was evident in the fact that the adoption of the slogan of overthrowing the new Indian Government had little appeal to the masses.[18]

The progressive National Conference of Sheikh Abdullah had launched a 'Quit Kashmir' Movement against the very unpopular and despotic Hindu maharaja of the Muslim majority state of Kashmir.[19] When Sheikh Abdullah was arrested on 20 May 1946 while leading the movement, Nehru rushed to the support of the Kashmiri leader and was arrested for defying the ban on his entry into Kashmir. Soon after this, negotiations with Kashmir's Prime Minister Kak began for a possible accession of Kashmir to India; Nehru agreed to protect 'Kashmiriat'—the identity of Kashmir, assured them of Article 370 which would allow Kashmir to have a special status in the Union of having its own legislature, non-transferability of land to non-Kashmiris, etc. At the prospect of losing Kashmir, Pakistani raiders invaded Kashmir which hastened the entry of the Indian Army and effected the accession of Kashmir into the Union, though almost half of it was occupied by the Pakistan raiders. This altered the outlook of the Princely States. Bhopal joined the union. Nehru who presided over the Gwalior session of the All India State Peoples' Conference (April 1947) warned that the states refusing to join the Constituent Assembly would be treated as hostile. Along with such verbal threats came promises too. Patel assured the princes that 'The Congress are no enemies of the princely order, but on the other hand, wish them and the people under the aegis all prosperity, contentment and happiness.'[20] While Bhawalpur succeeded in joining Pakistan, Junagadh did not. The Eastern States Union formed by recalcitrant princes crumbled in December 1947 in the face of powerful *Parajamandal* agitations in Nilgiri, Dhankanal and Talcher in Orissa.[21] Junagadh's Muslim ruler in Kathiawad tried to join Pakistan but his attempt was thwarted by popular agitation coupled with Indian police action.[22] The Congress exceptionally strong in Mysore since the late 1930s, launched a fairly uninhibited 'Mysore Chalo' Agitation on its own in September 1947, which forced substantial political changes in a democratic direction by 12 October.[23] By then, most of the states agreed to sign the Instrument of Accession to join the Indian Union acknowledging central authority of the centre over defence, external affairs and communication. The princes agreed to this fairly easily because they surrendered only what they did not have all this time and there was no change in the internal political structures yet. The myriad small states were merged with the neighbouring units to form unions like Kathiawad union, Vindhya and Madhya Pradesh, or Rajasthan while princes were made happy with the bait of a fat privy purse, some of them were made governors or rajpramukhs.[24]

As far as north-east India was concerned, Partition had devastated the region economically, politically and culturally. Following the prospect of the abolition of chieftainship, the oppressed Mizos of the Lushai Hills were inclined to join India while the Nagas wanted a ten-year of Interim Government after which they would decide their future. Manipur had an Assembly constituted by the people's representative after a long struggle for responsible government, but the Communist-phobia that had gripped this Indian state following Telengana, Punnapra-Valayar, Bengal (Tebhaga), Tripura, proved fateful. In fact, by the end of the War the CPI was in a position to claim to be the third biggest party after the Congress and the League and obviously weaker than them.[25] The inexplicable fear of

Communism was compounded by the worldwide spectre too—especially the events in China and Burma which bordered India's north-east. Home Minister Patel wanted to ban the party.[26] The Assam Chief Minister Bordoloi was willing to grant autonomy to Manipur so that its activities did not affect Assam.[27] The Communists were trying to organize a Telegana-like uprising in Manipur, which sealed the fate of this Princely State.[28] The neighbouring Tripura was already witnessing a similar uprising. The seize of Manipur became essential to stop the march of Communism into the Indian mainland.

NAGA HILLS

The Naga's appeal for independence failed to convince the British Labour Government as the Naga Hills and Naga areas were always considered a part of British India and were administered as such by the government. This was despite the fact that some British civil servants believed that the tribals of the north-east were not really Indians. Racially, culturally and otherwise they were projected as non-Indians even though they formed a part of British India. That is why plans of some local administrators to retain the control of some of these areas under Crown-Colony or Trust Territory were not favoured by the government. Moreover, the Labour Government, which had already decided on a complete withdrawal did not want to open up this ponderous issue at such a critical juncture. Therefore, the government maintained complete silence on the memorandum of the Nagas. The memorandum sent by the NNC to the British prime minister which sought to 'present the case of the Naga people for self determination' urged 'His Majesty's Government and the Government of India to set up an Interim Government for a period of ten years, at the end of which the Naga people will be left to choose any form of Government under which they will live'. The receipt of this memorandum was not acknowledged by the Secretary of State for India officially. But in a private top secret letter to Mountbatten, Sir Pethick Lawrence acknowledged its receipt and transfer to Sir Henry Knight. It was felt that the memorandum need not be taken seriously as the NNC was a self constituted body and not representative of all Nagas. It presented the view of the educated Nagas and not the traditional elders of the village. Knight felt that the underlying thrust of the memorandum was not political but the preservation of the economic equilibrium of the Naga Hills until the Nagas were educated enough to be able to compete with the free and independent Indian voters. This could be attained only by some form of Interim Self Government. Mere incorporation of Naga Hills in Assam might lead to the collapse of the Naga economy resulting in famines and to the relapse of the Nagas into head-hunting isolation.[29]

Lord Mountbatten in another private letter mentioned that he had clarified from the Assam Governor, Andrew Clow that although NNC was indeed a self constituted body it did have a representative character. He agreed that the Interim Government had to be a continuation of British rule. To put the Nagas under a Central Indian Government would mean the subjection of the tribes to the politicians of Delhi who would be more unaware of their needs than the Assam administrators. But if the tribals could be ensured some suitable safeguards within the framework of the Indian Constitution, they could themselves expect some share in the government and would have access and influence over it. The main hurdle was that these tribal areas were deficit areas and would need the support of other provinces. The thrust should be to ensure the protection of the tribals from exploitation and the preservation of their way of living.[30]

When the Prime Minister Lord Attlee had to reply to a question by Sir Walter Smiles on the Nagas' demand for an interim arrangement it was pointed out that Nagas should submit their problems to the Advisory Committee on Tribal Areas of the Constituent Assembly. In other words, the government had transferred the matter to the Indian leadership. What Andrew Clow told the Nagas (February 1947) was part of this policy. In a philosophical manner he advised the Nagas to reach an understanding and be accommodative with the people of the plains for their own benefit.[31] They should not think only in terms of what they could get but also what they could give. The Nagas who lived life in pure democracy could share their experience with the plains people and receive the benefits of development and progress from the Indian administration in return. The deputy commissioner of Naga Hills, Pawsey by now found that things were not working in his favour and that the Nagas were being obstinate in their demand for a sovereign Nagaland. He tried to remind the Nagas that they were still primitive and naked people forming a sullen minority of the subcontinent. As such the need of the hour was to remain united. He said,

> Changes in the Government of India are on their way and the Naga Hills too will experience changes. Fortunately here, there is no communal trouble and we

shall be spared of the bloodshed of Calcutta, Noakhali, Bihar and Punjab and if Nagas remain united, they will be able not only to administer themselves in a peaceful atmosphere but also will be able, through unity, to influence the adjoining areas where strife is prevalent. At all costs Nagas must remain united.[32]

But the new found enthusiasm and the prospect of ruling a sovereign Nagaland made the Naga elite insistent. They not only refused to give up their stance, they even encouraged the Mizos, Meithies and the Assamese, to declare themselves independent to strengthen their case. In a statement issued on 21 May 1947, the Nagas leaders called upon the Assamese, not to join the Indian Union, but form an independent Assam and work in cooperation with the federal Nagas state. It went on to say, that 'The Nagas who were determined not to allow themselves to be involved in a divided and chaotic India, are prepared to declare their own independence and can think of entering into a ten-year treaty with an independent Assam.'[33]

Amidst all these, the subcommittee on the future administration of the tribal and excluded areas, under the chairmanship of Gopinath Bordolio, constituted under the aegis of the Committee on Aboriginal Tribes under the chairmanship of Sardar Patel (under the Constituent Assembly constituted in November 1946) visited Kohima on 27 May 1947 to find out the wishes of the Nagas. In his welcome address to the subcommittee, T. Sakhrie the secretary of the NNC said, 'You have come to find out from us, the desire of the Naga people on the question of how their land should be governed when the British power withdraws from India. I am sure the members of NNC who are all present in this house will make your task easy, in that Nagas are indivisible and have one voice, I hope you will do all that is in your power to help the Nagas achieve their demand.'

The NNC then put forward their demands:

1. The Nagas want autonomous status under the guardianship of India for ten years, at the expiry of which they would be free to decide their future.
2. The Interim Government of the Naga people will rule over the people of Nagaland having full powers in respect of legislation, executive and judiciary.
3. Nagaland belongs to Naga people and will be inalienable.
4. The Interim Government of the Naga people will have full powers in matters of raising revenue and expenditure, an annual

subversion to cover the deficit being given by the guardian power.

5. For defence and aiding civil power in case of emergency a force considered necessary by the Naga National Council will be maintained in Nagaland by the Guardian Power.[34]

Bordoloi however was not convinced of the demand. He tried to impress upon the members of the NNC, the benefits that the Naga Hills would derive being a part of India. On the issue of evolving a device to integrate the administration of the hill people with those of the plains, and taking into consideration the fear, apprehensions and demands of the Naga people, Bordoloi recommended in his report that 'All the tribes of provinces other than Assam should be treated as a minority. As regard Assam, conditions in the hill districts in which Naga Hills, the Lushai Hills and North Cachar Hills have been included are on a totally different footing and the atmosphere, partially in the excluded areas is one, which is not to be found elsewhere. There areas must therefore be treated separately from the rest.'[35]

The committee then went on to lay down a number of provisions for the Tribal and Excluded Areas of Assam. These recommendations subsequently formed the provisions of the Fifth and Sixth Schedules of the Constitution of India.

On the failure of the mission of the Advisory Committee to arrive at any agreement with the Nagas on the future constitutional setup, Sir Akbar Hydari, ICS, the Indian Governor of Assam who succeeded Andrew Clow was sent to Kohima on 26 June 1947 to impress upon the Nagas the realities of the situation and negotiate with them to come to an agreement and merge with India. In his welcome address to Hydari, T. Sakhrie, the secretary of the NNC said,

> As is known to your Excellency, the Naga people have submitted a memorandum to His Majesty's Government and the Government of India asserting their rights for self determination and demanding the setting up of an Interim Government of the Naga people for a period of ten years, so as to enable the Nagas to be so schooled so as to make a responsible choice at the end of ten years. Apart from the reply given by the Prime Minister of England to a question of Sir Walter Smiles, seen in the Newspaper columns, no reply to this memorandum of the Naga people have been received. The Naga National Council still looks for a reply and reiterates the statement made in the memorandum that 'A constitution drawn by people who have no knowledge of Nagaland and the people will be quite unacceptable to the Naga people'. It is our desire to make it plain to your

Excellency that it will not be enough to say in the end that a constitution has been drawn upon the lines suggested by the Cabinet Mission. We know that your Excellency will concede that the Naga people have as much right for self determination as any other people. Our request to your Excellency is to do all that is in your power to enable the Nagas to stand on their own feet, so that they may be worthy members of a civilized world.[36]

After a series of hectic meetings and discussions with the members of the NNC and the Deputy Commissioner Pawsey for three days—27, 28 and 29 June 1947—on the question of the ten-year interim demand put forward by the Naga leaders, Governor Hydari expressed his full sympathy for the legitimate rights of the Naga people to an honourable life and worked on a compromise formula known as the Hydari Agreement comprising nine points with full consent of Nehru and Bordoloi.[37] The agreement recognized the rights of the Nagas to develop themselves according to their free wishes. The Naga Government would be given full legislative, executive and judicial power as far as Naga people were concerned and as in the case of Kashmir, legislation passed in central or provincial legislative bodies would not be effective on the Nagas. While the Naga Government will be responsible for the imposition, collection and expenditure of taxes, if at all, the Naga lands and its other resources could not be alienated to a non-Naga. The clause nine of the agreement specified that 'The Governor of Assam as the Agent of the Government of the Indian Union will have a special responsibility for a period of ten years to ensure the observance of this agreement; at the end of this period, the Naga National Council will be asked whether they require the above agreement to be extended for a further period or a new agreement regarding the future of the Naga people arrived at.'

The ninth clause of the agreement was formulated and agreed to after considerable discussion. This needs to be elaborated upon because subsequently this particular clause sealed the fate of the agreement. Narrating the events, Aliba Imti, who was the secretary of the NNC wrote in his memoir:

The (first days) discussion went on freely and with open-hearted attitude from both sides without any reservation. The first days meeting ended at 5 O'clock. Next morning the meeting's discussion was (sic) centered on the word Interim and bit by bit the discussion progressed. The afternoon session was very tricky. On many occasions we put the Governor in a very tight corner. The Governor left the meeting at 5 p.m. requesting us to let him know the same evening whether NNC would agree to his amendment. The members' discussion continued upto 8 P.M. and the burden of going down to the Governor's camp with the discussion of NNC, was given to me. I invited some of the senior members to accompany me at least for physical support while meeting the Governor, but they preferred to send me alone.

The Governor and the DC were sitting in the Governor's camp and they looked at me with expectant eyes. To avoid an awkward situation I quickly told them 'Sorry Sirs'. Pointing out a chair to me the Governor said, sit down Mr. Imti. At his request I gave a short summary about the discussion, He said, alright I am contacting New Delhi immediately and shall inform your decision to the Prime Minister. Next morning he came up with a new proposal on the last point.The Governor's proposal on the very controversial point no. 9 was as follows:

That at the end of 10 years Nagas will be free to choose any form of Government provided they did not join Pakistan or Burma.

The whole meeting was spent only on this 9th point modification and was refused to change even a word of our decision. As it will be understood that the NNC wanted absolute freedom to choose their Government after 10 years and the Government of India may not be ready to that extent. The afternoon session continued and we came to an agreement with all the 9 points (with modification) of our original demands. The last modification of point 9 according to me was less effective than that of Governor's proposal. But I was amused with certain reservation that how the members quite willingly accepted the last proposal from the Governor, that the proposal was something like this (that at the end of 10 years the NNC or the Government in power at that time shall be asked by the Government . . .). And as such the famous 10-year Interim Government was made and the term of the agreement was signed by the Governor of Assam and myself on behalf of the NNC. We made three copies, Governor took copies with him and one copy remained with the NNC. That evening everybody was happy and since [*sic*] the Governor had promised us that if we come to an agreement, it would be implemented immediately, say within a month.[38]

It was a triumphant moment for the NNC. Aliba Imti declared that 'The foundation stone of our cherished goal is already laid down. Let the spirit of difference, if there be any, be taken away from your hearts. Come forward with a united spirit. Let us build a new Nagaland based on the spirit of goodwill and understanding. Let us remember "Rome was not built in a day" and let us also member "United we stand, divided we fall".'[39]

For India too, it was seen as a victory as it was a peaceful step to bring the Nagas into the Union of India by their own free will, so that their future lay within India.[40]

Akbar Hydari seemed to have accomplished an impossible feat by signing the agreement. He had made his intention clear to the Naga leaders on the same evening of the agreement without any opposition or hostile reaction to it from the NNC leaders by categorically stating to them off the record that (if) after the expiry of ten years, the Naga's might change the administrative pattern with India with a view to securing an honourable place but the refusal of which would bring a display of force upon them.[41]

But though both parties went home happy after the agreement, trouble started in their respective headquarters over the Ninth Clause. There were some problems regarding the interpretation of the clause and despite Akbar Hydari's best efforts, the Constituent Assembly refused to ratify the agreement and hence it could not be implemented. Hydari had given the impression that he had Nehru's approval in farming the clause but obviously some interested camps disapproved of the last clause.[42] The NNC leaders suspected it was the Assam Premier Gopinath Bordoloi who wrecked the agreement. In Aliba Imti's words: 'I believe it was the misfortune of the Nagas that the Governor had to belong to a minority community—a Muslim . . . later on we came to learn that the Governor had not been fair and I do not know who was behind/(who was) against the agreement. Was it G.N. Bordoloi or some mysterious hands in New Delhi. The Governor [deteriorated] [*sic*] from his original stand.'[43]

A similar polarization took place within the NNC. While the moderates led by Aliba Imti and T. Sakhrie were happy with the agreement, the extremists—led by Zapu Phizo who had just joined the NNC—felt that it was a sell-out specially due to the last clause. It now began to find ways to undermine the agreement and gave a new interpretation of the last clause by saying that the Nagas had the freedom to opt out of India at the expiry of the stipulated ten years.[44] Deeply influenced by the separatism of the Muslim League and its success in carving out Pakistan out of the Indian subcontinent,[45] Phizo accused the NNC leadership of submission to the Indian Union. Phizo demanded a suitable interpretation of the Ninth Clause, so that it would guarantee the independence of the Nagas after the expiry of the ten years period.[46] But the moderates led by T. Sakhrie who were participants in the making of the agreement tried to convince the extremists that so long as the provision of the agreement remains effective the Nagas could maintain their independent life which was guaranteed by it. This 'liberal view' irked Phizo. Thus, in a bid to assess the views of the people on the subject, Charles Pawsey, the British D.C., Naga Hill District, stationed at Kohima asked the members of the NNC to put the issue to vote.[47] The pro-agreement

Sakhrie group won by a majority while Phizo's group protested that the Hydari Agreement could not be accepted under the present conditions until it guaranteed, the independence of the Nagas after the ten-year period. Following this defeat, Phizo withdrew from the NNC and formed the People's Independence League for sovereign Nagaland.[48] Phizo toured their villages to mobilize support in his favour and envisaged the formation of a sovereign Nagaland which would include the Naga Hills, Tuensang Hills, and contiguous Naga areas of Manipur and Burma. He projected his League to be more dynamic and purposeful than the moderate NNC. But Phizo's League could not win much public support. Its following was small and as a political force extremely weak. Inevitably, the League soon folded up and Phizo was left with no alternative but return to the NNC. But he was soon able to create a lobby within the NNC and persuaded it to agree to his interpretation of the Ninth Clause. In early July, there was a stormy meeting of the NNC, where the leaders who were instrumental in the making of the agreement were severely attacked and called 'moderates'. 'There was much stormy and heated argument about the Governor's agreement. I (Aliba Imti) was also criticized unfairly. I feel (while criticizing me for participating in the subcommittee) my colleagues conveniently forgot that some month before, the NNC had passed a resolution and written to the president and vice-president of the Interim Government to include one Naga in the subcommittee. I felt that to defend myself was not as important as to work unitedly in the fast changing pace where we had to work out something solid for the Nagas.'[49]

The meeting decided, not unanimously but amidst acrimony, to send a plenipotentiary delegation to New Delhi seeking clarification on the Ninth Clause and categorically assert the NNC's interpretation which would be that after the expiry of the ten year period the Nagas would be free to declare themselves independent. The makers of the agreement felt that it would amount to going back on the agreement but failed to convince the extremist faction. They also felt that the visit at this critical juncture would be impractical, 'to suddenly send a plenipotentiary delegate to Delhi on the verge of Indian Independence was, I felt impractical. Who to meet in Delhi? Who had the power to give independence to any part of the so-called India territory I explained to the meeting but they were adamant to send this delegation. I objected and refused to be a member of this delegation.' (Aliba Imti even resigned from the post of joint secretary at the end of the meeting.[50])

Nevertheless, a seven-member delegation of the NNC consisting of Phizo, Khrisnisa, Kughato, Kezehol, John Angami, T. Sakhrie and Lhousituo led by Rev Longri Ao was sent to New Delhi. As foreseen by Aliba Imti the delegation could not meet any of the Interim Government members. The imminent withdrawal of the British, the transfer of power, the issue of partition and the fierce communal riots all around were matters that kept the national leadership on their toes. The hectic political activity seemed to be never-ending. The only alternative for the delegation was to meet Gandhi who seemed to be relatively free. The delegation therefore met Gandhi on 19 July 1947 at his Bhangi colony, New Delhi residence.[51] On being asked by the secretary to place before Gandhi the purpose of their visit, the delegation presented the history of the Naga people highlighting the fact that they had never been a part of India including the brief period during which the British conquered them. Even the British kept them 'excluded'. Now that the British withdrawal as 'imminent', the authorities offered them district autonomy. But the Nagas wanted complete independence and that they were going to declare themselves independent unilaterally on the 14 August 1947—a day prior to the independence of India.

Gandhi reportedly tried to convince the delegation that the foundation of free India was love, brotherhood, non-violence and non-coercion. He promised that once India was free, Nagas like other citizens would be treated with honour. 'Nagas have every right to be independent. We did not want to live under the domination of the British and they are leaving us. I want you to feel that India is yours. I feel that the Naga Hills are mine, the matter must stop there. I believe in brotherhood of man. I do not believe in force or forced union.'[52]

On being told that the Nagas would declare themselves independent on 14 August, Gandhi retorted, 'Why not now? Why wait for August 14th?' On being told that Sir Akbar Hydari had threatened them with the use of force, on the evening of 29 June 1947, if they dared opt out of India, Gandhi characteristically said, 'Sir Akbar is wrong. He cannot do that. . . . I will come to the Naga Hills. I will ask them to shoot me first before one Naga is shot.'[53]

The Naga extremist leaders recalled this event after Gandhi was assassinated and made political capital of it in a memorandum submitted to the President of India on 1 November 1957.

On that historic day, the Naga delegation discussed the affairs of the Nagas fully with the Father of Indian Nation, and they made the Naga position clear to him without ambiguity. What he said was not a sudden impulse of the willingness of the father of a great nation trying to be obliging. He was sincere. He saw the undeniable right of the Nagas which should not be violated. We took his word as final as far as Nagaland and India were concerned. Gandhiji interpreted not only his own good nature but it was in full confirmation of the politically and publicly avowed policy of the great India National Congress not to be a party to coercion. And in this he was not only upholding the attributed national tradition of India as a country which claims to love not peace alone but 'she had never waged war against any nation'. The glory and pride of India was more important to Gandhiji and thus he laid the corner stone to build-up a greater heritage for future India.[54]

However on their return they found that the Nagas Hills were going to be a district of the province of Assam after independence and it would be administered as per the provisions of the Sixth Schedule of the Indian Constitution which was being prepared. The Naga extremist faction campaigned that the Constituent Assembly was not ready to accept the 'Hydari Agreement' which the NNC had already rejected. This activated Naga politics with more vigour. It was not only a triumph of the extremist faction of the NNC led by Phizo but it agitated the moderate sections too which had participated in the making of the agreement. Their stand had not been vindicated and this virtually amounted to loss of face. They were thus compelled to join the extremist line of action. The NNC was under the virtual control of Phizo who emerged to be a more pragmatic leader. Almost overnight Phizo emerged as the undisputed leader of the Nagas whose suggestions were accepted without much questioning while the erstwhile leaders responsible for setting up of the NNC like T. Sakhrie and Aliba Imti were relegated to insignificance.[55] What petrified both the factions was that if the government also rejected the agreement then the Naga future was sealed forever and the options that were given in the agreement would not be available to them anymore.

On the eve of Indian independence the NNC had a two-day meeting on 13 and 14 August 1947. Aliba Imti was elected the president of the NNC and a Council of Action was formed.[56] The Council sent a telegram to the Government of India on 14 August 1947 informing them that at the end of the ten year period of the Hydari Agreement 'the Naga will be free to decide their own future' but it failed to produce any reaction from the government. Another telegram was sent to the United Nations that the Nagas did not accept the Indian Constitution and at the end of their discussion with India, the Nagas would be independent. The Council asked the Nagas to boycott the celebration of Indian Independence on 15 August 1947. In the stormy NNC meeting of 13-14 August, representatives of many tribes participated and discussed the strengths and weaknesses of the agreement.[57] With Mr Rushukhrie in the chair and Mr Kumho as the secretary, the meeting decided that the NNC which stood for the solidarity of the Nagas, should continue to work for the 'good' of the Naga people. It set up a subcommittee comprising Kevichusa, Mayangnokhcha, Zopianga, Krusiehu, Nchemo, Kezuke and Subongnoklu to draft a constitution for the future government of Nagaland.[58]

On the morning of 15 August 1947, India was independent. As part of the boycott of the celebration, the Naga boys worked through out the night making posters and pasting them on Kohima's walls, trees and rocks. And included posters which said, 'outsiders (Indians) let us separate as friends and live like good neighbours', 'Indians, it is better to go from Nagaland without any delay,' 'Nagaland is for the Nagas', 'Naga people want peace'.[59] But the Kohima Police—now a part of the Indian administration of which Nagaland was now a district of the Assam province—had done a better job by removing almost all the posters before anyone could read them.[60] It became evident that Nagaland was now a part of India.

THE MIZO HILLS

On 20 February 1947, Clement Attlee announced that the British would leave India by June 1948.[61] The Cabinet Mission had recommended the constitution of an Advisory Committee to suggest constitutional devices to protect the rights and interests of the minorities and tribals.[62] This committee could be a part of the Constituent Assembly which was to frame the Constitution of India.[63] Attlee's announcement of 20 February 1947 also stated that unless the Constituent Assembly became the Constitution by June 1947, the British Government would have to consider to whom the powers could be handed over.[64] Accordingly the Constituent Assembly set up an Advisory Committee on the North-East Tribal and Excluded Areas under the chairmanship of the Assam Premier Gopinath Bordoloi.

CONSTITUENT ASSEMBLY AND INTEGRATION OF MIZO HILLS

By this time, the tribals in north-east India were already worried about their political future. The Constituent Assembly, which was to frame the future Constitution of India could not ignore the specialized requirements of the excluded and partially excluded areas. To assist the Assembly for the purpose a committee was formed to report on the North-East Frontier (Assam) Tribal and Excluded Areas which was popularly known as Bordoloi Committee after its chairman. The Committee was to work under the Advisory Committee on Fundamental Rights, Minorities and Tribal and Excluded Areas of which Sardar Patel was the chairman. The Committee was to have Gopinath Bordoloi, the Assam Premier as the chairman, and B.N. Rau, Constitutional Advisor to the Constituent Assembly, and a civil servant who had spent several years in Assam as its member. The other members were J.J.M. Nichols Roy, the leader of the Khasis and a minister in the Bordoloi Cabinet, A.V. Thakkar a Gandhian social worker, Rup Nath Brahmma, a prominent plains tribal intellectual and Mayang Nokeha. The last member was subsequently replaced by Aliba Imti Ao, the president of the Naga National Council.[65] The Committee which was officially formed on 27 February 1947 extensively toured the province of Assam which included visits to he Lushai Hills, North Cachar subdivision, Mikir Hills and the Naga Hills district.[66] In addition the representatives of the tribes visited the headquarters. The Committee received memoranda from various representative and political organizations and also recorded evidence given by prominent citizens and officials. The Committee co-opted two members from each of the district it visited.[67]

Among the Mizos, both the Mizo Union which was a new political party and the District Conference—comprising leading members of the Mizo society—claimed to be the representative organization. The Bordoloi Committee accepted the Mizo Union as the representative of the Mizo people rather than the Conference stating that

> the District Conference convened by the Superintendent of the Lushai hills as an elected body (was) purporting to be representative of the whole of Lushai hills. The election to this body which consisted of twenty chiefs and twenty commoners with the Superintendent himself as President was boycotted by the Mizo Union which was the only representative body of the Lushai at that time and (hence the Conference) could not be regarded by us as representing more than a section of opinion largely that of the officials and chiefs controlled by them.[68]

In fact, the district superintendent wanted that the District Conference to be treated as the representative of the Mizo people. The refusal to do so by the Bordoloi Committee and appointing co-opted members from the Mizo Union Party infuriated the superintendent no end. He complained to the Committee that the co-option had been done without consulting the district authority.[69]

According to its provision, the Committee had sent a request to the Mizo Union Party to select its nominees to be co-opted as members of the Committee. Earlier Bordoloi had invited Vanlawma to be one of the members of the Committee. But the situation had changed as the Mizo Union now had a new set of office bearers. While the Mizo Union nominated its president Khawtinkhuma and leader Saprawnga to be the members of the Committee, Vanlawma urged Khawtinkhuma not to accept the invitation because the Assam premier had earlier promised the Mizos full membership but now they were being given only co-opted membership. But the Mizo Union accepted the co-opted membership and joined the Committee.

Being members of the Committee had important implications for the Mizos. Since the Constituent Assembly was set up to frame the constitution for free India, participating in it implied consenting to be a part of the Indian mission. Due to this reason the Nagas who had joined the Committee, later withdrew from it as they decided not to join the Indian Union. The Mizos had no representative in the Constituent Assembly but the Bordoloi Committee was an integral part of it and its recommendations were going to be incorporated while framing the constitution of India. Hence, joining the Committee would imply acceptance of Nagaland's merger with the Indian Union. This sparked off a public debate among the Mizo leadership. On the eve of the visit of the Bordoloi Committee, a public meeting was organized in Aizawl, where Mizo leader Vanlawma, the former secretary of the Mizo Union made a scathing speech referring to his meeting with the Assam premier, at a time when the future of Assam was in jeopardy, had 'begged' the Mizos to side with Assam so that it could join India rather than Pakistan. And now that the Cabinet Mission proposals have been rejected and the crisis was over, the Assam Government was even refusing to offer the Mizos full membership in the Committee. He added, if this was any indication of the things to come in the future, the Mizos should insist on remaining independent.

But unperturbed by these developments, the Committee visited Aizawl, the headquarters of the Lushai Hills district on 17 and

18 April 1947[70] along with two of its Mizo members. During this visit it noted that the people, even though isolated from mainstream political life due to the device of 'Excluded Areas' 'were not found lacking in political consciousness'.[71] 'The people of Lushai Hills who have benefited by the activities of the missionaries among them cannot be said to be behind the people of the plains in culture, education and literacy. In literacy particularly they are in a better position than a good number of the plain areas and the general percentage of literacy among them is about 13 per cent while among men only is about 30 per cent'.[72]

The Committee through the evidence it had collected and memoranda 'noticed' school of thought among the Mizos, which favoured 'independence'.[73] The Committee suspected this to be the influence of 'instigation by certain elements'. The Committee also noted that the district conference convened by the district superintendent had drafted a 'constitution' by which Mizo Hills would manage all its affairs while surrendering only the area of defence to the Government of India. A treaty to that effect could be signed with the Government of India.[74] The Committee also appreciated the anxiety expressed by the hill people about their land and its exploitation by the advanced sections of the peoples of the Indian plains. Hence, they favoured the continuation of devices like the Innerline Regulations introduced by the colonial authorities and also the introduction of new protective laws which would not only ensure the preservation of the life and culture of the tribals but also grant them maximum autonomy.[75]

With the visit of Committee, the political climate in the Mizo Hills was activated again. The factions of the Mizo Union intensified their rivalry. Both the parties submitted separate memoranda to the Committee, the Right wing in their memorandum stated that the Mizos differed from the rest of Indians in every way and hence their position would not be secure if they integrated with India. Hence, they wanted to revert back to their independent status as they were prior to the British conquest of the Mizo Hills. Thus, the memorandum of the Right wing made the 'official' demand for independence for the first time.

According to the schedule prepared by the superintendent both the rival groups presented themselves before the Committee.[76] The Mizo Right wing was led by Pachunga and Vanlawma while the Left wing was by Dengthuama and Saprawanga. Even though they could not present any common political demand. The Right wing supported the proposals of the district conference.[77] The Left wing was in favour of joining India provided the interests of the tribals were provided constitutional safeguards. But it insisted on the provision for a review of the present arrangement after a period of ten years.[78] The essence of all the evidence presented before the committee was that of apprehensions about the plainsmen and insecurities of a small community while merging with a massive nation with whom they had very little in common. Hence, although they favoured joining the India Union, they demanded maximum autonomy for the district to rule themselves and protection of their rights and interests against exploitation by plains people. Even Mcdonald, the district superintendent made similar demands in his evidence before the Committee.[79] H. Vanthuama, general secretary of the Union (Left wing) stated that the Lushai Hills would be within Indian Union only as long as it was economically backward. As soon as it become economically viable it would part with India. In fact, he stated that after ten years the Mizos would secede from India.[80] Panchunga, a Right wing leader, wanted the Lushai Hills to be directly under the jurisdiction of the Government of India.[81] R. Thanlira, Dengthuama and Bawichuaka pleaded for maximum autonomy. Bawichuaka demanded the unification of all the Mizo inhabited areas under one administration and the setting up of a National Council with an independent judiciary, legislature and executive to administer the district. But he insisted on a ten-year period following which the Mizos would have the right to self-determination.[82] It should be noted that the members of the Mizo Union (Left wing) presented their views before the Committee which were then condensed and systematically presented in the form of a memorandum to the Bordoloi Committee. The Mizo Union had a conference on 22 April 1947, wherein it drafted a memorandum regarding the future of the Mizo Hills and submitted it to the Committee. The memorandum signed by Khawtinkhuma and Vanthuama concerned the future of Mizoram:

> At the time when India becomes independent, the Lushai Hills district will also be federated with the province of Assam and be connected therewith in certain subjects which shall be desired by negotiation between the provincial legislature and the Mizo National Council. The district will henceforth be called Mizoram including the contiguous areas of Cachar, Chittagong hill tract, Manipur and Tripura. . . . The village with its village council will constitute the unit and basis of administration within Mizoram. . . . The financial provision should be made by

the center from year to year until such time as the Mizos shall assert that they are able to maintain their territorial integrity and self-determination without this financial provision . . . all the points suggested by the party shall be subject to revision after ten years.[83]

MIZO SECESSIONISM

The visit of the Bordoloi Committee witnessed the intensification of the separatist movement. This happened because it was felt that joining the Bordoloi Committee and expression of the desire to be integrated into the Indian Union by the Left wing Mizo Union whom the committee had accepted as the mouthpiece of the Mizos had given it the seal of finality. Now a concerted effort had started in favour of independence. Pachunga, the president of the Right wing Mizo Union along with Dahrawka and Hmartawnpunga published a political pamphlet. In this excerpt they exhort the Mizos to work for their freedom:

We Mizos have nothing in common with the Vai (Indians). If we commit ourselves under the Indian government, we will be swallowed by the Indians because they are much more in number than the Mizo people. Until the British came, we Mizos had nothing to do with the Vai, now that the British are leaving we should get out of the British government to be as we were before, namely, free. The Mizos are neither slaves nor possessions; therefore we should not allow ourselves to be treated as such, having to change owners. The Mizos should stand firm together and defend Mizoram for the Mizo people. Whatever may come Mizoram is for the Mizos.[84]

On 5 May 1947 a pamphlet written by D. Ronghaka, *Zoram Independent*, persuading Mizos to declare themselves independent was published and distributed in Aizawl. The following is an English translation of the Mizo language pamphlet,

Every nation in the world strives for independence. India had struggled long to secure their independence. If the Mizo does not fight for their independence, they will remain slaves (Tuk Luh Bawi) which practise has been abolished long ago. We should fight for independence to avoid becoming salves again. The fact that we speak one language (which proves that we are one people) is reason enough for us to strive for independence. Some of us are of the opinion that we should remain within India for the present and seek independence later. But this would prove very difficult. In time there would be some other pharaoh who had power and did not remember our Joseph and if he ordered you to kill your first son you would not be able to disobey it if you are part of India. Our succeeding generations would be in a difficult situation. If we are independent, all of us will be happy because then we will be working for our own future. It might be difficult at the initial period but it would be a worthwhile struggle.

We have heard people say that Mizoram is a rich country. We have deciduous evergreen trees, bamboos, vines and many other plants from which medicines and herbs can be made. We have plenty of trees bearing fruits. We can increase the number of such trees and sell the fruits to our neghbouring countries. We will also increase our handicraft. We will improve our education. We will have the power to make machines. While the British government ruled us, we could not even make a gun because they provided it to us. We can make anything we want, if we are independent.

Because of our religion alone we should be away from the Indians. All around us, different religious groups seem to form their own countries. The Burmese are Buddhists. The Indians are Hindus and the Pakistanis Muslims. Why should not we Mizos who are Christians have our own sovereign country. As prophet Isaiah said, Have faith and it will be done. Let us say, if these people can have separate country, we Mizos can have one too. This is the time for us to take our religion seriously. If Prophet Isaiah had been alive He would have said, Believe in God and start your own government. At the moment some of us are concerned about their own selfish interests. But let us look at the future not just our present. Let us strive to keep this country for our own children and grandchildren, not just think about ourselves.[85]

Following this, a plethora of pamphlets were distributed in Mizoram resulting in a country-wide debate on whether Mizos should remain within India, join Burma, remain under the British or declare themselves independent. Thus, the more closer the Indian independence came, the more polarized the Mizo leaders became over the issue of joining India or remaining independent. The pro-India group was led by Vanthuama. The anti-merger group was led by Pachunga who was stripped of his MU position and hence was a dissident. There was also debate over the issue of whether to remain a part of Assam or be governed by the Government of India directly if the Mizo Hills merged with India. In the midst of all this both the parties seemed to agree with the point raised by Rev Zairema and R. Thanlira, the editors of *Mizo Daily* that Mizos should demand as much autonomy as possible even if merger was agreed upon. H.K. Bawichuaka demanded that the Mizos should be given adequate representation in the Assam Legislature, along with maximum possible autonomy and amalgamation of all the Mizo inhabited areas into one unit. A member of the Pachunga faction wanted the Mizos to join the Mizo areas of Burma and form a separate province within that country.

The MU faction led by Vanlawma and Pachunga continued their

campaign for an independent Mizoram. Vanlawma wrote a persuasive piece called *Khawi Lamah Nge I Kal Dawn? Quo vadis* (Where are you going).[86] He refuted the argument that the Mizos were 'too stupid' to govern themselves. He provided instances from the Bible saying that like the philosophers of Israel who were afraid to leave Egypt were guided by a fire till their destination was reached, Mizos were saved from Japanese invasion. Similarly, this time too God would certainly save them from the idol-worshippers (Hindus). Therefore, Mizos should not be afraid of seeking independence.

Pachunga was keen that the British should not desert the Mizos till they were able to govern themselves. He sent memoranda to the Constituent Assembly, British Prime Minister Attlee and the opposition leader Churchill to the effect that the British should not leave the Christian Mizos to the mercy of the Hindus.[87] A similar pamphlet was circulated by K. Zawla, which lamented the prospective merger of the Mizos with India and advocated its independence.

> It is most beneficial for the Mizos to have the British remain in Mizoram. Instead of having a limited, autonomous district attached to Indian government or Burma government it would be preferable to a limited state attached to the British. Before it is too late, let us consider carefully what is best for us. Imagine the state of things in the near future with Hindi as the official language, because virtually no Mizo spoke Hindi. If you allow the British to leave now, you will greatly regret it later. . . . To acquire the desired Mizoram and to make Mizoram a place in which Jesus could be happy to live, let us ask God for guidance.[88]
>
> When I would go to have a quiet moment alone, not knowing exactly why, I would cry for all the Mizo men in the Mizoram villages because they were forced to carry baggage for the Indian and the British Officials, but now I cried for the Mizos who had formal education, because they wanted to sell Mizoram to the Indian government. As soon as the Mizos joined the Indian government, they would have to pay such taxes as poll tax, land tax, home ownership tax, vehicle tax, bullock tax, car tax and school tax. They will pay more taxes than they ever paid to the British government. In effect, we will be slaves to the Indians.
>
> Therefore, the best thing we can do is to remain under the rule of the British government here in Mizoram. If the British stay in Mizoram for 3 to 5 years and meanwhile we learn from the British how to run our own government, this will be a happy occurrence. If the British remain in Mizoram, our Chiefs will be ruling under some constitutions, and they will not be too much of a burden for the common people; and the Superintendents, knowing the British occupation in limited will not become corrupted by an abundance of power. After 3 to 5 years, if we feel that we want to join either Burma or India, we can join them. We can always be the slave of the Indians.

Let us not hesitate in expressing our desire for the British to extend their stay in Mizoram. We must let the British know how we feel immediately.

Countries such as India, much wealthier than we are, have been granted a degree of autonomy under the British since 1937. To help us set up out own government 3 to 5 years is an obligation which is essence, the British owe us Remember, when the Superintendent McCall asked the Mizos to declare war against the Japanese, even before the British Indian government declared war officially on Japan, at the beginning of World War II, he spoke in the name of the King of England and said that after the British won the war, those of us who fought against the Japanese would be granted whatever we asked.

General Slim of the 14th British Army said, 'The Lushai have clearly shown your friendship to the British. When the British lacked man and ammunition, and the Japanese seemed unbeatable, our summer friends deserted us. Contrary to our summer friends, the Lushai carried on their traditions of honesty and bravery: the British officers and their Chief determined to defend their country and worked hard to do so. And when the enemy arrived at the India-Burma border, the Lushai Scouts were in the front lines, and stopped the Japanese. Mizo bravery and honesty will never be forgotten by us. In my opinion, those Mizo Scouts should be awarded a new status that of Soldier of the Empire'.

Look at the good words said about us in the above quotation. General Slim will obviously cooperate with us in whatever area we desire. Let us not get involved unnecessarily in the turbulent politics outside of Mizoram. Let us believe and have faith in God. If Mizos want to be parasites, why not continue to be parasitic to the British. . . .

Question: We Mizos are rather insignificant. Would the British be willing to help us?

Answer: We don't need to worry about that now. The British are obligated to teach the Indians for 11 years. The British are obligated to help us learn to govern ourselves.

Although it may seem not practicable for the British to help us in this matter, remember that the British have many colonies, we are not the least of them.

Question: Will the Indian government release us now that we are already a part of it?

Answer: Let us stop worrying about what the Indians will do; remember the Indians just want us as their salves. Mizoram is not really a part of India; it is actually an 'excluded area'. If you want to appeal your case belongs to the Superintendent, you have to appeal to the Governor, not to the Assam Legislature. The British government includes Mizoram under British India. The aid we have received from the British government is not from the Assam Legislature, but from the British Assam Governor. While the Hindus and Muslims were rulers in

India, we never were a part of them. Therefore, we have a good opportunity to choose our own future today.

Question: Will it not be an embarrassment to the British, now that they have stated their intention to leave India, to remain indefinitely in Mizoram?

Answer: The British government is giving cooperating with its former colonies in granting conditions under which independence is to come about. This is why Pakistan exists today. Some countries now feel that freedom means any states in which the British are gone, but if we define freedom for ourselves as involving the temporary continuing presence of the British, that is our right.

For those people in the 'excluded area', which included Mizoram, the British have appointed an Advisory Committee. This Advisory Committee will see that the wishes of the tribal peoples in 'excluded areas' are carried out, especially since many tribal representatives have been appointed to the Committee. If we demand what we desire to, the Indian, rather than the British will be embarrassed by the British presence in Mizoram.

Question: The fact the Mizoram has no outlet to the ocean, will India or Pakistan allow the British to pass through their territories in order to get to Mizoram?

Answer: I am certain that India and Pakistan will allow the British free passage. If they offended the British, they will find it difficult to trade with any country in the world since the British controlled most of the world's seas. . . .

As I said, it is most beneficial to the Mizos to have the British remain in Mizoram. Instead of having a limited autonomous state, attached to the Indian government or the Burma government, it would be preferable to have to limited autonomous state attached to the British. Before it is too late, let us consider carefully what is best for us. Imagine the state of things in the near future with Hindi as the official language, virtually no Mizos spoke Hindi. If you allow the British to leave now, you will greatly regret it later. I am eager to know how many of you agree with me. To acquire the desired Mizoram and to make Mizoram a place in which Jesus could be happy to live, let us ask God for guidance.[89]

As a culmination of this process on 5 July 1947, another party known as the United Mizo Freedom Organization surfaced under the leadership of Lalbiakthanga an ex-Brumese Mizo military officer. He assumed presidentship of the organization while Hamingliana and L.H. Liana were vice president and general secretary respectively. Lalbiakthanga believed that it would be difficult to talk of an independent Mizoram after 15 August 1947. Therefore, he felt that complete independence and the unification of all the contiguous

Mizo areas should be sought now before the boundaries between India, Pakistan and Burma were demarcated. Given a choice the UMFO did not mind joining Burma. The party received a boost, when all the MU members of the Pachunga group, except Vanlawma joined the UMFO.[90]

Apart from the Right wingers, the party was supported by the rich and the chiefs' council.[91] Its secessionist character and objective as was evident from the name of the party, earned it the support of the chiefs and rich businessmen who provided it with financial assistance. The chief's council selected Lalmawia, the founder leader of the Lushai Students' Association and an ex-army officer from Burma to work out a modified plan to keep Mizoram out of India and also mobilize public opinion in favour of it.[92] (Lalmawia became the president of the party when Lalbiakthanga left it.) But when the party prepared its constitution it did not make its secessionist character very explicit. This was done to show that the party's aim did not differ from the (Left wing) Mizo Union Party which was immensely popular among the masses.[93] The constitution listed the objectives of the party as:

1. To look for a country with which we could identify ourselves and which we admit and which can provide us the benefits.
2. To promote true democratic spirits where people can choose their own leaders and to reject all traces of authoritarianism.
3. To make our country as strong as possible so that it need not depend on other countries.
4. To improve our culture.
5. To try to better our communication and understanding between ruler and the ruled.
6. To develop the best way of self administration.
7. To ensure freedom of speech and press.
8. To ensure freedom of religion.[94]

Lalmawia who had served in Burma had contacts with the tribal chiefs of Burma. It is said that on the instructions of the chiefs' council, he discussed with the tribal chiefs of Falam-Zahrelian the feasibility of forming a Union of the hill areas of Burma and the Lushai Hills. Lalmawia and the chiefs agreed to unite. But the Burmese Government did not encourage the idea of merging Mizroam with Burma as it had already opted for India.[95] As a result the UMFO movement for merger with Burma fizzled out and so did the party because by then India had become independent.

One of the most important contributions of the UMFO was to initiate a movement for joining Mizoram with Burma. For a brief period the movement caught the fancy of certain sections of the Mizo people. The arguments advanced in favour of merger with Burma included the fact that the Mizos were ethnically very close to the Burmese and that their languages were very similar. In terms of commerce, the party felt that along with Burma, the Mizos could enter the international market with bamboo and other products. Politically they believed that it would be more advantageous to join Burma as it was smaller than India and hence would grant the Mizos a voice in mainstream politics.[96]

However, there was very little time to popularize UMFO or mobilize public opinion in support of its programmes. It could not make any inroads into the Mizo Union stronghold. The base of the Union were the masses, who were not receptive to the ideas of the UMFO. People wanted to be rid of the chiefs whereas the UMFO was the party of the chiefs. In fact, the party was known as the Zalen Pawl[97] or the 'Party of the Privileged'. Hence, they rejected the UMFO and without the support of the common people the party faded out.

In view of the increasing momentum of the secessionist movement the Mizo Union seemed to be a losing its strength. To gain lost ground they started sending volunteers to the villages and interior areas to campaign for the merger of Mizoram with India and popularize the issue of Indian independence. Vankhama and Lalrinliana were sent to Sialsuk (east of Aizawl); Vanlalliana (son of Pachunga) and Challeta were sent to Champai (east of Aizawl), Nagura and his friends to the north-east and Thangridema and Thantuma were sent of Baktawng.[98] However, these volunteers, during their extensive tour in the interior of Mizo Hills to accomplish the above mission, discovered that the common people had no idea of the impending British withdrawal. Reeling under the oppression of the chiefs these villagers did not about the future of Mizoram whether it planned to join India, Burma or emerge independent. What they desired was to get rid of the chiefs. Two Mizo folk songs of that period reflect this desire effectively,

bai thak arva
artui khawn leh
lal hnungzui reng ka ning tawh

kawltu chawi lai daltu an ni
sazai lian pui an ni

(We are fed up of submitting to the chief's orders. He wants us to do all his work. He demands eggs and chickens. We have to always carry out his orders and in this process get delayed for our own work. This is indeed a severe punishment).

zalen muhil lo tho r'u
ni a chhuak sang tawh em e
in kawmawl ahho reng hi
a lum lua e ka ti

(People awake, the sun has risen high. Free yourselves from the oppressors, it is getting too hot to bear).

The Mizo volunteers reported this to the party and the MU think-tank armed with this crucial feedback from the grassroots referred to the Congress pledge of abolishing the monarchy and *zamindari* system and obtained a promise from the Bordoloi Government that after the British withdrawal, it would abolish chieftainship. And this development was conveyed to the masses, which created a sensational turn in Mizo politics. Enthused by the promise, people rallied round the MU, describing the UMFO as the 'Party of the Privileged'. The Mizo Union organized a crusade against the chiefs and even launched a civil disobedience movement against them. The tempo rose as there was confrontation between the chiefs and the commoners. This polarization between the chiefs and the commoners weakened the Mizo independence movement and strengthened the merger movement.

This was also recorded in a classic Mizo folk song,

India zawm duh chu lal banna
independence duh chu lal lalna

which means that joining India would ensure the abolition of chieftainship, but independent mean its continuation.

And

union le union a dang manage
union vantlang kan tanrual laiin dawrpuii union ve che rual elna

(Though both the parties are called Mizo Union, they are different from each other. While the Mizo Union is trying to unite the people, the Dawrpuii (Pachunga) faction speaks ill of others and causes disunity).

In the meantime, McDonald was replaced by Penn for a short time who in turn was replaced by L.L. Peters as the District Superintendent. The extensive support for merger sidelined the UMFO and strengthened the Mizo Union. Enthused by this Khawtinkhuma, president of the Mizo Union prepared for a procession in Aizawal to celebrate India's independence on 15 August 1947. Hearing about it the Pachunga-Vanlauma faction tried to stop the procession and wrote to Khawtinkhuma to that effect.[99] And threatened that if the procession was not cancelled violent confrontation might break out. It also asked the district superintendent not to hoist the Indian flag in Mizoram on that day.

On the night of 14 August a MU meeting took place in Dawrpui Veng. As the situation had become very tense the procession was postponed. The superintendent called a meeting on the same day, in which about 50 Mizos were present and the following resolution was passed:[100]

1. Resolved that owing to the unexpected acceleration of the date of transfer of power by the British government and as the Lushei's have not yet been definitely informed in detail as to what is the proposed future constitution and form of administration of the district and as section (7) sub-section (2) of Indian Independence Bill does not clarify the situation, it is accordingly thought necessary that His Excellency the Governor of Assam should kindly inform them in writing as to what these are to be, also whether the Lusheis are at this stage allowed the option of joining any other Dominion i.e. Pakistan or Burma.

   Resolved further that the Superintendent Lushei Hills should communicate the above request of the Lusheis to the advisor to His Excellency the Governor of Assam in order to clarify these points.
2. Resolved if the Lusheis are to enter Indian Union their main demands are:

   (*a*) that the existing safeguards of customary laws and land tenure etc. should be maintained.

   (*b*) that the Chin Hills Regulation, 1896 and Bengal Eastern Regulation, 1873 should be retained until such times as the Lusheis themselves through parallel district authority declare that these can be abrogated.

3. That the Lusheis will be allowed to opt out of the Indian Union when they wish to do so subject to a minimum period of ten years.

The meeting was attended by both the MU factions but the pro-independence faction however was in a minority. However, on 15 August there was no untoward incident when the Mizo Hills formally became a part of India. The resolution was the final acceptance of the inclusion of Mizoram in the Indian Union signed by the accredited leaders of the Mizo people. The integration of the Mizo Hills with the Indian Union, was thus given legitimacy.

MERGER OF MANIPUR

The British paramountcy came to an end of 15 August 1947. Ripples of India's celebration reached the shores of Manipur too. The Indian tri-colour fluttered everywhere—roads, maidan, markets and villages. Strains of *Bande Mataram* were heard far and wide: 'There was none including women and children who did not feel their hearts with abandon on this particular day.'[101] The maharaja of Manipur gained full control of his state's administration once again after 86 years. But this was a critical juncture in Manipur's history. On the one hand, it witnessed a massive movement for responsible government and on the other, there were preparations underway among members of the Congress to effect its merger with the Indian Union. The then Dominion Agent, Debeshwar Sharma, was pressing the Centre for integration of Manipur as a district of Assam, there was even a suggestion that Manipur should be merged with West Bengal.[102] In mid-September, Sardar Patel mooted a scheme for the formation of a Purbanchal Pradesh consisting of Manipur, Cachar, Lushai Hills and Tripura.[103] Irabat found the whole idea of Purabanchal Pradesh 'nauseating'.[104] He felt that such a move would be a threat to the distinctive social, cultural, political and historical identity of Manipur. And strongly opposed the idea and implored the people to fight tooth and nail against it.

The dilly-dallying tactics of the maharaja in granting a responsible government generated public hostility against him. On 4 October 1947 the Congress Working Committee passed a resolution for 'immediately granting responsible government'—giving the deadline of 1 April 1948.[105] The maharaja assured the people of adult franchise, elected legislature, and a ministry of elected representatives. But as he was not trusted by political leaders, demonstrations and picketing in front of state offices, at the residence of the government officials, were resorted to. This non-stop agitation completely paralysed the functioning of the government and normal life in Manipur.[106] On 10 November the government threatened retaliation and stoppage of 'war compensation'.[107] But this intensified the movement, which compelled the chief minister of the Interim Council to make a declaration on 23 November that a responsible government would be introduced within six months. The election was held on 11 June 1948 under the supervision of the Francise Subcommittee.[108] No party could secure an absolute majority in the election though the Congress emerged as the largest majority. Consequently, a non-Congress coalition government was formed and Maharaja Kumar Priyabrata Singh became the first Chief Minister. The maiden session of the Assembly took place on 18 October 1948.[109]

The election results gave a jolt to the aspirations of the Congress party. It also sealed the fate of the idea of a Purbanchal Pradesh. The local Congress unit established closer links with the area. It invited Prafull Chandra Ghose an eminent Congressman from Bengal who in his speech favoured the idea of a Purbanchal Pradesh. But peoples' opposition to the idea made the situation tense.[110] At a public meeting held on 18 September, the leaders of both the hills and plains strongly opposed the move and declared that the people of Manipur would resist any type of imposition of the proposed province. The Government of Manipur also opposed the idea.[111] Due to such strong opposition the proposal of the Manipur State Congress for the creation of a Purbanchal Pradesh was nipped in the bud.

Irabat Singh who had contested on the Krishak Sabha ticket and was returned from the Utlou constituency, not only opposed the Purbanchal Pradesh idea, but demanded that Kabaw Valley which had been transferred to Burma be returned to Manipur. The workers of his Krishak Sabha and Praja Sangha started mobilizing villagers and organized several village meetings. Irabat was a confirmed Communist by now and his activities roused suspicion in the government circles.[112] Sir Akbar Hydari the Governor of Assam, visited Manipur to study the situation. The political activities of Irabat specially were minutely observed and studied. This had become essential in view of the increasing rumour of a Communist coup in Manipur and Irabat's opposition to the merger of Manipur with India.[113] It was reported that the higher level officials of the Indian Government felt that if Irabat was allowed to move freely it would be impossible to effect the merger. Irabat was also held responsible for all the disturbances in Manipur. The Manipur Government in a move to curb his activities banned the Krishak Sabha, Praja Sangha, Mahila Sammilla and the Student Federation—the organizations Irabat was associated with.[114]

Irabat on the other hand, founded the state unit of the Communist Party of India after the second Congress of the CPI was held in Calcutta, 28 February-6 March 1948.[115] This was the time when peasants were engaged in armed struggle in Telengana, Bengal and Tripura. Irabat's days as a free moving citizen came to an end on 21 September 1948. On this day as attempts were being made to arrest him Irabat went underground. From his hideout he started popularizing Communist ideology and programmes, and also started mobilizing and organizing the peasants. Irabat was trying to start a Telengana-like uprising in Manipur and establish an 'Independent Peasant Republic of Manipur'.[116] In fact, one the reasons that the Home Ministry of India hastened the process of Manipur's merger with India was the rising spectre of a Communist armed struggle in various parts of India which had given rise to this phenomenon called 'Communist Menance'.[117]

The Indian National Congress favoured the inclusion of all the former Princely States into the fold of the Dominion of India. At its session of 15 June 1947, the Congress party adopted a resolution which declared that 'they could not admit the right of any state in India to declare its independence and to live in isolation from the rest of India'.[118] This process of integration was to be achieved before India was declared a 'Republic'. As far as Manipur was concerned, the India Government desired to settle the merger issue by means of 'conciliation and pressure'.[119] As a first step, they asked the maharaja to sign the 'Stand-Still Agreement'.[120] The maharaja desired to establish a close relationship between Manipur and the Dominion of India and hence he agreed to the conditions of this agreement and signed it on 11 August 1947.[121] According to the agreement the Government of Manipur accepted to entrust the responsibilities of defence, communication and external affairs to the care of the Indian Government. Apart from this other ancillary subjects like custom, excise and coinage, etc., were also surrendered to the Government of India. The internal administration was the sole authority of the maharaja and the Government of India assured the protection of internal autonomy and authority of Manipur. But unfortunately, it had not specified the future political status of Manipur.

After independence the office of the Dominion Agent was established who was to be the Indian resident representative in Manipur. Debeshwar Sharma was appointed for the post. The nature of the position was such that it gave immense opportunity and power to the agent to interfere in state politics and take sides on issues. Sir Akabr Hydari's report on Sharma, after his visit to Manipur not only let to his dismissal but also to the abolition of the post of the Agent and in his place a dewan was appointed. Akbar Hydari's sudden death brought Sri Prakash as the Governor of Assam. His visit created panic in the state as it was rumoured that he was sent there to bring about Manipur's merger with the Indian Union.[122] Sri Prakash, sensing this, declared that he had no intention of destroying the political identity of Manipur.[123] But his actions proved otherwise. There were intelligence reports about the preparations for a Communist coup in Manipur. The state Superintendent of Police, S. Patil had covered a vast area to confirm that some workers of the Communist Party of Manipur were actually trying to collect arms and ammunitions and had launched a propaganda campaign in the Nungbung Awangba area, some 32 km east of Imphal to win the Naga tribals in their favour.[124] Strict vigil and army patrol was maintained in Nambol—the constituency of the Communist leader Irabat which was viewed as the potential center where the uprising could start. The unconstitutional appointment of Major Rawal Aman Singh as the dewan of Manipur by the governor was a move to counter the Communist insurgency. In a confidential letter to the Advisor to the Governor of Assam, Nari Rustomji, Major Singh stated that he was doing all he could to put a check on the activities of the Communists in the state, but there was collaboration between the Manipuri and Brumese Communists and he would not be surprised if there was some kind of a flare up.[125]

The function of dewan in Manipur was to provide general supervision and guidance in the matters relating to the state's administration. The dewan was also to hold the direct charges of (1) law and order, and (2) the administration of hill areas and relations with the Government of India. Thus, the dewan was made the virtual overall in charge of Manipur's administration which annoyed the helpless maharaja. Major General Rawal Amar Singh was appointed as the dewan with Major Khating as his deputy.[126] By the middle of 1949, the Government of India had apparently decided to integrate Manipur within the Indian Union. The intention of the Indian Government to accede Manipur into India was becoming manifestly clear. Even the secret conferences between the state Congress unit and the AICC had become an open secret.[127] The Praja Shanti Sabha a strong political party took strong exception to the negotiations and opposed the impending merger.[128] In a meeting (25 August 1949) it pleaded with the Government of India to maintain the *status quo* and retain the separate identity of Manipur outside India. But, the writing on the wall was clear. On 8 September 1949 a public meeting way organized by the Youth Socialist League where except the state Congress every other party spoke against the merger and asked the maharaja not to sign any document in favour of the integration.

Soon after the Manipur State Congress got instructions favouring merger from the High Command they share it with the people called a public meeting in Imphal on the 3 August 1949, in which they promised to convey to them the assurances received from the Indian leaders. The people expected to hear assurances against the possible merger. (The Congress workers had taken photographs of the assembled crows to be sent to New Delhi as proof of the mass support to the Manipur State Congress.) But when they found that the assurances were for the merger of Manipur with the Indian Union and that the meeting itself was not a 'public meeting' but that of Congress workers, they immediately held another public meeting at the Ghandi Maidan, Imphal, on the same day under the joint presidentship of Solet Haokip Kuki, Habi Dewan Mohammed and Nandalal Sharma. The following resolutions were adopted at the meeting:

1. The big gathering of today's protest public unanimously passes the resolution that the *gaddi* cannot be abolished and the State cannot be integrated or merged.
2. This meeting unanimously resolves that the Manipur State Congress is a deceitful one.
3. This meeting condemns the Manipur State Congress in their act of selling the Manipur prajas to India without taking public opinion and by falsely alleging that they had the support of the people. This meeting further expresses its utter denial of the deceitful plan for a public meeting on their return from Delhi. The Praja Shanti Sabha be requested to perform the function of informing the Manipuri public and all authorities concerned clearly explaining all these faults and cheatings of the Manipur State Congress.[129]

On 15 August 1949, the Manipur State Congress had celebrated the Independence Day in Imphal peacefully. Some 4,000 people took part in the meeting and there were processions with National Flags, music, etc. Krishnamohan Singh had presided over the meeting and with people shouting *Bande Mataram, Shadhin Bharati Ki Jai, Down with Maharaja and Down with Gaddi*. The Manipur Student's Federation has observed *Dibashpalan Day* by hoisting black flags at Iril Khongnangkhong (Porompat). Only 200 people had attended the function and passed a resolution condemning the Congress Government. N. Binoy Singh, son of Dr Leiren who had been a minister, hoisted the black flag. This flag hoisting ceremony was reported in detail in the daily *Praja Tantra* of 17 August 1949, under the title 'Shameful News',

> On the 15th August, 1949, the Manipur Student's Federation held a protest meeting by hoisting a Black Flag at Prompat. Cyclostyled bulletins were also distributed. Last year, Dr. Leiren Singh, the present Minister-in-charge of Education held a procession by hoisting a black flag on the 15th August, 1948, at Khurai (lamlong). By that time this gentleman had not been selected a Minister. This year Srijut N. Binoy Singh, who is the son of this gentleman has performed the function on behalf of the Manipur Student's Federation.[130]

Immediately the Manipur State Police along with the help of a platoon of the Manipur Rifles started searching the houses of all those suspected of being members of either the Communist Party of Manipur or the Manipur Student's Federation. On 22 August 1949, houses of the active workers were searched and Communist propaganda leaflets were seized.

All members of political parties besides the State Congress in the Legislative Assembly adopted the following resolution opposing the merger.

> If integration or merger be imposed here irrespective of our unfortunate helpless circumstances and (by violating) the principle of Bapuji, without the consent of the people, the present moral submission of the Manipuris to India, which is most precious, may disappear bidding good-bye to the physical control of imposition and the bitter experiences thereof, may be a sort of handicap in the political race of India with other countries; a double loss for India and Manipur. If the people have been sinned against and wronged, the people themselves have to be watched over in addition to the watch over across the frontier.[131]

In contrast to this the Manipur State Congress adopted a resolution strongly favouring the merger.[132] They even even decided to send a three-member delegation of the party to meet the AICC leaders in New Delhi to expedite and facilitate the merger. According to them, the merger was necessary in view of the following reasons:

1. incapability of the Government of Manipur to maintain law and order situation in the country;
2. the apprehensions from the activities of the Communist revolution in Burma; and that
3. the merger would ensure peace and development in Manipur.[133]

The maharaja was not unaware of the developments and the impending crisis. But he was controlled and virtually dictated to by the dewan. The relationship between the two had deteriorated on account of the dewan's constant interference in the states internal administration. Annoyed with the interference the maharaja left for Shillong—the capital of Assam—on 15 September 1949 and reaching there on the 17 September. The governor was happy to receive[134] the maharaja and offer him hospitality. He seized this unexpected opportunity and laid the trap. The governor had already been briefed by the dewan that the maharaja was in the hands of unscrupulous individuals which became an excuse for him not to negotiate with any other individual or bodies except the maharaja himself. When the maharaja reached the Government House in Shillong, he was extremely disturbed by the sudden developments. He was informed by the governor that the Government of India had instructed him to complete the negotiations with the maharaja regarding the merger before 20 September 1949.[135] The maharaja wrote a letter to the governor on 18 September that he wanted to talk to the representatives of the people in the Manipur Assembly. He observed, 'Now that the sovereignty of the state has been vested in the people, it would be in the fitness of things to hear the people's voice and learn their sentiments so that the line of action may not in any case be unconstitutional.'[136]

After his first meeting with Sri Prakash the Governor of Assam in the forenoon of 18 September, Maharaja Bodh Chandra initially thought that he could perhaps slip away from Shillong and thereby evade a final decision on the governor's unpleasant proposition about the integration of Manipur. He could not yet imagine himself to be a prisoner in the hands of Sri Prakash and his Advisor, N.K. Roustomji since it was only on 18 September, that the Redlands—the maharaja's residence in Shillong—had been encircled by armed security personnel, and plain-clothes men were keeping track of people entering and existing the building. The maharaja and his party were absolutely cut off from the outside world. Not a single letter and not even a telegram from Manipur (except one in Manipuri about Sri Govindajee's *puja*) had reached them, and no information could leak out from the royal residence, though many letters and telegrams were dispatched from either side. In addition, the Redlands had no telephone connection. The maharaja's bodyguards—eight riflemen from the Manipur Rifles—were nothing more than ornamental, specially as the number of forces surrounding the maharaja were significantly increased in the subsequent days. Since Sri Prakash did not pay any attention to the maharaja's appeal to withdraw the armed security personnel from his residential quarters, the officiating private secretary to His Highness the maharaja of Manipur decided to request the superintendent of police, Shillong, to withdraw the security guards:

> I am directed to convey the grateful thanks of His Highness the Maharaja of Manipur for your sending guards for the protection of His Highness during his stay here in Shillong. Indeed, His Highness feels glad at the gesture.
>
> But since His Highness has brought adequate guards for himself, His Highness does not like to cause any trouble to you. Hence, you can please arrange to withdraw your guards forthwith.[137]

On the same evening of 18 September 1949, Sri Prakash had informed Maharaja Bodh Chandra to come to the Government House the next day (19 September) at 9.30 in the morning in order to complete the discussion on the morning of 18 September. The governor had further stated that he had been given definite instructions by the hon'ble minister of states to complete the 'negotiation' by 20 September 1949 positively. Maharaja Bodh Chandra was not unaware of the fact that the subject matter would certainly involve the fate of future Manipur. He could not deny the fact that he had received a number of representations and resolutions from the people of Manipur concerning 'this very important affair'.

Although to keep up appearances Maharaja Bodh Chandra had shown a little resistance to the governor's proposition, he was personally satisfied to learn from the governor's adviser that if the administration of the Manipur state had to be taken over by the Central Government in New Delhi, he would be entitled to a sum of Rs.2,25,000 per year as privy purse for his lifetime. Maharaja Bodh

Chandra had shamelessly requested the governor to persuade the Government of India to raise the amount to Rs.4,00,000.[138]

In the early morning of 19 September 1949, Maharaja Bodh Chandra expressed a desire to leave Shillong for Imphal in the afternoon of the same day. Since there was no reply from the governor to the contrary, he even informed Sri Prakash that all the papers connected with the discussions of 18 September may be returned to Imphal. But the governor wrote to the maharaja to come at once in order to finalize the issue of merger. Sri Prakash had already communicated to the States Ministry in Delhi, late in the night of 18 September, all that had transpired at their meeting held earlier the same morning. And he had received back very 'strict instructions' that the negotiation should be completed before Maharaja Bodh Chandra left Shillong. Sri Prakash had telegraphed Sardar Patel saying that the maharaja 'threatened to return to Manipur without holding any discussions' and the response had been that he 'must not under any circumstances be allowed to return to Manipur'.[139] Sri Prakash had sought authority to detain the maharaja if need be. The Sardar simply required 'whether he had not a Brigadier in Shillong'.[140] The maharaja knew very well that if he was compelled to work independently of his people, his actions could become unjustifiable. Therefore, he sought the governor's permission to go back to Imphal and thus bring a speedy solution to the matter. But Sri Prakash said the he was under the strictest orders of the Government of India to have the negotiations completed without any further delay. He cunningly referred to one of Maharaja Bodh Chandra's letters (Secret Memo of 11 August 1949) wherein His Highness had requested the governor to grant an interview in Shillong regarding the affairs of the Manipur state. It was, Sri Prakash said, in compliance of the maharaja's request that the meeting had been arranged:

> I have had the opportunity, since, to have discussions with the Hon'ble Minister of States, and have, therefore, no alternative but to communicate the decision of the Government of India to Your Highness and negotiate the final settlement of Your Highness's Privy Purse on the lines of the instructions that have been given to me.[141]

A meeting was held between the governor, and the maharaja on 20 September at Governor's House. In the meeting they discussed a subject of the 'greatest delicacy', and in the meeting the maharaja had been assured by Sri Prakash that the Government of India would certainly protect his ultimate interest. Sri Prakash further told the maharaja that he would be coming to the Redlands at 5 p.m. on the same day (20 September). But before the governor's arrival at the Redlands, Maharaja Bodh Chandra sent a very strange note to Sri Prakash reflecting a sudden change in his attitude. The following letter clearly indicated that the maharaja's will had snapped somewhere:

> Like all other patriots of India I too am a great lover of the Indians for whose welfare I am always anxious. The Manipuris are also Indians. I therefore, always have the good wishes of the people and India at heart. It is also in the best interest of India that the will of the people ought to be taken into consideration.
>
> I consider that I have a guardian in the person of Your Excellency who guides and helps me in my endeavour towards ameliorating the welfare of my people. The only thing is that this being a great change it should be done constitutionally and democratically with an eye to the will of the people whose co-operation I confidently hope we will secure.[142]

As per plan, Sri Prakash and his Adviser N.K. Rustomji came to meet the maharaja exactly at 5 p.m. and had their secret discussions. Later in the evening Sri Prakash wrote another letter to Maharaja Bodh Chandra stating that he was glad that they were able to conclude their discussions and happy note. He again invited the maharaja for a meeting on the 21 September at 9 a.m. Since Maharaja Bodh Chandra was tired and unable to come in the morning he suggested that half-past two in the afternoon would be convenient for him. In the meanwhile, Sri Prakash got the Merger Agreement typed incorporating all the additions and amendments made therein in accordance with the maharaja's wishes. In the last meeting with Sri Prakash at 2.30 p.m., maharaja Bodh Chandra put his royal signature on the Merger Agreement.

The Merger Agreement was signed on 21 September 1949 but under the Home Ministry's instruction it was officially announced on 15 October 1949 when the maharaja was back in Imphal. With that announcement Manipur ceased to be an independent monarchy and became a part of the Indian Union as a part 'C' state. It is interesting to note that Sri Prakash did not allow the maharaja to consult the legally constituted State Assembly or the Manipur State Council. It refused to recognize these duly elected bodies. Instead the Government of India stated,

> The Government of India have throughout dealt with you highness directly as

the Ruler of the State and are not prepared to make any deviation at the present stage from the procedure hitherto followed. Your highness may rest assured that the Government of India will take complete responsibility in matter of meeting whatever objection may be raised by the people of the State.[143]

Although Maharaja Bodh Chandra had signed the Merger Agreement on 21 September, people in Manipur move completely unaware of the drastic happenings in Shillong. An editorial published in the *Bhagyavati Patrika*, dated 20 September 1949, reflected the peoples' disapproval of the merger policy of the Indian Government:

There must be kinship, and we should not forget that Manipuri nation will surely wither away from the day it is abolished. Anarchy will then be the order of the day; people will lose moorings and not understand the very purpose of life.

We are insulting the honour of our forefathers if the consequence of an Independent India is going to be the enslavement of Manipur through dethronement of the Meitie King. Not a single patriot, not a single nationalist would support or agree to the abolition of the *gaddi*. We urge upon His Highness Maharaja Bodh Chandra Singh not to surrender the dignity and honour of the Manipuri nation. Kinship in Manipur must be protected.[144]

Another editorial published in the *Bhagyavati Patrika* of 21 September 1949, was somewhat prejudicial in tone which of course incited the people of Manipur to take recourse to murder and bloodshed if the state became part of the Indian Union. An excerpt from the editorial reflects its incitement to the public to revolt:

About 50 years ago, a British Chief Commissioner came to Manipur and he was killed here. There is again a rumour about another Chief Commissioner, and the people are reminded of the Chief Commissioner who lost his life. They ought to remember the incident, for it is now a critical point in Manipur's history. If an Indian Chief Commissioner arrives here, it might be the case of 'History repeats itself,' and, we are afraid, Manipur may witness a mini-scale war.[145]

NOTES

1. R. Suntharalingam, *Indian Nationalism A Historical Analysis*, Delhi: Vikas, p. 459.
2. Ibid. Also V.P. Menon, *The Story of the Integration of the Indian States*, Hyderabad: Orient Longman, 1956; reprint, 1961.
3. Ibid.
4. Ibid.

5. Ibid., Sumit Sarkar, *Modern India*, Delhi: Macmillan, 1983, p. 449.
6. Ibid., R.J. Moore, *Endgames of the Empire: Studies of Britain's Indian Problem*, London: OUP, 1988, p. 189.
7. R. Suntharalingam, op. cit., p. 460.
8. Ibid.
9. Ibid.
10. Sumit Sarkar, op. cit., p. 451.
11. R.J. Moore, op. cit., pp. 174-201.
12. Ibid.
13. Ibid.
14. Sumit Sarkar, op. cit., p. 441.
15. E.M.S. Namboodiripad, *National Question in Kerala*, Bombay: Peoples Publishing House, 1952.
16. Ibid., also Sumit Sarkar, op. cit.
17. Sumit Sarkar, op. cit., p. 443.
18. Ibid.
19. Ibid., p. 450.
20. V.P. Menon, op cit., p. 46, cited in ibid.
21. Sarkar, ibid.
22. Ibid., p. 450.
23. Ibid., p. 451.
24. Ibid., p. 413.
25. Ibid., p. 446.
26. N. Sanjaoba, 'The Genesis of Insurgency', in Sanjaoba (ed.), *Manipur: Past and Present*, Delhi: Mittal, 1990, pp. 245-90.

    In this letter to Patel, 26 May 1948, Bordoloi wrote, '. . . It has therefore been absolutely necessary that these trends towards separatist (Communist) uprising shall be observed from day to day and the Dominion Government and the Government of Assam should be kept appraised of them . . . while therefore I am completely agreeable to allow autonomy to the State of Manipur, I would not like the State Government of feel that all it should do is to satisfy the Governor of Assm personally and should have no other consideration for their conduct.' Cited in ibid.
27. As can be seen below.
28. Pethic Lawrence to Mountbatten, 12 April 1947, letter no. 134, and N. Mansergh (ed.), *Transfer of Power, 1942-47*,Vol. X, London: HMSO, 1981.
29. Mountbatten to Earl of Listowel, 24 April 1947, letter no. 210, in ibid.
30. Andrew Clow, public address in Mokokchung, February 1947.
31. Charles Pawsey, DC, Naga Hills District, address to the Nagas, cited in ibid., pp. 170-1.
32. Asoso Yunou, *The Rising Nagas: A Historical and Political Study*, Delhi: Vivek, 1947, pp. 170-1.
33. NNC Memorandum to G.N. Bordoloi, Chairman, Subcommittee on the Future Administration of the Tribal and Excluded Areas, Kohima, 27 May 1947.

34. As in note 32.
35. T. Sakhrie, welcome address to Akbar Hydari, 26 June 1947.
36. Asoso Yunou, op. cit., pp. 172-9.
37. T. Aliba Imti, *Reminiscences: Impur to Naga National Council*, Mokokchung: Author, 1988, pp. 66-8.
38. Ibid.
39. Asoso Yunou, op. cit., p. 175.
40. Ibid.
41. T. Aliba, Imti, op. cit., p. 68.
42. Ibid.
43. A. Yonou, op. cit., p. 200.
44. Ibid., p. 175.
45. M. Zinyo, *Phizo and the Naga Problem*, Dimapur: Author, 1979, p. 20.
46. A. Yunou, op. cit., pp. 200-1.
47. Ibid.
48. T. Aliba Imti, op. cit., p. 69. Aliba gives the date of the meeting as 23 July in his Memoir which cannot be correct as it preceded their meeting with Gandhi which took place on 19 July.
49. Ibid.
50. This is corroborated in the Government of India publication, *Collected Works of Mahatma Gandhi*, LXXXVIII, 25 May 1947 to 31 July 1947, Delhi, 1983, p. 373. And is based on the 'record of Pyarelal'. Gandhi mentioned about this meeting in his letter to Rammanohar Lohia on 22 June 1947. See ibid., p. 395. But the literal version given above is different from the one published by the Naga leaders although in essence the two are similar. Gandhi told them that if they don't even produce their own clothes they were slaves of foreigners. Even though no one could deprive them of their independence, they could not live in complete isolation. Gone are the days when one nation could use army to snatch the freedom of others and as far as India was concerned the Nagas were safe.
51. Ibid.
52. Ibid.
53. Phizo to the President of India, 1.11.1957, cited in ibid. Also Girija Kumar and V.K. Arora (eds.), *Documents on Indian Affairs*, Delhi: Asia, 1965, p. 108.
54. In fact, if anybody can be hailed as the father of Naga Nation it was T. Aliba Imti who was the maker of the Naga National Council. Similarly, T. Sakhrie was one of the former leaders of the NNC had been the core of the Naga thinktank. Angami Phizo was a relatively late entrant (June 1946). He was 'deeply convinced by the Muslim two-nation theory and the tactics employed by the Muslim League to create Pakistan'. A failure in his personal life, Phizo joined the NNC when it was in the thick of its movement and immediately 'tried to prevail upon the organization to lean more towards extremism'. Phizo had a firm belief that if India could

concede to the Muslim League, his own pressure tactics would win independence for the Nagas too. Phizo remained an ordinary member of the NNC until 1950. It was only in the aftermath of NNC-Akbari Hydari Agreement that Phizo with his rhetoric was able to factionalize it into moderate and extremist sections. Aliba and Sakhrie were realists and pragmatists in their approach and hence where dubbed as moderates. The rise of 'extremists' saw the obvious relegation of the moderates into insignificance. In fact, Sakhrie was subsequently murdered. The suspicion was again on Phizo.

55. T. Aliba Imti, op. cit., p. 70.
56. Ibid., p. 71.
57. Ibid.
58. Ibid., p. 70.
59. Ibid.
60. R.J. Moore, *Endgames of Empire: Studies in Britain's Indian Problem*, Delhi: OUP, 1988, p. 75.
61. B. Hanasaria, *Sixth Schedule to the Constitution of India: A Study*, Gauhati: Ashok, 1983, p. 8.
62. Ibid.
63. R.J. Moore, op. cit.
64. Report of the North East Frontier (Assam) Tribal and Excluded Areas Subcommittee (Report) reproduced in B. Hansaria, op. cit., pp. A-183-4.
65. B. Hansaria, op. cit., p. 8.
66. Report, pp. 184-5.
67. Report, p. A-184.
68. Ibid.
69. Report, p. A-192.
70. Ibid.
71. Ibid., p. A-190.
72. Ibid., p. A-192.
73. Ibid.
74. Ibid., pp. A-194-6.
75. S.K. Chaube, *Hill Politics in North East India*, Delhi: Orient Longman, 1973, p. 162.
76. R.N. Prasad, *Government and Politics in Mizoram*, Delhi: Northern Book Centre, 1987, p. 80.
77. Report of the North East Frontier Tribal and Excluded Areas Subcommittee, Vol. II, also with ibid.
78. Ibid.
79. Ibid.
80. Ibid.
81. Ibid.
82. Memorandum to the Bordoloi Committee by Mizo Union, 22.4.1947.
83. Pachunga, Dahrawka and Hmartawnpunga, *Independence*, Aizawl, 7 June 1947.

84. D. Ronghaka, *Zoram Independent*, 5 May 1947.
85. R. Vanlawma, *Khawi Lamah Nge I Kal Dawn*? *Quo Vadis*, 18 June 1947.
86. R. Sena Samuelson, *Love Mizoram*, Imphal: Goodwill Press, 1985, p. 51.
87. K. Zawla, *Zoram Din Hmun Dik Hmuh Chuah Theina Tur*, Aizawl, 29 July 1947.
88. Ibid.
89. R. Sena Samuelson, op. cit., pp. 47-50.
90. B.B. Goswami, op. cit., p. 136; S.K. Chaube, op. cit., p. 162, R.N. Prasad, op. cit., p. 255.
91. B.B. Goswami, ibid.
92. This was clarified by Vanlawma, *Ka Ram le Kei*, Aizawl, 1972, p. 216.
93. *Mizo Zalenna Pawl: Pawal Din Dan* (United Mizo Freedom Organisation: Constitution), Aizawl, 1947.
94. R.N. Prasad, op. cit., B.B. Goswami, op. cit.
95. Vanlawma, op. cit., p. 217.
96. B.B. Goswami, op. cit.
97. R. Sena Samuelson, op. cit., pp. 47-50.
98. Ibid.
99. *Proceedings of the Accredited Leaders of all Lushai Political Parties*, Aizawl, 14 August 1947.
100. *Bhagvati Patrika* (Editorial), 18 August 1947, cited in K.M. Singh, *Hijan Irabat Singh and Political Movement in Manipur*, Delhi: B.R. Publishing, 1989, p. 251.
101. Bimal Deb and Dilip J. Lahiri, *Manipur: Culture and Politics*, Delhi: Mittal, 1987, pp. 124, 159.

    Niharendu Dutt Majumdar, Minister, Government of West Bengal, wrote to Sardar Patel, Deputy Prime Minister, on 14 January 1980, 'with regard to the future of the state of Manipur, it is also to be considered whether it should not be merged in West Bengal. . . . I think the interests of Manipur will be better served by her merger in West Bengal than in Assam: cited in Kshetri Rajendra Singh', in 'Social Movements in Manipur: A Study of Two Movements among the Meitheis', unpublished Ph.D. thesis, Centre for Social Studies, Surat, 1987, p. 106. Also in Durga Das (ed.), *Sardar Patel's Correspondence*, Vol. 9, Ahmedabad, 1973, p. 253.
102. It had originated in the Manipur State Congress unit and supported by Manipur Socialist Party. It reportedly had Sardar Patel's blessings.
103. Kshetri Rajendra Singh, op. cit.
104. N. Joykumar Singh, 'Movement for Responsible Government in Manipur (1938-48)', *Proceedings of the North East India History Association*, Barapani Session, 1983, pp. 202-9. Also Ksh. Shyam Kanai Singh, 'The Merger of Manipur with India', *Proceedings of NEIHA*, Imphal Session, 1982, pp. 224-8.
105. Ibid.
106. Ibid.
107. Ibid.

108. Ibid.
109. Bimal J. Dev and Dilip Lahiri, op. cit.
110. Ibid.
111. Kshetri Rajendra Singh, op. cit., p. 107.
112. Irabat was already talking in terms of a people's republic in Manipur and working towards it which had reinforced the Indian Government's suspicion. The country was already witnessing peasant unrest in Telangana, Tebhaga (Bengal), Assam and Tripura. The second Congress of the CPI was held in Calcutta from 28 February to 6 March 1948, which supported these movements. This was followed by the inauguration of state unit of CPI at the District Organizing Committee level in Manipur. This was a red signal for the government.
113. S. Chattradhari, *Manipungi Itihassta Irabat*, Imphal, 1972, pp. 64-5, cited in Kshetri Rajendra Singh, op. cit., p. 109.
114. See note 99; also T. Bir Singh, *Comrade Irabat*, Imphal: Irabat Memorial Library and Information Centre, 1983, pp. 56-7.
115. Kshetri Rajendra Singh, op. cit., p. 111.
116. The Communist armed movement in Manipur had intensified and was viewed seriously by the Government of India specially because it came in the wake of rumours of Chinese hand in it and spurts of such movements in many parts of the country. Sardar Patel as the Home Minister confirmed in the Parliament (February 1951) that there had been a Communist uprising in Manipur of a serious nature but was presently under control. The *Times of India*, 28 February 1951, wrote in its editorial 'widespread terrorist activities are reported in the strategic north-eastern districts embracing Assam, Manipur and Tripura. Peking may not harbour expansionist designs but Communism in potentially expansive and explosive and anxiety is heightened by the Union Home Minister's reference of encouragement for the Assam terrorists from across the border.' The Communist phobia gripped the Assam Chief Minister Bordoloi so much that he asked Patel to allow Manipur autonomy so that Manipur did not influence Assam.
117. N. Joykumar Singh, op. cit.
118. Ksh. Shyam Manai Singh, op. cit.
119. N. Joykumar Singh, op. cit.
120. Ibid.
121. Ibid.
122. Ibid.
123. Confidential Report, 27 July 1949, Memo No. 78, CID, from S. Palit, S.P. Manipur to the Dewan.
124. D.O. No. DM.89/49, dated 29 August 1949, Imphal, from Major Rawal Amar Singh to Adviser to the Governor of Assam cited in K.M.M. Singh, op. cit., p. 346.
125. N. Joykumar Singh, op. cit.
126. Ibid.

127. Ibid.
128. Proceedings of a public meeting held at the Gandhi Maidan, 3 August 1949, cited in K.M.M. Singh, op. cit., p. 347.
129. *Prajatantra*, 17 August 1949, in a report by S. Palit, S.P. Manipur to the Dewan, 29 August 1949, in ibid.
130. Resolution of the meeting of MLA's belonging to the ruling Praja Shanti Sabha on 25 August cited in ibid.
131. Ksh. Shyam Kanai Singh, op. cit.
132. Op. cit.
133. From the Officiating Private Secretary to His Highness, Maharaja of Manipur, 18 September 1949, cited in K.M.M. Singh, op. cit., p. 354.
134. N. Joykumar Singh, op. cit.
135. Maharaja Budha Chandra to Sri Prakash, 18 September 1949, reproduced in *Resistance*, 25 September 1979.
136. From the Maharaja of Manipur to Sri Prakash, 18 September 1949, cited in K.M.M. Singh, op. cit., p. 354.
137. K.M.M. Singh, op. cit., p. 355.
138. Durga Das (ed.), op. cit., Vol. 8, p. 528.
139. Nari Rustomji, *The Enchanted Frontier*, Delhi: OUP, 1973, p. 109; R. Constantine, *Maid of the Mountain*, Delhi: Mittal, 1981, pp. 93-4.
140. Sri Prakash to the Maharaja of Manipur in 19 September 1949, cited in K.M.M. Singh, p. 355.
141. Maharaja Bodh Chandra to Sri Prakash, 20 September 1949, cited in ibid., p. 357.
142. Sri Prakash to the Maharaja, 19 September 1949, reproduced in *The Resistance*, 2 October 1979.
143. *Bhagyavati Patrika* (editorial), dated 20 September 1949, courtesy *The Resistance*, Vol. IV, No. 40, dated 9 October 1979, cited in K.M.M. Singh, op. cit., p. 358.
144. *Bhagyavati Patrika*, dated 21 September 1949, courtesy, *Resistance*, Vol. IV, No. 41, dated 16 October 1979, cited in ibid.
145. Ibid.

CHAPTER SEVEN

The Resistance

MANIPUR

'Now Manipur is finished' was the reaction of Irabat Singh at the merger of Manipur with the Indian Union.[1] Irabat who had dreamt of establishing an independent peasant republic in Manipur was disillusioned at the merger but refused to give up his ideal. Irabat had 'launched a revolutionary movement in the north eastern part of Manipur with the aim of establishing an "Independent Peasant Republic" with its headquarter at Nongda (1948)'.[2] Following the Second Congress of the Communist Party of India held in Calcutta (28 February-6 March 1948 famous for its Ranadive thesis) where the peasant armed struggle in Telengana, Bengal, Tripura was endorsed to bring about a 'peoples' democratic revolution' in India,[3] the state unit of the CPI at the district organizing committee level was formally set up in Manipur on 23 August 1948 under the leadership of Irabat, although he had never held any formal position in the party.[4] The party had adopted the decision to continue the armed struggle and bring about a Telengana-like uprising of the peasants. The Red Guard units were entrusted with the operational aspect. Since 21 September 1948, the party had operated as an underground outlawed outfit.[5] In view of the reports of a prospective Communist coup in Manipur, the fearful Premier of Assam Gopinath Bordoloi recommended complete autonomy for Manipur in his letter to Sardar Patel (26 May 1948).[6] During his underground years Irabat had taken up the task of strengthening the Communist Party in Manipur and was actively engaged in building up the Krishak Sabha in the villages. In the village set up, any three Communists would constitute a cell. He also kept sending memoranda and resolutions to the maharaja which were adopted and passed in clandestine Communist assemblies. His weekly paper *Anouba Yug* appeared regularly without interruption. He also managed to distribute letters, leaflets, pamphlets and political statements from time to time. He moved from village to village to organize and mobilize people for the uprising. In an underground meeting under his chairmanship, held on 29 October 1948, at a place called Top it was decided to intensify the underground Communist movement.[7] The movement took a violent turn after the merger of Manipur with India. As this development created problems for Irabat, he concentrated on the immediate course of his struggle. Sometime in March 1950, the Communist Party set up a secret organization known as the Red Guards the avowed object of which was 'to collect arms and ammunitions with a view to harassing and fighting the police and overthrowing the Government of India'.[8] The volunteers of the Red Guard were required to carry arms and therefore had to be well-trained in using arms and ammunition. The Red Guards had its camp at Kangmong, North Jiri and Bamdiyar (near Nambol). There were sporadic encounters between the state forces and the Red Guards at Hoijang, Angom, Bishenpur, Mayang and Imphal. The Communist armed struggle in Manipur intensified and was at its height in the late 1950s. Hijam Irabat is said to have secured the association of the Burmese Communist parties from May 1950 till his demise on 26 September 1951.[9]

The home minister at the Centre confirmed in February 1951, in the Parliament that there had been a Communist uprising of a very serious dimension in Manipur and that the situation was 'under control'.[10] The *Times of India* of 28 February 1951 wrote that 'widespread terrorist activities are reported in the strategic north eastern districts embracing Assam, Manipur and Tripura. India's eastern frontiers have intermittently been inflicted with violence and unrest since 1949. . . .'[11]

By early 1951, a heavy offensive was launched to counter the 'insurgency'. Most of the important leaders were arrested and prosecuted. Irabat continued to escape arrest and 'defied' all the detailed plans 'to get him', he continued to provide training to the Red Guard volunteers and at the same time devised strategies for the revolutionary struggle. But soon Irabat realized the futility of fighting a superior enemy without adequate man-or armpower. Therefore, after his last meeting in Manipur in North Jiri, Irabat went to Burma (*c.* early 1951) to contract and seek the help of Burmese Communists for establishing an Independent Socialist Republic in Manipur.[12] It was also a part of his strategy 'to arrange training for the Communists from Manipur and to depute Burmese Communists to function in the state'.[13] There were three Communist parties in Burma that were fighting against the Burmese Government independently of each other; they were the Communist Party of Burma (CPB); the Burma Communist Party (BCP) and Peoples' Comrade Party (PCP). Irabat succeeded in organizing a tripartite conference of the three parties and helped form a united front. The front established a United Front Liberation Government of Burma and reached an agreement with Irabat that the former will give back Kabaw Valley and Ango-ching to Manipur.[14] After more than three years of fighting underground, with his dream of carving out an 'Independent Socialist Republic' in South-East Asia, Irabat died of typhoid at Tangbaw village, his headquarter at Kabaw Valley, on 26 September 1951.

The Irabat led Communist movement in Manipur (1948-51) was part of an all-South-East Asia phenomenon of Communist organized peasant uprisings in Burma and China as well as Telengana, Bengal, Tripura, Assam in India. It is unfortunate that while Telengna peasant rebellion of the late-forties is well known, similar movements in this part of the country are not known.[15] Insurgency in Manipur dates back to 1948 when the Manipuri Communists under the charismatic leadership of Hijam Irabat, took up the cause of liberation of Manipur, which was in a state of semi-feudalism and semi-colonialism by resorting to the Marxist 'line of armed struggle against the power that be . . . the thread left by Hijam Irabat was taken up by the Revolutionary Government of Manipur which started its spadework of insurgency in March-April 1969.' The movement for a responsible government in Manipur and a popular Communist uprising were not superficial. Manipur in the past two centuries had witnessed monarchical autocracy, feudal oppression, Brahmanic domination, and colonial subordination and these factors were solely responsible for such popular outbursts seeking change from a claustrophobic and exploitative regime. The pre-colonial monarchical autocracy in Manipur was as oppressive to the people as it could be. It squeezed out the people through its taxation structure, compulsory services to the state and repression. This was compounded by the Brahmanic exploitation. Hinduism had entered Manipur only in the eighteenth century but the evils of the caste system, Brahmanic hegemony, and the idea of purity-pollution had crept deep into its structure by the nineteenth century. It is easy to discuss it by saying that the evils of Hinduism like the caste system, *sati*, *purdah*, taboo on food and drink were less intense in Manipur compared to the rest of India. But such a comparison would amount to trivilization of the issue because the casteist Manipuri society has to be compared with the pre-Hindu

Manipur which was more or less a society based on communal living. Brahmanic hegemony was not only repressive it was exploitative. At the slightest pretext common men could be declared polluted and excommunicated. The repurification required elaborate ceremony and monetary tribute to the Brahmins. In a society where most of the people were 'commoners' barring the small number of Brahmins and royal family members as Kshatriyas, this had far reaching consequences. The advent of colonialism did not help. Rapid monetization of economy, commercialization of agriculture, heavy taxation burden on the peasants and the monopolization of the trade and commercial sector by exogenous elements crippled the peasants.[16] It is these circumstances that made people launch the movement for a responsible government or 'a people's republic based on the principles of socialism'. They were merely seeking relief from the oppressive life through such a change. Both the state peoples' movement and even the Irabat led movement promised such a relief which explains their immense popularity. The merger with India did not promise any such change unlike in the Mizo Hills. People were neither sure that Indian rule would be different from British colonial rule, nor did the Indian State bother to explain to them and promise a hopeful future. On the other hand, while the Indian Government was involved in clandestine intransigence to effect the accession, a section of the Meitheis went all out to describe the prospective Indian administration to be as bad as the colonial regime. The fact that hurt the politically conscious Meitheis most was that the Indian Government should be more interested in hastening the merger process when people were reeling under the impact of a famine-like situation.

Manipur, in fact, had never recovered from the transition that its economy was forced into by colonialism. Famine-like situations were a recurring phenomenon especially in the post-Second World War period.[17] The Nupilan movement[18] salvaged the situation temporarily but the late 1940s witnessed famine, food shortage and starvation again. Between 1942 and 1945, there were constant disturbances in the Manipuri agrarian sector. The military officers however continued to buy army supplies of foodgrains from the peasants which included vegetable, rice, firewood and milk. In addition was the export of agrarian products by Marwari traders. Heavy induction of money by the army and constant crop failures led to a high rate of inflation in the state. Despite the government sponsored 'Grow more food' campaign, agricultural production declined. The price of rice rose from Rs.1.12 *annas* per *maund* in early 1942 to Rs.10 in April the same year. In March 1943, it rose to Rs.30 and by May it was Rs.50.[19] To aggravate the problem both the British as well as the Japanese armies very often resorted to forcible confiscation of whatever little the peasants produced.[20] In 1944, the British Army confiscated as much as 10,000 *maunds* of rice promising replacement.[21] The Japanese Army forcibly confiscated large quantities of consumer goods against forged Burmese and British currency.[22] During the post-Second World War period, the momentum of the economic activities declined considerably. Agriculture had been disturbed because of the continuing inability of the general masses to buy and also the non-availability of ploughing cattle which were either used for transportation or slaughtered as food for the army during the War.[23] The situation was further aggravated when the colonial authorities increased the land revenue to Rs.9 per *pari*, which was an increase of 50 per cent.[24] As a consequence there was large-scale sale of land rendering a mass of peasants landless. There were stringent forest and fishery rules and a heavy cycle of taxation. During 1946-7, the colonial authorities allowed a number of Marwari businessmen to enter Manipur and engage in trade and business which the local people strongly disapproved of due to the previous record of the Marwari business houses. The cumulative effect of all these factors was an acute food shortage and famine-like conditions in Manipur especially in the rural areas during 1947-8.[25] When the people of rural Manipur were starving to death the Indian State was busy manoeuvering to effect a hush-hush accession of the province to the Indian Union.

The merger proved to be a blow to the collective Meithei ego because it disregarded the people by not consulting their elected representatives. The manner in which the accession was effected gave the impression that the maharaja was forced to sign the Instrument of Accession at 'gun-point'. While this satisfied the aspiration of the ambitious pro-Indian section of the new middle class, it was a death blow to the aspirations of the pro-independence Meithei middle class who fancied themselves as the rulers of an independent Manipur. None really cared for the famine-stricken masses who were with Irabat Singh. Irabat's long and tested career proved him trustworthy and people rallied round him. If he opted for independence, they would be with him, if he desired merger they had no objection. Irabat had already understood the bourgeois nature of the new Indian State. Its repressive character was evident in its suppression of the

Communist movement in Telengana, Bengal and Tripura. He did not want to be a part of such a state and decided to continue with his struggle for an Independent Peoples' Republic in Manipur. His death brought an end to his aspirations. But the ground was still fertile. In 1953, a group called the Revolutionary Nationalist Party raised the banner of independence.[26] They resented Manipur's loss of responsible government. This group was not really secessionist initially. They met Prime Minister Nehru on his visit to Imphal (October 1952) and tried to impress upon him the need for an administrative setup that would be responsible to the people of Manipur instead of the Parliament in New Delhi. Nehru turned down their demand, and these leaders resented his refusal and formed themselves into the Revolutionary Nationalist Party and demanded independence. It decried the denial of democratic rights of the people. But the party petered out within a short period. The summer of 1965 was one of discontent for the Manipuris.[27] It was a time when people were on the verge of yet another famine which was the artificial creation of the unscrupulous Mayang traders. Not only did people face the pinch of rising prices, rice was not even available in the market. The situation threatened to starve people to death. This was not only true of Manipur the entire country was facing such a situation because of the Indo-Pak war. The pinch was felt more acutely in the north-east due to its proximity to the eastern front—East Pakistan (present Bangladesh). There was large-scale hoarding, black marketeering of food products and inflationary pressure. Throughout the north-east food products disappeared from the market and the government emergency distribution system was extremely inadequate. 'Cries and woes of hunger and starvation were the order of the day.'[28] According to a student leader who participated in the protest movement, the Marwari traders would not sell rice from their stock at any price whatsoever.[29] During the period 1939-40, the womenfolk had risen against the traders exporting rice at the cost of Manipur. In 1965, it was the student community who were up in arms against the government. On 27 August 1965, the students led a demonstration against the government's apathy towards peoples' misery. 'We are starving, give us rice',[30] was their slogan. But they received bullets instead. In the government ordered firing four students died, and several others were injured. The day was commemorated as the 'Hungry Marchers Day'. This event was taken as another instance of New Delhi's apathy towards the people of Manipur. Though Manipur had a chief minister and its own council of ministers, it was a Union

Territory and the state was virtually ruled by the chief commissioner. Therefore, the anger and hostility of the people was directed towards New Delhi. The event was politicized and peoples anger against New Delhi led to the revival of the movement for Manipur's independence. It was said that the Meitheis were slaves in the hands of the Mayang rulers in New Delhi. The activities of the Mayang traders and bureaurcrats fueled the fire and a strong anti-outsider feeling grew in the Imphal Valley. It was also the time when sections of people, who were critical of the merger agreement, pointed out the evils of merger with India.[31] Other groups too began to lose faith in the New Delhi pattern of administration. They highlighted the fact that despite peoples' demand, Manipur was not being granted statehood, whereas the Naga's were granted because they had resorted to secessionism and insurgency. The youths, among whom there were large numbers of educated unemployed—were told that they cannot achieve their goals through peaceful means. That secessionism and insurgency were the only means to realize their aspirations. The administration in Manipur was seen as a virtual Mayang administration because as a union territory most of its bureaucrats and officers were from New Delhi who were corrupt and apathetic to the interests of Manipuris. Manipuri language despite its acclaimed status had not been included in the Eighth Schedule. The elected representatives of the Manipur Legislative Assembly were denied the right to take part in the election of the president of India though the latter was directly responsible for the administration of Manipur. It was apparent that the Meitheis as citizens did not enjoy equal rights with their counterparts in the rest of India. Manipuris though proud Hindus failed to get into the civil services because they were not categorized as 'scheduled' and had to compete with the advanced section of Indians whereas the Nagas or Mizos from Manipur—due to their Scheduled Tribes status—could get into such services even if their scores were low. Even the posts in the state went to the tribals and Scheduled Castes by virtue of the government's reservation policy. Meitheis were not allowed to buy land and settle in the Hills of Manipur itself whereas a tribal could buy and settle down in the Imphal Valley. This peculiar situation is reflected in the life of Samarendra Singh one of the pioneers of insurgency and secessionism in Manipur. Samarendra was a graduate from Imphal who had obtained his master's degree from Pune. During his Pune days Samarendra regularly met L. Gyanendra in Bombay who was a hard-core Communist and one-time colleague of Irabat. Besides him the other person to influence Samarendra was L. Kanhai.[32] Emerging as a talented playwright in his youth, Samarendra appeared for UPSC exam but lost the civil service position to someone much junior. As we shall see latter, this failure was a turning point in Samarendra's life who along with Sudhir Kumar subsequently established the United National Liberation Front inaugurating the era of modern insurgency in Manipur.

Frustrated with the situation the Meithei youths believed that their affiliation with Hinduism was the reason for their predicament. These angry young people led a crusade against Hinduism and questioned Manipur's merger with India. A group of brilliant young Meithei boys started a movement which aimed at the de-Hinduization of Manipur, revoking the merger and restoring Manipur's independent entity through sustained efforts. Organizing themselves under the name Pan-Manipuri Youth League the group popularized its ideas through its party paper, *Resistance*. An excerpt from its journal is given below:

> The Manipur valley in the 1960's presented a picture of deep and varying contrasts—a contrast between the newly introduced bureaucratic set up and remnants of the old princely order; a contrast between promise and hopes, aspirations and the naked reality. Over and above this the decade also witnessed the resurgence of Irabat's ideas and inherent conflicts between Hindu identity and the pre-Hindu identity marked by a determined conscious process of de-Sanskiritization.[33]

The politicians also took advantage of the situation. A new political body, the Meithei State Committee emerged on the eve of the 1967 elections. Its avowed objective was claimed to be the independence of Manipur. It only fielded a handful of candidates for the 30 elective seats of the Assembly. The candidates were not only defeated but also lost their deposits. This made it clear that the people, though angry, could differentiate between students and unscrupulous politicians. The Meithei State Committee was reported to be the result of Phizo's manoeuvering, the Naga leader who visited Imphal and reportedly struck a deal with certain Meitheis.[34] Despite securing arms, etc., it could not pose a challenge to the state. As an underground body too it soon withered away.

But the youth led de-Sanskritization activity emerged as an effective movement. Naorem Phullo's ideas which did not become popular in the 1930s were now used with a vengeance and soon de-Sanskritization emerged as a movement. The Meithei Marup or

Meithei Association which was almost defunct now sprang into activity in 1963 with a spectacular debut by reviving an ancient Meithei festival called Mera Mentongber devoted to the Meithei pre-Hindu deity *Sanamahi*.[35] It also revived certain ancient Manipuri musical instruments and games like *mukna* (wrestling) and *kanjei* (country hockey) along with polo. The United National Liberation Front almost came up at the same time and was formed on 24 November 1964 with Samarendra as its general secretary.[36] It aimed to establish an independent Manipur and organized the so-called Revolutionary Government of Manipur (RGM). The famine as mentioned earlier, coupled with political unrest and a violent movement for separate statehood provided the backdrop against which UNLF and RGM appeared. The outfits burst into activity with a series of robberies and dacoities hitherto unheard of in Manipur.

The United National Liberation Front emerged to be a composite body in which the Khongjais (Kukis) and the Kabuis were also represented. It started organizing the Khongjais the Kabuis along with the dominant Meitheis of the plains. This was significant because so far the hill people had identified themselves with the Federal Government of Nagaland. Samarendra wanted a joint effort for the revolution along with the Nagas, the Khongjais and other minor tribes of the hills and therefore was keen on a dialogue with leaders of the hill tribes. He secured the association ofThangkhopao Singshit, an influential leader and the Thadou Chief of Ihang Karong who succeeded Lune as the president of the Kuki National Assembly.

In 1965, Samarendra met Tungkhupum Baite, president of the United Chin People Union, a guerrilla outfit composed of the Chin sub-tribes of the India-Burma frontier. By this time Tumkhupum had already established relations with the Pakistan Government seeking its assistance in their mission. Although Tunkhupum was thinking in terms of a Greater Chin Movement, Samarendra toyed with the idea of a Pan-Mongoloid Movement which would include all Mongoloid peoples of the Indo-Burma region. However, they agreed to collaborate as a joint rebel front. Though there was agreement in principle, a coordinated struggle could not be carried out in practice. The 1966, Tungkhupum Baite was assassinated by the Mizo Rebels of the Mizo National Front.

Samarendra then sought to coordinate his struggle with the Mizo National Front learning about its preparations to fight against the India State and serve independence. He sent his close colleague

Thangkhopao Singshit to Aizawl to have a dialogue with Laldenga, chief of the MNF. Laldenga who was prejudiced against the Meitheis told Singshit that 'the liberation of the Meithei should be kept as the second stage of the Mizo liberation and movement.'[37] Nevertheless, he informed Singshit that he would be sending his general secretary to meet Samarendra at Imphal. But, the general secretary never came.

In his bid to meet the Naga leaders, Samarendra went to Kohima to contact Imkongmeren Ao, who was the vice president of the Naga National Council. But not only was he refused a meeting, Lungshim Saiza—a Tangkhul Naga who had married Rano, a niece of A.Z. Phizo—reportedly made some derogatory remarks about Meitheis and asked Samarendra and his friend Yengkhom Pramod to meet the Nagas only when the time was ripe.[38] Peeved by the arrogance of the Naga spokesman, Samarendra came back with his friend Pramod and decided to concentrate on the Meitheis.

In the year 1967, Samarendra made a preliminary survey of the Manipuri people in East Pakistan through his volunteers and sent his foreign secretary, Sudhir Kumar to prepare the ground for his trip. Sudhir went to East Pakistan in the early spring of 1967 and returned after one month. After his report, a party led by Samarendra left Imphal for East Pakistan. They were stationed at Bhanubil and from there they proceeded to Dacca and contacted the Chinese officials at the Chinese Consulate General's office in Dhanmondi and pleaded for their cause.[39] Samarendra next met the Pakistani authorities for their help. The Pakistani authorities could not make any commitment on the subject though they expressed their sympathy and Samarendra understood that they suspected the seriousness of the commitment of his group. After repeating their request to the Chinese officials for help, Samarendra and his group returned to Manipur in early autumn.

By this time N. Bisheshwar, a young enthusiast and his friend R.K. Senajaoba who were close associates of Sudhir Kumar stressed on quick action whereas Samarendra wanted a steady approach. Consequently a misunderstanding developed between Samarendra and Sudhir. 'Both however agreed on the objective namely, the establishment of a Republic of Manipur as well as the means, the violent overthrow of the State apparatus. The difference was over the tempo of action. Sudhir wanted quick and spectacular deeds while Samarendra advocated slow but steady and firm action. Sudhir in pursuit of quick returns went to East Pakistan.' He wooed away a sizable number of volunteers.

The UNLF, at one point of time, had conceived of an ambitious pan-Mongoloid movement, the plan was to have a Monogoloid State in South-East Asia outside India. The Naga and Mizo secessionist movements along with the incipient Manipuri secessionism was its inspiration. But soon it petered out and Manipur became its concentration point. Thus, the UNLF finally settled down to work towards the goal of an 'Independent Republic of Manipur'.[40] But the organization did not have any mass base and depended on the youth and intellectuals for support. The state intelligence was alert already about this movement as it had come to know of its existence as early as 1965.

UNLF was an underground organization. Its most important body was the Central Council,[41] which consisted of seven members who assumed charges of portfolios such as president, vice president, home, defence, finance and publicity. The supreme authority of the Council was the president but in practise it was the general secretary who discharged the most important functions. A revolutionary co-ordination committee was also set up under the supervision of the Central Council which planned to establish a revolutionary unit in every village. Members were categorized as first and second hardcores. The second hardcore members were responsible for the task of mobilizing villagers and enlistment of new members. But this task was hardly done in practise which is why the UNLF never really was a successful and popular organization. It remained an insurgent outfit with hardly any manifest activity. The UNLF did not maintain lists of its members and had no mediating mechanism between the leaders and the activists. It had an overground wing called the Pan-Manipuri Youth League (PANMYL) which through its mouthpiece *Resistance* lamented the merger of Manipur with India and questioned the merger treaty.[42] It popularized the idea that Manipur was annexed at gun-point by India. It also lamented the loss of Kabaw Valley to Burma and blamed the Government of India for the transfer and the Manipuri leadership for surrendering to the wishes of the Indian State. The UNLF mainly remained a youth movement without any violent activity. It never came into open conflict with the Indian State. It merely organized schooling of its members in revolutionary political ideologies and some training in the use of arms. Around October 1965, the UNLF organized a military training camp for its members on a hillock near Khonbum which lasted for 15 days.[43] It tried to spread its ideology and objectives to the Manipuri students studying in Calcutta and New Delhi and even tried to obtain support from Pakistan and China.[44] But UNLF did not really adhere formally to any particular ideology. In fact, it went to the extent of abhorring Marxism, Maoism or any other fashionable ideology as 'foreign' and unsuitable for Manipur though its avowed ultimate objective was to secure Manipur's independence through armed struggle.[45] The UNLF as its founder leader stated was built on 'nationalist lines and patriotic fervour'.[46] But initially it did try to go beyond what it described as 'narrow nationalism' and work for the liberation of the Mongoloid people of south-middle Asia.[47] Condemning the Naga movement as narrow nationalism, the UNLF appealed to the common ethnicity and the cultural affinity of the people of this region and believed that only a new 'militant nationalism' of all the ethnic groups of the region can bring about an armed revolution. It held that the fact that the different ethnic communities in the north-east engaged in their 'private revolutions' were all Mongoloid should be the basis and the reason for the establishment of a 'common revolutionary banner'.[48] Based on this it conceived of a Pan-Mongoloid Movement (PMM) which offered a four-point programme as basic elements towards bringing an armed revolution in the region. The UNLF believes that 'Unity', 'Nationalism' 'Independence' and 'Democracy' were processes through which the people of south-middle Asia could get rid of 'bondage and alien rule'. And refused to be 'guided by foreign ideals and imported social outlook' but 'look back to our own way of life and not to imported ideals and philosophies'.[49] It did not like to resort to an immediate armed revolution but believed in doing the necessary spadework for the revolution. The revolutionary theories of Mao Tse-Tung or Che Guevera were regarded as outdated and not suitable to the changing conditions. It therefore laid down a 'new system of revolution'[50] which laid emphasis on international diplomatic contacts. India was a mighty military power vis-à-vis the struggle of the Nagas as had been proved. Therefore, the emphasis should be not on an outright armed revolt, 'but diplomatic contacts with other sovereign state of the world, neighbouring Asian countries and cultivate help and immediate recognition [*sic*].'[51] Since there was no positive response to the PMM from the Nagas or Mizos the UNLF decided to focus an Manipur.

Before UNLF could create any ripples in Manipur its organizers Sudhir Kumar and Samarendra parted ways. Sudhir Kumar went ahead and formed another organization in August 1968 with the same objective of liberating Manipur from Indian rule. The steering committee meeting of this new organization was held in August 1968. The new outfit was called Consolidation Committee or Consocom in short form. Sudhir Kumar offered the following reasons which necessitated the formation of Consocom.[52]

1. The UNLF did not try to bring all the 'revolutionary elements' and 'organizations' who are working for a nationalist revolution under a common ideology, or a common platform.
2. The UNLF did not want to reach a mutual understanding with the Mizos and Nagas.
3. The UNLF's idea of a revolution was urban based; it had been indifferent to mobilization and set up of organizational network in the rural areas. It even had a tendency to exploit the rural people.
4. Too much stress was given by the UNLF on establishing foreign contacts as a result its future and struggle depended on foreign aid.
5. There were no democratic principles working in the organization but a tendency to 'fascist military dictatorship'.

Apart from these matters of principle, ideology and mode of operation, the split between Samarendra and Sudhir Kumar Oinam was also due to personal differences and clash of egos and ideas. Samarendra was accused of being dictatorial and concentrating all power unto himself. He was also accused of favouritism and nepotism in the allocation of portfolios. Sudhir Kumar reportedly resented such concentration of power by Samarendra. But Sudhir in turn was accused of instigating young cadres against the central leadership and was manoeuvered to 'political isolation' which led him to break away from the UNLF and launch his own organization.[53] On the other hand, the Samarendra-camp alleged that Sudhir Kumar was a 'very restless person' and 'not politically conscious'.[54] It also claimed that it was Sudhir's ambition to assume the leadership of the organization which caused a bitter power-rivalry between the two and was the real cause of the split. However, what caused the ultimate split was the disillusionment of the younger cadres who only heard of the rhetoric of armed revolution but had not tasted any action.[55] The extremists who believed in armed struggle wanted to raise the socio-political consciousness of the masses before actually taking up arms and sought immediate action towards that end. The Consocom according to its pamphlet was formed primarily to bring together all organizations on a common platform through democratic means. It felt that, the talk of 'pan-Mongolianism' and fighting the Indian State under one banner by UNLF was all rhetoric and not substantive. Accordingly a Consocom delegation was sent to East Pakistan for the purpose of unifying all the organizations working in Manipur under one banner from a foreign base. Another objective was to internationalize the Manipuri cause. In April 1969, Sudhir Kumar and his lieutenant N. Bisheshwar travelled to Bhanubil a Meithei village in the Sylhet district of East Pakistan. Bisheshwar came back after the groundwork to send the first batch of cadres over to East Pakistan. Since it involved expenses, Consocom resorted to robbery. The first robbery took place on 15 May 1969 in the Imphal college when a sum of Rs.10,000 was looted from the cashier.[56] This money was spent on sending the first batch of cadres which reached Sylhet on 31 May 1969. By July altogether 53 activists were sent to Pakistan. After keeping them in jail for several days, the Pakistani Government suddenly ordered the activists except Sudhir Kumar to leave Pakistan without assigning any reasons. Towards the end of July 1969, Sudhir Kumar suddenly announced the formation of a parallel 'Revolutionary Government of Manipur' (RGM) in exile with himself as the chairman.[57]

It seemed that Consocom was either dissolved or Sudhir Kumar had dissociated himself from the organization. Another theory was that Consocom and RGM were not different.[58] The name RGM was selected from one of the Consocom pamphlets which had RGM as its title and had become immensely popular. Sudhir Kumar revived its existence while still in Pakistan. However, since then the insurgent activities in Manipur that came to be associated with RGM and Consocom sank into oblivion and there have been no claims or counter-claims to it but it did create immense dissension among Sudhir Kumar's colleagues. Some of the 53 members who had gone over to East Pakistan even accused Sudhir Kumar of being 'power-hungry' and resented his tendency of running a 'one-man-show'.[59] They held Sudhir Kumar responsible for the failure of the Pakistan trip. Indeed Sudhir Kumar's announcement took them by surprise and precluded all efforts at unification.

Meanwhile, the Consocom members who had not visited Pakistan held a secret meeting in the middle of July 1969, at Pangei, Imphal at the house of an advocate, Gourdas Singh, wherein 'it was resolved that a Revolutionary party be formed in order to overthrow the present existing Government by use of force with the help of foreign powers like Pakistan, Burma and China with a view of making Manipur a sovereign state'.[60] Accordingly a government of Revolutionary Party was formed afresh with Gourdas as the president and the following portfolios were allocated amongst its elected members: finance, external affairs, internal affairs, voluntary organizations and information.[61]

But even before RGM could accomplish anything it suffered a severe set-back. Between 1 and 6 August 1969, 56 Manipuri youth belonging to the UNLF and Consocom most of whom were coming back from East Pakistan after the so-called arms training, were arrested in Tripura. Immediately after this 8 members were arrested by Manipur police during the same month. The arrested persons were charged with 'conspiracy to overthrow the Government of Manipur after receiving training in arms in East Pakistan'.[62] Those arrested in Manipur were similarly charged and in a addition were accused of planning to make 'Manipur a sovereign state outside the Indian Union and wage war against the Government of India'.[63] From the interrogation it was learnt that a number of people did not know the organization for which they were working or about the organization called Consocom. Some members were recruited and told to undergo arms training to protect Manipur. It is believed that N. Bisheshwar—incharge of recruitment—did not like to divulge much to the new recruits. Specially facts such as the purpose of recruitment and the nature of organization that members were working for.[64] However, the literature on RGM and the statement of the arrested persons threw much light on the nature of the organizations.

Unlike UNLF, the RGM had no pretensions of addressing itself to the issue of uniting people of common ethnicity in the region though it certainly was not against the idea of a joint struggle. Its explicit aim was an independent Manipur and believed in an armed struggle.[65] For the RGM it was 'not a demand to the Indian Government but a fight for the restoration of the lost independence'.[66] It was also reported that the RGM was firmly against Communism like its predecessor UNLF. The RGM leadership held that the 'Meithei way of life', and its philosophy were ideals that were dear to the organization and wanted to revive them. It also felt that to be a Hindu was to be meek and less militant which was incompatible with the Meithei character who were generally a martial race. The RGM invoked the Meitheis to revert back to their pre-Hindu Sanamahi identity.[67] It also warned the Meitheis against the influx of outsiders into Manipur citing the example of Tripura where reportedly the indigenous Tripuris had become a minority in their own land. It led a vigorous attack on Sanskritization and campaigned for re-Meitheization. It lamented the loss of the cultural heritage and identity of the Meitheis due to Hinduization and was determined to stop and revert they process. To an extent, the RGM was thus successful in reinstating a sense of identity among the Meitheis, awareness regarding the influx of outsiders, monopolization of Manipur's trade and commerce by outsiders, and exploitation by *Banias*.[68] In fact, it was even able to generate a hostility against the outsiders in the Meithei mind by pointing out that the non-Meitheis were the root of all evil.

The arrests of the cadres in Tripura and Manipur at the very outset and their detention by the government under various charges had completely demoralized the hard-core supporters of RGM. And with the liberation of Bangladesh in 1971, the RGM base was completely shattered. This was followed by Manipur's upgraded status as a full-fledged state in 1972 resulting in people's jubilation that outshone their enthusiasm for the RGM. Sensing this, the Government of Manipur granted general amnesty and rehabilitation in the form of cash support to the RGM members.[69] This further weakened the organization. The remaining structure of the organization was weakened by the cold war between Sudhir Kumar and Bisheshwar.[70] There were complaints against Sudhir Kumar's dictatorial attitude, high-handedness and hunger for power. To retrieve the situation Bisheshwar proposed that Sudhir Kumar should offer a public apology for his behaviour. Sudhir Kumar not only refused to comply but branded his opponents as 'Naxalites'.[71] The arrest of Sudhir Kumar and Bisheshwar marked the death-knell of RGM.

As a result of the amnesty Sudhir Kumar was back in action, but in a new garb. He was found to be close to the Chief Minister R.K. Dorendra Singh. He was even seen campaigning for the Congress party in the 1977 elections,[72] Sudhir Kumar was thus seen as a sell out and an ideological bankrupt. The government patronage could not prevent his liquidation by his adversaries. His assassination (14 January 1979) however did not mark the end of insurgency, but inaugurated a new and so far the most important phase in the history of insurgency in Manipur.

MIZORAM

One of the first actions of the Indian Government after independence was one that directly opposed the desires of the hill people of Assam. The Bordoloi Committee's final report submitted in July 1947 had stated that the Chittagong Hill Tracts of the Chakma, Bohmong and Mong circles, which were inhabited by the Masho Chakma and Magh people were strongly averse to their inclusion in Bengal.[73] It further stated that the people of these areas wished to live in an autonomous district area. But the Chittagong Hill Tracts were transferred to East Pakistan for no particular reason (even the Muslim League had not demanded it) and that the southern part of Tripura Hills (Jampui Hill area) inhabited by the Mizos were ceded to Bengal and later to Tripura, thereby splitting the Mizo people geographically, culturally and economically. Another issue that left a sense of betrayal among these people was the dominant issue of abolition of chieftainship. The Indian Government seemed to have forgotten the promise it had made to abolish chieftainship.[74] This troubled not only the common man but also the Mizo Union. The MU was able to secure public support because it promised to abolish chieftainship. To keep up the momentum it asked the people not to pay the customary taxes to the chiefs and not obey their orders. But the chiefs held their position, taxing villages for goods and services and using villagers as coolies. There was much confusion as the villagers felt that they could refuse to obey the chiefs on the strength of the MU backing. But the chiefs also insisted on being obeyed. Thus, when the Indian Government supported the chiefs, the MU used it as a campaign issue in the 1952 election.[75] In an additional effort to eliminate the office of the chiefs, village councils were created through the 'Mizoram Village Council Constitution and Mizoram Administration of Justice Rules 1953'. The 1953 rules required that every village with at least 60 houses have a village council composed of 5 members. The councilmen were elected by popular vote for a three year term and the village council had a president, vice president and a secretary. The establishment of village councils did much to curtail the powers of the chiefs as the council became responsible for distributing land for cultivation, and the general administration of the village. Immediately after instituting the village council system, a bill was proposed to abolish chieftainships. But the bill did not succeed as there was opposition from some of the MU members. The Assam State Legislature however passed a bill abolishing chieftainship on 4 August 1964. The chiefs were compensated with a sum of Rs.16 lakh, which brought to an end one of the oldest Mizo institutions.

In 1952, no Mizo contested for a seat in the Indian Parliament although a non-Mizo belonging to the Congress was elected from the Mizo Hills-Silchar joint constituency.

The UMFO also contested the 1952 election but fared miserably winning one seat against fifteen of the MU. But following the election, the tribal leaders of undivided Assam were disturbed by the nomination of non-tribals to the District Councils by the governor as this could harm the tribal interests. A protest meeting was held in Shillong on 30 May and 1 June 1957, where all tribal leaders participated (except the Nagas) and it was decided to form a new party of the tribals called the Eastern India Tribal Union.[76] The objective of EITU was to secure the formation of the North-East Tribal State comprising the tribal areas of Assam and the north-east.[77] These developments indicated a change in the politics of the north-east, which were visible in the results of the 1957 election. The MU led by Khawtin Khuma was committed to the Congress party and hence the EITU and Congress confronted each other in Mizoram in the ensuing election. The MU won 13 seats, Congress 1, and the EITU and UMFO 2 and 8 respectively. The EITU was later joined by the UMFO and some MU members too. The victory of EITU did succeed in getting a tribal into the Assam cabinet. Captain Williamson Sangma was made the first tribal-minister in the Assam cabinet. During the 1950s the talk of Mizo independence seem to have died a natural death. Vanlawma who pioneered the concept of Mizo independence founded the Mizo Cultural Society—a non-political organ which had prominent Mizos as its members.[78]

THE FAMINE

In October 1958, the Mizo District Council predicted the imminence of famine on the basis of the Mizo calendar and cycle, following the flowering of bamboos, and passed a resolution that the state administration take precautionary measures. The tradition worked in the following way. 'Reverting to the chronological sequences, the next event of importance was the Mautam in 1959, and the consequential famine in the following year.'[79] The Mizos have for ages dreaded the flowering of bamboos. It was noted that the flowering of bamboos was invariably followed by an unprecedented increase in the rat population in the countryside which in turn created havoc to the standing crops leading ultimately to famine. The Mizos named these unusual occurrences after the bamboo species. One is called *Mautam*, the other *Thingtam*. *Mautam* or *Thingtam* were known to recur periodically at intervals of every 50 years. The Mizo elders have recorded these occurrences in the following chronological order:

Mautam	—	*c.* 1862
Thingtam	—	*c.* 1881
Mautam	—	*c.* 1911
Thingtam	—	*c.* 1929
Mautam	—	*c.* 1959
Thingtam	—	*c.* 1977
Mautam	—	2007 (due)

On the basis of this cycle the resolution of the Mizo District Council asked the governor of Assam to take precautionary measures and sanction a sum of Rs.1,50,000 relief money to be spent on the Mizo districts including the Pawi-Lakher region to ensure measures against the imminent famine.[80] the Assam Government rejected the request, dismissing the prediction of famine as a tradition of the 'primitive people'.[81] But the prediction proved right. Bamboos flowered in 1959 and the next year rats multiplied in millions and ate up the standing crops, grains, fruits and everything that was edible. The catastrophe occurred with such suddenness and so completely that the Government of Assam was caught unawares. As a result relief supplies were slow in coming and very inadequate as the government was not aware of its severity. Moreover, the lack of infrastructural development in terms of roads hampered the quick delivery of relief measures. The Riang and Chakmas were eating wild *arami*, a kind of grass and there were reports of starvation deaths and flights of people from the famine-hit areas before the relief arrived.[82] The indifference and the callousness of the Government of Assam alienated the Mizos.[83] When the relief was found to be slow in coming the District Council charged the government with 'incapability'. Vanlaibiaka, a member of the District Council was quoted as saying. 'If we continue to be neglected . . . the people's feeling will be for secession from Assam.'[84] He recalled that even the British had gone all out to help the Mizos when such famines occurred during the colonial period. The Assam Government on the other hand, charged the District Council which was dominated by the Mizo Union with 'non-cooperation',[85] which was not quite correct. To help supplement the government's weak relief measures the Mizo Cultural Society formed a new group called the Mizo National Famine Front to render voluntary services to the people most affected by the famine. They helped the villagers by ensuring that they received their share of government aid. In doing so they had earned the goodwill of the people and villagers even recognized them as leaders of the Mizo people. The initial bottlenecks and red-tape in providing relief measures were remedied belatedly by the Assam Government and caused serious discontent among the people. The cases of starvation deaths officially reported by the District Council were denied by the Assam Government. When Captain Williamson Sangma the Minister for Tribal Area Development visited Aizawl a demonstration was organized to pressure the Assam Government to declare Mizoram as a famine affected area. The Government of Assam sanctioned a sum of Rs.190 lakh for a famine affected population of 3,32,390. The amount of money spent under the various heads were as follows:[86]

Gratuitous relief	— Rs.04.90 lakh
Relief work	— Rs.28.00 lakh
Subsidy on transport of grains	— Rs.66.00 lakh
Purchase of vehicles	— Rs.13.00 lakh
Cost of petrol, etc.	— Rs.03.00 lakh
Accommodation to IAF and IAC personnel	— Rs. 0.87 lakh
Construction of rice godowns	— Rs. 0.62 lakh

As the famine subsided it had its political fallout. The Mizo Union's image was tarnished as it was an associate of the Congress party which was at the helm of affairs at the District Council during the famine. At the same time due to the slow reaction of the Government of Assam to the famine, relations between the Chaliha Government of Assam and Mizo Union led autonomous District Council reached its lowest ebb.[87] The Mizo Union leaders who were staunch supporters of the Congress Government at one time gradually drifted away and became increasingly critical of the government in their public utterances. The District Council felt that the Assam Government did not care enough for the famine ravaged people of Mizoram and even by-passed the District Council in matters of crucial importance. The hostility became evident when trivial questions were raised as to whether the District Council was entitled to use 'service' stamps; whether the District Council members were entitled to occupy Inspection Bungalows, etc.[88] Things came to a head and the Mizo Union eventually parted company with the Congress following sharp differences on the famine relief and the more serious question the State Official Language of 1960. The Assam Government sought to introduce a bill which would force every non-Assamese to learn Assamese. This confirmed the worst fears of the tribals. There was a massive movement in the rest of Assam against the bill. The Mizos too joined in opposing it.[89] In order to undermine and weaken and Mizo Union, the Assam Chief Minister, B.P. Chaliha encouraged the Mizo National Famine Front to convert itself into a political organization which could effectively check the monopoly of the Mizo Union in Mizoram.[90] The MNF had already earned the gratitude of the people for their good work during the famine and nurtured political ambition. It published a daily newspaper *Mizo-Aw* (Mizo Voice) edited by Laldenga—an accountant in the Mizo Union dominated District Council. The Front received a grant of Rs.1500 for the publication of this newspaper. On 28 October 1961, the MNFF reorganized and declared itself as a political party with Laldenga as its president and S. Lianzuala as the general secretary. A summary of the party's objectives is given below:[91]

1. To serve the highest sovereignty and to unite all Mizos to live under one political boundary.
2. To uplift the Mizo position and to develop it to the highest extent.
3. To preserve and safeguard Christianity.

The party was renamed as Mizo National Front. Right from the beginning it made its military and secessionist intentions clear to the Mizo people, specially the youths.[92] It laid emphasis on the indoctrination of the youth and even promised to give arms to each of them. The political campaigns of the party began with prayers. Laldenga used his oratory skills to indoctrinate the youths by narrating and popularizing the Mizo past in glorifying terms. Lectures were organized on nationalism and the preservation of Christianity from the domineering Hindu nation. A section of the youths, drivers, conductors, businessmen, ex-chiefs, ex-servicemen and individuals who were anti-Mizo Union were easily won over by the objective and ideology of the Mizo National Front. For this group Laldenga had become a cult figure. In the general elections of 1962, the Mizo Union contested and won two State Assembly seats while the third seat went to a Mizo Union supported nominee of the Eastern India Tribal Union, another constituent of the APHLC (All Party Hill

Leaders Conference). Then due to a directive from the APHLC both the Mizo Union nominees resigned their seats on 24 October 1962, but the EITU candidate refused to resign his seat. The two by-elections were held in 1963 and were contested by the MNF. It proved its increasing popularity by winning both the seats that it contested from Aizawl west and the Lunglei constituency. In the 1963 election to the village councils the Mizo Union secured 228 seats against MNF's 145, the Congress got 16, EITU 12 and independents 10. When the third legislative seat in the Mizo Hills fell vacant due to the resignation of Thanhira (EITU), who was appointed as member of the Assam Public Service Commission the by-election was won by the Mizo Union president Chunga in 1964, although the MNF mustered all its strength to win this seat for its candidate, P.B. Rosanga a young commerce graduate.[93]

The MNF meanwhile stepped up its activities specially of indoctrination, campaigning and mobilization.[94] It propagated that before the coming of the British the Mizos were an independent nation.[95] In fact, they were a 'distinct nation created, moulded and nurtured by God and nature', and that the administration of the chiefs was close to the 'Greek city states'. They considered the MU led merger of Mizoram with India an act of political immaturity, ignorance and absence of farsightedness.[96] The MNF leaders in their speeches demanded their 'human rights' and freedom.[97] The newspaper *Zalenna* (Freedom) under the editorship of a seasoned activist R. Vanlawma was used to propagate their ideas. Simultaneously pamphlets were also used with regularity for the same objective. The MNF also brought in the religious factor.[98] It depicted India as a land of Hindus with Mizoram consisting of Christians who faced persecution under Hindu rule. Lalthangliana alleged that the Indian officials intentionally used Sundays for their official visits to Mizo Hills, so as to prevent the Mizo Christians from offering their prayers. 'They want us to pay less regards to our sacred days', he observed.[99] The Mizos would refuse to be dominated or assimilated into that fold of idol worshippers. He promised that under the MNF rule Mizos would be free to practise their Christian religion without any hindrances. The MNF also manage to create occasional brawls between the Mizos and the non-Mizos to derive a wedge between the tribals and non-tribals in Mizo Hills. The MNF manifesto declared that 'Mizoram is for Mizos'.[100] To counter the MNF influence the MU also initiated a movement for the separation of the Mizo Hills from Assam and to constitute it into a state within the

Indian Union. It vowed to achieve it through Gandhian methods and recruited volunteers for this purpose.[101] The situation became explosive due to the confrontation between the MU and MNF. To avoid a possible conflict between the two organizations the neutral Mizos organized a conference at Churachandpur (Manipur) in January 1963. It was attended by members of both the organizations. The MU agreed to postpone the movement for statehood for Mizoram while the MNF agreed to drop its demand for secession of the Mizo Hills from the Indian Union and adopt constitutional methods to achieve its ends.[102] The Churachandpur Conference however resolved to work for the integration of all the Mizo area of north-east India into one state unit. Accordingly in October 1965, a MU delegation waited on the Prime Minister Lal Bahadur Shastri and submitted a memorandum for the formation of the state of Mizoram. Shastri assured the Mizo Union leaders that he would 'have a word' with H.V. Pataskar, Chairman of the Hill Areas Commission, so that the latter examined the Mizo Union's demand while going into the administrative arrangement proposed under the Nehru plan of autonomy.[103] But the PM's sudden demise and the refusal of the Pataskar Commission to consider the demand for a separate state made both MU and MNF active again. Dissatisfied the MU boycotted the Pataskar Commission. The rejuvenated MNF submitted a memorandum to the new prime minister demanding freedom for the Mizos (30 October 1965):[104]

> The Mizos from times immemorial lived in complete independence without interference. Chiefs of the different clans ruled over separate hills and valleys with supreme authority and their administration was very much like Greek city states of the past. Their territory and every part thereof had never been conquered or subjugated by their neighbouring state.. scattered as they are divided (by the British) the Mizo people are inseparably knitted together by their strong bond of tradition, custom, culture, language, social life and religion wherever they are. The Mizos stood as a separate nation even before the advent of British Government, having a nationality distinct and separate from that of India. In a nutshell they are a distinct nation, created, moulded and nurtured by God and nature. . . .
>
> In other words, the Mizos had never been under the Indian Government and never had any connection with the politics and policies of the various groups of Indian opinion. When India was in the threshold of independence the relation of the Mizos with the British Government and also with British India were fully realised by the Indian National Congress leaders. . . . Due solely to their political immaturity ignorance and lack of consciousness of their fate, representatives of

the Mizo Union, the largest political organisation at the that time representing all political including representatives of religious denominations and social organisations that were in existence submitted their demand and chose integration with free India imposing condition *inter-alia* 'that the Lushai will be allowed to opt out of Indian Union when they wish to do so subject to a minimum period of ten years. . . .'

During the fifteen years of close contact and association with India, the Mizo people had not been able to feel at home with Indian or in India nor have they been able to feel that their joys and sorrows have really been shared by India. They therefore do not feel Indians. Being created a separate nation they cannot go against nature to cross the barriers of nationality. They refused to occupy a place within India as they consider it to be unworthy of their national dignity and harmful to the interest of their prosperity. Nationalism and patriotism inspired by the political consciousness has now reached its maturity and the cry for political self-determination is the only wish and aspiration of the people *ne plus ultra*, the only final and final perfect embodiment of social living for them. Their only aspiration and political cry is the creation of Mizoram a free a sovereign state to govern herself to work out her own destiny and to formulate her own foreign policy. . . .

Though known as head hunters and martial race, the Mizos commit themselves to a policy of non-violence in their struggle and have no intention of employing any other means to achieve their political demand. If on the other hand, the Government of India brings exploitation and suppressive measures into operation employing military might against the Mizo people as is done in the case of the Nagas, which God forbid, it would be erroneous and futile for both the parties for a soul cannot be destroyed by weapons.

For this end it is in goodwill and understanding that the Mizo nation voices her rightful and legitimate claim of full self-determination through this Memorandum. . . .

The situation was tense. There was dissatisfaction in the Mizo Hills with the administration of the Government of Assam. The MNF used the situation to its advantage. In attracted the younger generation on account of its radicalism and romantic idealism. The loyal Mizos foreseeing danger advised the government to take the final decision and concede all reasonable demands forthwith in one installment rather than allow itself to be bumped from one concession to another. Even the Governor of Assam Vishnu Sahay was of the same opinion.[105] but the Government of Assam was indecisive. Vishnu Sahay even suggested that the Mizo Hills should be constituted into a separate administration like Nagaland, Tripura and Manipur before insurgency erupted there. But the Assam Chief Minister Bimala Prasad Chaliha was totally opposed to such an idea.[106]

Meanwhile the MNF had prepared itself for a *coup d'état*. It trained its cadres—members of the Mizo National Army (MNA)—for a simultaneous multi-pronged attack on government offices in different parts of the Mizo Hills. The main targets being the Assam Rifle concentration in Aizawl and the treasury offices of the government. The plan was to take the government as well as the paramilitary forces completely by surprise with an armed attack. And that before the Government of India could send its army, the MNF would declare independence which hopefully would immediately be recognized by some countries. This would compel the Indian Government to withdraw its forces from the Mizo Hills. Accordingly, the attack was launched on 28 February 1966 which continued till 1 March 1966. About 800-1300 armed MNF soldiers took part in the violent action that took place simultaneously in Aizawl, Lunglei, Vairangte, Chawngte, Chimluang, Kolashib, Champai, Saireng and Demagri. The MNA looted the treasury, kidnapped government officials, killed security personnel, damaged property and set fires to the bazaar. They disrupted communication lines and blocked roadways to prevent the Indian Army from reaching the Mizo Hills.

Within hours of all these violent activities, on 1 March 1966 the MNF declared unilateral independence and set up a parallel government in exile with Laldenga as the president of this Mizoram *Sawrkar*, Lalnunmawia as the vice president, Sainghaka as the home minister, C. Lalkhawliana as the finance minister, R. Zamawia as the defence minister, Ngurkunga the information minister, and John F. Manliana as the chief justice. The declaration of independence observed:[107]

> In the course of history, it becomes invariably necessary for mankind to assume their social, economic and political status to which the laws of the nature's God entitle them. We hold this truth to be self-evidence that all men are created equal and that they are endowed with inalienable fundamental human rights and dignity of human persons and to secure these rights. Governments are instituted among men deriving their just powers from the consent of the governed and whenever any form of government becomes destructive of this it is the right of the people to alter, change, modify and abolish it and institute a new Government laying its foundation on such principles and to organise its powers in such forms as to them shall seem most likely to effect their rights and dignity. The Mizos created and moulded into a nation and nurtured as such by nature's God, have been intolerably dominated by the people of India in contravention of the laws of nature.

THE NAGAS

The year 1947 did not obviously mark the beginning of a stable life for the Nagas: It became more tumultuous, violent and hectic as the year progressed. The assassination of Mahatma Gandhi was another setback for the Nagas. The Naga National Council (NNC) had a meeting on 1-2 February 1948 and sent a condolence message to Gandhi's family.[108] At the meeting Z. Phizo in an attempt to usurp power, tabled a motion stating that since the NNC members had all been elected anew, the president too should be elected afresh. But the motion was defeated by 17-4 votes. Nari Rustomji had just joined as the Advisor to the Governor, and meeting him was important for the NNC. The advisor gave his personal view on the whole Naga issue but the NNC stuck to its original demand on the governor's agreement.[109] It refused to use the agreement as the basis of its discussion. The Council finally selected Phizo, Longri Ao and Khelhoshe as Working Committee members. On 16 February Phizo and Aliba Imti joined Longri Ao in Jorhat to discuss ways to form the Working Committee and start functioning as the provisional government of the Naga people.[110] In between they met Premier Bordoloi in Gauhati to seek clarification on the 'agreement'. The meeting took place on 21 February.[111]

Back in Kohima, the working committee members were once again involved in serious discussions. In one such meeting (25 February) Phizo urged the NNC to exercise the 'right of secession'.[112] Aliba Imti was of the opinion that they were not empowered to work on 'secession', but only on the 'agreement'.[113] The discussion continued till 26 February but without any progress due to 'difference of opinion'. The month of March was also spent discussing the agreement and other related issues. The next Mokokchung meeting of NNC also ended without any tangible result as Phizo was firmly opposed to the agreement.[114] He reportedly said in the meeting, 'As an Angami I agreed to fight for the agreement but as an individual I want independence.'[115]

In the first week of May, Phizo and 'some of his men' went to Shillong to discuss the Naga problem but he did not submit any report to the NNC office about the meetings or their outcome.[116]

In the meantime, there were apprehensions that the NNC-Hydari Agreement had become null and void. This was greatly frustrating for the moderate Nagas. But the Assam governor[117] as well the chief minister[118] assured that the clauses of the agreement would be included in the Sixth Schedule of the Constitution. The advisor to the governor asked the NNC to speed up 'the work on the agreement'. Copies of the agreement were sent to all the tribal councils to study and submit their reports to the NNC. The NNC Working Committee meeting was held in Mokokchung (21-27 June 1948) and Aliba Imti wrote from there to the governor on the implementation of the agreement. He left for Shillong (30 June) to meet the advisor to the governor about his visit to Kohima and further discussion. The advisor reportedly told Aliba that he would visit Kohima in the first week of September. But on 9 July Phizo had been arrested in Shillong on charges of sedition. From the Presidency Jail in Calcutta, Phizo wrote to the Governor-General of India, C. Rajagopalachari (21 November 1948) reiterating that Nagas were not Indians and therefore the question of Nagas being hostile to India did not arise.[119] He pointed out that there existed a profound antipathy between the two due to their racial and cultural differences and even during the British rule there was no communication between them. Thus, though living under the same government, they remained strangers to each other. 'Nagas know Indians very little because Indians, as foreigners, are not allowed to enter Naga territory freely except on fringes where the Assam Railways was made to pass through our territory.'[120] In his 44-page letter Phizo also reiterated that the Nagas became independent the day British left Nagaland and India.[121]

But tragedy struck Phizo on 4 December 1948 when his wife Jwane and their two year old son met with an accident on the road between Jotsoma and Khonoma village. While his wife was injured, the son was killed in the accident. Subsequent to this Phizo was released on compassionate grounds on 18 December 1948 for a short period which was later extended and Phizo and his wife were sent to Shillong for special treatment at the Welsh Mission Hospital.[122] The government bore the expenses.

For sometime it looked like Phizo had given up politics. He told Nari Rustomji, the then Advisor to the Governor of Assam that he had been misunderstood.[123] Rustomji was convinced that the personal tragedy had changed his life and ambition. It was on Rustomji's recommendation, who was reputed to have had close associations with the tribals that Phizo was released unconditionally from jail.[124] With Aliba Imti also resigning from NNC and active politics, the Naga Hills seemed to be heading for a peaceful alliance with India.

But soon after his release Phizo came back to Naga politics more vigorously[125] and on 11 December 1950 was elected as the president of the NNC succeeding Visiar Angami, a position which he did not relinquish till his death. Naga politics entered a new phase with this election. The failure of the NNC-Hydari Agreement was a blow to the moderate Nagas. Phizo took this opportunity to cleanse the NNC of the moderate elements and put the house in order by selectively picking up his own men from the People's Independence League, purged all his opponents and pledged to fight for the sovereignty of Nagaland. Phizo's stature grew as even the Assam Government recognized him as the 'representative spokesmen of the Nagas'.[126] The rejuvenated NNC rejected the Sixth Schedule of the Indian Constitution as contrary to the spirit of the NNC-Hydari Agreement and refused to send any Naga representative to the Indian Parliament. Instead it organized on its own a plebiscite on the question of Naga independence in the Naga Hills. Despite the Assam Government's opposition the Government of India let Phizo hold the plebiscite.[127] The youth wings of the NNC, NYM and NWS enthusiastically went about collecting thumb impressions and signatures of the Nagas in favour of Naga independence. The moderates and even the pro-Indian and neutral Nagas were too terrified of Phizo's men to refuse to sign.[128] But the move to include Burmese Nagas in it failed as the Burmese ambassador in India in a statement declared that the border Nagas had no interest in the plebiscite.[129] The plebiscite claimed that 99 per cent of the Nagas favoured severance from India and independence but the Government of India refused to give it any importance.[130]

When Indian Prime Minister Nehru and the Congress president visited Assam in December 1951, a five member Naga delegation met him to put forward their claim to independence. Nehru related to them how India's sovereignty was transferred by the British Government and how through a process of integration the Naga Hills had become an inalienable part of India. Nehru said to the delegation:

> I consider freedom very precious. I am sure that the Nagas are as free as I am, in fact more free in a number of ways. For while I am bound down by all sorts of laws, the Nagas are not to the same extent bound down by such laws and are governed by their customary laws and usages. But the independence Nagas are after, is something quite different from individual or group freedom. In the present context of affairs both in India and the world, it is impossible to consider, even for a moment, such an absurd demand for independence of the Nagas. It is

doubtful whether the Nagas realise the consequence of what they are asking for. For their present demand would lead them to ruin.[131]

At the same time Nehru gave them assurance that everything possible would be done to accommodate Naga aspirations within the Constitution of India. In March 1952, another interview was granted to the Naga delegation which reiterated its demand for independence. It enraged Nehru so much that he reportedly said that even if heavens were to fall or India went pieces, Nagas would not be granted independence.[132]

The next step for the NNC under Phizo's leadership was to boycott the General Election of 1952. As a result of NNC's declaration, no one contested the elections to the District Council, Assam Assembly or Indian Parliament. Though the government went about with the preparation, the Naga boycott of the elections was almost total.

In December 1952, Phizo quietly left the Naga Hills to establish contacts with the rest of the world to raise the question of Naga independence in the United Nations. But the Burmese police intercepted Phizo and sent him back to the Naga Hills.[133]

Nehru visited Kohima with the then Prime Minister of Burma U Nu, on 30 March 1953. A huge crowd gathered to listen to him. But when a group of Nagas wanted to hand over a memorandum to Nehru personally, Barkakaty, the Assamese Deputy Commissioner of Naga Hills prevented them from doing so. Denied of representation the Naga crowd walked out of the meeting halfway. Nehru never visited Naga Hills again although the Nagas apologized for their behaviour later which they said was their form of 'protest' and not meant to 'insult' the prime minister.[134] This deliberate discourtesy not so much to him as to U Nu stiffened Nehru's attitude. The Naga leaders were informed that by such a behaviour, the Naga National Council had put itself beyond the pale and the government would not hereafter recognize or deal with it.[135] Following this event, the Assam Government issued arrest orders for eight Naga leaders who were reportedly behind the episode.[136] Police raided the house of T. Sakhrie, the general secretary of NNC. Meanwhile, other leaders held secret meetings to decide whether to court arrest or go underground to evade arrest. The situation further deteriorated with the movement of Indian Army into the Naga Hills, house to house raids, arrests and the death of Zasibate Angami, a judge of the Angami Tribal Council. Several Naga leaders and Naga youth went underground to evade harassment by the army. This was the beginning of a new phase in Naga history—the underground movement. The NNC newspaper *Naga Nation* and the *Naga Herald* were banned. The Naga leaders were also refused interviews with Rajendra Prasad, the President of India and the Congress president in New Delhi and on his visit to Manipur (December 1953).[137] The Nagas retaliated by launching a non-cooperation movement against Assam and Indian officials. They refused to work for them or sell food item and render porter services. There was a boycott of everything Indian. The publicity wing of the NNC led by the able T. Sakhrie launched a massive propaganda which immensely influenced the Naga minds.[138] To quell the tension, a goodwill mission of the Nagas visited Assam between 30 November and 15 December 1953. The mission brought a goodwill massage of the people of Naga Hills to the people of Assam.

On its part the Assam Government decided to concentrate on development works in Nagaland proclaiming that these were what the Nagas really wanted and dismissed the demand for independence as the work of a handful of Naga leaders.[139] Bimala Prasad Chaliha also met a number of Nagas to improve the situation and workout an agreeable formula for undertaking such work. Rajkumari Amrit Kaur, the Central Health Minister during her visit to Imphal (30 November 1953) also met a Naga delegation.[140]

PUSHED UNDERGROUND

Meanwhile, the NNC propaganda from underground continued. These included eloquent essays, speeches, appeals, statements, patriotic calls, counter appeals, national poems, marching songs, etc. In this atmosphere even a small incident could tilt the balance either way. An army vehicle accidentally ran over a Naga riding a scooter which vitiated the peace again. As a result, the extremists once again gained an upper hand and demolished the work of the moderates. The NNC soon gave up its peaceful demonstrations and petitions. The extremists now began preparations for an armed uprising from the Tuensang area, the free Nagaland as they called it, the international frontier area touching China and Burma. Thereafter, Nehru declared a change in policy and decided 'to bring this area under more direct administrative control to enable them to share the benefits of a welfare state, subject to the protection of their distinct social and cultural pattern'.[141] There was also the fear of China taking advantage of the turmoil in the frontier area.[142] But the tribes reacted to the administrative mission of goodwill and civilization as an act of intrusion into their territory. They appealed to the United Nations by stating that they were in free Nagaland and that India was invading their territory.[143]

Subsequent to the entry of the Assam Rifles into that area the underground Nagas organized themselves and on 18 September 1954, the Federal Government of Nagaland or Hongking was announced in Tuesang. Inter-tribal feuds, also broke out in the area around the same time which complicated the situation further. Violence, head-hunting, and inter-tribal attacks were rampant. The Government of Assam blamed the NNC factions for engineering this inter-tribal feud and reviving head-hunting.[144] The NNC however denied the allegation and said that the Tuensang area was free Nagaland under the so-called Hongking Government and the NNC had no influence over it. The Government of Assam also went full scale to deal with the situation without really grasping the forces working behind it. The Tribal Councils were abolished; the Kohima High School was closed down, and promulgation of regulation to requisition porter services were made. The Naga people were aghast at these developments and saw it as Assamese domination.[145] The extremists took advantage of this situation to again control. The situation worsened in March 1955 when fierce fighting broke out between the Assam Rifles and the Hongking Army in the Tuensang area.[146] The NNC appealed to the government to preserve peace. A Naga delegation consisting of Phizo, Jasokie and three other leaders met Bishnuram Medhi, the Assam Chief Minister in Shillong on 15 August 1955 and signed a declaration condemning terrorism and promising that the NNC would use peaceful means in achieving its goals.[147]

It was clear that the NNC had no control over the extremist elements active in the Tuensang area. Meanwhile, NNC itself was going through a crisis. Internal dissension and intrigues were plaguing it. T. Sakhrie, Jasokie and others who were disillusioned with Phizo's leadership held a series of secret meetings from September 1955 onwards to reorganize the NNC and find a peaceful solution to the Naga problem.[148] On the other hand, in his report placed before the Lok Sabha on 30 September 1955, Prime Minister Nehru pointed out that the tribes differed greatly from each other, some being 'rather primitive' while others were 'remarkably developed and advanced'. It was the British rule which kept the tribal areas 'almost completely cut off from the rest of India'. Even in post-independent India the 'legalistic' and bureaucratic approach' of certain officials had led to 'a certain lack of confidence among the tribal folk'. 'The situation in the Naga Hills would have been much better if it had been handled a little more competently by local officers, and if some officers who were notoriously unpopular had not been kept there.' Nehru felt that the Nagas were 'proud and sensitive and do not like being treated as subject people or being looked down upon in any way'.[149]

The Nagas sent their representatives to meet the Assam chief minister in October 1955, issued leaflets for peace and had a number of public meetings at the end of the year. Thus, the moderates who had lost the organization to Phizo were again gaining ground.[150] Such development made an insecure Phizo who was underground to try and destroy the moderate elements and to make efforts to achieve freedom for Nagaland by organizing a strong armed force (Home Guard) and establishing a parallel Federal Government, whose sovereignty would extend over all Naga areas in Assam, Manipur and Burma.[151] In January 1956, Sakhrie, Phizo's cousin and an expert writer of propaganda material, who was opposed to a violent doctrine was kidnapped from his house, tied to a tree and murdered brutally by the extremists with a view to striking terror in the hearts of the 'traitors'.[152] Since then the moderates and extremists parted company almost for good. Fierce fighting broke out all over the Naga Hills which prompted the government to declare it as a 'disturbed area' (31 January 1956). The Naga Hills Disturbed Area Ordinance and Assam Maintenance of Public Order Act were promulgated by the government. As the Indian armed forces replaced the Assam Rifles battalions, the Special Powers Act was also enforced in the Naga Hills in order to take necessary measures to maintain law and order and to stop violence and bloodshed.

On 22 March 1956 the Phizo group declared the establishment of the Federal Government as a *de facto* government at Phensinyu village in the Rengma area. He claimed that it was done according to their constitution, adopted and signed by the head of the state, president and the commander-in-chief of the Naga Army. The Naga national flag bearing the red, green and white with three blue stars was hoisted with great traditional ceremony and feast.[153]

The Naga freedom movement had thus had a metamorphosis: from then on it took the form of an organized insurgency. From an overground activity the Naga movement had become an underground movement in the face of the onslaught of Indian State and the weakening social base of the movement itself.

NOTES

1. S. Chattradhari, *Manipurgi Itihasta Irabat*, Imphal: State Krishak Sabha, 1972, p. 69. Cited in Kshetri Rajendra Singh, 'Social Movements in Manipur: A Study of Two Movements among the Meitheis', unpublished Ph.D thesis, Centre for Social Studies, Surat, p. 42.
2. Th. Boro, 'Manipurda Communist Party Amasung Kutlai Paiba Lalhou' in *Neengshing Chephog* (85th Birth Anniversary of Irabat Commemorative Publication), Imphal: Irabat Bhawan, 1981, p. 15. Cited in Kshetri Rajendra Singh, ibid., p. 41.
3. Sumit Sarkar, *Modern India*, Delhi: Macmillan, 1983. Irabat attended the conference as a delegate from Assam.
4. Thokchom Bir Singh (comp.) *Comrade Irabat*, Imphal: Irabat Memorial Library and Information Centre, 1983, p. 51.
5. On this day a protest meeting against the so-called Purbanchal state was convened at the MDU Hall. Watching the massive turnout of people despite the ban on such gathering the police resorted to repressive measures and sought Irabat's arrest. Sensing impending arrest, Irabat went underground. See ibid., p. 53.
6. Naorem Sanjaoba, 'Genesis of Insurgency', in his (ed.), *Manipur: Past and Present*, Delhi: Mittal, 1990, pp. 245-90.
7. Th. Boro, op. cit.
8. Ibid.
9. Thokchom Bir Singh, op. cit., pp. 57-60.
10. Cited in V.B. Singh, *The Red Rebel in India*, Delhi: Associate Publishing House, 1968, p. 65.
11. The *Times of India*, 28 February 1951.
12. Thokchom Bir Singh, op. cit.; S. Chattradhari, op. cit.
13. V.B. Singh op. cit.; also Thokchom Bir Singh, op. cit.
14. Ibid.
15. *Weekend*, April 1980. Even Sumit Sarkar, op. cit., does not mention it.
16. A good study of this can be found in N. Lokendra Singh, 'Socio-Economic Roots of Popular Movements in Manipur Valley', unpublished Ph.D. thesis, Manipur University, Imphal, 1990.
17. Ibid.
18. An account of Nupilan Movement can be found in Sanamani Yamban, 'Nupilan: Manipur Women's Agitation 1939', *Economic and Political Weekly*, Vol. XI, No. 8, 21 February 1976, pp. 325-31. Also N. Lokendra Singh, op. cit.; N. Joykumar Singh, *Social Movements in Manipur*, Delhi: Mittal, 1992.
19. N. Lokendra Singh, op. cit., p. 325.
20. Ibid.
21. Ibid.
22. Ibid.
23. Ibid.

24. Ibid., p. 34.
25. Ibid.
26. R. Constantine, *Manipur: Maid of the Mountain*, Delhi: Mittal, 1981, p. 94.
27. Kshetri Rajendra Singh, op. cit., p. 136.
28. Ibid.
29. Cited in ibid.
30. All Manipur Students Union, *27th August: Hungry Marchers Day*, Imphal, 1984, cited in ibid.
31. Kshetri Rajendra Singh, op. cit., also Manipur Territorial Congress Committee, *Case of Manipur: Manipur Demands Statehood*, Imphal, 1968, Appendix A. The rest of this section relies on Rajendra Singh's study op. cit.
32. Based on Samarendra's interview in M. Bharati, 'Insurgency in Manipur', Imphal, 1992, pp. 7-8, unpublished M.A. thesis, M.S. University of Baroda, Vadodara, 1992.
33. R. Constantine, op. cit., pp. 89-90.
34. Ibid.
35. Ibid., pp. 70-1.
36. As in note 32.
37. Ibid.
38. Ibid.
39. Ibid.
40. Kshetri Rajendra Singh, op. cit., p. 151.
41. Ibid.
42. The 'Resistance' serialised the documented story of Manipur's merger with India to show how the maharaja was cornered into signing the agreement.
43. Kshetri Rajendra Singh, op. cit.
44. *The pan Mongolian Movement* is an unsigned and undated eight page leaflet found in the collection of the materials on recent insurgency in North-East India preseved by a journalist from North-East India, at Guwahati. Also cited in Kshetri Rajendra, ibid., p. 152.
45. Cited in ibid.
46. Ibid.
47. Ibid.
48. Ibid.
49. *Why Our Revolution needs Special Emphasis on International Deplomatic Work?*, ibid., three page leaflet dated 13 August 1967. Cited in ibid.
50. Ibid.
51. Ibid.
52. Consocom, *The Revolutionary Government of Manipur: A Review*, The Consocom Office, Imphal, n.d., pp. ii-iv.
53. Ibid.
54. Kshetri Rajendra Singh, op. cit., p. 194.
55. Ibid., p. 195.
56. Ibid., pp. 196-7

57. Ibid., p. 198.
58. Ibid.
59. Ibid.
60. Ibid., pp. 199-200.
61. Ibid.
62. Ibid.
63. Ibid.
64. Ibid.
65. Ibid., p. 236.
66. Ibid., p. 237.
67. Ibid.
68. R. Constantine, op. cit., pp. 96-8. While listing the factors responsible for the outburst of insurgency in Manipur, Samarendra, one of the pioneers, declared the exploitation of Manipuris by non-Manipuri business classes as one factor.
69. Kshetri Rajendra Singh, op. cit., p. 157.
70. Ibid.
71. Consocom, *The Revolutionary Government of Manipur*, op. cit., pp. xiii-xiv.
72. Kshetri Rajendra Singh, op. cit., p. 204.
73. Vumson, *Zo History*, Aizawl: Author, n.d., p. 259.
74. The details of the situation is presented in Vanlawma, *Kan Ram Le Kei*, Aizawl: Zoram Printing Press, 1972, p. 158.
75. Vumson, op. cit.
76. S.K. Chaube, *Hill Politics in North East India*, Delhi: Orient Longman, 1973, p. 114.
77. Ibid.
78. Vanlawma, op. cit.
79. Lalbiakthanga, *The Mizos: A Study in Racial Personality*, Gauhati: United Publisher, 1978, cited in Vumson, op. cit., p. 265.
80. V. Venkata Rao et al. (eds.), *A Century of Government and Politics in North East India*, Vol. III, *Mizoram*, Delhi: S. Chand & Co., 1981. The resolution read:

    'On 29 October, 1958, the Mizo Hill District Council resolved: with the flowering of the bamboos in the Mizo District, (the) rat population as phenomenally increased and it is feared that in the next year (1959) the whole district would be affected. As a precautionary measure against the imminence of famine, following the flowering of the *bamboos*, the District Countil feels that the government be moved to sanction to the Mizo District Council a sum of Rs.15 lakh to be expended on a test relief measure for the whole of the Mizo districts including the Pawi-Lakher region.'
81. Ibid.
82. Vumson, op. cit.

    The *District Census Handbook* (Mizo Hills) recorded, 'That the entire population was affected by the famine.' The Finance Commission which visited the district recommended after studying the food situation that 6 trucks and 180 jeeps should immediately be put in use to reach foodstuff to the famine affected areas. See, B.B. Goswami, *The Mizo Unrest: A Study of Politicisation of Culture*, Jaipur: Alekh, 1979, pp. 141-2.

83. V.V. Venkata Rao, op. cit., p. 236.
84. Ibid.
85. S.K. Chaube, op. cit., p. 164.
86. S.H. Pautu, 'Mizoram Separatist Politics', unpublished M. Phil. thesis, Department of Political Science, North-Eastern Hill University, Shillong, 1989, p. 45.
87. Ibid., p. 46.
88. Ibid.
89. H.C. Barua, *A Glimpse of Assam Disturbances*, Gauhati, 1961; Narayan Chowdhury, *Ashamer Bhasha Danga* (in Bangla), Calcutta, 1963.
90. S.H. Pautu, op. cit., p. 48. See Saprawnga's statements in Amrita Rangasami, 'Mizoram: Tragedy of Our Making', in *Economic and Political Weekly*, 15 April 1978, pp. 653-62.
91. Tlangchuaka (ed.), *Mizoram Politics Chanchin* (in Mizo), MNF Headquarters, Aizawl, 1973, p. 19. Cited in John V. Hluna, *Church and Political Upheavel*, Aizawl: Author, 1985, p. 88.
92. S.H. Pautu, op. cit., p. 48.
93. The above details are available in Animesh Ray, *Mizoram: Dynamics of Change*, Calcutta: Pearl, 1982, p. 135.
94. B.B. Goswami, op. cit., p. 144.
95. *Memorandum to the Prime Minister of India by MNF*, Aizawl: MNF Headquarters, 30 October 1965.
96. Ibid.
97. Ibid.
98. B.B. Goswami, op. cit., pp. 149-50.
99. Lalthangliana, Secretary, External Affairs MNF, Government of Mizoram (in exile) to Stanley Nichols Roy, General Secretary, APHLC Lt. No. 20(1), EA/66, dated 13 March 1967, Aizawl, cited in J.V. Hluna, op. cit., p. 90.
100. J.V. Hluna, op. cit., p. 92.
101. V. Venkata Rao, op. cit., p. 238.
102. Ibid.
103. Ibid.
104. Same as note 95.
105. V. Venkata Rao, op. cit., p. 240.
106. Ibid.
107. MNF Declaration of Independence, 1 March 1966, Aizawl.
108. T. Aliba Imti, *Reminiscence: Impur to Naga National Council*, Mokokchung, Author.
109. Ibid.
110. Ibid.
111. Ibid., p. 75.

112. Ibid.
113. Ibid.
114. Ibid.
115. Ibid.
116. Ibid.
117. NSCN, *A Brief Political Account of Nagaland* (n.d.), p. 11. Also Memo No. 490/C, dated 11 June 1948. N.K. Rustomji, Advisor to the Governor to Secretary, NNC.
118. Memo No. 88-C/47-570-72, Gopinath Bordoloi to secretary, NNC, 22 June 1948.
119. A.Z. Phizo to C. Rajagopalachari, Governor-General of India, 22 November 1948.
120. Ibid.
121. Ibid.
122. Mhiesizokho Zinyo, *Phizo and the Naga Problem*, Dimapur: Author, 1979, p. 24.
123. Ibid.
124. Ibid., also P.D. Stracey, *Nagaland Nightmare*, Bombay: Allied Publishers, 1968, p. 83.
125. In fact, Stracey found that many Indians blamed Nari Rustomji for recommending Phizo's release which was described as a 'rash act' prompted by a 'softhearted advisor'; see Stracey, ibid., p. 83.

    Rustomji however stood by his recommendation and said that permanent detention of Phizo in the prison would not in any way have altered the political crisis of Nagaland because 'the seeds of unrest were already deeply laid. The movement might have taken a different shape in the absence of Phizo's leadership, but it would be a foolish over simplification to suppose that it would have fizzled out. The tribal people are not insensitive and would have been angered and embittered more if government had not shown humanity and decency to Phizo's family at the time of their distress', in Nari Rustomji, *Enchanted Frontiers*, Delhi: OUP, 1972, p. 103.
126. Mercus, F. Franda in *Economic Weekly Annual*, 4 February 1961, p. 155, cited in Asoso Yunou's, *The Rising Nagas: A Historical and Political Study*, Delhi: Vivek Publisher, 1974, p. 201.
127. Asoso Yunuo, ibid., p. 202, note 1.
128. Personal interview of a Naga Elder, Lower Chandmari, Kohima, October 1991.
129. Asoso Yunou, op. cit., p. 202.
130. Ibid.
131. Nehru to NNC Delegation, 29 December 1951, aboard S.S. *Lusai* (steamer), on river Brahmaputra, Silghat, Assam.
132. Nehru to NNC Delegation, 11 March 1952, Delhi.
133. M. Horam, *Thirty Years of Naga Insurgency*, Delhi: Cosmo, 1990, p. 51.
134. Ibid.

135. Nehru to J. Daulatram, 4 April 1952, cited in S. Gopal, *Jawaharlal Nehru: A Biography*, Vol. 2, Delhi: OUP, 1975, p. 208.
136. M. Horam, op. cit.
137. Asoso Yunou, op. cit., p. 205.
138. M. Horam, op. cit., pp. 55-8.
139. On 2 December 1953, Bishnuram Medhi the Chief Minister said, 'I cannot think of any demand for independent sovereign Naga state raised by a few handful of Naga leaders, mostly Christians. And probably this demand was raised by interested foreign missionaries to keep them isolated from the rest of India. During the pre-independence days, the British administrators also were greatly responsible for giving the idea of independence among a handful of Naga leaders under the influence of foreign Missionaries.'

    In 1954, again Bishnuram Medhi reiterated this in the Assam Legislative Assembly, 'The (common) people of Naga Hills want jobs, schools, dispensaries, new roads and . . . other facilities . . . the Nagas in Burma have accepted the constitution of Burma Government, the Nagas in the Mikir Hills, North Cachar Hills, etc., do not want independence, the Nagas in the NEFA also do not want independence. Why this handful of persons want independent Nagaland. . . . It is desirable to allow things to settle down so that the Nagas may realise the futility of pursuing a sentimental agitation for Nagaland.'
140. Asoso Yunou, op. cit., pp. 209-10.
141. Nehru, cited in ibid., p. 211.
142. See notes 10 and 11 above. Phizo reportedly sent emissaries to China for recognition of Naga independence to which the latter did not respond. Although the underground Nagas refused to seek assistance from China for the latter's adherence to Communist ideology which the former felt was opposed to the proposed Christian-state. This however did not reduce the Communist phobia that had gripped the ruling community.
143. Asoso Yunou, ibid., p. 211.
144. Ibid., p. 212.
145. Ibid.
146. Ibid.
147. The statement signed on 13 August 1955, read, 'The declared policy of the Naga National Council is of non-violence and we the undersigned, reiterated the same and condemn any violence that has been committed in different parts of the Naga Hills District by some miscreants. We assure the Government of Assam and India and remind the Nagas that whoever indulges in any act of violence will go against the best interests of the Naga people and in general for preservation of law and order and to help the administration in restoring peace and order . . .', ibid.
148. Ibid.
149. Jawaharlal Nehru, A Note on the North Eastern Frontier Areas, 19-25 October 1952, pp. 1-28.

150. Asoso Yunou, op. cit., p. 214.
151. Ibid.
152. M. Horam, op. cit., pp. 78-9. Official circles held Phizo responsible for the murder and a case was registered against him by the Kohima police. See ibid. M. Zinyo put it on record that 'according to several eyewitnesses at Khonoma, it was no other place than Khonoma itself, that Phizo first blew the gaff which was in his mind about the necessity to wipe out Sakhrie. The same eyewitness testified that Phizo had ominously pronounced that . . . Nagas could never attain independence until T. Sakhrie was eliminated . . . Phizo compared T. Sakhrie to a leaking hole in the boat of Naga independence . . . which needs to be checked immediately.' M. Zinyo, op. cit., p. 37. Phizo however pleaded not guilty: 'I could never have authorised such a killing for it would destroy the whole fabric and the very foundation of the Naga community organisation', in *New Statesman*, 3 September 1960, cited in ibid., p. 38.
153. Asoso Yunou, op. cit., p. 215.

CHAPTER EIGHT

The Negotiation

The Nehru Government of free India had not foreseen the snowballing of seccessionist movements in the post-colonial India. The Indian nation seemed to have consolidated itself except in the case of Kashmir and the Naga Hills. The miniscule Naga population vis-à-vis its own size and might, had made the Indian State complacent about the eventual Naga acceptance of Indian suzerainty.[1] Nehru knew that the Nagas were a tough people and was therefore against any hasty attempt to absorb them.[2] He felt that 'if government keeps it head cool and restrains its hand the whole movement may gradually fizzle out, because it leads to nothing.[3] But the situation deteriorated with the unfortunate event of March 1953 in Kohima when the Nagas walked out of the meeting Nehru was to address. Nehru blamed the Assam Chief Minister Bishnu Ram Medhi for the mishandling of the Nagas who in turn sacked the deputy commissioner.[4] Nehru even put it on record that the Naga situation worsened due to its mishandling by certain officials.[5] To avenge the misconduct the Assam Government cracked down on the Naga National Council activists. The NNC office and the NNC secretary, T. Sakhrie's place were raided. The *Naga Nation*, the NNC mouthpiece was banned. Following the declaration of the Tuensang area as Free Nagaland, formation of a parallel government in exile and a bitter factional fight amongst the Nagas, the Indian Army moved into the Naga Hills. On 31 January, the entire Nagas Hills was declared as a Disturbed Area by the promulgation of the Naga Hills Disturbed Area Ordinance and the Assam Maintenance of Public Order of 1953. The Assam Police was replaced by the Indian Army. The Armed Forces Special Power Act was promulgated for added power to the army. As secessionist activity did not diminish or disappear and military operations too did not bear substantial results in curbing them, more power was given to the army authorities through the Nagaland Security Regulation Act of 1962 and the North-East Armed Forces Special Power Act, 1972. The Armed Forces (Special

Power) Act of 1958 as amended by the Armed Forces (Assam and Manipur) Special Power (Amendment) Act of 1972 were mooted as and when required and then enforced in the area. Similarly, the MNF in Mizoram was declared unlawful in the wake of its attempted coup in March 1966. The Extraordinary Gazette Notification of the Government of India published on 6 March 1966 declared that the MNF activities were 'prejudicial to the security of the Mizo district in the state of Assam and the adjoining parts of the territory of India'. The Central Government by effecting necessary amendment ordered that Rule 32 of the Defence of India Rule, 1962 shall be applicable to the MNF. Simultaneously various other orders similar to that of the Naga Hills were passed to provide additional power to the armed forces, which will be discussed later. The provisions of Disturbed Area Act were extended over Manipur on 21 July 1978 and the Armed Forces Special Power Act, 1958 was also imposed. Although the government was forced to withdraw the imposition on 1 August 1978 these were reimposed on 8 September 1980. The army was called in to deal with the insurgency. A separate 'M' (Mike) sector was opened specifically to counter the Meithei insurgents. Since then Manipur has virtually been under army rule.

Although the Indian State did not formulate any conscious anti-insurgency policy, its method of dealing with insurgency situation developed a pattern over time. It preferred to ignore secessionist movements in the initial period when such movements were weak. But should a movement develop significant strength it would be declared illegitimate and force would be resorted to crush it. Simultaneous efforts would also be made to win over the moderate section of the secessionists by conciliation and thereby alienate the extremist elements. The emphasis was to get the secessionist movement to peter out on its own. But even after army operations if it continued to pose problems to the polity, accords were be entered into with the leaders of the movement whereby major demands of the insurgents that could be implemented would be granted while the secessionists would be expected to give up their claims to sovereignty.

THE STICK: ENTER THE ARMY

While moving the army into the Naga Hills, Prime Minister Nehru's reported instructions to the chief of the army staff was to deal with the Nagas as 'fellow Indians' and use 'moderate force'. Following this the order issued by the chief of the army staff to the armed forces were in the same spirit:

> You must remember that all the people of the area in which you are operating are fellow Indians. They may have a different religion, may pursue a different way of life by they are Indians and the very fact that they are different yet form a part of India, is a reflection of India's greatness. Some of these people are misguided and have taken to arms against their people and are disrupting the peace of the area. You are to protect the mass of the people from these disruptive elements. You are not here to fight the people in the area but to protect them. You are fighting only those who threaten the people and who are a danger to the lives and properties of the people. You must therefore do everything possible to win their confidence and respect and the help them feel that they belong to India.[6]

But when the movement took the form of organized insurgency, the Government of India concluded that they had no option but to deal with it for all practical purposes as a purely military solution though it was never officially acknowledged as such.[7] Nehru was successful in vetoing the suggestion of the use of machine guns from the air.[8] The failure of the army to effectively deal with the Naga movement also did not harden Nehru. 'It must always be remembered that if the Nagas are made to feel that they have no alternative but to fight and die, they will prefer doing so.'[9] So Nehru urged the army to act swiftly but not brutally. Thimayya, the most distinguished of the senior army commanders was ordered to take charge immediately. But Nehru's objective of 'win(ing) the minds and hearts of people, not to terrify or frighten them' did not succeed. It ended up doing what it did not intend to do. The army, frustrated by failures to tackle the insurgency did not act with restrain. Enormous power was given to the army as a result of the enactment of various acts by successive governments, especially during Prime Minister Indira Gandhi's rule. For example, under Section 4 of the Armed Forces Special Power Act and its amended version of 1972, any commissioned officer, warrant officer, non-commissioned officer or any other person of equivalent rank in the armed forces may in a disturbed area,

> (*a*) if he is of opinion that it is necessary to do so for the maintenance of public order, after giving such due warning as he may consider necessary, fire upon or otherwise use force, even to the causing of death, against any person who is acting in contravention of any law or order for the time being in force in the disturbed area prohibiting the assembly of five or more persons or the carrying of weapons or of things capable of being used as weapons or of fire-arms, ammunition or explosive substances;

(*b*) . . . destroy any arms dump, prepared or fortified position or shelter from which armed attacks are made or are likely to be made or are attempted to be made, or any structure used as a training camp for armed volunteers or utilised as a hideout by armed gangs or absconders wanted for any offence;

(*c*) arrest without warrant, any person who has committed a cognisable offence or against whom a reasonable suspicion exists that he has committed or is about to commit a cognisable offence and may use such force as may be necessary to effect the arrest;

(*d*) enter and search without warrant any premises to make any such arrest as aforesaid or to recover any person believed to be wrongfully restrained or confined or any property reasonably suspected to be stolen property or any arms, ammunition or explosive substances believed to be unlawfully kept in such premises, and may for that purpose use such force as may be necessary.[10]

As can be seen the laws on surveillance were so carefully phrased that no offence needed to be committed, nor even contemplated by the tribals to enable any petty *havildar* of the Indian Army to take drastic actions against the former. The Nagaland Security Regulation Act of 1962 conferred special provisions for search giving the same latitude to the police officer to determine intent. The police had a right to search 'any street, alley, public place or open space' to check whether a person is carrying 'in contravention of the law' not only corrosive substances or explosives 'but any article which (the police have) reason to believe is being or is about to be used in contravening any order'.[11] Although there were no references to any power to the army to burn down civil habitation, villages and granaries were systematically burnt down by taking shelter under the provisions in Clause (b) mentioned earlier in this chapter. Section 5 of the Armed Forces Special Power Act, 1958 also stipulated that 'any person arrested and taken into custody under this regulation shall be made over to the officer in charge of the nearest police station with the least possible delay together with a report of the circumstances occasioning the arrest'. But taking advantage of the ambiguous phrase 'least possible delay' the army would deal with the suspect themselves sometimes leading even to his death without handing him over to the local police. The government also armed itself with the right to obtain information. The government could by an order ask any person to produce any such information or article in his possession. The government also was empowered to impose collective punishment—not for commission of offences that may be held to be cognizable but for failing to fulfil responsibilities that it had demanded from the tribals. Section 7 of the Assam Maintenance of Public Order Act stated that:

> If it appears to the State that the inhabitants in any area are concerned in or abetting the commission of offences pre-judicially affecting the public safety or the maintenance of supplies or services necessary to the life of the community or are harbouring persons concerned in the commission of such offences are failing to render all assistance in their power to discover or to apprehend the offender or are suppressing material evidence, that state government may impose a collective fine.

As against these, Section 6 of the Armed Forces Special Power Act, 1958 (Amended in 1972) assured for good measure complete autonomy and immunity to the members of the armed forces personnel engaged in all such operations from being called upon to account for their actions: 'No prosecution, suit or other legal proceedings shall be instituted, except with the previous sanction of the Central Government, against any person in respect of anything done or purported to be done in exercise of powers conferred by regulation.'[12]

While the armed forces personnel were thus given a free hand without any accountability, the tribals were not provided any legal redress. Section 34(1) of the Nagaland Security Regulation Act of 1962 stipulated that 'no court shall take cognisance of the provisions of this regulation or of any order made thereunder, except on a report in writing of the facts constituting such contravention made by a public servant'. The tribals therefore could not seek redress from courts against all the arbitrary powers that the state had over him: requisition of his property, destruction of his food stock, burning of his habitation, removing him without so much as a right to raise a slogan against the state, and deprivation of his access to his forest resources without providing him with any alternative for his subsistence.

Having thus been armed with such absolute power the Indian Army set out to crush rebellions in the respective states of Nagaland, Mizoram and Manipur. Reporting the uprising in Mizo Hills, which necessitated the deployment of the army, Gulzari Lal Nanda, Minister of Home Affairs said to the Parliament on 3 March 1966:

> Sir, we have been in touch with the Government of Assam in regard to certain serious incident's that have occurred in the night of February 28-1st March in the Mizo Hills district. The position as ascertained from the State Government,

is that between 10.30 p.m. on the 28th February and 3 a.m. on the 1st March, some tribals resorted to acts of lawlessness and violence at Lungleh, Aijal, Eayrangte (Vairengte), Chawngte and Chinluang (Chhimluang) in thier attempts to disrupt communications and overawe public servants. The total number who took part in all these places is about eight hundred to one thousand three hundred. There are reasonable grounds to believe that these tribals are led by extremist elements in the Mizo National Front. The first attack was at about 10.30 p.m. on 28 February on the sub-treasury at Lungleh. A gang of five hundred to one thousand strong attacked a camp of Security Forces and an Assam Rifles post. This attack was beaten back and some of the attackers were stated to have been killed. On our side, two men of the Assam Rifles were killed and three wounded. The whereabouts of the sub-divisional officer of Lungleh who was surrounded are still not known. The latest reports to reach from Lungleh indicate that some firing is going on at Lungleh. At about 2.00 a.m. on the 1st March, a number of persons attacked the telephone Exchange at Aijal and an hour later the District Treasury was also attacked by about one hundred to one hundred fifty persons who took away ten rifles, two bayonets, some rounds of 303 ammunition and cash from the single lock of the Treasury. They tried to break open the double lock but they did not succeed. At about 1.30 a.m. on the 1st March, a gang of one hundred to one hundred and fifty people armed with lathis (clubs) surrounded the sub-divisional officer, Public Works Department, at Eayrangte (Vairengte) and asked to get out of the district. The mob took the key from Chowkidar (caretaker) and took over the departmental stores and the jeep. There were similar encounters at Coinluang and Chawngte at which a number of persons belonging to the Mizo National Front were killed. No fresh incidents have been reported from the morning of the 1st March, but delayed reports of the rebels seizing two police stations on the 1st have been received. While full details of all these incidents are yet to be gathered. I learn from the Chief Minister that the situation at Aijal is now fully under control. The Commissioner of Silchar Division, the Inspector General of the Assam Rifles and a senior Army Officer have visited Aijal and made an on the spot assessment of the situation.[13]

Nanda continued his report as follows:

As a result of this, the Army has been asked to deal with the situation in Mizo Hill District. Transport of troops to Aijal by helicopter has been going on this morning and troops are also moving by road to Aijal and are expected to reach there by noon today. The armed police forces have been placed under the operational control of the Army for dealing with the disturbances. The Army will be in charge of the operation for as long as necessary in support of the civil administration. Curfew has been imposed and intensive patrolling has been started. The State Government issued a notification declaring Mizo Hill District area under the Armed Forces (Assam and Manipur) Disturbed Area Act and under the Assam Disturbed Areas Act. This confers special powers on the Armed

Forces and the State police. The report that a pirate radio is functioning inciting the Mizo tribals to declare independence and resort to lawlessness is being checked up. The Director General, All India Radio is arranging to monitor the transmission if any of the pirate radio and steps are being taken to find out the location of the transmitter if in fact it exists. There is enough evidence to come to the conclusion that these acts are part of a campaign by misguided extremist elements in the Mizo National Front to back their demand for independence. Government are determined to put down the disturbances with the utmost firmness and speed, and to restore peace and order. They are confident this will be achieved within a short period.[14]

Immediately on receipt of information about the out-break of violence in Mizoram, the government sent a team of officers, consisting of the commissioner of the division, the inspector general of police (Assam Rifles) and a senior officer of the army to Aizawl to study the situation on the spot and suggest ways and means to quell the rebellion. It suggested that the area should be handed over to the army. On 2 March 1966, the Government of Assam declared the district as a disturbed area. The army reached Aizawl on the evening of 6 March. The security forces gained complete control of the district headquarter, after which the army marched towards Lunglei but the town was completely under the control of the rebels. The army threatened to bomb it. The church leaders interfered and requested the army not to bomb the town and that they would secure its surrender. The troops entered Lunglei on 13 March, Champai on the next day and Demagri on 17 March. All the important towns and posts were cleared of the influence of the MNF armed forces. The MNF volunteers took to the jungles of Pakistan and Burma.

On 6 March 1966, the MNF was declared unlawful. The State Government air-dropped one lakh leaflets in the district to inform the people of the facts of the situation and warn them not to participate in any unlawful activities. The army took over the area and launched the counter-insurgency operation. The counter-insurgency combing operation of the Indian Army also followed a set pattern in all the three areas under discussion. On the strength of a tip off from the state intelligence official or local informers a particular village or a locality, where the insurgents had reportedly taken shelter, would be marked. Curfew would be imposed in the area all of a sudden in the early morning hours when everybody was asleep and no one could run away. The area then would be cordoned off and announcements made over loudspeakers that curfew had been imposed and no one should venture out of their houses. Then an operation would be launched to screen and frisk children, women and old people inside houses and the rest would be taken out in the open field where tents were built for interrogation through an identifier.[15] Occasionally, during such operations, encounters broke out between the insurgents and the army resulting in casualties.

THE GROUPING OF VILLAGES

The Indian State took its lessons in anti-insurgency measures from the British and the Americans in Malaya and Vietnam respectively. In fighting the Malayan Races Liberation Army in Malaya the British General Briggs had mooted what was known as Operation Starvation.[16] Its object was to deprive the guerrillas of their source of food and stop them from taking shelter in the villages. Besides imposing restrictions on the selling and distribution of food items, the army also rearranged the Chinese settlements and regrouped the tin and mine workers so as to check the infiltration and exfiltration of the guerrillas with the settled population. The population was no longer scattered. It was concentrated in units of 40,000 moved into just 400 villages, which made it easy to keep a strict watch over them.[17] The device was later tested by the Americans in Vietnam. Field Marshall Manekshaw advocated the application of the same in the insurgency affected areas of Nagaland and Mizoram[18] where the army did not have much success allegedly due to the cooperation of the villagers with the insurgents. Tarlok Singh, Member of the Planning Commission, visited Mizoram in 1966 and approved of the regrouping of villages euphemistically described as *economically viable villages*.[19] Replicating the arrangements made by the British and American armies in Malaya and Vietnam respectively, the Indian Army would move and surround the notified villages before dawn, issue quick notices to the villagers to take their bedding, etc., and move them to the new site. Here identity cards were issued to them and barricades constructed to restrict their movement. The old and abandoned villages with their granaries were then burnt. About 50 to 100 villages were initially shifted from their original sites and settled along the highway and placed under the charge of the army so that this can be kept isolated from the insurgents and a strict vigil can be maintained. Although the regrouping facilitated army operation it caused acute human trauma to the villagers.

In many instances villagers were forced to move out of their old dwellings at gun-point because they were reluctant to leave what had been their home for generations. In most cases the villagers had to leave on a day's notice. There was no time to pack their belongings and it was not possible to carry everything at one time. Animals had to be killed foodgrains had to be hidden in the forest. If there was no time to hide foodgrains they were burnt with the houses. As soon as the people left the place the army personnel ransacked the houses, valuables were kept for themselves and then burnt them down. Hidden foodgrains in the forest when discovered were taken away by the troops and hoarded or villagers were ordered to burn them.[20]

The regrouping not only drastically altered the settlement pattern of the Mizos, it had a substantial impact on their socio-economic and cultural life. Before the introduction of the scheme, there were 764 villages distributed in the three sub-divisions of Aizawl, Lunglei and Chhimtuipui excluding the two towns of Aizawl and Lunglei. Of these 764 villages 516 were evacuated and grouped into 110 grouping centres while 138 villages were excluded from the grouping scheme.[21] Thus, at the completion of the grouping of villages in 1970, the total number of villages in the districts had been reduced from 764 to 248. In the Aizawl sub-division alone the 456 villages before 1967 had been reduced to 112 villages involving a population of 1,88,923 or approximately 95 per cent of the rural population. One set of grouping took place along the Silchar-Aizawl-Lunglei Champai highway and another along the secondary Lunglei-Lawngtai-Selling Champai, Darhgawn-Bungzung-Khawbung-North Vanlaiphai Serchip Road. The grouping was done under four distinct categories: Protected and Progressive Villages, New Grouping Centres, Voluntary Grouping Centres and Extended Loop Areas. Although the Indian Government claimed that the grouping was necessary for the economic development of these distant villages, the operation was carried out under the Defence of India Rules, 1962 and Assam Maintenance of Public Order Act, 1953.

Such forcible resettlement shattered the very foundation of the economic and social structure of the Mizos. Excepting the areas where wet rice cultivation was practised (Bilkhawtlir, Champai, Thenzawl) the *jhoom* method of cultivation experienced total dislocation[22] because:

1. The amount of cultivable land had been drastically reduced as the ratio of people to land had been with the use of force vastly increased and the curfew compelled the villagers to cultivate those areas only which was within half-a-day's reach.

So that they could go to the field and come back home before the curfew hours.

2. *Jhoom* cultivation, the basic method of agriculture of the tribals became virtually impossible as *jhoom* went only with scattered habitation. To exacerbate the situation further the tribal institution of *tlawbawk*, a hut built near the *jhoom* for camping during harvesting and weeding, was abolished. Thus, villagers had to waste precious time in travelling to the fields and returning home for mid-day meals.
3. Harassment in the initial checking of identity cards and periodic curfews for collective interrogation or for re-checking identity cards further reduced working hours on the fields.
4. Male labourers on whom agriculture in Mizoram depended heavily were rounded up and sent off to work on border roads in Kashmir or were forced to act as porters for the troops during movement.
5. Access to the forest beyond the prescribed limits for vital additional food gathering was denied to the tribals by the army.
6. Since possession of even small arms were prohibited, hunting the only alternative during famines also became impossible. As a cumulative result there was a drastic fall in agricultural production and acute food shortage. Famine-like conditions were experienced through out 1968, 1969 and 1970. Landlessness emerged as a new phenomenon. In a resettled area where 400 families grouped, out of 100 persons 90 did not have any land. As a result the villagers became wholly dependent on the rations supplied by the government which was denied to them at will causing immense suffering. Soon there was a large scale migratory movement towards the towns of Aizawl and Lunglei where educated and pauperised people began to crowd around the white-collar employment sector.

VIOLATION OF HUMAN RIGHTS

Although the prime minister and the chief of the army staff claimed that the 'army had shown remarkable patience in the face of considerable provocation' human rights organizations reported widespread abuse of human rights in Mizoram, Nagaland and Manipur. As early as 1956 the army killed a veteran Naga physician Dr Haralu that sent shock waves throughout the Naga Hills. Prime

Minister Nehru himself admitted of the death of Dr Haralu during one of the army operations and described it as 'one of the most regrettable mistakes'.[23] Armed repression was gradually mounted. 'There was heavy deployment in the Tuensang area.' Gavin Young of the *London Observer* visited the Naga Hills from 20 February to 10 March 1960 to study army activities in the area and subsequently published his report in the form of a book entitled *The Nagas, An Unknown War—India's Threat to Peace*. As a result of such reports the Naga People's Movement for Human Rights was formed to campaign against the army excess in Naga Hills. In the Mizo Hills which was disturbed by the army atrocities, Brig. T. Sailo—an ex-armyman—set up the Human Rights Committee. In 1974, two public leaders from north-east India, G.G. Swell, MP and J.J.M. Nicholas-Roy, MLA prepared a report in the violation of human rights in the region and submitted it to the Indian Parliament.[24] According to these reports many forms of repression were used by the military and paramilitary forces: execution in public, mass raping, deforming of sex organs, mutilating limbs and body, electric shock, puncturing of eyes, hanging people upside down, putting people in smoke-filled rooms, burning down of houses, food-stocks and crops, concentration camps, suffocating a person by covering him fully with a dripping wet blanket, economic blockade, forced starvation, and forced labour.[25] The last one in this list was practised widely by the British in the Naga Hills while fighting to subdue the Nagas. Women were specially singled out; Indignities like rape, parading nude in the open and assaulting pregnant women were committed. The Human Rights Committee set up by Brig. T. Sailo collected detailed evidence on 36 cases of army atrocities ranging from rape and torture to execution listing the names and ranks of the army officers involved. The most shocking incident being the mass rape at Kolashib (1966):

> In Kolashib, 50 miles of Aizawl, the army rounded up all the menfolk of the village, about 500 of them. They were collected, made to lie down on the ground on their stomachs and then were kicked, beaten, trampled upon and confined for the night. At night groups of soldiers moved about the village. They broke into the houses, helped themselves with everything of value—clocks, sewing machines, clothes, etc . . . and raped the women.[26]

Another incident in the same village was the 'case of a woman in an advanced stage of pregnancy—Lalthumai wife of a cultivator, Lalkhangliana. Five soldiers appeared in her house one night, took the husband out of the house at gun-point and then while two soldiers held the woman down, the third committed rape'.[27]

Sailo's report created a furore in the Indian Parliament.[28] The pattern was all too similar in the Naga Hills. The Amnesty International, which also compiled a report on the human rights violations in the area recorded cases of sexual abuse by the Assam Rifles personnel and even knew their names.[29] At least three women complained of having been raped by a commanding officer. On 24 January 1986 Miss Luingmla was murdered by two army officers when she resisted rape. A belated general court martial was held on 11 July 1988 in which the main accused in the above case Lieutenant Mandhir Singh was sentenced to life imprisonment and cashiered for murder.[30] However, the army threatened and harassed the social workers who protested against this crime by taking recourse to the provisions of the Armed Force Special Power Act to deny jurisdiction of the Chief Judicial Magistrates Court which had taken cognizance of the crime (16 May 1986). A horrific incident took place in Oinam on 9 July 1987. Fifteen men were tortured to death by the Assam Rifles, another six died of continuous torture like starvation and standing in the open on one leg for the whole day. Six babies also died of starvation and lack of medical facilities.[31] Two pregnant women were forced to deliver their babies in full view of the *jawans*. About 125 houses were burnt or dismantled, valuables taken away and *jhoom* crops destroyed. On receiving complaints from some social workers the Guwahati High Court directed the Session Court in Imphal to record first-hand evidence from the villagers about the alleged offences by the Assam Rifles *jawans*. The Naga People's Movement of Human Rights moved a *habeas corpus* petition on behalf of the two women whose husbands were taken away by the 21 Sikh Regiment never to be returned.[32] The two men—a pastor and a school teacher—were reportedly not connected with insurgent activities. In a historic judgement in the *Sebastian Hongray* versus *Union of India Case* (*AIR*, 1984, SC 1626) the Supreme Court of India directed the army to pay Rs.1,00,000 in damages to each of the widows and directed the district superintendent of police to begin prosecuting the guilty army men. The Kohima Baptist Women's Union submitted a memorandum to the prime minister of India reporting such atrocities because they felt that the 'reports of such incidents that occur in our state' were not heard by him and that 'our moans and wails are muffled and lost in the deep gorges of thickly forested mountains in this part of the country':[33]

> We do not believe that the army officers were directed by the Government of India to act so. They seem to be here with the high and mighty attitude of the ancient barbarian conquerors. We pray that misdeed of a small section of the security forces must not be allowed to undermine the very basis of decent human existence and bring disrepute to the good name of the Indian army.[34]

The incident narrated here took place on 11 July 1971 when a strong column of the Maratha Regiment came to Yankeli, a village in the Wokha sub-division of the Mokokchung district of Nagaland, at about 6 p.m. They herded all the womenfolk into a house. Then the captain 'handpicked' four girls amongst the crowd who were taken to the church building. One Mr. Peleo was also taken along with the girls. Once inside the church, Peleo was sent back and a 17 year old girl named Shachano was stripped naked, her hands and legs were tied against the chair and after a brief interrogation she was taken to the pulpit and was raped by a captain and second lieutenant by turns. She was then led out, allowed to dress and sent away. The same treatment was meted out to Mseno, Sukrumo, and Tungteno aged 15, 12 and 11 respectively. In August 1977 Rano Saiza an MP from Nagaland narrated this incident to a shocked audience at a Convention of Political Prisoners in New Delhi while citing instances of human rights violations in the Naga Hills.[35] In the Matikhru village of Phek district the Indian Army rounded up all the menfolk, executed them, hounded the women out of the houses and then razed the villages down. Six Naga students of the Pfutsero Government School were kidnapped by the Indian Army and later reportedly butchered. In Ignasumi village a pregnant woman was shot at while harvesting in the field and her dead body was dragged along the jungle route. When the villagers went to retrieve her battered body they found it with the protruding head and limbs of the aborted baby. On 11 July 1977 the pregnant wife of a pastor was stoned and kicked so badly that the woman subsequently (30 July) suffered an abortion and a dead child with a broken skull was delivered. On 4 March 1977 a young girl was raped in Nagaprum village of Ukhrul district of Manipur by Major Pundir and Captain Negy of the 95 Border Security Force. The girl who was raped in front of the villagers subsequently committed suicide.

The army fury was worse if the insurgents killed any of the army personnel in an ambush. The army in such cases retaliated with a vicious and inhuman attack on the villagers to avenge the murder of their colleagues. In one such ambush 22 army *jawans* were killed by the NSCN on 19 February 1982; the retaliation was on the villagers of Ukhrul, the base of the insurgent organization. The villagers suffered untold atrocities at the hands of the rampaging army men.[36] At a Convention on Political Prisoners, the Naga human rights activist L. Luithui observed that 'The only freedom the Nagas know is the freedom to obey and submit to the military authorities. . . . But none of us love this freedom. We hate it bitterly because this freedom means the freedom to be insulted, tortured and raped in public. . . . In deep agony we wonder how all these things are going on in our land without any protest from the great Indian people. . . .'[37]

The army atrocities and the trauma caused to the people by the counter-insurgency measures have since become a part of the tribal folklore. There is a Naga folk song about an Angami girl who was raped by a member of the Indian Army which goes:

She was a happy child
She went out to the rice fields
Singing like a free bird. She was born of the rugged mountain.
But one day a soldier came to her land
She was tortured and raped
He took her dignity away
Her home is where she belongs
And she will rise up again to
Sing in glory and
Tell her people a new story.

The inhuman trauma caused to the tribals by regrouping of villages has been movingly captured in the following Mizo folk songs composed by the village bard Sukliana of Sialsuk:[38]

Pity of Pities, our villages are grouped
Everywhere in Zoram, life has lost its beauty
Women, Children, men gathered from every hill
Feel homeless and stranded like Riakmaw bird
In the new place where friends and loved ones gathered
I still pine for our old motherland (village)
where the gentle prince (God) who loves us also dwells.

I dare not contemplate this grief of our land
Departed are our civilized white skinned mentors
Oh, God, who succour the poor, I pray thee
set our tottering land on its feet again.

Silent are the countrysides and the Churches
where we lived and sang with our near and dear ones,
Lovely doves yearning for their mates haunt them now
and frequented by flock of birds they now lie forlorn.

O Lord, forgive us all our sins and trespasses
(which have caused us this uprootedness) guide us on,
Holy spirit, Zions fair flowers
Hold me with your powerful hand that bless men
Till I reach your sweet and bright heavenly homes.

POLICY OF ACCORDS

Neither in Nehru's time nor later did the military solution bear any substantial result; rather it succeeded in alienating the citizens who were not sympathetic to the rebels. Nehru observed that the military solution had landed in a 'deadlock and we should explore ways of getting out of it'.[39] In fact, Nehru was worried about the Nagas:

> This worry is not due so much to the military or other situations but rather to a feeling of psychological defeat. Why should we not be able to win them over. I do not like being pushed into repressive measures anywhere in India. . . . This long-drawn out business has a bad effect, both internationally and nationally and if I may say so, personally on me. I am, therefore, prepared to consider any reasonable approach to this problem which promises a settlement.[40]

By May 1957, a political settlement of the Naga problem had become urgent. With the world drifting towards war and a crisis developing in India's relations with Pakistan, it was risky to tie up a considerable portion of the army in the Naga area.[41] Not that the army operation had yielded any substantial result. On the contrary a number of Indian officers and troops were being killed in regular battles. As far as the Nagas were concerned, the army operation served to alienate the moderate citizens. Although Nehru made a defiant statement that 'it is fantastic to imagine that the Government of India is going to be terrorised into some action by Phizo and company',[42] privately he admitted that 'total suppression (of the Naga revolt) was out of question and partial suppression would serve only as an irritant . . . the Nagas are a tough and fine lot of people and we may carry on for a generation without solving the problem'.[43] In other words by this time Nehru and given up his optimism that the Naga movement would fizzle out in its own.[44] What was more serious, was the damage to India's image to the international community. Phizo's escape to England and the adverse publicity given to the Naga issued by Michael Scott and David Astor about the army atrocities in the Naga Hills was hurting India's image abroad. On his visit to London to the Conference of Commonwealth Prime Ministers, Nehru had already realized that the Naga problem along with Kashmir, was causing great harm to India's interest.[45] He was, therefore, willing to concede anything less than independence to the Nagas. His task was made easier by the people's initiative for peace in the Naga Hills.

PEOPLE'S MOVEMENT FOR PEACE IN NAGA HILLS

Nehru's visit to the north-east and his confession that the Naga situation had worsened due to its mishandling by certain unpopular local officials and 'a certain lack of confidence among the tribal folk' brought fresh hope of a solution to the Naga problem. But not only did he continue to underestimate the hold of Phizo over the Nagas, the Assam Government too continued to treat it as a mere law and order problem.

Meanwhile, the Naga commoners were caught in the fierce factional fights between the Naga insurgents and the Indian Army. To put an end to the continuous harassment and human trauma of the people the Nagas held a number public meetings, appealed to the underground Nagas as well as the Indian Government and distributed leaflets for peace. A Naga delegate met the Assam chief minister to request him to make efforts for peace. Sensing the peoples' mood and desire for peace the moderate element which had been marginalized due to Phizo's rise tried to recapture the NNC leadership. This section of the leadership found immediate approval from the traumatized Naga people and propelled them to go ahead with the peace efforts. These moderates formed a Reform Committee within the NNC, under the chairmanship of Thepfulo Nakhro (T.N. Angami). The committee issued a statement on the 18 February 1957 opposing violence, military methods and pledged to restore peace and order by trying to win over the 'hostiles'. It also expressed its confidence in the prime minister's assurances and desired the establishment of a separate administrative unit for the Nagas within the Indian Constitution which would protect and preserve the Naga customs and traditions. It also agreed to send its representative to the Indian Parliament. Accordingly it sent Khelhoshe, Chubatemsu and Subedar Satsuo to fill the three Assam Legislative Assembly seats for the Naga Hills uncontested in India's second general election. This trend continued with the forming of the Naga People's Convention which included about 1765 traditional representatives of the different Naga tribes belonging to the Naga Hills as well as the Tuensang area, and about 2,000 observers from other Naga areas. The convention was held in Kohima from 22 to 26 August 1957 under the chairmanship of Dr Imkongliba which unanimously endorsed that:

> Being deeply grieved by the killings and the widespread sufferings caused by burning of houses and granaries the destruction of crops, grouping of villages, restriction of freedom of movement and speech, forced labour without payment, the resultant diseases and hunger, we, a convention of the Naga people, drawn from every tribe and area of the territories now known as the Naga Hills district of Assam and the Tuensang Frontier division of NEFA, having met in Kohima on the 22 August 1957, in search of a solution to end the infinite sufferings and bloodshed, do hereby resolve as follows:
>
> We maintain that the only answer to the Naga question is a satisfactory political settlement. In as much as a large number of our people are still underground and there is no freedom of movement and speech under the present conditions in the Naga Hills district, we feel no full discussions can be held among the people preliminary to negotiations. . . .[46]

The convention desired that the Naga Hills district of Assam and Tuensang Frontier division of the North-Eastern Frontier Agency (NEFA) along with the reserved forests—transferred out of the Naga Hills district after the reforms of 1921—should be constituted into a single administrative unit under the External Affairs Ministry of the Government of India with the governor of Assam acting in his discretion as the agent of the president of India, 'so as to ensure with our active help, a genuine, general amnesty, speedy end of hostilities and relief to suffering'.[47]

It also appealed to the armed Nagas to give up violence, and sent 'prayers' to all men of goodwill, both underground and overground and in government services to work towards a lasting and honourable peace in the Naga Hills.

However, during the deliberations at the convention, the pro-hostiles and moderates quarrelled over the phrase 'within the Indian Union' which the latter wanted to incorporate so that the convention's opposition to the demand for independence became apparent. At last, the imbroglio was resolved in a compromise resolution, which was passed on 26 August and sent to the governor of Assam. The governor who was already aware of the positive developments sent a goodwill message a day earlier to the convention which said: 'if delegates really desire satisfactory political settlement and ending of Naga trouble, as I am sure they do, the resolution must clearly state that political settlement will be within the Union of India. Any settlement to be practical and acceptable must be within the Indian Union. It will also be, as far as I can see, in the best interests of the Naga people in whom we are all interested. I have great hope in the collective wisdom and practical sense of the assembled delegates.'[48]

The convention also elected a nine-member delegation headed by its president, Dr Imkongliba to continue political negotiations with the Government of India, at the Centre.

As recommended by the Assam Governor, Fazl Ali the nine-member delegation met and presented the convention's resolutions to Prime Minister Jawaharlal Nehru in New Delhi between 23 and 25 September 1957.[49] While Prime Minister Nehru objected to the concept and practicability of an overall sovereign independent Nagaland, he promptly consented to the immediate demand for a separate Naga administration that would no longer be part of Assam, but under the Central Government. He also announced that the Centre would grant amnesty to the rebels, 'in respect of all offences committed against the State in the past', though the amnesty would not cover future offences.[50] He also gave an assurance that the necessary amendments to the Constitution would be considered by Parliament during its next session in November-December 1957.

The bill for amendment of the Sixth Schedule of the Constitution was introduced by the Home Minister, G.B. Pant in the Lok Sabha on 20 November 1957 and passed on 25 November. It was subsequently passed by the Rajya Sabha on 28 November and received the assent of the President, Dr Rajendra Prasad on 29 November. Thus, the Naga Hills-Tuensang Area Act, 1957 was passed by the Parliament of India. Speaking of the bill, Pant said that although for a territory of 3,50,000 people, with an annual revenue of less than Rs.40,000 to aspire to full independence was not feasible in the modern world the Central Government had taken all steps to fulfil the assurances given by Nehru to the Naga delegation in September.

According to this Act, from 1 December 1957, the Naga Hills district of Assam and the Tuensang Frontier division of NEFA covering an area of 6,236 sq. miles with a population of about 3,69,000 living in 718 villages were constituted into a single administrative unit.

The Select Committee of the convention then set out to plan the future of Naga Hills on the basis of the assurances given by the prime minister. It met on 11 and 12 December 1958 and appointed a Drafting Committee, which thrashed out a 16-Point Plan culminating in the decision to establish a Nagaland state within the Indian Union.

The underground Nagas strongly objected to these developments, yet undeterred the convention stood by their demand for a Nagaland state. In fact, the third convention of the Naga People held in Mokokchung from 22 to 26 October 1959 not only approved of the Draft Constitution but also appealed to the underground to accept the government's offer of amnesty and cooperate with the proposed new government of Nagaland. The convention set up a committee to mediate between the underground Nagas and the Central Government.

In pursuance of the resolution of the Third Naga People's convention a delegation of 15 Naga leaders headed by Dr Imkonliba, the president of the convention entered into an agreement with the Central Government on 30 July 1960 for the establishment of a Naga state within the Indian Union.

There were serious objections to the grant of statehood to the Nagas from members of the Jan Sangh as well as the Assamese politicians. The Chief Minister of Assam, Bishnu Ram Medhi even threatened to resign if the administration of Naga Hills was taken away from the Assam Government.[51] Fazl Ali, the Assam Governor also felt that granting statehood would be a show of weakness on the part of the Government of India.[52]

Undeterred, the Nagaland Statehood Bill was introduced on 28 August by the prime minister in the Lok Sabha and was also debated on the same day. In the Rajya Sabha the bill was passed on 3 September 1962. It received the president's assent on 4 September as a result of which Nagaland became the sixteenth state of the Indian Union with a number of protective measures for its people. These measures included the provision that no act of Parliament in respect to the religious or social practices of the Nagas, Naga customary laws and procedure, ownership and transfer of land and its resources would apply to the state of Nagaland unless the Nagaland Legislative Assembly so decided. An interim body looked after the administration till Nagaland was formally inaugurated as the sixteenth state of the Indian Union by President Dr Radhakrishnan in Kohima on 1 December 1963.

DECLINE OF UNDERGROUND REBELS

The peace activities of the Naga People's Convention which was a peoples movement was enough reason for Phizo to panic. It was clear that the traumatized Naga people were willing to settle for less than sovereignty for peace, which meant a dwindling support base of Phizo and the underground Nagas. Indeed, the support for Phizo as well as the underground recorded a massive decline since the beginning of peace efforts. By 1962, it had progressively declined to its lowest point from which Phizo was never able to recover. This decline was inevitable due to the resurgence of the moderate leadership and a sharp rise in factionalism among the underground rebels. The convention's defiance of Phizo's leadership and its efforts for a Nagaland state within the Indian Union greatly disturbed him. On 30 July 1960 he issued a statement from London, where he had been granted political asylum, that the Naga struggle had been for 'a completely sovereign, independent Naga state having international recognition' not for any constituent state within the Indian Union. At best, he felt that Nagaland could have a treaty relationship with India on the basis of equality and reciprocity. He denounced the Naga People's Convention as a 'puppet assembly', and declared that any agreement entered into by this convention regarding the future of Nagaland could not be recognized. According to him, the only persons authorized to enter into any agreement were those who were fighting for the Naga cause and hence were the true representative of the Naga people. Denouncing the proposal of a Nagaland state he said,

> In occupied France, Norway, Belgium, there also came 'moments when responsible people chose co-operation instead of futile warfare'. They were tragic moments, laying up a store of hatred, division and bitterness for the future. Just as the mass of the people of those countries wished the struggle to end in their country's total liberation, so do the Naga People Convention who have signed an agreement with India for statehood within the Indian Union are well-meaning people driven to a desperate and short-sighted manoeuvre by the years of suffering and massacre which India has inflicted on Nagaland. Far from denouncing these men, I have appealed to the Nagas to forgive them for the betrayal they have foolishly brought about. The Naga people will not accept the Indian bribe of statehood, nor India's offer of 'internal autonomy' as something to be eulogized: it is only a means to conceal her heinous crime against humanity. Neither Nagaland nor India can honestly work it out in good faith, which could bring about full independence.[53]

To reactivate the underground movement as retaliation to the peace process the Federal Government stepped up its guerrilla activities in Naga-inhabited areas of Assam, Manipur and Burma. The Indian armed forces too tightened their belts to counter it. The rebels attacked the railways in Assam, which constituted a threat to the state's food supply. All trains had now to be protected by military escorts. The guerrillas shot down an IAF Dakota on 26 August 1960 and captured four crewmen 'to demonstrate, through physical violence, their disapproval of the Government of India's agreement with the Naga People's Convention'.[54]

Phizo's denunciation and the activation of the underground movement however had little impact on the peace process. In fact, the interim body of the Nagaland state declared in its fourth session that Phizo had no right to speak for the Nagas since he had become a British citizen in 1962 and even went to the extent of describing him as a man 'condemned by his own people and the law of the land'. Sensing the hostility of his own people towards him and his waning base even in the rank and file of the underground Nagas Phizo wrote to the Government of India offering to fight against the Chinese who had just declared war on India attacking its north-east frontier. In return, at the end of the war, Phizo wanted India to grant sovereignty to the Nagas, which the Government of India was, prompt to reject. Phizo followed this proposal with another letter through Michael Scott to Nehru (21 February 1963) seeking to meet him. Nehru in turn referred the letter to the Nagaland Executive Council which felt that though there was no harm in meeting Phizo, but this might not be the most appropriate and propitious time for it. Nehru therefore replied to Phizo through the Indian High Commission in London expressing his willingness to meet him provided the rebels would stop all violent activities forthwith and surrender their arms whose rehabilitation would be the responsibility of the Indian Government. Phizo replied to Nehru proposing that Rev Michael Scott should be permitted to meet the NNC to ask them to observe a ceasefire from 14 April 1963 and that a similar ceasefire instruction should be given to the Indian armed forces. The Naga Executive Council headed by Shilu Ao however objected to Scott's visit to the Naga Hills and denounced Phizo's proposal as being 'vague' and did not recognize the present status of Nagaland. Seizing the opportunity the Government of India in reply to Phizo's letter stated that:

> Willingness to work with the people of Nagaland state within the present constitutional arrangements . . . and to co-operate in the maintenance of law and order as the essential preliminaries to any further constructive steps for rapprochement between the underground hostiles . . . and the people of Nagaland. If, as he states, Phizo shares the general desire to restore peace and normalcy in Nagaland, he can immediately advise all those indulging in hostile activities . . . to give up violence, release those they have kidnapped, and be prepared to come overground, surrender their arms, and get rehabilitated as normal citizens of Nagaland. After such a statement is issued by Phizo, the Government of Nagaland will make a policy declaration indicating the nature and extent of rehabilitation and resettlement facilities they are prepared to give to those who come overground. . . . The Government of India . . . will at the same time issue instructions to the security forces not to take any punitive action against those who have stopped all violent activities.[55]

Thus, the Government of India's reply handed over to Rev Scott on 20 April 1963 had offered the rebels an amnesty and rehabilitation if they ceased hostilities and surrendered their weapons.

Phizo's statement in London on 8 May 1963 that the government's demand for 'unconditional surrender' was unacceptable[56] however brought an end to the peace process initiated by the underground and again it was left to the civilians to renew the peace efforts. In the same spirit the underground elements operating in the Naga Hills also declared that the 16-point agreement signed with the Naga People's Convention was not acceptable to them. They newly created Nagaland state within the Indian Union was dismissed as a *puppet state*. There was also a rise in the number of militants among the younger elements of the NNC. The vacuum created by the sudden exit of Phizo to London as a British citizen without proper organization of the movement was thus filled by those who were not only critical of the 16-point agreement but also of him.

INSURGENCY TO ACCORD IN MIZO HILLS

A three-member Mizo Union deputation met the Prime Minister on 22 June 1966, and informed him that the Assam Chief Minister Chaliha must be held responsible for the outbreak of insurgency in the Mizo Hills district. They questioned Chaliha's propriety releasing Laldenga and demanded the formation of the state of Mizoram.[57]

From 15 September 1966 onwards the MNF resumed its armed attacks. About 100 Mizo hostiles attacked the police station at Jairampunji in the Cachar district bordering the Mizo Hills district with rifles, grenades and automatic weapons. Three constables died in this encounter. Such ambushes continued up until 1970.

After the liberation of Bangladesh, the Mizo hostiles had to leave their sanctuary in East Pakistan. Some took shelter in the jungles of Arakan and then infiltrated into the Mizo Hills district to murder the loyalists.[58] This was facilitated by the government's removal of some of the restrictions imposed on the free movement of citizens. It enabled the hardcore elements in the MNF to terrorize the people loyal to the Indian Government and the administration.

In December 1971, Bangladesh was liberated which resulted in the virtual collapse of the MNF. The Chittagong Hills in Bangladesh had served as an excellent sanctuary for the MNF. It was from this area that the Mizo hostiles launched their attacks against the security forces. East Pakistan was also the perennial source of supply of arms and ammunition to the Mizo insurgents. Once these sources were lost, the MNF was demoralized and the insurgents in large numbers came out of their hideouts and accepted the rehabilitation benefits offered by the government. Laldenga with his family left Dacca, went to Burma and from there went to Islamabad in West Pakistan.

In 1974, however, the hard-core members of the MNF regrouped their forces to launch an attack on the Indian security forces from the hill tracts of Burma, Arakan and Chittagong.[59] Some of the MNF members infiltrated into Mizoram and collected funds forcibly, and recruited volunteers of both the sexes and terrorized and intimidated the loyalists. To hoodwink the government, the MNF proposed talks for the solution to the Mizo problem. The government, in good faith, sent a military helicopter to fly the MNF representatives from their hideouts. Malsawma Colney came to Aizawl for talks. While the talks continued for about a month, preparations were underway for an attack on the Indian security forces. Nothing came out of the talks, and Colney returned to his hideout in the Arakan Hills in Burma.

The MNF even had ambushed the convoy of the Lieutenant Governor of Mizoram and injured him. But the most daring act was one that occurred in broad daylight in the heart of Aizawl town. On 13 January 1975, the MNF desperadoes, entered the police headquarters in the heart of the Aizawl town and shot dead the inspector general, deputy inspector general and superintendent of police when they were in conference and quickly drove away into the near jungle. This brutal act shocked the nation. It created the impression that the MNF was the *de facto* ruler in Mizoram. The

Government of India was rudely shaken. The home minister accompanied by the senior officers of the Home Department arrived at Aizawl and reorganized the administrative machinery. A new group of police officials were brought into replace those that had been assassinated. And an able police officer was appointed as the chief secretary, which was an unusual practice and a tough policy, but was adopted to deal with the underground forces. These measures were effective. The security forces and the police launched a vigorous campaign against the MNF. Among the assassins of the three police officers all but one were shot dead and later the lone absconder was also nabbed. Large quantities of arms and ammunition were seized and 266 MNF volunteers were captured.[60]

All these measures disabled the MNF and its leader Laldenga. Under these circumstances Laldenga offered peace talks. New Delhi readily agreed to the proposal.

Laldenga arrived in New Delhi on 24 January 1976, and the talks began on 11 February. On 18 February the MNF and the Government of India arrived at an understanding. The MNF delegation agreed to instruct its members to stop all hostilities, to collect all underground personnel with their arms and ammunition in mutually agreed camps, and had over the arms and ammunition within one month. The Government of India agreed to provide suitable subsidy for the maintenance of the camps and to suspend all operations by the security forces.[61]

The MNF Emergency Convention was held from 24 March to 4 April in Calcutta. The convention accepted the agreement of 18 February and authorized the president of the MNF to negotiate with the Government of India. Accordingly negotiations were held and on 1 July 1976 an agreement was arrived at, according to which the rebels were to abjure violence and continue talks for an amicable settlement.[62]

The agreement was widely welcomed by the people of Mizoram who were anxious for peace and tranquility in their fatherland. The Government of Mizoram celebrated the event by declaring 7 July 1976 as a Thanksgiving Day. Church bells rang throughout Mizoram and prayers were offered. The Chief Minister of Mizoram Chhunga declared that all those interested in coming back to the mainstream of national life would be welcomed with open arms and rehabilitated as far as possible.

But this happiness was short-lived. The agreement was not acceptable to a number of the underground rebels. Laldenga was in a fix. To salvage the situation he said that it was not an agreement but an understanding. At the same time he sent tape recorded speeches to his followers in Mizoram asking them not to surrender arms and ammunition and personnel to the authorities because the basic problem was yet to be settled.

Meanwhile, the MNF hostilities continued, and the government launched vigorous military operations against them. Cornered Laldenga again pleaded with the Home Ministry for suspension of counter-insurgency operations agreeing to solve the problem within the framework of the Indian Constitution. Accordingly military operations were suspended in December 1976. But there was no progress in negotiations. Amidst all this there was a change of government at the Centre in 1977. The new home minister summoned Laldenga and asked him to state clearly the MNF demands for settlement. Laldenga evaded the issue by handing over charge to the Mizo National Council. Sensing his waning base and his cunning tactics Laldenga was accused of anti-Indian activities and was directed to leave the country by 6 July 1977.[63] This intimidated Laldenga who felt that he was losing his bargaining position. He met Prime Minister Morarji Desai and agreed that the implementation of July agreement and peace talks should go on simultaneously.[64]

Accordingly Laldenga drafted a scheme for the implementation of the agreement and sent it to the MNF headquarters. The MNF headquarters modified the scheme but the modifications were not acceptable to the Government of India. Talks collapsed again and Laldenga was asked again to leave the country by 21 November 1977. An anxious Laldenga who was well aware of Phizo's plight—who had lost his following during his exile in London—had no intention of leaving India. Since it was important for Laldenga to stay in the country he wrote to the Home Ministry promising to solve the Mizo problem and to implement the July agreement by 26 January 1978. But he demanded statehood for Mizoram with himself as the chief minister of an interim government. He also demanded that the Mizoram Legislative Assembly elections to be held in 1977 be stopped. The Government of India rejected the demands and the talks broke down. The government had found Laldenga to be undependable and directed him again to leave the country on 26 November 1977. But Laldenga was not prepared to leave the country. So he wrote to the Home Ministry on 14 November 1977 promising to lay down arms and ammunition unconditionally and that the surrender of the MNF personnel would be completed by 26 January 1978. The Government of India allowed him to stay. Laldenga instructed the MNF headquarters that it should lay down arms and ammunition unconditionally at suitable places.[65]

The MNF National Council refused to agree to these proposals.[66] Instead they invited Laldenga to the headquarters for discussion. The Government of India allowed him to go to the headquarters but he refused. Instead he wrote to Tlangchhuaka on 25 February 1978 and sent it through Zoramthanga. But Zoramthanga was arrested at Champai and brought back to Delhi as he was suspected of carrying instructions contrary to the contents of the letter addressed to Tlangchhuaka. On 20 March 1978, the home minister announced in the Lok Sabha that he was breaking off his talks with Laldenga as the latter could not be trusted.[67] Laldenga was arrested along with his son and was chargesheeted for waging war against the Government of India. Subsequently when the Janata Government at the Centre fell and the Congress party under the leadership of Indira Gandhi came back to power, charges against Laldenga were dropped and negotiations for a peaceful settlement of the Mizo problem were renewed.

Although the MNF suspended their terrorist activities after the ceasefire, there was no surrender of the volunteers, arms and ammunition. On the other hand, the MNF continued to recruit volunteers and collect taxes. It succeeded in infiltrating into the Students' Associations. Student riots took place, educational institutions were burnt down and state transport buses were destroyed on 28 October 1981.

The talks meanwhile continued in New Delhi between G. Parthasarathy, Mrs Gandhi's emissary and Laldenga. The list of 23 demands put forward by Laldenga included full statehood for Mizoram; special constitutional provisions guaranteeing the state complete autonomy; dismissal of the Sailo Government, dissolution of the Mizoram Legislative Assembly; appointment of a council of advisers to the Lieutenant Governor headed by Laldenga himself, pending fresh elections; inclusion of all the areas inhabited by the Mizos even those that were part of other states of the Indian Union and independent countries like Burma and Bangladesh; a separate flag for Mizoram; membership for Mizoram in the UN; and a separate university for Mizoram. The government agreed to grant statehood to Mizoram and a separate university for Mizoram, but rejected the other demands. The Government of India also insisted that the Lieutenant Governor should have the power to control finance, law and order and also internal security. Interestingly the Mizoram unit of the Congress also supported some of the MNF demands, particularly the dismissal of the Sailo ministry of the People's Convention Party.[68] The Government of India was intrigued by the frequent changes in Laldenga's attitudes. Therefore, on 12 January 1982, it terminated the talks, and declared the MNF and its military wing as unlawful. The official announcement accused the MNF that:

> It had openly declared as its objective the formation of independent Mizoram, comprising the Union Territory of Mizoram and the adjacent Mizo and Kuki inhabited areas of Assam, Manipur and Tripura; has been continuing its activities to achieve the end and bring about secession of the said areas from the Union of India. It has been employing an armed force, the so-called Mizo National Army and other bodies set up by it. In furtherance of this objective, it has been attacking the security forces, civil government and civilian forces.[69]

On 22 January 1982, the home minister said that Laldenga had used the talks as a cover to undermine the lawfully constituted authority in Mizoram and that he was intransigent in his attitude and had never wished to settle the matter. Laldenga was ordered to leave the country.[70]

As expected Laldenga, who was exiled in London, offered peace talks in 1985 when a new popular government was installed at the Centre under Rajiv Gandhi.[71] The Government of India agreed and invited him for talks, which continued and on 23 December 1985, an agreement was signed on the constitutional aspects. On 25 June 1986, a political agreement was signed in New Delhi by Arjun Singh, the then vice president of the AICC(I) and Laldenga. According to the agreement, the then existing Congress(I) Ministry in the state was to be dissolved and an Interim Coalition Ministry was to be formed consisting of the MNF and the Congress, headed by Laldenga. The MNF would have four seats and the Congress(I) five. The then Chief Minister Lalthanhawla was to be the Deputy Chief Minister.[72]

The main accord was signed on 20 June 1986, by R.D. Pradhan, the Union Home Secretary on behalf of the Government of India, Laldenga on behalf of the MNF and Lalkhama the Chief Secretary of the Mizoram Government on behalf of the Mizoram Government.[73]

THE MEITHEIS: IDEOLOGICAL METAMORPHOSIS

While serving a sentence as a RGM activist in Tripura Jail, N. Bisheswar came in contact with the Naxalites who were also serving jail terms. He was indoctrinated by them in the Marxist-

Leninist and Maoist ideologies. By the time Bisheswar came out of the jail he was total a convert to Maoist ideas.[74] Back in Manipur Bisheswar reorganized his group and led a 20-member Meithei youth delegation to China, which left Imphal on 16 April 1976.[75] This group underwent training in guerrilla warfare as well as ideological indoctrination in Maoist ideas in Lasha during April 1976 and February 1978. Complete with armed training and ideological indoctrination, this group under its chief Bisheswar set up a new outfit known as the People's Liberation Army (PLA) in September 1978 and burst into Manipuri politics 'signalling a continuity' after a 'lull in the hotspot'.[76] The PLA professed to be a military organization, which believed in the Maoist line of thought and action. It announced the dissolution of the ten-year old RGM and of reorganizing the group into a strong party representing all nationalities and the broad interests of the masses. The PLA charged the RGM of representing 'reactionary Meithei chauvinism' and described themselves an 'advanced, progressive section who believed in Marxism-Leninism-Mao Tse Tung thoughts'.[77] It declared that the 'political line' of the RGM was wrong and therefore had failed to represent the interest of the majority of the Manipuri people and other nationalities.[78]

Due to this radical change in ideology, insurgency was resurrected in the Imphal Valley. With the granting of statehood to Manipur and the euphoria over it, the memory of RGM had faded from the mind of the people till this trained group started its activity. The intelligence outfit of the Government of India already had information about the presence of some young radical elements in Imphal. But somehow they had given them the slip while others had been intercepted at Siliguri in north Bengal. By June 1978, the PLA had consolidated its urban cells. But it did not possess any sophisticated weapons.[79] Some of their leading men had country made pistols and a small quantity of hand grenades. Therefore, the PLA's first task was to concentrate on acquiring weapons. Almost simultaneously, they had to get the necessary finance to sustain the movement. Accordingly they made the first move to accomplish their goal on 29 June.[80] A couple of boys snatched the pistol from an unwary might patrol soldier of the Manipur Rifles, and shot him with it and fled. The second incident occurred on 17 July. A sub-inspector and a constable, escorting a prisoner to the court, were gunned down in broad daylight on the main highway leading to the airport. The police officer was on a bicycle and the constable in a rickshaw with the prisoner when they were ambushed at point-blank range. While both the policemen died, the boys vanished with the inspector's service revolver. On the following day, a branch of the United Bank of India was looted by a group of boys who decamped with Rs.20,000. On 19 July a passenger bus was attacked at a stop, killing a soldier and snatching away some arms and ammunition.

With this spurt in violence and crime Imphal was jerked awake. This was the first time after many years that a systematic wave of violence was rocking the valley. The Imphal Valley was declared as a 'disturbed area' two days (21 July 1978) after these incidents. Condemning the declaration, *Resistance*, the organ of the Pan-Manipuri Youth League observed that: 'This action is unprecedented in Manipur which had witnessed the armed peasant movement under the leadership of Hizam Irabat in the early fifties, the violent activities of the Meithei state committee which continued up to mid-sixties and the incipient insurgency of the so-called Revolutionary Government of Manipur in the late sixties.'[81] Another newspaper in Imphal compared the government's reaction to using a sledge hammer to kill a fly.[82]

But the security network had discerned a pattern behind the violent activities of the young people. An estimated fifty of these young radicals were believed to be engaged in the hit and run raids in the valley. That they were divided into small groups of two to three boys to elude the police was also obvious. The sense of fear and insecurity was almost total in the valley. There was also a growing gap of communication between the government and the people. Most people, both among the younger and the older generations, were steeped in corruption which earlier was unknown to the valley. The state had large numbers of educated-unemployed youths who were angry because jobs could only be obtained through bribes:

> These boys were rebelling against the fossilised first generation leaders who seemed too stubborn to change their old ways thereby producing increasing distrust among young radicals yearning for a change. And in an environment of growing violence, the leaders of the extremist factions were busy formulating the theoretical line and making it known to the people. What compounded the situation was that besides an underground movement, a growing campaign was soon discerned against the *mayangs* or outsiders.[83]

For the first time in the history of insurgency in the valley it was clear that unlike previous occasions this spate of violence was well-planned. It was systematic, perfect and regular. In all the incidents the civilians were not attacked or hurt—only those representing the state were killed or hurt. It restored the confidence of the panic-stricken civilians but the government was alert. There was a simultaneous campaign against the government not only by the PLA mouthpiece *The Dawn* and its pamphlets but also by newspapers like PANMYL's *Resistance*. The *Resistance* compared the Lynda Airport massacre to 'Munich Tragedy' and described the assassinations as 'Naxalite annihilation of class enemies'.[84] It observed that 'while the culprits stand condemned by their inhuman action, the government cannot escape responsibility for having forced the youths into such extreme postures of protest', and that 'the seeds of rebellion lies in the misdeeds of the government and its allies in exploitation. The wonder is why the people have tolerated it for so long.'[85] However with the declaration of Imphal as a disturbed area and the promulgation of the Armed Forces Special Power Act, 1958, combing operations were started beginning in the southern part of the valley. *Resistance* reacted to this action of the government wondering 'whether the government was justified in rushing for the hammer or it was a case of panic by a government which have become strangers to the people they were supposed to serve will be answered by history'.[86] Weighed down under popular pressure the government withdrew the orders on 1 August. But the rebels struck again on 18 November when they raided the Imphal police station. This was followed by the assassination of Sudhir Kumar, Bisheswar's former chief who was described as a counter-revolutionary and as being pro-establishment. This was followed by a spate of murders, assassinations, gun-snatching and arm-gathering, ambush and encounter with the state army for almost a year. The state had to be declared a disturbed area once again in 8 September 1980 and the army was deployed for the first time in Manipur to deal with the Meithei insurgency. Over and above this a separate 'M' (Mike) sector was opened specifically to counter the Meithei insurgency and conduct counter-insurgency operations.[87] The state was virtually under army rule with curfew, ambush, encounters being the order of the day. By the middle of 1982, about 1089 extremists were arrested, 80 security men, 97 alleged extremists and 93 civilians were killed; Rs.13.2 lakh were looted; and 252 extremists surrendered to the government. The PLA accounted for 341 of the arrested extremists, 45 out of the 62 extremists were killed by security personnel, 7 were killed by enraged villagers and 9 by rival factions and 28 out of the 251 surrendered. On 6 July 1981 PLA chief Bisheshwar himself was captured by armymen at Tekcham, a hamlet about 30 km from Imphal after a heavy encounter.

But on 9 August 1981,[88] 12 top-ranking PLA activists fled from the Imphal Central Jail in a daring jail break-out. This was followed by another jail break-out on 11 January 1982 when 22 extremists made a great escape by digging a 27 m long tunnel. In addition 22 army personnel were killed in an ambush by the PLA-NSCN joint attack on 14 February 1982. But the army struck back on 13 April 1982 by killing Ojha (a reverential mode of address used by PLA activists for their leaders) Kunjabihari along with 12 members of the PLA in a bloody operation.[89]

Kunjabiharis death following Bisheshwar's arrest was a severe setback for the PLA. The leadership crisis led to the rise of factions within the organization. The new chairman Manikanta assuming office on 17 April, faced hostility from other aspirants.[90] One such individual Temba, the last of the Lasha trained members wrested power from Manikanta on 8 June 1982 and took over as the new chairman. By the end of 1982, and early 1983, about 50 more guerrillas, this time including females undertook a long march to China through the Kachin forest in northern Burma.[91] The long march was undertaken to boost the fading image and strength of the PLA by acquiring arms and training in China. In addition, the image and position of the new chairman Temba required consolidation. But the most serious blow to the PLA movement came when the founder chairman Bisheshwar and three of his colleagues decided to participate in the Assembly election held on 27 December 1984.[92]

Many theories have been forwarded to explain the reason why the PLA chief chose to participate in the democratic political processes of the Indian State against which he had been fighting for so long. The most plausible being the crucial illness that he had suffered during his imprisonment and his reluctance to continue in jail in that condition.[93] His fading youth and the crumbling strength of the PLA against the might of the Indian State too must have influenced his decision. But there were sharp reactions to this decision from many quarters where he was regarded as a charismatic leader. His PLA colleagues initially reserved their comments though a new chief had taken over the organization, but the RGM colleagues termed it as going back on his stand of liberating the Manipuris. Others felt that Bisheshwar had something else in mind behind this 'capitulation'.[94] Bisheshwar defended himself saying that it was an attempt to bridge the gap between Indians who were free and those still in bondage. He said that his participation in election was not a change in his stand or ideology, but mere change in strategy. 'Change of policy', he said, 'should not be equated with change in our stand but be regarded as a case of changing means to achieve our, goal.' Of the four PLA men who contested the Assembly elections from jail, two emerged victorious. Bisheshwar from Thongju constituency and Deven from Lamsang constituency. Subsequent to their victory, they were released from jail. But Bisheshwar's participation in the election did not bring any tangible result: neither did it bring any negotiation between the state and the insurgents nor did it end insurgency in the valley. If anything, it worsened. However, even when they were still in jail Bisheshwar along with Deven, Ibochomba and Shyam formed a political party—the Democratic Independent Front (DIF)—implicitly indicating that it was still a wing of the PLA. The DIF general secretary said that, 'Though ideologically the party is still guided by the tenets of Marxism-Leninism, it would try to achieve their goal politically within the framework of Indian Constitution.'[95] As an organization the DIF announced that the 'insurgents have decided to change their line of battle from bullet to ballot to achieve their objective of a Manipur free of corruption and injustice, within the framework of the Indian Constitition'.[96]

RENEWAL OF PEACE EFFORTS: THE SHILLONG ACCORD

The creation of Nagaland as a state neither brought the desired peace in the hill areas nor ended what had come to be known as 'insurgency' by now. Though it was coined by the Indian State it soon caught on as a description of the Naga underground movement. The people of Nagaland along with Church leaders again took the initiative to end the bloodshed and bring about peace in the state through an understanding between the underground Nagas and the Indian Government both of whom seemed to be adamant.

In a convention held at Wokha on 24 February 1964 the Nagaland Baptist Church leaders urged the Government of India and the Federal Government of Nagaland to form a Peace Mission. The convention nominated B.P. Chaliha the then Chief Minister of Assam, Jayaprakash Narayan the noted Sarvodaya leader, Shankar Rao Deo and Rev Michael Scott, a British citizen to explore ways and means for the restoration of peace and normalcy in Nagaland. Shankar Rao Deo, however, declined the offer, and the Peace Mission was composed of only three members.

The first task of the Peace Mission was to negotiate for a ceasefire between the Government of India and the underground Nagas.

The ceasefire came into force with effect from 6 September 1964. Meanwhile, negotiations for a political settlement between the Government of India and the underground, called 'peace talks' began on 23 September 1964 at Chedema Peace Camp. These peace talks consisted of two phases: the first, at the government level as many as seven rounds of talks were held; the second, at the ministerial level spread over six rounds of talks. During the first phase, the Indian delegation was represented by Y.D. Gundevia the then Foreign Secretary, N.G. Santok, Deputy Secretary in the External Affairs Ministry, U.N. Sharma and Shilu Ao the Chief Minister of Nagaland. The inclusion of Shilu Ao was vehemently objected to by the underground Nagas on the ground that they did not recognize the Nagaland State Government. However, after much persuasion Shilu Ao was later allowed to attend the talks as an 'observer' from the Indian Government's side. The Naga Federal Government was represented by Isac Swu, the foreign secretary, Zashi Huire, governor (Ang) and Brigadier Thinuselie of the Naga army.

Since the underground stood firmly by their demand of sovereignty and the Government of India insisted on a solution within the Indian Constitution, the talks reached a deadlock. The Peace Mission in a bid to break the deadlock, prepared a set of proposals known as 'The Peace Mission Proposals' which were issued on 20 December 1964.

The Government of India delegates welcomed the proposals and urged that the 'dissident elements' in Nagaland should agree to join the Indian Union of their own volition, 'and the Government of India, for their part, would see what further adjustments they could make in regard to autonomy of the state of Nagaland'. In response the underground Nagas demanded a plebiscite on the issue of joining the Indian Union so that Nagas could decide their future according to 'their own volition', and also demanded that the status of the Union Government's delegation, at the negotiation, be upgraded to the 'ministerial level'.[97]

The two delegations met again finally on 4 and 5 May 1965, and during this talk the Nagas came up with the fresh demand that Phizo should be associated with the next higher level talks. The Government of India agreed to this proposal but Phizo refused to come to India for talks.

Political negotiations which had been suspended were resumed after seven months. The venue was shifted to New Delhi and as the Nagas had desired the talks were upgraded to the ministerial level.

There were as many as six rounds of ministerial level talks between the Government of India led by the prime minister and the underground Nagas led by their prime minister Ato Kilonser. The talks spread over a period from February 1966 to October 1967. The atmosphere deteriorated when there were strong reports in the press accusing Rev Michael Scott of being 'soft and partisan' to the Nagas. In August 1965, Scott went to England for medical treatment. And on his return to India, he submitted a paper, titled 'The Naga Problem: A Point of View' to the Prime Minister, Mrs Indira Gandhi. Simultaneously in a paper circulated to the press Scott questioned the legitimacy of India's rule over Nagaland and asked for the setting of an Indo-Naga Commission to investigate the allegations made by the Nagas and the 'crime sheet' prepared by him in 1964-5. On 3 May 1966, the External Affairs Minister, Dinesh Singh announced in the Rajya Sabha that Rev Scott had been served with orders to leave the country 'immediately'! Scott's exit weakened the morale of the Nagas considerably. In the fourth round of talks held on 27-29 October 1966 some basic proposals were put forward by the Naga leaders. Kukhato, the leader of the Naga delegates, submitted a 14-point agreement to the prime minister. The points were studied in minute details and at the close of talks, the prime minister held up to the Naga leaders the economic backwardness of Nagaland thus indicating that Nagaland would not be 'economically viable'. The prime minister also explained the 'strategic consideration' from India's point of view. The Naga delegates were however assured by the prime minister that Nagaland could have the maximum autonomy with the 'Indian Union'. The Government of India permitted the Naga representatives to visit England to consult with Phizo before any final decision was reached. 'Accordingly Suisa and Vizol were sent to England where it is believed that Phizo gave the two Naga leaders a cold reception refusing to meet them and snubbing Suisa with whom he was very annoyed.[98]

FORMATION OF THE REVOLUTIONARY GOVERNMENT OF NAGALAND

As soon as the Naga leaders returned from New Delhi, the Naga Federal Parliament (*Tatar Hoho*) and members of the Indian Parliament roundly blamed the Naga leader, Kukhato Sukhai, and held him responsible for the failure of the talks with the prime minister of India. The Federal Parliament also moved a resolution to the effect that 'in spite of the direct talks having been established between the Indian leaders and the Naga leaders it is unfortunate that the Indians were adamant in not recognizing the sovereignty of Nagaland'. In a 'no-confidence motion' against Kukhato's leadership in *Tatar Hoho*, he was defeated and made to resign from the post of prime minister. Sukhai tendered his resignation on 24 October 1967. In place of Kaito, Mowu Angami was appointed as the Naga federal army general. In the administrative set-up also Mehiasiu Angami of the Angami tribe was appointed as the president. He replaced Scato Swu Sema and assumed the 'overall executive powers'.

The appointment of Z. Ramyo as home minister of the Federal Government of Mehiasiu caused further jealousy in the underground ranks. As it is the entire Naga underground movement was full of inter-tribal rivalry and struggle for hegemony.[99] The appointment of a Tangkhul to such a coveted post therefore, resulted in considerable resentment. Yet another extremely coveted post of the general secretary of the Naga National Council was taken by a Tangkhul, Thuingaleng Muivah (commonly called Th. Muivah) with a Master's degree in Political Science, Muivah hailed from Somdal which is one of the most educated villages of the Tangkhul tribes. The Tangkhul hegemony following the Angami ascendancy prepared the ousted Semas to retrieve the political initiative.[100] While all this inter-tribal hostility was going on—General Kaito was assassinated by an unknown person on 3 August 1968 in Kohima.

His death further deepened the tribal feud among the Nagas and drove a wedge of hatred between the Semas and the Angamis. Motivated by tribal rivalry the Semas kidnapped president Mehiasiu Angami and Z. Ramyo and kept them in an 'unknown place' for several months. The Sema group then announced the formation of a new political party called the Council of the Naga People (CNP) and declared at the same time the dissolution of the Federal Government of Nagaland Party:

1. The chapter of Federal Government and the army government declared closed.
2. Reasons for creating new party: (*a*) failure to bring about a negotiated settlement of the Naga political problem by NNC and (*b*) failure to hold Naga People together by non-recognition of smaller communities and co-workers.
3. Policy: (*a*) peaceful solution of the Naga political problem, (*b*) continuance of the ceasefire and resumption of talks with

the Government of India, (*c*) unity of Naga people, and (*d*) upholding principles of democracy.

4. The name of the political party shall be called 'Council of Naga People' (CNP).
5. The representative of the people unanimously elected Mr. Sukhai to be the president at on 1 November 1968.
6. Declaration of the government will follow soon.

The CNP met on 2 November 1968 and a new government called the Revolutionary Government of Nagaland was formed. The meeting also ceremoniously declared that it would be a parliamentary form of government. Mr Scato Swu, the erstwhile president of the Federal Government of Nagaland was unanimously elected the prime minister of the Revolutionary Government. The new government pledged for: (*a*) the integrity of Nagaland, (*b*) peaceful coexistence, (*c*) peaceful solution of the Naga political problem, (*d*) preservation of Naga culture and tradition, (*e*) achieving national and individual liberty and freedom from external pressures.

As expected the Federal Government of Nagaland and the NNC denounced the formation of the Revolutionary Government and refused to recognize it. Its leaders were charged as 'renegades and traitors' and branded it as quislings helping the Indian Government. On 14 August 1970, the twenty-third anniversary of the Naga independence the federal president, Mehiasiu Angami in the course of his address said:

> The error of the catch phrase that Nagaland is an integral part of India is identical to India is an integral part of Asia. National distinction cannot enforce a physical geography. Nagaland is never an integral part of Independent India. I hold India guilty on all counts for the criminal act of aggression against the territorial sovereignty of Nagaland. In this hour of trial, it the highest honour for the Nagas to defend their homeland.[101]

THE SHILLONG ACCORD: THE DISCORD

In a bid to explore fresh avenues of approach leading to the final political settlement of the Naga question, on 8 August 1974 the NPC (Nagaland Peace Council) submitted a 4-point memorandum to Governor L.P. Singh. This memorandum suggested that as a preliminary step the underground Nagas should, (*a*) desist from firing, and (*b*) stop recruitments, collection of levies and import of arms.

On 27 August 1974, a public meeting was held in Kohima.

This all Naga Public Peace Conference included 5 representatives from each tribe, 16 representatives from various Christian associations and conventions besides public leaders from both NNO and UDF parties. They endorsed the call earlier given by the Nagaland Peace Council and urged the underground Nagas and the Government of India to come to an early political settlement. By September 1975, the Liason Committee of the Nagaland Peace Council had successfully arranged to have top-ranking underground leaders brought to the Chedema Peace Camp under safe-conduct arrangements. The Council formulated two principles, namely, that the solution should be 'honourable' to all concerned and that it should be 'acceptable' to both sides.[102] In early November 1975, the Council was thus instrumental in bringing together both the parties for talks. The six-member underground delegation led by Kevi Yallya (Phizo's brother) met L.P. Singh on 10 November 1975, at Raj Bhavan, Shillong. The talks were a subdued affair, and most of the meetings were held in camera. The following agreement was the outcome of the discussions and was signed on 11 November 1975.

1. The representatives of the underground organization decided, of their own volition, to accept without condition the Constitution of India.
2. It was agreed that the arms, now underground, would be brought out and deposited at appointed places. Details for giving effect to this agreement will be worked out.
3. It was agreed that the representatives of the underground organizations should have reasonable time to formulate other issues for discussion for final settlement.

During the talks in Shillong, a few terms were presented to the governor which included the return of Naga forests, the integration of all Naga-inhabited contiguous areas, changes in the election system and structural alterations in the administrative and judicial system. But the jubilations at the signing of the accord was short-lived.

NOTES

1. It was only after the secessionist threats from the Tamils, Kashmiris during the dangerous decade of the 1960s that constitutional safeguards were evolved against secessionism. The Indian Constitution was amended

(sixteenth) which sought to prevent fissiparous trends engendered by regional and linguistic loyalties and preserve territorial integrity of the country. Amending Article 19 (referring to the freedom of speech) it enabled the legislatures to penalize any individual who questioned the sovereignty and integrity of the country.

2. S. Gopal, *Jawaharlal Nehru: A Biography*, Vol. 2, Delhi: OUP, 1979, p. 207.
3. Nehru to B.R. Medhi, 25 May 1951, cited in ibid., p. 208.
4. M. Horam, *Thirty Years of Naga Insurgency*, Delhi: Cosmo, 1990, p. 44.
5. Jawaharlal Nehru, 'A Note by the Prime Minister on his tour of the North Eastern Frontier Provinces', Shillong, 1952.
6. Cited in V. Elwin, *Nagaland*, Shillong: Govt. of Assam, 1961, pp. 60-1.
7. 'Statement made by the Prime Minister in the Parliament 23rd August, 1956', Shillong, 1956, pp. 1-4.
8. Nehru to Defence Secretary, 19 June 1956, in S. Gopal, op. cit., p. 211.
9. Nehru to K.N. Katju, Defence Minister, 28 July 1956, in ibid., p. 212. 'Disturbed Area', Editorial, *Economic and Political Weekly*, 15 April 1978, p. 633.
10. Also cited in Amrita Rangasami, 'Mizoram: Tragedy of our Making', in *Economic and Political Weekly*, 15 April 1978, pp. 653-62; N. Haksar and M. Luithui, *Nagaland File*, Delhi: Lancer, 1984, pp. 176-86.
11. Ibid.
12. Ibid.
13. Parliamentary Debates, Vol. 55, Nos. 10-22, 28 February-17 March 1966, Rajya Sabha, Govt. of India, Delhi, pp. 2125-6.
14. Ibid., pp. 2126-7.
15. Sreekant Khandekar and Raghu Rai, 'The Army Takes Charge', *India Today*, 1-15 December 1980, pp. 14-21, Pramila Dandavate et al., 'Report of a Fact Finding Team', in A.R. Desai (ed.), *Repression and Resistance in India*, Bombay: Sangam, 1990, pp. 291-308.
16. Edgar O'Ballance, 'Malayasia: The Communist Insurgent War', cited in Amrita Rangasami, op. cit.
17. Ibid.
18. S. Chatterjee, *Mizoram Encyclopaedia*, Vol. 2, Delhi: Jaico, 1990, pp. 355-6.
19. Ibid.
20. Vumson, *Zo History*, Aizawl: n.d., pp. 284-5.
21. C. Nunthara, 'Grouping of Villages in Mizoram: Its Social and Economic Impact', *Economic and Political Weekly*, 25 July 1981, pp. 1237-40.
22. Ibid., Amrita Rangasami, op. cit.; Chaitanya Kalbag, 'The North-East: The Human Tragedy' (Mizoram Group Therapy), in *India Today*, 31 October 1982.
23. Nehru's speech in the Lok Sabha, 23 August 1956.
24. G.G. Swell and J.J.M. Nichols Roy, *Suppression of Mizos in India: An Eye Witness Report*. This report was submitted to the Govt. of India in 1966. A smuggled copy of which was later published in Pakistan by Feroze Sons, Karachi, n.d.

25. Govinda Mukhoty, 'The Army Atrocities in Naga Areas: People's Union for Democratic Rights', Delhi, 1987, Pamphlet.

    Amnesty International, 'India: Operation Bluebird: A Case Study of Torture and Extra Judicial Executions in Manipur', NSA, 20/17/90, DISTR: SC/CO/GR, London WC IX, 8DJ, UK, 1990, M. Luithui and Nandita Harksar, 'Nagaland File: A Question of Human Rights', Delhi: Lancer, 1984, pp. 234-40; Report of NPMHR, in A.R. Desai (ed.), op. cit., pp. 289-91.
26. Swell and Nichols Roy, op. cit., p. 5.
27. Ibid., pp. 5-6.
28. Vumson, op. cit., p. 29.
29. Op. cit., see note 24.
30. Luithui and N. Haksar, op. cit.
31. Amnesty International, op. cit.
32. Luithui and N. Haksar, op. cit.
33. Memorandum to the Prime Minister, From Kohima Baptist Women's Union, Kohima, 22 August 1971.
34. Ibid.
35. Rano Saiza's speech cited in People for a New India, *Disturbed Areas: The Roots of Repression in Nagaland, Mizoram and Andhra Pradesh*, Bombay: People for a New India, 1979, p. 11.
36. Chaitanya Kalbagh, op. cit.
37. People for a New India, op. cit., p. 16. A Report on the Army atrocities was published in *India Today*. See Chaitnya Kalbag, op. cit.; International Work Group for Indigenous Affairs (IWGIA), *The Naga Nation and Its Struggle against Genocide*, Copenhagen, 1986, pp. 135-229.
38. Cited in V. Venkata Rao et al., *A Century of Government and Politics in North East India*, Vol. III, *Mizoram*, Delhi: S. Chand & Co., 1987, pp. 269-70.
39. Nehru to B.R. Medhi, 9 March 1953, in S. Gopal, op. cit., Vol. 2, p. 210.
40. Nehru to Fazl Ali, 22 January 1957, in S. Gopal, op. cit., Vol. 3, p. 29.
41. Ibid., p. 28.
42. Nehru to Fazl Ali, 9 September 1956, in ibid.
43. Nehru's note, 9 December 1953, cited in S. Gopal, op. cit., Vol. 2, p. 210.
44. Nehru's hope of Naga movement fizzling out was mentioned in his letter to B.R. Medhi, 13 March 1952, in ibid., p. 208.
45. S. Gopal as in note 41, p. 28.
46. Asoso Yunou, *The Rising Nagas: A Historical and Political Study*, Delhi: Vivek, 1974, p. 222.
47. Ibid., for details of the peace process see, M. Aram, *Peace in Nagaland*, New Delhi: Arnold-Heinemann, 1974. Also M. Horam, *Thirty Years of Naga Insurgency*, New Delhi: Cosmo, 1990. Jayaprakash Narayan, *Nagaland Ka Sawal* (in Hindi), Varanasi: Sarva Sewa Sangh, 1965.
48. Ibid.
49. Ibid., p. 244
50. Statement of Government of India, 25 September 1947, *The Hindu*, 26 September 1957.

51. B.R. Medhi to Nehru, 22 May 1957, cited in S. Gopal, op. cit., Vol. III, p. 30.
52. Fazl Ali to Nehru, 25 May 1957, cited in ibid.
53. *The New Statesmen*, London, 3 September 1960, cited in Asoso Yunou, op. cit., p. 236.
54. Prem Bhatia's report, the *Times of India*, 13 September 1960.
55. Asoso Yunou, op. cit., pp. 248-9.
56. Cited in ibid.
57. V. Venkta Rao et al., op. cit., p. 245. Also see Nirmal Nibedon, *Mizoram Daggers Brigade*, Delhi: Lancer, 1980, pp. 77-103.
58. Ibid.
59. Ibid., p. 246.
60. Ibid., p. 247.
61. Ibid., p. 248.
62. Ibid.
63. Ibid.
64. Ibid. A critical analysis of the peace talks is available in 'Mizoram: The Laldenga Factor', *Economic and Political Weekly*, 13 May 1978, p. 786.
65. Ibid.
66. Ibid.
67. 'Mizoram: The Laldenga Factor' as mentioned in note 64.
68. V. Venkta Rao, op. cit.
69. Ibid.
70. Ibid.
71. Ibid.
72. Ibid.
73. Ibid.
74. The indoctrination took place when Bisheshwar was confined with the Naxalites in Tripura Jail. Gangumei Kabui, 'Insurgency in Manipur Valley' in B.L. Abbi (ed.), *North Eastern Region: Problems and Prospects of Development*, Chandigarh: CRRID, 1984, pp. 233-9.
75. Kshetri Rajendra Singh, 'Social Movements in Manipur Valley: A Study of Two Movements among the Meitheis', unpublished Ph.D thesis, Centre for Social Studies, Surat, 1987, p. 204.
76. PLA, *PLA Gi Lanjangbu Sougatppiya*, a Leaflet dated 6.11.1980 cited in ibid., p. 204.
77. PLA, *Dawn*, Vol. II, 1979, p. 30.
78. Ibid.
79. Kshetri Rajendra Singh, op. cit., pp. 205-6. Also *Resistance*, Vol. III, No. 29, 25 July 1978, p. 1.
80. Cited in Nirmal Nibedon, *North East India: The Ethnic Explosion*, Delhi: Lancer, 1981, p. 71.
81. *Huyen Lanpao* (Manipuri), 21 July 1978, Imphal cited in ibid.
82. Ibid.

83. *Resistance*, Imphal, Vol. III, No. 29, 25 July 1978.
84. Ibid.
85. Ibid.
86. Ibid.
87. 'Manipur: the Army Takes Charge', *India Today*, Delhi, 1-15 December 1980, pp. 14-21.
88. Huyen Lanpao (Manipuri), 21 February 1985.
89. Kshetri Rajendra Singh, op. cit., p. 211.
90. 'PLA Leader Rises from Grave', *Indian Express*, Bombay, 24 July 1982; also ibid., p. 211.
91. Ibid., p. 212.
92. Kshetri Rajendra Singh, 'From PLA to MLA', *Frontier*, Vol. 19, No. 20, 3 January 1987, pp. 4-6.
93. Ibid.
94. Ibid.
95. *Times of India*, Delhi, 22 December 1984, also ibid.
96. *Amrita Bazar Patrika*, Calcutta, 24 December 1984, also ibid.
97. M. Horam, *Thirty Years of Naga Insurgency*, Delhi: Cosmo, 1990, p. 44.
98. M. Horam, op. cit., p. 134.
99. Ibid., pp. 142-3. This was another phase when intra-tribal feud overtook the Naga freedom struggle. Horam also shows the details of intra-tribal rivalry over hegemony of the underground movement.
100. Ibid.
101. Ibid., p. 148.
102. Ibid., pp. 177-8.

CHAPTER NINE

The Ramifications

The exit of Bisheshwar did not result in the demise of the People's Liberation Army. Almost simultaneously with the PLA another outfit had emerged known as the People's Liberation Army of Kangleipak (PREPAK) led by the late R.K. Tulachandra, a young graduate of D.M. College, Imphal. This was also an outfit with Maoist ideology and was led by Maipak Sharma after Tulachandra died in an encounter with the Indian Army. The activities of the PREPAK and the Kangleipak Communist Party (KCP) were overshadowed by the imposing image of PLA. The PREPAK aimed at the installation of a 'socialist sovereign state in Manipur by suppression all counter revolutionary people, destruction of class enemies which included capitalist politicians, bureaucratic officials, the capitalists in the society, the contractors and anti-social elements.[1] It termed the bureaucratic imperialist Indian Government which exploited the traditional economy of Manipur, supported outsiders and unleashed military force against Kangleipak (Manipur) as a neo-colonialist enemy. It envisaged the setting up of collective farming, nationalization of all trade and business and a judicial system of people's court. It believed in armed protest against the racial policies of the Government of India. It also planned to coordinate all the movements in north-east India into a pan-Mongoloid offensive against the Indian State. Gradually the PREPAK elements were absorbed into the PLA and KCP. The PREPAK elements were believed to be mere 'enthusiasts' and hence had been liquidated gradually.

By March 1986, PLA itself seemed to have three major factions led by Temba, Binoy and Bisheshwar, respectively. In April 1986, a PLA leaflet announced the return of Manikanta as the new PLA leader. According to it Temba, who while acting in connivance with the enemy had been captured and was to be kept in the PLA jail until his fate was decided by the party.[2] The Manikanta group also owned responsibility for the murder of four persons belonging to USRP and an executive engineer of the Manipur Public Works

Department on 2 March 1986 at Thongjon. While this indicated the existence of PLA as an active force nothing much was heard about their insurgent activities. On the other hand, some of the erstwhile PLA members were reported to have earned state patronages after giving up arms and were flourishing in one of the highly lucrative enterprises of the north-east: government supplies.[3]

The turn of the decade saw some uneasiness again and insurgent activities seemed to have re-emerged with PLA leading the scene once more. This time PLA was declared as an armed wing of the Revolutionary People's Front claiming to be the largest militant outfit in Manipur. It is worth mentioning that this re-emergence coincided with the turmoil in Assam which now had a secessionist organization of its own—the United Liberation Front of Assam (ULFA, 1979). The PLA's existence was confirmed when Vandana Malik, a lady IPS officer was killed in Imphal in a sudden attack and the gunning down of Rajee Mangang—a PLA leader reportedly active in initiating a negotiated peace process in Manipur. Simultaneously came the '*nashabandi*' (liquor prohibition) order of the PLA. Despite government's assurance of protection the terror-stricken liquor sellers closed their shops. The PLA now had a new president—Irengam Bhorot alias I. Chaaren. In a significant interview the outfit's vice president and chief of the army staff M.M. Ngonba (originally Monohar Mayum Praveen Sharma) revealed that the Revolutionary Peoples' Front was a guardian organization fighting for 'total freedom and independence of Manipur', the PLA was its armed wing.[4] For the first time it declared its founder-chairman turned legislator N. Bisheshwar as a 'betrayer'.[5] It also repudiated any possibility of a negotiated settlement with the Indian State. With almost a phoenix-like revival the long forgotton UNLF and PREPAK too reappeared in the Imphal Valley in the early 1990s and have since been constantly in the news for insurgent operations. It was reported that the Khaplang faction of the NSCN, the ULFA of Assam and the revived UNLF of Manipur led by R. Meghan had formed a united front called the Indo-Burma Revolutionary Front which did not make much headway initially.[6] This is evident in the massive counter offensive launched by the Burmese Army in early 1992 against the multiple Burmese insurgent outfits like the Kachin National Army, Karen National Army and others, active in the Indo-Burmese frontier region creating terror in the rank and file of these outfits which might have weakened the strength and strategy of the IBRF.[7] However, the revived PLA resumed its ambushes. On 14 March the

PLA ambushed an Indian para-military force at Langthabal on the outskirts of Imphal killing five *jawans* of the Special Service Bureau (SSB). Within a week of the massacre the state's border district of Ukhrul, the hub of lingering Naga rebellion came alive with the Muivah faction of NSCN executing two alleged informers. In face, one of the reported informers was dragged from the bazaar, shot and then thrown on the lawns of the deputy commissioner's office. Simultaneously came the announcement that PREPAK and the KCP along with PLA have closed ranks to float a unified command called the Revolutionary Joint Committee (RJC).[8] The RJC was formed for coordinating cadre training, exchanging tactical intelligence and conducting joint ambushes on government security forces. This 'much-dreaded' merger of the leading secessionist groups was the second serious attempt made by the rebel outfits in the past two years. It came as the culmination of a series of attempts in a enclave in Khongjom on the Indo-Myanmar road in the late February 1992. Insurgency watchers in the state read much significance into the merger as it indicated that the PREPAK and the KCP after years of obscurity finally succeeded in coming alive. The NSCN had also been in touch with the new PLA supremo M. Parveen Sharma.[9]

NEW PHASE IN NAGA STRUGGLE

The Shillong Accord created major discord among the underground Nagas. The federal leader 'general' Th. Muivah who succeeded Phizo, denounced the agreement and issued a stern reprimand to the signatories of the accord. The underground politician Veni Chakesang had refused to be a party to the accord and later went over to Burma where Muivah was said to have given him letters to be carried back into India.

Phizo also made several characteristic moves. He sought an audience with Prime Minister Morarji Desai while the latter was in London (June 1977). Phizo told Desai that the Nagas had been 'suffering for a long time' and that despite a 'wide gap' between the Indian understanding of the Naga problem and the Naga people's own understanding of the same, 'the problem is more serious than an argument' which is how Mr Desai was treating it.[10] Phizo claimed that he had tape recorded the 'talk' during this meeting and the text of the Phizo-Desai talks would soon be circulating in Nagaland.[11]

Soon after the Shillong Accord[12] was signed, not only the anti-accord groups, but even the signatories of the accord backed out of it. In the meantime, the leadership of the underground movement shifted from the hands of the Semas to the Tangkhul Nagas which itself was a cause of resentment in the feud-ridden Naga community. There was growing opposition to the leadership of Phizo too. The underground members felt that Phizo, exiled in London, was no longer capable of providing leadership to the Naga independence movement. As a result of these development a militant group of Naga leaders announced the formation of the National Socialist Council of Nagland on 31 January 1980. The three trusted lieutenants of Phizo, Isac Swu, S. Khaplang and T. Muivah led this breakaway group. The manifesto of the NSCN declared that:

> The facts must be admitted and it is a fact that the most ignominious sell out in the history of the Naga people ever since the time of the first bullet of freedom was fired, is beyond dispute the notorious 'Shillong Accord'. That Accord deserved an outright official and open condemnation. Indeed, the Naga National Council is spent; it had termed it to be treacherous and reactionary. Any effort to revolutionise it is stifled. It has neglected to carry its solemn national trust through to the end. It has totally failed. The resort being made to 'peace' and 'unity' is simply a desperate attempt at covering up and making virtue of their obvious treason. . . .
>
> It is deplored that the leadership acted in the past completely independently of the actual conditions and in total isolation from the people. . . . We do not think it proper either, on the part of the leadership to stay away from the people even when there is fatal danger at home and against the appeal of the people to come back and illuminate their way . . . the contention that a particular leadership staying away in a foreign land has sustained the existence of Nagaland thus far and that he alone will bring the final victory too needs immediate correction. . . .[13]

The circumstances leading to the formation of the NSCN was described by the group follows:

> These acts (The Shillong Accord and Phizo's patronisation of the signatories of Accord) constituted almost a national insult and created adverse impact on the crucial issue. Nation wide danger thus hung around. In view of that an outright official condemnation became indispensable as the sovereign rights of the Nagas were to be safeguarded and kept intact for all time to time. Reinforcing the earlier condemnation of it, the National Assembly held on 15th-17th August 1976, totally condemned the accord as the work of the sole traitors once and for all. The Assembly elected Mr. Isak Chishi Swu and Th. Muivah in their respective capacities as the Vice President and the General Secretary, NNC.
>
> [Even after the failure of Phizo] the stalwart Nagas however were never deterred. Rather they were irrevocably opposed to the leadership which could

not prove itself in the most crucial hours of national trials, for them to be buried together with him was out of question. They knew of a certainty that the noblest task to save the nation from the precarious state of affairs was incumbent upon them. They would not fail whatever the ordeals; they had to see through the end. Accordingly, they revoked all confidence and stakes, took fate into their own hands from the treacherous mess and entanglement which portends nothing but disaster, beyond salvage. They gave an outright unsparing rebuff to the NNC's Shillong Accord. Further, they were determined evermore against the NNC's all-out satanic attempt at physical liquidation of the unquestionable patriots through direct collaboration with the Indian and the Burmese troops. But, notwithstanding the overwhelming challenges, this group managed to close ranks behind them and formed themselves into a force most authentic and formidable to defend the right of the Naga's sovereignty against external invasion and NNC's capitulation, at all costs. The long awaited historic Merger of the East and West was also formally made at Nokpa village on the 30th Jan. 1980. Subsequently they came to be known as the National Socialist Council of Nagaland with their Manifesto solemnly declared on the 31st Jan. 1980. . . . Being absolutely committed to the cause of the people NSCN solemnly declared themselves to the people that they would stand for the line enshrined in the Manifesto which ensured beyond doubt the best attainable for the people. In the NSCN system sovereignty of the nation and freedom of the people in all fields against exploitation and oppression is first and foremost. Their stand for justice and for the welfare of the people does not admit of distortion.[14]

The group then went on to form an alternative front called Peoples' Republic of Nagaland and sprang into action. The NSCN vowed not only to lead the struggles of the Indian Nagas but also the Nagas living within the Burmese frontier. A base was established in the Burmese side of the border. Systematic training of cadres were carried out. Massive mobilization was attempted among the Nagas on both sides of the frontier. Besides providing them primary and political education, the NSCN also propagated Christianity, instructed them on terrace cultivation, sanitation norms, banning poppy cultivation, and discourage opium consumption. According to the NSCN, there was a large area of unsurveyed, unadministered area inhabited by the Nagas stranding the Indo-Burmese frontier, where 'the impact of the outside world was virtually nil. Head chopping was held high as a manly honour until early 1980'.[15] These people were also included by the NSCN in their mobilization efforts even though 'their sovereign rights had not yet been snatched'. These Nagas were convinced that the 'NSCN alone stood for their future salvation'. And this was achieved through NSCN's educational programme, and training in better cultivation of food crops to alleviate conditions of food scarcity. A large number of the Nagas were addicts. Hence, opium growing, its consumption and selling or buying was forbidden. Alongside, the NSCN also had substantial success in converting these Naga tribals to Christianity. In this task the NSCN went about with strict professionalism by its own admission. It neither failed to appropriate peoples' religious sentiments nor their hopes of miracles. In fact, NSCN claimed that 'God worked with the NSCN to do His will.'

> To magnify His name further some women blessed with healing power, worked miracles. Through the name of our lord, Jesus Christ, many people were healed of incurable diseases of years. A few instances may be cited. A man of forty-five years old who had been laid up in bed 20 years with paralysis was completely made whole, who in turn witnessed the glory of God of the people. A man suffering from oozing blood in his private part for 30 years was cured. Lepers including one who suffered 20 years were nicely cleansed. Advanced cases of T.B. was successfully healed. Seniors' eyesight problems were treated well. Demons were cast out from the possessed.[16]

Simultaneously, it launched its offensive too. On 12 May 1981 the NSCN led a major attack on the Indian outpost at Fakmali in Tuensang killing twelve armymen and carried away 2 light machine guns, 2 stenguns, 3 rifles, 1 wireless set and a large quantity of ammunition. Thus, began another chapter in the history of insurgency in north-east India. Reportedly, the NSCN then established links with the PLA operating in Manipur and became a member of the Indo-Burmese Revolutionary Front. On 2 July 1980 the NSCN General Secretary Th. Muivah issued the following message to the people of north-east India:

> It is high time to do away radically with the delusion in the paper-Indian-Constitutional-guarantees of equality, justice, protection and so on and prudently guard against the repetition of being befuddled with the sweet promises of New Delhi Bosses. . . .
>
> Leave not any longer the fate of our people adrift on the surging waves of the massive Indian domination and exploitation, Blame not the angles, not the devils, Be resolute in purpose and undeterred in the face of reverse. Hold on to your gun, you are not alone; we are your comrades in arms, your can count on us.

The NSCN manifesto declared violence as the means of achieving its goal: 'We rule out the illusion of saving Nagaland through peaceful means. It is arms and arms alone that will save our nation and ensure freedom to the people.'[17]

The rejection of the Shillong Accord and the regenerated insurgency by the NSCN created fresh enthusiasm amongst certain sections of the youth. The NSCN took advantage of this and launched a massive recruitment drive. And no wonder it was reported to have a 3000-strong army trained in modern weaponry. To ensure financial viability the NSCN collected taxes and rations periodically from villages. The business community of Dimpur and Kohima, and the forest contractors of Tizit paid huge sums as taxes to the NSCN. Activities like bank robberies, attack on government officials, ambush of army personnel and elimination of persons suspected to be informers were stepped up in the post-1984 period. Since 1984, the NSCN is reported to have killed 3 government officers, 32 army and para-military officers, ambushed the army on 10 occasions, and in the 11 incidents of bank robberies it carried away about Rs. 2.4 crore.[18] It killed a former Chief Minister of Manipur Yangmaso Shaiza and an ex-finance minister of Manipur for being opposed to the cause of the NSCN. It had also killed 111 persons on suspicion of being informers. In its attack of 9 July 1987 on the Assam Rifles post at Oinam in the Senapati district of Manipur, the NSCN killed 9 *jawans* and carried away a huge quantity of arms and ammunition. The three tonnes of ammunition that they took included 90 self-loading rifles, 10 light machine guns, 22 stenguns, 28,052 rounds of ammunition, 396 handgrenades, 300 detonators, 60 bombs and two light mortars.[19]

But it was not just the Indian Army that the NSCN was combating. Since its target was to free the 'Burmese-occupied Naga areas' too, the Yangon (Rangoon) regime also launched a military offensive against the NSCN which was intensified in 1992. The Burmese military operation against the ethnic guerrilla groups also had an all out reprisal against members of the respective ethnic communities leading to a large scale exodus of the Karen villagers into Thailand, Arakan Muslims (Rohingiyas) into Bangladesh and the Burmese Nagas into India. According to an estimate of the State Government of Nagaland the total number of Burmese Naga refugees in India following the military crackdown was about 1,00,000 by mid-1992. It also meant the loss of shelter for the NSCN guerrillas in the Karen villages of Burma.

Taking advantage of this confusion the New Delhi regime reportedly initiated efforts to unify the two factions of the NNC as well as the NSCN, so that negotiations could begin with the underground groups.[20] But the Indo-Burmese Revolutionary Front stepped in to forbid any individual insurgent organization to hold talks with the Indian State. The NSCN(M) chief Muivah himself doubted the sincerity of the intentions of the Indian State in negotiating peace with the underground Nagas. He felt that the Indian State was wrong in presuming that the underground Naga organizations had become weak on account of the Burmese offensive. On the contrary he felt that it was the Indian State which was facing disintegration due to the various dissident constituent nationalities:

> We have a solid ideology (of a independence Nagaland) which sustains our struggle. But the ideological force essential to sustain the Indian Union has almost fainted. It can only depend on the army to hold the Union together. Given its present plight of growing disintegration due to uprisings in Kashmir, Punjab, Assam and other parts of India if the Indian State continues its armed intervention to contain these uprisings, it can only be to India's own detriment. We are, therefore, in an advantageous position to fight a protracted war. Time will bear out whether Nagaland will disappear first or India becomes ten.[21]

The emergence of ULFA (the United Liberation Front of Assam) and the already existing MNF (Mizo National Front) only reinforced the NSCN activities. The intermittent ambush, robbery and killings continued. In November 1989, internal squabbles and power-feuds led to the expulsion of S.S. Khaplang from the organization. This was followed by the formation of a parallel NSCN led by Khaplang which since then has been known as the NSCN-Khaplang faction, while the other one is known as the Muivah-Swu faction. In the meantime, there was also a split in the NNC; Adino Phizo leads one faction while Khodao Yanthan leads the other.

S.S. Khaplang was instrumental in uniting all the insurgent outfits of north-east India and Burma under one banner which came to be known as the Indo-Burmese Revolutionary Front (22 May 1991) at Mukpa in West Burma.[22] The IBRF was organized as a supervisory body comprising of representatives of various insurgent outfits, and coordinated their struggles. It provided the necessary training, encouragement and inputs that an infant insurgent body needs. Since 'isolated and separate strategies by the guerrillas land them nowhere' IBRF helped in the coordination of the insurgencies.[23] The IBRF defined Indo-Burma as 'the region between India and Burma comprising the so-called north-eastern region of India and the present north-western Burma' which 'is one of the few regions in world which remains to be liberated from colonial rule'. The IBRF admitted that 'the long struggle for national independence of various ethnic groups in the region had made little headway; rather many of these as in Mizoram and Tripura had gone down the road to capitulation'. It ascribed the reasons of this setback to the failure of these organizations in challenging the Indian State to realize the 'historical limitations of ethnicism which made their leaders unable to see the potential strength of the region as a whole'. Following this realization that 'separate and isolated struggles' would lead nowhere, the IBRF 'a united front of the revolutionary forces in the region was formed as a historical necessity'. Though the IBRF has been in existence for over three years, its activities have been confined to theoretical and ideological discussions of revolutionary strategy and tactics. On the ground its actions as a 'front', collectively, were hampered because of the lack of coordination of the forces of its component units active in widely separated areas. On the reported move of some of the active insurgent organizations to hold negotiations with the Government of India, the IBRF issued stern warnings to the front's partners and declared that any talk could be held only with the IRBF leaders.[24] Moreover, all such talks would have to be held without any preconditions and 'not on India's terms'. It was also categorical in stating that it would never compromise on the question of sovereignty and independence of the ethnic people of the region. 'There shall be no talks with the Government of India unless the national rights of the people of this region is fully recognized.' The signed statement of the IBRF further stated that the organization was slowly and steadily progressing in its efforts to build up a united struggle for independence of the nationalities in Indo-Burma. 'The ideas being propagated by the Front has spread all over Indo-Burma.' Although it too desired peace, it felt that 'genuine peace could be brought about only if the national rights of the people of the region are fully recognized' and added that there could surely be no genuine and lasting peace as long as the 'colonial exploitation by India' existed. It concluded the statement saying

> our struggle for independence will be a long-drawn out struggle. In the process the enemy will do all in its power and resources to divide and suppress our struggle. What will be decisive is the united strength of the entire population of Indo-Burma. No power on earth will be able to suppress such a united people for all time to come. This is history and the history of national struggles will repeat itself in Indo-Burma again.[25]

In May 1992, the IBRF, in a written statement invited 'all other revolutionary forces in the region' to join hands with the IBRF to fight together for a 'common goal'—the 'liberation of the Indo-Burma region'. The component units of IBRF had already established bilateral links with other 'revolutionary forces' active in their home territories. Thus, the ULFA for instance had a working relationship with the Bodo Security Force in Assam; valley-based insurgent group in Manipur had a working relationship with both the factions of the NSCN though serious differences divide these factions. Later the PLA too joined the IBRF. Given the growth of this complex network, the active involvement of PLA, not an original member of the IBRF, in this body marked an important tactical and strategic advance of the political objectives of IBRF. The split in the NSCN weakened the organization considerably, and was evident from the fact that from 1987 to 1990 it did not launch any intensive attack. In 1990, it came back to the news headline with its attempt on the life of S.C. Zamir, the then Chief Minister of Nagaland. Though Zamir escaped unhurt, his wife sustained bullet injuries and two of his bodyguards were killed. This was immediately followed by an ambush on a police patrol party killing three policemen. On 4 August 1991 the NSCN struck again. It attacked the convoy of the then Speaker Mr Thenochu who escaped unhurt but ten policemen were killed.[26] In yet another incident, the NSCN killed eight CRPF *jawans* (December 1991) and made off with lakhs of rupees the *jawans* were carrying. The was followed by another attack (June 1992) on an army convoy in Phek district in which five commissioned officers and several *jawans* were killed.[27]

The 1990s saw a transformation in the basic character of the insurgent outfits which began to take upon itself the role of a social reformer focusing on popular causes. This method was profitably used by the ULFA in Assam[28] which helped it gain respect among the rural masses and build a Robinhood like image for itself. The ULFA settled village feuds, helped by pooling manpower to build embankments and bridges, big wells and construct roads and houses for the village collectively. It also ruthlessly eliminated the moneylenders and those exploiting villagers and provided social justice. In fact, the strategy was so successful that by the late 1980s, the ULFA ran a parallel administration complete with a judiciary and executive in rural Assam. The NSCN in Nagaland and the PLA in Manipur also adopted a similar approach. To begin with the NSCN prohibited drug and liquor consumption, gambling, and prostitution in rural Manipur.[29] In February 1991, it threatened to 'execute' all prostitutes, 'drug addicts' and those 'suffering from AIDS in Manipur and other north-eastern states', as these social evils were threatening to ruin the Naga society.[30] The PLA too decided to fight such social evils in Manipur. It declared Manipur to be a dry area and that anyone found buying, selling or consuming liquor or drugs would be exterminated. Though there was no ban on selling or drinking liquor by the state the fear-stricken public observed the PLA's dictate. Despite the State Government's assurance of security, all liquor shops were closed down and suddenly Manipur became a 'dry-area' though there were no orders from the State Government.[31]

But the NSCN and the PLA were not as successful the ULFA in resolving social problems due to regional differences where the respective outfits functioned. But the change in the NSCN's approach to issues was noticeable especially in the context of the construction of the Thoubal multipurpose dam in Manipur.[32] The construction of the Thoubal Dam envisaged to irrigate 17,000 ha of agricultural land which would ensure 3 crop facilities, provide 10 million gallons of drinking water per day, generate 7.5 megawatt of electricity and control floods along the river basin. The insurgency in the north-east took a new dimension when the NSCN decided to oppose the construction of the dam across the Thoubal river unless the compensations it demanded for the six to-be-affected villages were paid in advance. According its official sources, two of the hamlets each consisting of 28 to 70 hutments have already reached an agreement with the government and have been shifted to alternative sites. And that the remaining four villages would not be affected until four years after the dam was constructed and the gorge in which they are situated is submerged. A total area of 1,215 ha would be submerged once the reservoir reaches its full capacity of 880.75 cm elevation. Other than the village steeds, of the six tribal villages totalling 120 ha another 595 ha forest land and 800 ha of cultivable land of the six villages and other adjoining villages would be affected. According to a government survey, the forest land was mostly under shifting cultivation and the forest cover was very sparse. As per the same assessment 286 families having a total population of 1,735 would be displace. The NSCN felt that these figures were disputable and the actual figures in terms of people and property were much higher. The NSCN demanded compensation of Rs.1 lakh against that of Rs.80,000 per acre offered by the government. And if this demand was not met the NSCN threatened to stop them from continuing the work on the dam. The NSCN spelt out its threats into action in

September 1990 when the swooped down and set ablaze Rs.2 crore worth of construction equipment belonging to two firms—Progress Construction Ltd. and Ansal. Simultaneously, it also destroyed Rs.10 lakh worth of official property. The insurgents struck again on 11 February 1992 setting aflame a government bus at the project site. It also threatened the workers at the dam with grave consequences if their continued to work. On 25 June 1992 two workers were shot dead and two were injured by the NSCN at the construction site. Since then, with threats of more such raids, work at the site ground to a halt. Though the authorities were determined to complete the Rs.140 crore project within the stipulated year 1994, the terror of NSCN raids continued to cause uncertainty in the Thoubai Valley. The year 1992 witnessed other major developments. In a phoenix-like fashion the defunct United National Liberation Front of Manipur with a sudden revival made its presence fell as effectively. While the ever-present defence personnel and banks were its immediate target, it also involved itself in various reformatory social work. The UNLF commandos warned the unscrupulous businessmen in Imphal town against selling contraband drugs to addicts in Manipur.[33] In many such moves these commandos seized truck loads of these drugs and burnt them publicly.[34] It also launched a vigorous drive against pornographic books and video cassettes which were contributing to the rising number of sexual crimes in Manipur. Many non-Manipuri businessmen who continued with the lucrative trading of contraband drugs despite warnings were given notices to quit by the UNLF. They were even threatened with capital punishment. As mentioned earlier this was a new approach of wining public support that was popularized by the ULFA in Assam and then followed by the PLA in Manipur. The NSCN came up with another surprising move, it shifted its area of operation. From mid-1992 there were a series of violent attacks on the tea gardens of North and South Cachar in Assam.[35] The sustained attacks on the tea gardens of North Cachar by the NSCN struck terror in Assam's plantation economy because the prosperous tea sector, mostly owned by outside businessmen, had already been the target of extortion and violence by militant organizations such as the ULFA, BSF (Bodo Security Force) and the HPC (Hmar People's Convention).

While such confrontation continued well into 1993, a momentous event took place in the history of Nagas. On 23 January 1993 the Naga community represented by the NSCN, was admitted as a member of the Unrepresented Nations and Peoples' Organization

(UNPO) with its headquarters at the Hague.[36] The UNPO, is an international organization, that is fast growing in importance. The UNPO manifesto describes the outfit as follows:

> An organization of nations and peoples not adequately represented in the international community. It was set up by these nations and peoples themselves to promote their own aspirations through peaceful means. A non-aligned organization dedicated to non-violent programmes and solutions, UNPO offers and international forum as well as much needed services for those nations and peoples whose causes and needs are not adequately addressed in existing international bodies. . . . UNPO provides a community of support for those nations and peoples who have long felt alone in their struggle.[37]

This was a significant development because it already had 26 member nations consisting of approximately 50 million people which included Abkhazia, Armenia, Assyria to the Turkomans, Kurds, Tibet and other such nations. The UNPO manifesto goes on to observe:

> Throughout the world, many nations and peoples struggle to regain their lost countries, maintain their cultural identity, and establish basic human and economic rights. Some of these groups live under occupation or have been dispossessed of their countries, while others are ethnic minorities and indigenous peoples who exist as second class citizens in the land of their ancestors. Most of these nations and peoples feel isolated in their struggle and have no international forum in which to be heard. . . . It is UNPO's position supported by international laws, that human rights, including the right to self-determination, are not issues exclusively within the domestic jurisdiction of States.[38]

It was in early January 1993 that the NSCN leaders had slipped out of India through Nepal to present the case of the Naga people to the UNPO and other world bodies subsequent to which they were admitted to the UNPO along with the Chakmas of Bangladesh. Besides Amsterdam the NSCN leader Muivah visited the United States, British and German missions in Geneva, Paris and Bonn, and addressed a Human Rights Convention in Geneva.[39] Since then Muivah has been functioning from Cox's Bazar in Bangladesh. Although the Khaplang faction of the NSCN refused to give much credit to this development,[40] it was nevertheless an important milestone in Naga history. The Khaplang faction of the NSCN soon had another foe within its area of operation; the Kuki National Organization—an outfit formed in 1992 with the aim of setting up Kukiland that would include the Kuki inhabited areas of India and

Burma. The Kuki National Army strongly objected to the NSCN claim of suzerainty over the three Kuki villages in interior Manipur and their right to collect taxes from them.[41] According to the NSCN these villages belonged to Nagaland. Consequently, the two outfits started attacking Kuki and Naga villages which between January and April resulted in the loss of about 90 lives, destruction of property and exodus of people to safer areas. The NSCN described the KNA as a ploy of the Indian Army, and as a retaliatory measure launched an economic blockade of the Imphal-Moreh-Pallel road (National Highway No. 39) where large-scale trans-frontier trade in contraband goods took place and which was the mainstay of Kuki life. The Kukis in turn blocked the Imphal-Ukhrul road, which was the base of the NSCN guerrillas. The army had to move in to resolve the crisis.[42]

Before the violence subsided another unprecedented development rocked Manipur. Manipur has a sizeable Muslim population, who are locally know as Pangals. So far the relationship between the two had been cordial. But on 3 May 1993 a fierce riot broke out between the two communities and within a span of three days about 150 people were killed and many were injured.[43] Again there was an exodus of panic stricken people to safer areas. What sparked off the genocide had again something to do with the myriad insurgent outfits that frequently surface in the Imphal Valley. One such new outfit called the People's Republican Army had advanced money to some Muslim arm peddlers of Lilong in Imphal. Since the arms were not delivered on time members of the organization went over to Lilong and demanded the refund of their money. This resulted in a scuffle and when the gun-runner called for help, his people came to his aid and beat up the three insurgents and handed them over to the police. But by then there had been retaliatory attacks on Muslims in other areas of Imphal. The scale and the viciousness of the riot was an indication of the fragile nature of the apparent social fabric of Manipur. It also showed that even a distant corner of India where anti-Indian sentiment supposedly thrived could not escape the vicious impact of the post-6 December communal riots that had rocked the entire country. The riot also revealed some other important aspects. True to their ideology and progressive character most of the insurgent outfits were unequivocal in condemning the riots. In fact, the revived PLA got into the act and threatened that it would kill anyone who was found rioting. According to newspaper reports the PLA had actually killed one such person. But on the other hand, N. Bisheshwar, the founder of PLA and currently in its hit list due to his counter-revolutionary and reformist activities was arrested. He was accused of leading the Inreipak Kanba Lup (Save Manipur Group) which indulged in extorting money from people and writing inflammatory pieces in Imphal's vernacular press.[44] His dislike of non-Manipuris in Imphal was evident in his earlier writings, and this added another dimension to his prejudices. In fact, it was the UNLF which made sustained efforts to expose Bisheshwar and his outfit. The significant point that emerges as a result of these new developments is that though there are a number of insurgent organization in the Imphal Valley (other than NSCN and KNA) there was no inter-outfit rivalry in recent times like that of the Naga outfits. There was a move to coordinate their activities for a joint struggle. This was evident in their call for observing 15 October 1992 as a Protest Day against the merger of Manipur with India which took place on that date in 1949. But given the history of insurgency in any part of the world the sustainability of such unification seemed a remote possibility.

NOTES

1. V. Venkata Rao, et al., *A Century of Government and Politics in North East India*, Vol. IV, *Manipur*, Delhi: S. Chand & Co., 1991, pp. 183-7.
2. Kshetri Rajendra Singh, 'Social Movements in Manipur Valley: A Study of Two Movements among the Meitheis', unpublished Ph.D. thesis, Centre for Social Studies, Surat, 1987, p. 217.
3. Ibid.
4. 'Plea for United Efforts', interview with I. Chaoren, the *Sun* (north-east), Delhi, 14-20 September 1991, pp. 181-2.
5. Ibid.
6. *The Telegraph*, Calcutta, 27 September 1991. Also ibid.
7. Ibid.
8. 'Back to the Battlefront', *Sunday*, 12-18 April 1992, p. 94.
9. Ibid.
10. 'Exterminating Angels', *Economic and Political Weekly*, Vol. XII, No. 35, 3 August 1977.
11. For the text of this recorded version, see M. Horam, *Thirty Years of Naga Insurgency*, Delhi: Cosmo, 1990, App. VII, pp. 290-2.
12. For the full text of the agreement, see ibid., App. V, p. 267. Also 'What is Shillong Agreement', *Economic and Political Weekly*, 27 May 1978, pp. 859-60.
13. *Manifesto of the National Socialist Council Nagaland*, Oking, 31 January 1980, signed by Isac Chishi Swu.
14. NSCN, *A Brief Political Account of Nagaland* (n.m., n.d.), pp. 33-5.

15. Ibid., pp. 35-8.
16. Ibid.
17. As in note 13, also Statement of the NSCN, 3 January 1984.
18. V. Venkata Rao, op. cit., pp. 187-8.
19. Ibid.
20. Sumanta Banerjee, 'Dangerous Game in Nagaland', *Economic and Political Weekly*, 18 July 1992, pp. 1525-7.
21. Ibid.
22. *The Telegraph*, Calcutta, 27 September 1991.
23. Ibid.
24. Statement by IBRF in *The North-East Times*, 28 July 1992.
25. Ibid.
26. 'New Turn to NSCN Struggle', *The Sentinel*, Guwahati, 29 June 1992.
27. Ibid.
28. Sajal Nag, 'The ULFA Phenomenon', Surat: Centre for Social Studies, 1991.
29. 'NSCN strikes against all addicts, whores in Ukhrul', *The Nagaland Post*, Dimapur, 15 May 1991.
30. 'Threat to AIDS Victim', *The Nagaland Post*, 3 April 1991.
31. As in note 4.
32. 'NSCN Opposed to Project', *The Meghalaya Guardian*, 11 July 1992.
33. 'Blue Day the Drug Dealers', in *The Sun* (north-east), 7-13 May 1992, p. 18.
34. Ibid.
35. 'Explosions in Assam', The *Indian Express*, Vadodara, 15 October 1992; '4 Jawans Killed', *Times of India,* Ahmedabad, 13 October 1992.
36. 'NSCN admitted as member of UNPO', *Naga Banner*, 10 March 1992.
37. UNPO Manifesto, The Hague, 1993.
38. Ibid.
39. 'Naga Leader attended World Meet of Militants', *The Telegraph*, Calcutta, 30 March 1993.
40. 'In Nagalands Not Netherlands', *The Nagaland Journal*, 7 April 1993.
41. 'Ethnic Strife, Strikes Adding to Insurgency in Manipur', *Shillong Times*, 23 April 1993.
42. '25 Killed in Community Clashes in Manipur', *Shillong Times*, 5 May 1993; 'CM Rules Out Division of Manipur', *Shillong Times*, 24 April 1993.
43. '60 Feared Killed in Manipur Violence', *Meghalaya Guardian*, Guwahati, 4 May 1993; 'Survival Key Issue in Manipur', *The Telegraph*, Calcutta, 5 May 1993; 'Manipur Riot Toll Mounts to 108', *The Telegraph*, Calcutta, 5 May 1993.
44. 'IKL' and 'N. Bisheshwar in a Nutshell', *The Sun* (north-east), 7-13 May 1993, pp. 18-ii and iii.

CHAPTER TEN

The Transformation

The last decade of the twentieth century marked a transition in the history of insurgency in north-east India. Transition here meant a fluid state where the future course of insurgency was uncertain. Following this phase was a transformation in the character of insurgency in the region. To be precise this transformation became evident from 1995. As such the year 1995 was a watershed in the history of insurgency because it brought a metamorphosis in the nature of insurgency and its related activities. Insurgent activities, so far, involved guerrilla warfare with the Indian armed forces, formation of a government in exile, training and camping in the jungles, and occasional killing of officials representing the Indian State. In other words, the confrontation between the Indian State and the insurgents, was confined mainly to the jungles and remote areas. It hardly ever disturbed civilian life. In fact, it was the army which disturbed the life of the civilians during their counter-insurgency operations. Insurgency was viewed by the ordinary citizens of these areas as a struggle for lofty ideals, where supreme sacrifices were made for a sacred goal and insurgents were seen as special people, with haloes, to be helped, supported and emulated. But by the year 1995, the activities of the insurgents were hardly noble and became involved with extortion, kidnapping, abduction, looting of banks and exchequers, collection of exorbitant and arbitrary amounts of money as taxes, bomb blasts and killing of civilians. And such activities were resorted to mainly by the NSCN (Isac-Muivah) and the insurgent outfits it sponsored. Thus, insurgency had come down from jungles to the urban areas and from lofty sacrificial acts to ordinary law and order problems. There had obviously been a massive change in the nature of insurgency in north-east India. In this chapter we shall study the change and attempt to examine the reasons for it. We shall also discuss the recent developments that constitute the history of insurgency in north-east India.

The collapse of the Soviet system, its ramification on the East

European Communist conglomerations, and the disintegration of the old nation states making say for the new ones were all significant new developments in the world. The late 1980s, saw the breakup of the Russian, Yugoslav and Czechoslovak states into a number of new nations. It also saw the unification of the divided Germans, Vietnamese and the Yemenis. It witnessed the independence of South Africa and these secession of Eritrea. It saw the return of peace in Ireland and autonomy for Scotland. The impact of these new developments was also felt in India. Though India did not have any *perestroika* or *glasnost*, it was plagued by secessionism, subnationalism, communalism and provincialism—experiencing insecurities as a nation.[1] This insecurity was evident when in the wake of the disintegration of Eastern Europe, there were deliberation on whether India too was going to breakup. Several newspapers articles speculated on the possible areas, which might secede, states that could form independent nations and even the possibility of formation of a commonwealth of Indian nations. Several academicians participated in such discussions to provide a serious dimension to the debate.[2] On the other hand, it also raised hopes among Communities which were struggling to secede from India that perhaps they would now be able to secede from the Indian Union. Among them were the Nagas who felt that pressured by the international political climate the Indian State would now allow them to form an independent nation state. The admission of the NSCN(IM) to the Unrepresented Nations and People's Organization (as discussed in an earlier chapter) raised the hopes further. But no such thing happened. As the situation in Eastern Europe and the consequent political climate settled down, the international pressure on India eased and the hopes of the Nagas petered out. The time was appropriate for retrospection, regrouping, rejuvenation and working out new strategies. And this explains the lull during the period 1993-4.

The events and developments in the subsequent period that is 1995 onwards indicate a new phase in the history of insurgency. It is marked by activities, which were hitherto not associated with insurgents. These were essentially criminal acts, which amounted to the breach of law and order. This change in the nature of insurgency related activities was not spontaneous nor did it mean any dilution of the ideologies of the insurgents or any change in their declared goal of attaining Naga sovereignty. A careful study and analysis of the nature of this transformation suggests that such a change was the result of a carefully worked out strategy. Such a strategy was necessitated by the Indian State's policy of perpetually ignoring the struggle of the Nagas or Mizoram as long as it did not affect the developments in the rest of India. As far as the north-east region was concerned, the Indian State was content in imposing a semi-permanent presence of the army and paramilitary forces in the affected areas. It was accompanied by a liberal dose of cash inflow to the State Government which instead of development, bred corruption and uneven distribution of wealth.[3] Such neglect of the Naga and Meithei problems only protracted their struggle without providing any hope for the future. The East European developments did not have the desired impact on the Indian State as far as the Naga or Meithei aspirations were concerned. Moreover, the successful achievement of an accord and the consequent peace and prosperity in the Mizoram also led to a debate about the need for peace and tranquility in Nagaland and Manipur too. In such a situation the NSCN(IM) could no longer remain quiet and wait for the Indian State to initiate a move towards the settlement of Naga problem. It evolved a strategy of disturbing peace in not just Nagaland, but the entire north-eastern region so as to attract the attention of the Indian State and compel it to take the Naga problem more seriously than it ever did. Spreading insurgency throughout the region, creating law and order problem for the government, sponsoring terrorism and internationalization of the Naga problem were some of the elements of this carefully evolved strategy.

SPREADING INSURGENCY

The 1990s saw a sudden spurt in the rise of new insurgent outfits in the north-eastern region, and a consequent increase in terrorist violence. These outfits were in addition to the already existing ones and emerged in areas that had been peaceful, representing ethnic/tribal communities which had never showed any sign of discontent with the Indian State. Some outfits also emerged in areas where assertive democratic movements were active. For example, the failure of the six-year long foreign national movement in Assam led to the crystallization of the United Liberation Front of Assam (ULFA). Though organized in 1979, its presence was beginning to be felt only in the 1990s. The Indian Army sources reported that it was the NSCN(IM) which strengthened the ULFA by supplying arms and providing training to it. Similarly, the Bodos and the Karbis were in the thick of a peaceful democratic movement demanding separate states for themselves. The rejection of their demands brew discontent among the two tribes. But the movement became violent as underground wings emerged, which resorted to terrorist methods to attract the attention of the government. With the emergence of the Karbi National Volunteer (KNV) the demand for autonomy graduated to secession. Two insurgent organizations emerged among the Bodos which unleashed terror in the region. Similarly, Tripura had experienced massive violence during 1980-5 for which the outfit called Tripura National Volunteers (TNV) was responsible. The accord between the TNV and the Government of India was expected to bring peace in Tripura. But here too, two new insurgent outfits appeared shortly after the accord—the All Twipra Tiger Force (ATTF) and the National Liberation Front of Twipra (NLFT). At least one of these—the NLFT was engineered by the NSCN(IM), which had successfully implanted insurgency even in the most peaceful of areas. One such area was the Karbi Anglong district of Assam, which we have already mentioned. The other being the North Cachar Hills of Assam. These hills are inhabited by one of the most peaceful tribes of north-east India—the Dimasas who had no articulated discontent so far. The NSCN(IM) first used this area as a transit route for their guerrillas and subsequently set up their base in the dense forests of the hills.[4] This was followed by the setting up of an underground organization named Dimasa National Security Force (DNSF). Under the chairmanship of Bharat Langthasa this outfit advanced secessionist demands but its main activity was extortion and murders related to it. But soon the NSCN(IM) withdrew its support to the outfit and formed a counter-outfit called Dima Halom Daoga under the chairmanship of Jewel Burman. This outfit too mainly indulged in extortion from businessmen and government employees. It was reported that DHD was a front organization of the NSCN(IM) and that 70 per cent of the money collected through extortion was to be deposited with the NSCN(IM). The seeds of insurgency were also sown in the peaceful hills of Meghalaya, where the NSCN(IM) sponsored two organizations—the Achik National Volunteers Council (ANVC) to operate in the Garo Hills and the Hynnewtrap Achik Liberation Council (HALC) to function in and around the city of Shillong. Although both were secessionist groups, their main activity was extortion and murder of businessmen and officials. In Manipur, which had a number of such outfits, the NSCN(IM) sponsored another one called the Kanglei Yawol Kanna Lup (KYKL).

Through the NSCN(IM) did not declare its policy on the

expansion of insurgency in the region, it seems that it had a twofold motive. One, to have as many front organizations as possible through which it could collect its finances and two, to create acute turbulence in the region. Both would attract the attention of the Indian State to the region and compel its to negotiate with the NSCN(IM) as a solution to the Naga problem would neutralize other outfits too. The immediate attention of the Indian State was sought also because the Naga issue and the Naga underground movement had been too protracted with no sign of any prospective solution. In the meantime, the prolonged struggle had eroded its mass base and resulted in a dwindling cadre structure.[5] As against this a large chunk of the Nagas were frustrated and had settled down to the fact of being the sixteenth state of the Indian Union.

TURBULENCE IN CIVIL LIFE

Throughout its history, the NSCN(IM) had so far never disrupted the civil life or inflicted violence on the common people or resorted to extortion from the Naga or non-Naga citizen of the Naga Hills. The only 'extortion' it had even indulged in was the collection of an annual amount from the government servants working in Nagaland as 'taxes' which was a source of revenue to run the underground movement. The amount was small and collected with due receipt without any threat or violence. But significantly, from the 1990s it not only indulged in extortion, threat, violence and abduction it also resorted to bomb blasts which killed innocent civilians. It thus marked another change in the pattern of insurgency: degeneration to criminal activity and shift of insurgency from the jungles to urban areas.[6] It was no more just the army which had to deal with insurgency; from now on the state police force was also involved in controlling insurgency as it was part of the maintenance of law and order. For example, on 25 February 1995, there was a massive bomb blast in a train near Nailung near Lumding.[7] The army claimed it to be a handiwork of the NSCN(IM) which it did not deny.[8] In Karbi Anglong and the North Cachar Hills the NSCN(IM) and its front organization had launched a massive extortion drive from businessmen, and government and bank employees. The situation was so bad that the banks operating in the area were eager to withdraw from the region[9] and the employees working in the area sought immediate transfer. The business houses were either shifting to safer areas or closing down. On 5 February 1995 a massive bomb exploded near the Manipur Raj Bhavan in Imphal.[10] Following the deterioration the situation, the Chief of the Indian Army, General Shankar Roy Choudhury, toured the north-east and hinted at a large scale army deployment. But he emphasized that a military solution would provide only a temporary relief; for a permanent solution to the insurgency problem, dialogue with the insurgents was essential.[11] On 27 December 1994 there was a massive shoot out between the NSCN(K) and the Indian Army in the Mokokchung town of Nagaland resulting in the death of seven people including civilians.[12] On 5 March 1995, any army convoy coming from Imphal to Kohima was fired upon by the NSCN(IM) (subsequently it was reported that there was no firing but the sound of a tyre burst from the nearby area). The panic stricken Rashtriya Rifles too opened fire in the middle of the Kohima town resulting in the death of 8 civilians.[13] This act of the army earned widespread condemnation. But by March 1995 more than 150 persons including 13 policemen, 18 army personnel and 112 civilians had been killed by the insurgent groups in the renewed escalation of terrorism and violence.[14] This compelled the Government of Nagaland to promulgate the Disturbed Area Act, 1958 in the state with immediate effect (3 March 1995).

As the situation became volatile, the army launched Operation Golden Bird by which it flushed out the 200-strong group of ultras from the Mizoram-Myanmar border and compelled them to abandon their traditional transit route along this route. The simultaneous escalation of violence in Manipur led the army to launch Operation Sunny Vale there from 4 August 1995. This operation was to counter the Meithei insurgents like PLA, UNLF, PREPAK, KYKL which were operating in Manipur. But the situation showed no signs of improvement.

Another shift in the activity of the NSCN(IM) was evident in its involvement in the tea gardens of Assam along the Assam-Nagaland border. It served extortion notices to a number of tea gardens demanding exorbitant amounts and threatening dire consequences if they are not paid. On 17 October 1995 a tea garden executive was kidnapped from Nowgong.[15] Two days later another tea executive was kidnapped.[16] A powerful bomb exploded in Diphu town on 29 October reportedly by the KNV.[17] The United Liberation Front of Assam had also begun to exort money from a large number of tea planters. As a consequence panic gripped the tea industry of the region.[18] The NSCN(IM) also involved itself in the border dispute with Assam. It supported the concept of a greater Nagaland which meant disturbing the territorial integrity of Assam and Manipur. The NSCN(IM) claimed a large chunk of Assam territory as part of Nagaland which was rejected by its erstwhile comrades in the ULFA.[19] Apprehending claims on Manipur's territory, the Meithei insurgents also protested to the NSCN(IM).[20] As a follow up of its claim on Assam's territory the NSCN(IM) attacked a border post at Lakhimijan near Sibsagar killing some state police personnel.[21] It was also involved in the ambush of an army convoy in Halflong killing several civilians in the process which included a lady and a nine-month-old baby.[22]

Although such disruption of the civil life was resorted to only by the NSCN (IM), other outfits like the ULFA, NDFB, BLTF, ANVC, NLFT, KNV and the DHD too were creating a volatile situation in the entire region. A sense of terrible panic gripped the minds of the people as life became insecure. Bomb blasts and explosions were rampant, and dead bodies were found frequently in most neighbourhoods. Besides the army launching counter-insurgency operations through out the region, paramilitary forces patrolled the affected areas round the clock. The Railway authorities and to rescheduled the departure and arrival timings of trains so as to avoid night operation

These newer forms of terrorism and violence even led the Human Rights activists to denounce the acts of the insurgents. It was a significant shift because all along these bodies were severe critics of the army and their mode of operation, and sympathized with the underground rebels. The National Human Rights Commission Chairman Justice Ranganath Mishra stated that the insurgents too were guilty of human right violations because all violence is an antithesis to human rights.[23]

ESTABLISH NSCN (IM) HEGEMONY

As is evident from the above presentation that from 1995 the insurgency scene in the north-east was entirely dominated by the NSCN(IM). While Mizoram had settled down to peace and development after the accord, the Meithei outfits were confined to the Manipur Valley. As against this the NSCN(IM) which was hitherto confined to the Naga Hills now extended their operations throughout north-east India. In some areas it functioned directly while in others through its front organizations like the KNV, DHD, NDFB, ANVC, HNLC and NLFT. In doing so it not only succeeded in spreading insurgency but also had established itself as the premier insurgent outfit with hegemony over the others. In fact, the NSCN(IM) had been struggling to establish its supremacy over others all along its history. After the Shillong Accord (1975) it broke away from the NNC and formed NSCN(IM) but it still had to contend the NNC as its rival organization. For a short period the NNC was relegated into insignificance but the NSCN(IM) itself broke into two factions—the Isac Swu Muivah group and Khaplang group. Since then the two faction had been fighting an extremely bitter battle to establish their respective supremacy. Now by having so many front organizations which looked up to the NSCN(IM) as their parent body, it finally established its hegemony in the region. To further strengthen its position it tried to set up an umbrella organization under which all the insurgent outfits of the region would function with the NSCN(IM) being the supreme body. One such umbrella body, the Indo-Burmese Revolutionary Front was already there but in this body the NSCN(K) was supreme. Therefore, the NSCN(IM) now formed the United Liberation Front of Seven Sisters (ULFOSS) with the other members such as the United Liberation Front of Assam, Hmar People's Convention, United National Liberation Front (Manipur), and People's Liberation Front of Manipur.[24] These outfits could now buy arms and ammunition from the Bangkok and Singapore market through this body. The Indian Army sources reported that the Inter Service Intelligence of Pakistan was also involved in this regrouping. The ULFOSS was formed in December 1993. Subsequently, on 30 November 1994 it redrew its strategy by forming another umbrella organization called the Self Defence United Front of South East Himalayan Region to coordinate the activities of the constituents.[25] According to the solemn declaration signed by 23 individuals representing various outfits, its objective was to 'fight Indian expansionism and the Indian State terrorism'. The signatories were the NSCN(IM), HALC, NLFT, KNV, HPC, KYKL.[26] It is evident that the constituents of this body were outfits which had been sponsored by the NSCN(IM). Needless to say therefore that the NSCN(IM) was the commanding voice in this organization.

The other method that the NSCN(IM) adopted in establishing hegemony over others, was to set up counter-organizations against the existing one. Thus, it created NLFT against the ATTF in Tripura; NDFB against the BLTF in the Bodo area, and KYKL against the other Meithei outfits in Manipur. It first created the DNSF in the North Cachar Hills but when it fell out with it, it countered it by creating the DHD. In fact, some outfits were able to see through the games of the NSCN(IM). In a press statement the United Liberation Front of Manipur accused the NSCN(IM) of trying to create divisions not only among the Meitheis by creating front organizations like the KYKL but also trying to destroy the traditional bond between the Nagas and Meitheis in Manipur.[27]

INTERNATIONALIZATION

Since the beginning of the movement, the Nagas have been trying to internationalize the Naga issue. It was imperative to create international diplomatic pressure on the Indian State to release the Nagas. This process of internationalization was started by Phizo. The NSCN(IM) continued the effort. It was a major achievement for the NSCN(IM) when it got admission to the Unrepresented Nations and People's Organization. As a result of their persistent endeavour, the NSCN(IM) was able to raise the Naga issue at the United Nations Commission for Human Rights Conference[28] held at Geneva in December 1996, the Working Group on Indigenous People around the same time and the International Convention of Ethnic People in Geneva in July 1994.[29]

CRACKDOWN IN THE NEIGHBOURING COUNTRIES

Alone with the Indian military operations the underground rebels had to face crackdowns in the neighbouring countries too in the 1990s. Such crackdowns meant immense difficulties to the insurgent outfits because most of them had their main base office and training camps in neighbouring countries like Bangladesh and Bhutan. As the pro-democracy movement resuscitated in Myanmar from 1994, the Military Junta in Myanmar began its suppression drive again. The various Burmese groups like the Karens and the Kachins who were leading an underground movement to secure independence from Myanmar also became victims of this suppression drive. The NSCN(IM), both Khaplang and Swu-Muivah factions also had to leave the area as a result of their persecution. The situation worsened with the change in the Government of Bangladesh. Khaleda Zia's Government had encouraged the Indian underground outfits to establish their bases in the Bangla territory. But the new government headed by Sheikh Hasina sought to improve its relationship with India. As a goodwill gesture the Hasina Government decided to stop insurgents from using the Bangla territory against India.[30] As a first step, the bank accounts of the insurgents were frozen[31] and the ultras were asked to leave the Bangla territory by 15 April 1997.[32] The two governments then agreed to jointly fight the ultras. In February 1997, the Bangladesh Government officially launched a crackdown on the ultras and their base camps were busted.[33] The ultras were reported to be shifting their bases back to the jungles of Myanmar[34], while the Brahmaputra Valley based ultras like the ULFA and NDFB were moving to Bhutan.[35] To add to their woes, the Government of India negotiated with the Government of Bhutan not to allow sanctuary to the Indian insurgents. As a follow up the two governments agreed to launch a joint operation against the ultras from November 1997.[36] These developments were serious setbacks to the underground organizations because without these base camps outside India it was extremely difficult for them to operate.

PEACE PROCESS: END OF INSURGENCY?

While the ultras were on the run outside the country and facing combined military operations inside India, the common people of north-east India were facing greater hardship. Caught between the insurgents and the army, repeated curfews and counter-insurgency operations, their normal life was paralysed. Such a volatile situation created a strong desire for peace and normalcy among the people. The Nagas, especially, sought an urgent solution to the 50-year old Naga problem. The change of government in New Delhi facilitated the peace initiative when the new Prime Minister H.D. Deve Gowda during his north-east visit invited the underground leaders for negotiations.[37] It was later confirmed that the prime minister had actually met some insurgent leaders to initiate the peace process.[38] Prominent Naga citizens and organizations decided to seize the opportunity and strengthen the initiative. In a significant move, the Naga citizens decided not to leave the initiative either to the government or the underground alone and to create pressure on both the parties to finally settle the Naga issue. Since the Government of India had expressed its willingness to talk to the underground rebels, the onus was now on the NSCN(IM). The factionalism of the Naga underground was the main obstacle.[39] The Naga people decided to take the initiative to get the NSCN(IM) agree to unification and then sit for the talks. Thus, the Naga Hoho (the summit conference of the Nagas) along with prominent NGOs like the Naga People's

Movement for Human Rights, Naga Mother's Association, Naga Student Federation and Church leaders held discussions to start the peace process. A United Naga Conference was held on 6 February 1997 to deliberate on the subject.[40] on 4 March 1997, the prime minister announced in the Lok Sabha that he had met some insurgent leaders to discuss the Naga issue. The Home Minister Indrajit Gupta subsequently told the Rajya Sabha that the prime minister's talk with the underground leaders did not make any headway due to their insistence on secession from India which was unacceptable to the government.[41] As a result of this failure the Indian Army expressed its doubt over NSCN(IM)'s sincerity in holding talks with the Centre. 'Our past experience shows that this sort of move (acceptance of talk offer) was used by militants as a reprieve and also to redefine and consolidate their present position.'[42] The NSCN(IM) too expressed its dissatisfaction over the Centre's attitude. It set certain pre-conditions for further discussions: (*i*) that the talks be held in a third country, and (*ii*) and that the negotiations be settled by a third country.[43] In the meantime, the Kukis (a tribe in constant conflict with the Nagas) urged that they be included in the negotiations because any settlement would have to take care of their interests too.[44] The Khaplang faction of the NSCN(IM) dissociated itself from the talks.[45] But despite these bottlenecks the first round of talks between the NSCN(IM) and the Indian officials were held in Bangkok in July 1997 and were able to break the ice.[46] As per the desire of the Naga Hoho and as a goodwill gesture to create a congenial atmosphere for negotiations, the Government of India offered a ceasefire agreement to the NSCN(IM) which the latter accepted. As a result the ceasefire came into effect in Nagaland from 1 August 1997. After almost 50 years guns were silent in the hills of Nagaland.

Meanwhile, the Naga Hoho and NGOs kept up their pressure on the NSCN(IM) so that the peace initiative did not fizzle out. The Baptist Fellowship of America organized a convention of Nagas at Atlanta (USA) in August 1997 to mark the 125th year of the advent of Christianity in Naga Hills. The convention wanted to use this opportunity to work out a lasting solution to the Naga problem. The Naga Hoho made the NSCN(IM) agree to participate in the convention. In fact, it even got the Khaplang faction to agree to come to the convention. The eight-day long convention was attended by about 10,000 Nagas and had successful deliberation on the Naga issue. Its major success was to get the Khaplang and Swu-Muivah factions of NSCN(IM) to join the peace process and not to impede solution to the Naga issue.[47] Addressing a UNPO Conference in Geneva (15th session) Isac Swu of the NSCN(IM) stated that the Government of India had agreed to the NSCN(IM) condition that: (*i*) talks between them be held without either side stipulating any precondition, (*ii*) that the talks be held at the highest level (prime ministerial), and (*iii*) at a venue anywhere outside India or Nagaland.[48] In pursuance of the agreement the second round of talks were held in Geneva. The date and deliberations of the meetings were not known as they were kept secret. But the Government of India and the Naga Hoho were hopeful about the progress of the negotiations. To continue the peaceful atmosphere the Government of India extended the ceasefire further which continued up to the middle of 1999. There were hopes all round that the half a century old Naga problem was going to be solved and the insurgency and violence was going to give way to peace and prosperity.

Meanwhile, the United Front Government was dislodged from power and a new government led by Atal Behari Vajpayee assumed power. But the change did not affect the peace process. The new government extended the ceasefire and appointed Swaraj Kaushal, a prominent lawyer and former Governor of Mizoram as prime minister's emissary to the negotiations. Talks were subsequently held in Manila, Zurich and Amsterdam. The Amsterdam talks were held in March 1999. A joint Ceasefire Monitoring Cell was constituted by the NSCN(IM) and the Government of India to monitor the progress of ceasefire and breach if any. The next round of talks were scheduled to be held by the end of June 1999. This time the Government of India wanted to hold the talks in any Indian city but the NSCN(IM) insisted on a foreign country.[49]

The period under discussion acquired more significance for other reasons too. Due to the pressure of the Naga Hoho, the Khaplang faction of NSCN(IM) agreed to observe the ceasefire. It now appeared that the Naga Hoho was in position to control the Naga situation. It agreed with the NSCN(IM) to observe 16 May as the Plebiscite Day' and accordingly it was solemnly observed throughout Naga areas. In May (8 1999) the Naga underground leaders Th. Muivah and Isac Swu returned to Nagaland after 33 years and since then have been camping there to monitor the ceasefire, the peace process and to assess the ground realities in Nagaland. In an interview Isac Swu said 'since we are entering into serious discussions with India (after initial rounds) we have come here for consultations'.[50]

Muivah stated that 'the people here are very anxious about the developments taking place outside. Our movement as such is people based and unless people understand what is going on there will be a gap.'[51] While in India, the NSCN(IM) renamed itself as National Socialist Council of Nagalim (Lim stood for land). The visit of the underground leaders raised the hope of the Naga people about arriving at a lasting solution to the Naga issue and the coming of the long awaited peace and tranquility which would enable them to lead a normal life, that had so far eluded them. But the conflicting statements issued by both the parties raised doubts about the end of insurgency. Naga leaders declared that they could not accept any solution that is not 'honourable' after fifty years of struggle and that sovereignty was inalienable,[52] while the representative of the Indian State, Swaraj Kaushal ruled out sovereignty for the Nagas.[53] He stated that any solution has to be worked within the framework of the Indian Constitution.[54] With both the parties refusing to negotiate 'Naga Sovereignty' it is feared that the talks were heading for a deadlock. This would mean despair and agony for the Naga people. But the question remains, can the Naga underground leaders and the Indian State continue to ignore the Naga peoples' desire for peace and the right to normal life. The onus therefore is on the Naga people represented by the highest body—the Naga Hoho.

However, in the July-August (1999) peace talks the ceasefire was again extended, this time for a year signalling another positive development. There were a number of meetings between the NSCN(IM) and the Govt. of India negotiator Swaraj Kaushal in Bangkok, Zurich and Paris and twice in Amsterdam. But then suddenly Kaushal resigned from the post of negotiator. Internal politics within the Bharatiya Janata Party of which Sushama Swaraj, wife of Kaushal was a prominent leader was said to be the reason.[55] K. Padmanabhaiah, retired Home Secretary was then appointed as representative of the government in the peace talks who continued the peace discussions with the NSCN leaders. In a meeting held in 29-30 July 2000 in Bangkok the two parties agreed to extend the ceasefire by another year. But following this an unfortunate event took place. The NSCN leader, Th. Muivah was arrested by Thailand Police on charge of travelling on fake document and put him in jail. With the leader in jail the continuation of the peace talk was in peril. There was another lurking danger to the peace process: the question of extension of ceasefire in all the areas of north-east where there is a preponderance of Naga population.

CEASEFIRE AND GREATER NAGALAND

On 26 August 2000, Mr Isac Swu of NSCN(IM) wrote to the Prime Minister of India alleging his government of betraying its commitment on the ceasefire issue. Padmanabhaiah had reportedly agreed to the extension of ceasefire provision to all Naga inhabitated areas of north-east, not just Nagaland. The NSCN argument was that observing ceasefire only in Nagaland but continuing the fight between the NSCN and the Indian Army in other areas did not prove meaningful. It vitiated the atmosphere for the continuation of peace discussion. Swu warned that the NSCN(IM) would no longer be under any obligation if the Indian Government does not officially implement the ceasefire in all Naga areas by 5 September 2000.[56] In reply in 11 September 2000, K. Padmanabhaiah replied to Swu stating that none of the government representative has agreed to extend the ceasefire in all Naga areas. He also pointed out that the Government of India would consider extension of ceasefire with NSCN(IM) to other areas in north-east subject to the condition that NSCN(IM) accepts and agrees to issue a statement that extension of ceasefire to other areas will not be interpreted by them as a step towards recognition of their claim to Greater Nagaland.

Padmanabhaiah's statement had a context. The Naga underground organizations have long been demanding that all the contiguous areas of Nagaland which has a preponderant Naga population, such as Assam, Arunachal Pradesh and Manipur should be amalgamated into a single Naga unit. From this emerged the concept of greater Nagalim. In fact for these organizations it was not just the sovereignty of Nagaland but the carving out of a greater Nagaland was also part of the goal. But problem resulted from the irrelevantly opposition from those states—Assam, Manipur and Arunachal Pradesh protested and opposed the idea of greater Nagaland and refused to part with even a fraction of their respective territory. As soon as the Swu-Padmanabhaiah's dialogue became public. There was vociferous objection in these states which compelled the Prime Minister to convene a meeting with the Chief Ministers of these states. In this meeting of 28 September 2000 the Chief Ministers of Assam, Manipur, Arunachal Pradesh and Meghalaya opposed the extension of ceasefire in their respective states on the ground that this would legitimatize the claim of the Nagas on the territory of these states in future. In fact it would become the basis of their future claim of Greater Nagaland. Secondly, the ceasefire extension over these areas would provide free access to the NSCN to construct their camps, carry their tax collection and extortion drives, recruit local youths in its cadre and give birth to dummy insurgent outfits. All these were sure to disrupt these otherwise peaceful areas. In fact even the Nagaland Chief Minister S.C. Jamir in its meeting with the Home Minister L.K. Advani said that the extension of ceasefire beyond Nagaland was fraught with dangerous consequences.[57.]

But the NSCN(IM) was not ready to continue peace discussion without such extension. Since it decided to call off the negotiation if ceasefire to all Naga areas were not implemented, the Government of India in a significant move on (14 June) 2001 decided to agree to ceasefire 'Without territorial limits'.

THE FALL OUT

The fall out of the this extension of ceasefire over areas of other states was cataclysmic. The state of Manipur was up in arms led the students union, the state experience unprecedented violence in the form of protests. The State Assembly building was burnt, legislators threatened and Government establishment attacked. The uprising continued unabated for almost a month. With more and more people joining the protest, women and youth coming in the forefront and defying State's repression and prohibitory orders the movement continued to gain strength. Gradually the protest movement spread in other areas of the region too—in Assam and Arunachal Pradesh. While students organizations and political parties protesting against government decision it threatened to become violent when insurgent organizations like Dima Halom Daoga and United Liberation Front of Assam also joining the protest. The situation became volatile and threatened to erupt in violence. In Manipur the amity between the Meithei and Nagas also on the verge of breach. Terrified of violent attack on them, the Nagas of Imphal Valley evacuated to safer place. The Kuki and Vaiphei, etc., non-Meithei tribes of Manipur also supported the protest of the Meitheis.

Taken aback by the unprecedented protest, the Govt. of India convened a series of meetings with the protesting groups as well as the Naga organizations. On 27 July 2001 a high level meeting was held at the 7 Race Course, New Delhi, the Official Residence of the Prime Minister. Subsequent to this, the Home Minister announced that while ceasefire continued the words in the agreement 'Without territorial limit' was being withdrawn. In other words the status quo was maintained and ceasefire would now be continued only within Nagaland. It was also added that the Government of India representatives had discussed the matter with the NSCN(IM) which was agreeable to the decision.

While the announcement quelled the disquiet in Manipur, Assam and Arunachal Pradesh it had the expected repercussion on Nagaland.

The people of Nagaland as well as the Nagas of Manipur rose in protest against the about turn which they termed as 'betrayal'. To make matter worse the NSCN(IM) stated that contrary to the statement of the Government of India it had not agreed nor is agreeable to this 'reversion'. The breach of agreement was done unilaterally by the Government of India. Although the latter insisted that despite the setbacks the negotiation with the NSCN(IM) would continue, the future seems to be uncertain yet again. The only hope was the Naga Hoho, Naga Mother Association and Naga People's Movement for Human Rights which is making untiring efforts to bring the peace process back to its track.

NOTES

1. Sajal Nag, *Nationalism, Separatism, Secessionism*, Jaipur: Rawat, 1999.
2. Ibid.
3. Kuldip Nayyar, 'Defiance by the Nagas', in *The Sentinel*, 8 March 1995.
4. *The Sentinel*, 27 February 1995.
5. Ibid., 26 May 1997. It was reported that to attract youngmen, the NSCN(IM) was offering Rs.5 lakh to each recruit.
6. Ibid., 23 March 1995.
7. Ibid., 26 February 1995.
8. Ibid.
9. Ibid., 27 February 1995.
10. Ibid., 10 February 1995.
11. Ibid., 9 February 1995.
12. Ibid., 28 December 1994.
13. Ibid., 6 March 1995.
14. Ibid., 23 March 1995.
15. Ibid., 18 October 1995.
16. Ibid., 20 October 1995.
17. Ibid., 30 October 1995.
18. Ibid., 18 October 1995.
19. Ibid., 24 August 1997.

20. Ibid.
21. Ibid., 3 February 1996.
22. Ibid., 8 February 1996.
23. Ibid., 4 November 1956.
24. *The Shillong Times*, 27 December 1993.
25. Kamrupi, 'NSCN(IM) Redress its Strategy', in *The Sentinel*, 21 February 1995.
26. Ibid.
27. *The Sentinel*, 23 February 1995.
28. Ibid., 6 January 1997.
29. Ibid., 26 April 1995.
30. Ibid., 27 July 1996.
31. Ibid., 14 September 1996.
32. Ibid., 18 April 1997.
33. Ibid., 19 April 1997.
34. Ibid., 1 March 1997.
35. Ibid., 4 March 1997.
36. Ibid., 20 and 26 June 1997.
37. Ibid., 25 October 1996.
38. Ibid., 5 March 1997.
39. Ibid., 26 May 1997. The main fight was between the Khaplang and Muivah-Swu faction. Khaplang was a Myanmarese Naga while Isac Swu was a Sema and Muivah was a Tangkhul. The bulk of the cadre were Konyaks. In 1988, the Konyaks murdered 88 Tangkhuls leading to the separation of the Khaplang and Muivah factions.
40. Ibid., 18 February 1997.
41. Ibid., 15 May 1997.
42. Quotes in *The Sentinel*, 19 December 1996.
43. *The Sentinel*, 30 December 1996.
44. Ibid., 21 May 1997.
45. Ibid., 30 July 1996.
46. Ibid., 3 July 1997.
47. Ibid., 31 July 1997.
48. Ibid., 2 August 1997.
49. *The Telegraph*, 12 June 1999.
50. Interview with Isac Swu and Th. Muivah in Nuland, Dimapur, Nagaland, 27 May 1999, *The Sun* (North-East), 15-30 June 1999.
51. Ibid.
52. *The Northeast Daily*, 4 June 1999.
53. *The Telegraph*, 12 June 1999.
54. Ibid.
55. 'A Couple of Problems', in *Outlook*, 10 August 1999.
56. 'Recent Turn of Events', in *The Sun* (North-East), 15-31 October 2001.
57. Ibid.

CHAPTER ELEVEN

The Discourses

The granting of statehood by the Indian Government to the Naga Hills in response to the wishes of a large section of the Nagas was a severe blow to the extremists who had been demanding independence from India. This not only meant the reinforcement of Indian authority in the Naga Hills but also the victory of the moderates. It was a set-back for the politically ambitious extremists who had been considering themselves as the legitimate ruling community of the prospective Naga nation state. The event was all the more meaningful because it signified the polarization of the mass base. The moderates had control over a large section of these polarized masses who, caught between the violence of the Indian Army and the faction-ridden underground insurgents and traumatized by the bloodshed and harassment, were willing to settle for little less than complete freedom for the sake of peace. The enthusiastic response to the inauguration of the Naga Hills as the sixteenth state of the Indian Union also proved the weaning away of its support base. What was immediately required was the stepping up of the mobilization and indoctrination process as well as a sustained and massive propaganda campaign. But the banishment of the extremists as secessionists and insurgents and the launch of a gigantic counter-insurgency military operation pushed them to the underground. The Naga insurgency since then has taken an organized form. The emergence of an organized insurgency coincided with an organized, systematic and rigorous presentation of the Naga national question. The same was the case with the Mizos as well as the Meitheis. In this phase as compared with the earlier phases we get a relatively sophisticated construction of the Naga national question. However, as far as the Nagas were concerned. Phizo was responsible for raising these issues.

In this phase we find Phizo for the first time declaring India as an aggressor nation. It implied that Phizo had by then realized the inefficacy of his appeals to the conscience of the new Indian nation as well as his threats. The post-colonial Indian State responded by demonstrating its military might and in self-interest maintained a conciliatory approach towards the moderate section of Naga leadership. Phizo's reaction to the conferment of statehood in the Naga Hills was to declare India as an aggressor nation:

> Any Government which invades another territory is an aggressor and Nagaland is being invaded by free India under the direction of her External Affairs Ministry. Their forces have committed genocide by wiping out community after community and they are now heavily occupying our country. . . .
>
> Today the Naga citizens who are in the hands of the Indian Armed Forces have no human rights. Those who are still free are hunted and killed as if they are animals. Mass killings and wholesales massacre started years ago and has been going ever since.[1]

The Federal Government of Nagaland, which functioned from exile, continued the same line of argument consistent with its predecessors. It decried what it described as Indian occupation of Naga Hills. It asserted that the Nagas were not seeking secession from India as it had never conquered the Nagas. In fact, according to the Federal Government Nagaland became independent on 14 August 1947, i.e. the day the British, who had conquered the Nagas, had withdrawn from India.

The construction of the Naga national question reached a level of abstraction with the emergence of the National Socialist Council of Nagaland (NSCN, 1980). The NSCN began its exposition of Naga nationality by observing that:

> The concept of human race, internationalism and myth of nations could in no sense deprive the Nagas of the basis of being a family and a national of their own existence. This self determination is their righteous cause and Nagas shall always be the people of this noble cause. It is, however, submitted that notwithstanding the feat of patriotism and valour, Nagas found themselves being self-defeated now and then. It is purely due to, in the first place, parochialism practised in the highest circle of national affairs. Also the path the people have to tread was not illuminated, *sine qua non* of clarity of the way to their salvation was absent. The masses were by the large led along in the name of nation alone.[2]

It then described the Nagaland-India tangle as:

> The rulers of India and their strong men could not understand Nagaland and her people. They only know that the Nagas were naked and on this account despised

them and disregarded all their historical rights. However, Naked Nagas also have their homeland and it have never been conquered by the Indians nor by the Burmese. Neither have the Nagas ever joined the Indian Union nor that of Burma by consent. As the Indians and Burmese took recourse to force, Naga people knew for certain that the problem had involved a challenge on our stand on the basic issue of principle, to face which we have come into being. Indians demanded total surrender. They also boasted stating that to finish the Nagas was a matter of a day and took pride in it. The Generals and the strongmen who were the hope of India, were sent one after another to Nagaland to conduct the unprecedented theatre of cruel war. Hundreds and thousands of troops operated and ravaged the land, indiscriminately putting out thousands of lives. They resorted to endless devices of tortures and killings . . . (then) they had to change their stand from total surrender to negotiation. The one day has turned out to be a quarter of a century. . . . However it is clear that India would muster all the traitors and organize them into an active puppet front to attain their objective which is expressed in lucid terms by Morarji Desai, a one-time Prime Minister of India as 'I will exterminate the Nagas without any compunction.[3]

The NSCN then went on to depict India as a colonial nation which not only subjugated the Nagas but the other weak nationalities of the region. These nationalities, it was prophesied, would soon revolt to exercise their right to self-determination, which would cause the eventual disintegration of the Indian Union:

Moreover, it is evident from the present day phenomena that India, not to speak of forcing the Nagas into the union, would not be able to hold together all its component parts for all time to come. The discontented peoples and nationalities are bound to rise up to save themselves from perishing altogether in Indian society where suppression, discrimination and all sorts of corruption abound. India would soon be bound up in internal turmoil. The mighty problem of poverty and hunger shall loom ever more. India can gain no ground to defeat us.[4]

Having said so, it also cautioned the Nagas about the silent invasion of Indian capital with the aim of a political conquest. Such a conquest it was said was already being facilitated by the migration of Indians to Nagaland.

Along with the occupation of Nagaland by sheer military might, one started witnessing the process of Indianisation of the Naga people on full massive scale (for the purpose of cultural conquest). Therefore, the struggle of the Nagas was not only 'to defend Nagland's independent existence' but also 'safety from the doom of Hinduism'.[5]

It then philosophized:

> In this would of bitter history where powers and unruly ambitions make life insane, the only way for a people to hold out their salvation is to cling to their freedom. Because it is freedom and the love for it that give meaning to life. Therefore, freedom the very precious most, shall on no occasion be yielded to whatever guests history may still afford. The desire for domination has not ended desire the horrors it has brought about. The just aspirations of the weak and the poor are left downtrodden in justification of the sheer interests of the aggressors and that is the worst side of politics everywhere. Aggressors never teach themselves justice; peace is still a long way off, and it is the problem. But passivity to unjust domination is unmitigated evil, which needs thorough eradication from people's mentality, for a people that do not uphold their rights have nothing here in this world which they can call theirs. They are homeless in their own home with all the ceaseless miseries of domination. Because in their passivity they have committed the genesis of political crime. The most beautiful country for a people is the country they are born in and her freedom is above all treasures. But preparedness to rise in defence of the freedom whenever called for is the finest of all politics anywhere. The strong throws his weight about and the unprepared to stand up to it are always the victim and it wouldn't stop. If not crushed, they are strung along to perpetuate the grips on them with promises of 'constitution guarantees' which is, of course, a beautiful modern sophistry. But those who trust in it are no longer a free people. People void of confidence in themselves are no people. They are lost. They exist for no cause. Such people know neither shame nor glory. A people are a people but only when they are the master of themselves. Therefore, to survive with meanings, a people must hold to the truth that they are the master of themselves; they must have faith in themselves. They should know for sure that they are competent to determine their future, that they are most able to do justice, that their future is secure in their own hands alone, for the world belongs only to the prepared. We profoundly share weal and woe with the aggrieved wherever they may be. They are our fellow travelers. To us, the most miserable world ever to live in is the one where truth is suppressed and where there is no hope for salvation. We shall hold fast to our freedom, for what remains when it falls! Yes, we will never back down from our principles; they are all the world to us. This is our treasured philosophy. The fate is decided; it is in our hands. We shall live only in freedom.[6]

The Mizo National Front came into being in 1961 and since then has been working for outright independence from India. In its demand for Indian withdrawal from the Mizo Hills, the MNF construction of its national identity was very similar to those of its predecessors in the Naga Hills. The MNF Memorandum to Prime Minister Lal Bahadur Shastri dated 30 October 1965 began by stating:

> The Mizos from times immemorial lived in complete independence without

interference. Chiefs of the different clans ruled over separate hills and valley with supreme authority and their administration was very much like the Greek city state's of the past. Their territory and every part thereof had never been conquered or subjugated by their neighbouring state . . . scattered as they are, divided (by the British), the Mizo people are inseparably knitted together by their strong bond of tradition, custom, culture, language, social life and religion wherever they are. The Mizos stood as a separate nation even before the advent of British Government, having a nationality distinct and separate from that of India. In a nutshell they are a distinct nation, created, moulded and nurtured by God and nature. . . .

In other words, the Mizos had never been under the Indian Government and never had any connection with the politics and policies of the various groups of Indian opinion. When India was in the threshold of independence the relation of the Mizos with the British Government and also with British India were fully realized by the Indian National Congress leaders. . . . Due solely to their political immaturity ignorance and lack of consciousness of their fate, representatives of the Mizo Union, the largest political organization at that time. Representing all political including representatives of religions denominations and social organizations that were in existence submitted their demand and chose integration with free India imposing condition *inter alia* 'that the Lushai will be allowed to opt out of Indian Union when they wish to do so subject to a minimum period of ten years. . . .'

During the fifteen years of close contact and association with India, the Mizo people had not been able to feel at home with Indian or in India nor have they been able to feel that their joys and sorrows have really been shared by India. They therefore do not feel Indian. Being created a separate nation they cannot go against nature to cross the barriers of nationality. They refused to occupy a place within India as they consider it to be unworthy of their national dignity and harmful to the interest of their prosperity. Nationalism and patriotism inspired by the political consciousness has now reached its maturity and the cry for political self-determination is the only wish and aspiration of the people *ne plus ultra*, the only final and final perfect embodiment of social living for them. Their only aspiration and political cry is the creation of Mizoram a free, a sovereign state to govern herself to work out her own destiny and to formulate her own foreign policy. . . .

Though known as headhunters and a martial race, the Mizos commit themselves to a policy non-violence in their struggle and have no intention of employing any other means to achieve their political demand. If on the other hand, the Government of India brings exploitation and suppressive measures into operation employing military might against the Mizo people as is done in the case of the Nagas, which God forbid, it would be erroneous and futile for both the parties for a soul cannot be destroyed by weapons.

For this end it is in goodwill and understanding that the Mizo nation voices her rightful and legitimate claim of full self-determination through this Memorandum. . . .[7]

When the MNF declared unilateral independence and formed a government of its own in exile (1 March 1966) its declaration of independence observed:

> In the course of history, it becomes invariably necessary for mankind to assume their social, economic and political status to which the laws of the nature's God entitle them.
>
> The Mizos created and moulded into a nation and nurtured as such by Nature's God, have been intolerably dominated by the people of India in contravention to the laws of nature.[8]

The PLA had however reiterated the significance of ideology as an inseparable part of the movement it led. It revived the Marxian ideology of 'liberation movements' in north-east India after Irabat. In sharp contrast to its predecessors, the PLA treated the issue as a class question. Following the Maoist line, the PLA declared that 'armed struggle is always the main form of our struggle throughout the period of our new democratic revolution'. To bring about this democratic revolution and liberate the people from 'the colonial yoke of the reactionary rule of the Delhi Bandits' it had adopted the ideas of revolution evolved and experimented by Mao in China, which it considered to be the most scientific theory of revolution without which it said, 'we cannot successful fulfil the task of our motherland and we can never lead the revolutionary cause of our people successfully'.[9] In this struggle the question of class was placed over nationality.[10] It felt that the struggle of the Nagas, Mizos and the Meitheis in the past had failed because its strategy was erroneous. It failed to analyse the class dimension of their respective societies and to locate its class enemies and friends. It also failed to see the history of mankind as the history of class struggles. 'The Phizo-led revolutionaries did not study the Marxist-Leninist and Mao Tse-Tung thoughts and thus failed to analyse the class nature of Naga society.'[11]

It attributed the failure of the Naga movement to its emphasis on the 'Naga nation theory' and 'over emphasis on Christianity' which it termed as 'chauvinism'. It found the case of the Mizos similar.[12] The Meitheis too had, in the past, wanted to revive the old indigenous religion and establish a great Meithei land. But PLA considered such ethnic oriented struggles as 'narrow nationalism' and condemned the theory of 'Meitheis for the Meitheis', 'Mizos for the Mizos' and 'Nagas for the Nagas'.[13] It felt that these movement therefore were destined to fail and invoked them to a joint battle against the Delhi

Bandits. There was a need of unity of all the nationalities and also to 'arouse the neighbouring states of India and help guide the Indian working class'.[14]

In a remarkable departure from other insurgents of the north-east, the PLA declared the peasants and proletariats of India to be its real friends and the motivating force of the revolution. 'The poor have no motherland' it said. It also recognized the role of intellectuals in such a struggle saying 'without the participation of revolutionary intellectuals, no revolution can be successful'.[15] However, it felt that the intellectuals could not lead the revolution until they were re-educated in objective realities. The PLA considered the Meithei society as feudal, which was witnessing feudal as well as colonial exploitation. The 'national bourgeoisie' and the 'proletariat' both were slaves of the same masters—the Delhi Bandits, the term used for the New Delhi regime was derived from the Maoist phrase 'Chiang Kai Shek bandit gang'. According to them such an exploitative regime could be replaced through a new democratic revolution wherein the targets need not be the petty bourgeoisie but the compradors. In fact, except the latter, all should get united in which the chief target would be feudalism and colonialism. 'We know that the bourgeoisie are always antagonistic to the proletariats. However, at the present stage, the bourgeoisie (except the compradors) are not the main target of our revolution but to be united. Because our revolution is a new democratic revolution, we unite with the bourgeoisie in order to overthrow and defeat the treacherous Delhi bandits.'[16]

It was obvious that the PLA did not want to alienate certain sections of the Meitheis. From a pragmatic point of view by declaring that they were safe from the PLA men it wanted to send the message that they were included in the battle.

The PLA also proclaimed itself to be internationalist and extended its support to various international proletarian movements. It however was very critical of the Communist Party of India (CPI) and charged it as a party 'which betrayed the revolution of Indian working class'. And was also branded as the chief agent of the 'Delhi Bandits' and 'puppets of Moscow'. It even decried the Soviet Union as 'the chief betrayer of the world revolution' and described it as 'expansionist'.[17]

The PLA's professed motto was 'from the masses to the masses',[18] and the peasantry was to be leading force of its revolution. Their targets were not the common Indians but the Indian ruling class that was feudal and neo-colonialist in nature. It wanted to repeat the 'Nanchang uprising' in Indian, and felt that 'the nature of Chinese revolution is undoubtedly applicable to us and we have to apply it'.[19] Though the PLA believed in an armed struggle, it conceded that peoples' consciousness was superior to arms. 'It is the consciousness of men that is decisive in winning a war, though arms play a role in it.'[20] The PLA also guaranteed people religious freedom along with the freedom of criticizing religion.

The PLA's internationalist image and rhetoric of a joint struggle with the Indian peasants and working class to overthrow the common enemy—the Delhi regime—created a dilemma for those who wanted to characterize it as a secessionist organization. The PLA planned on forming a Revolutionary Front covering Manipur, Nagaland, Mizoram, Assam, Tripura and Aruanchal Pradesh and proclaimed that 'the future of revolution is bright. . . . The unity of all nationalities including the Nagas, the Mizos, the Chins, the Kukis, the Meitheis and so on can arouse the neighbouring states of India so that the Delhi-regime can be overthrown by joint force.'[21] What is required, 'at the present stage is a real Marxist party, guided by Marxism-Leninism and Mao Tse-Tung though—a party which by mobilizing the whole masses can lead the people to an armed revolution'.[22] Such an objective and ideology seemed to be consistent with other Maoist groups like the CPI(ML) and its Naxalite wings which were not characterized as secessionists even by the Indian State. Consistent with this ideology the PLA condemned the 'political ideology (which) was based on Meithei fanaticism, chauvinism and revivalism' which it felt to be the reason 'why it (the earlier revolutionary movements in Manipur) collapsed so soon'.[23] Invoking the working class parties in the rest of India, it said that 'it is time for the Indian working class to jointly sit together, sacrificing all kinds of personal difference and settling the problems through consultations and discussions, so that unity can be achieved and once the Indian working class is united, the success of the Indian revolution is in sight.'[24] The PLA said that the Indian peasants and working class were its ally and it felt that only Marxism can help in the survival of the poor and the downtrodden.[25] But Bisheshwar went back to the position that others took before him when he wrote his autobiography which reveals his personal predilections. He felt that the people who labelled him as a secessionist were naive.[26] He considered himself equal to any Indian leader and emphasized that he was opposed to violence and was for peace. 'I love democracy. A strong and great motherland is always my motto.'[27] He also declared that the Meitheis were not anti-Indian as it was generally believed but were 'non-Indian Indian'.[28] He amplified the phrase to mean that Meitheis are Indians but 'less equal than the Indians'. They are 'a semi and illegitimate or an abandoned Indian Hindu yet to be recognised by the Indian Hindu'.[29] Thus, the PLA struggle was 'a struggle of the unfreed Indians against the freed Indian'.[30]

Bisheshwar in his autobiography, which is a collection of disjointed, inconsistent statements says:

> To me, my people of the north east in the eyes of India are pseudo or self-styled Indians, unrecognized or illegitimate Indians, indeed abandoned Indians, like step brothers of the foster mother India or may I say a colony of or a dominion status of the Indian empire. This is supported by the fact there are many kinds of armed or other form of uprising or rebellion in the north east for the last many a decade.[31]

He goes on to explain:

> when I say north east is a colony, it does not imply that the citizens in the region have anti-Indian attitude but it only means that we are made to feel inferior. . . . We have to bend our heads low, when our Indian bosses call us.[32]

As far as the Meithies are concerned:

> They become [*sic*] extinct in the form of a soluble salt in the mainstream of Indian ocean. . . . Today the Meitheis are facing a threat to their very existence. They get [*sic*] extinct. They have no motherland of their own in India and in Manipur. . . . Are we joining the Indian Union to get wiped out? Should India build its empire on debris of the Meitheis.[33]

Bisheshwar then went on to describe how the Meitheis were confined to the plains of Imphal and not allowed to settle in the hills which was 'once their own'.[34] Also, there had been as incessant influx of non-Manipuri Muslims, Nepalese and Bengalees who threaten to reduce the Meitheis to a minority in their own land. Foreigners of non-Indian origin were not allowed in Manipur by the Indian State though the Meitheis wanted their free mobility. Manipuri language, of which Meitheis are so proud was not recognized by the Indian State (it has since been included in the Eighth Schedule). Manipur had a 'meaningless' representation in the Central Legislature (only 2 members of Parliament) whereas states like Uttar Pradesh alone have 85 members which was ethnically speaking, unequal and due to which Meitheis had no political power at the Centre. He continued:

> Considering the Indian Government's attitude towards me and my people I hate to call myself Indian. I have tasted the flavour of the Indian pudding. Indians are sour, no bitter [*sic*]. It's law is blind and its Government has no room for justice and humanity. In short India is barbaric. The so-called Indian democracy, the religious India, the land of saints, the Gods, the old Indian tradition, the rich cultural heritage all come out to be a shield or a camouflage to conceal the dirty national image of India.[35]

He blamed the Indian State for 'starting' insurgency in Manipur by sending its army. In the name of tackling the insurgents they succeeded in antagonizing the entire civilian population. He also believed the Indian State to be biased against the north-east. The activity of the Naxalites who conducted armed struggles in several states was not called 'insurgency' and not tackled by the Indian Army, but the PLA, MNF and NSCN who were admittedly a handful of rebel groups, were condemned as insurgents.[36]

The PREPAK another Maoist organization aimed at the installation of a Socialist Sovereign State in Manipur by suppressing all counter revolutionary forces, destruction of class enemies which included capitalists, politicians, bureaucrats, contractors and anti-social elements.[37] The PREPAK termed the Indian Government as bureaucratic-imperialist which exploited the entire traditional economy of Manipur, supported outsiders and unleashed military force against Kangleipak (Manipur). India was described as a neo-colonialist enemy. It envisaged the setting up of collective farming, nationalization of trade and business, and people's courts. It believed in armed protest against the Government of India for its racist postures. It also planned to coordinate the movements in north-east India into a pan-Mongoloid offensive against the Indian State. Gradually the PREPAK elements were absorbed into the PLA and KCP. The PREPAK elements were believed to be mere 'enthusiasts' which is why it was liquidated gradually.[38]

The Nagas had used the word 'self determination' in 1929 which to them meant the 'right to live the inherited life'.[39] But the breakdown of the NNC-Hydari Agreement changed the Naga attitude totally. The Indian refusal to grant freedom if they so desired after ten years, seemed to confirm their worst fears of Indian domination already. The Indian attitude brought about a change in the Naga perception of independence and sovereignty: it meant resistance to Indian domination. It was the British who had conquered the Nagas and made them a part of British India. The Naga elite use self-determination to mean reversion to their original independent status after the British withdrawal. As such the continuation of Indian hold over Nagaland was seen as an act of aggression. India was described as a colonial power in the 1960s and was accused of the 'criminal act of aggression against the territorial sovereignty of Nagaland and using coercive power against the nationalist people of Nagaland'. The Indian rule in Nagaland was described as 'subjugation' and the Naga struggle for independence as a 'nationalist movement'.[40]

The coercive policy of the Indian State strengthened the extremist sections of the Nagas whose projected image of India as a colonial and aggressor nation got reinforced at the popular level. The spokesmen of the Naga independence movement also began to conceptualize the idea of independence and sovereignty according to theories and jargons of modern nationalist discourse. The original Naga ideas of independence and sovereignty—based on Naga folk perception and tribal outlook was now being given a sophisticated shape. In 1956 the undergrounds rebels set up the Federal Government of Nagaland in exile which adopted a modern constitution called 'Yezabo' written in English which pledged to promote democracy, equality, justice, liberty and fraternity and set up a parliament called Tatar, consisting of two houses—Kimhhao (Upper House) and Tatar House (Assembly of Representatives). It adopted a national flag and anthem.

The National Socialist Council of Nagaland formed by the breakaway faction of the NNC revolted against Phizo's leadership and formed an alternative government in exile called the People's Republic of Nagaland. It declared itself Maoist and had the goal of setting up a socialist society in Nagaland. 'It is definitely socialism alone that can assure the fairest deal to the community as a whole as it is the only social and economic system that does away with exploitation and oppression.'[41] To them Socialism meant a system, 'where virtually all the means of production, transportation and communication and other essential functions are to be owned by the state or by the community as a whole. It is only in the dictatorship of the people through a Revolutionary Council that the principle of people's supremacy is upheld to its meaning, the free existence of Nagaland could be safeguarded and socialism could be realized. . . .'[42] Elaborating on the actual policies to be followed in Nagaland it stated that:

> . . . all means would be nationalized; there shall be economic ceiling. There shall

be national programme for raising the living standard of the poorest family to the richest. In order to raise the living standard of the people, agricultural methods shall be modernized. Every house shall be electrified. Discrimination and exploitation of any form shall be illegalised. However, import of things that are repugnant to the taste of a Christian people would be prohibitied.[43]

The NSCN declared that in their scheme of things Christianity would be the state religion of Nagaland, though a Christian state practice of other religions would be permitted. But it was opposed to the influx of Indian capital as well as Indian nationals as it might lead to colonization and Indianization which virtually meant Hinduization. Nagaland would be ruled in the spirit of love for God and Men which was the essence of Christianity. It did not find the concept of Socialist state contradictory to a Christian state because 'the spirit of Christianity and socialism were not antithetical'.[44] Under its rule the Church would function as an independent organization. 'Since religion is a creative force and inseparable from people's life, the state needs it as much as individuals need it.'

The NNC and NSCN refused to see the Naga independence movement as a secessionist movement. They argued that the question of secession did not arise as Nagaland was never a part of India. No Indian had ever conquered the Naga Hills. Since it was the British who had conquered the Naga Hills and administered it for nearly sixty years, with their withdrawal Nagaland should have automatically become free again. The Indian State could not inherit it from the British. The Indian attempt to extend its rule over Nagaland was therefore seen by these groups as an expansionist design of a neo-colonial power.

Unlike the NNC, NSCN did not believe in a peaceful struggle. It believed that it was 'arms and only arms' which could wrest Naga freedom from the massive Indian domination.[45]

The merger of the Mizo Hills with India did not however usher in the rosy future the Mizo's had looked forward to. Although along with the *zamindari* system Chieftainship was abolished by the Government of India, this was replaced by a new kind of domination by another group of people—the outsiders. Their worst fears seemed to be coming true.

The people whom the Mizos called *vais* (people of the Indian plains) began to pour in as administrators, businessmen and so on in their hitherto closed and exclusive territory. While the Mizos were traditionally wary of the *vais* and consequently became careful and insular, the attitude of the Indians was one of 'superiority'.[46] Soon the situation was complicated. Not only did the Assamese government officials enter Mizo land, the Assamese were attempting to dominate the hill people by the imposition of their language and culture. According to the hill leaders the merger resulted in several problems. The hill people had to learn as many as four languages: English, Hindi and Assamese besides their own, due to the new state: policies and not one of these languages was close to their Tibeto-Burmese mother tongue. The Assamese constituted 50 per cent of the state population but controlled 75 per cent of the seats in the Legislature; monopolized 90 per cent of the seats in the state cabinet and 70 per cent of the civil services. All technical and non-technical institutions were in the Brahmputra Valley whereas even road-construction in the hills, so basic to the development process, was neglected by the Assam Government since proceedings in the Legislature were conducted in the Assamese language the tribals were unable to understand it. The tribal officials were compelled to learn Assamese. Caste-conscious, the Hindus continued to treat the tribals as 'untouchables';[47] Hydro-Electric dams were constructed in the hills flooding the agricultural lands of the tribals but the power generated from the dams benefited the people of the plains.[48] The hill people had no role in the preparation of the Five-Year Plans but there was a rapid acquisition of tribal lands by the plainsmen who drove the tribals out their ancestral land.[49]

The real blow came when the periodic famine, which had been predicted by the tribals occurred in the Mizo Hills and people were left to fend for themselves by the state and central governments. Despite the warning of the Mizo elders neither any precautionary steps were taken to fight the famine, nor was the Mizo District Council equipped to do so. The District Council's request to sanction an advance of Rs.1,50,000 was rejected by the Assam Government. But when the famine finally came even in grant of Rs.190 lakh proved inadequate. The belated relief could not prevent the famine from taking a heavy toll. There were starvation and diarrhoeal deaths. The Mizos, as a result showed considerable bitterness and antipathy towards the Indian State and its people especially so when they recollected that even the British imperialists had made an all out effect to help the community during a similar famine.

This variety of famine was a periodic occurrence in the Mizo Hills and the Mizos had always collectively fought it successfully. For the first time, they were adversely affected by the famine because they no longer governed themselves and had relied on the *vai*-administration to tackle it. It was clear that if they had not opted for India and were self governed themselves they would not have suffered in this manner. The Mizos bore acute hostility and hatred for India.

This hostility and hatred was represented by the MNF, which was a product of the famine situation. It would be wrong to say that the MNF appropriated the feeling of the Mizos. It had actually given vent to the Mizo feelings. No wonder the word '*vai'* which was Mizo equivalent for the Indian plainsmen began to be used pejoratively. In the MNF campaign the term '*vai*' came to connote hostility and hatred. Though this term was not such a strong one before the late 1960s.[50] While Indians were described as *vai* their rule was known as '*vai*-rule' or 'alien-rule'. This concept was stretched to depict India as a colonial power from which the Mizos had to free themselves. The MNF was projected as an agent which would liberate the Mizos from colonial subjugation by India. It projected the term '*hnam*' as a Mizo equivalent to the word 'nation', and '*ram*' as a Mizo equivalent to Mizo country. Originally these two terms meant a village community or social group or a community and area/territory belonging to a particular Mizo group. Freedom from Indian rule was defined as 'freedom to pursue their (Mizo) happiness, freedom from the feeling of insecurity and freedom from ignorance, poverty and wants'.[51]

The MNF vowed to unify all the Mizos living in the Mizo Hills, Tripura and Manipur and described the distribution of the Mizos in different states as a part of the 'Divide and Rule' policy of the Indian State. It also declared Christianity to be the state religion of the prospective Mizo sovereign state which would be a 'Christian Kingdom'.[52] The MNF believed that secession from India and the consequent independent status of Mizoram would 'improve the social, economic and political condition of the Mizos and safeguard Christianity which was in danger of being exterminated by Hindustan.'[53] It assured that 'Mizoram would be only for the Mizos'. It talked of the 'Mizo' community as an ancient unified nation with a long glorious history even though the word 'Mizo' was a construction of the 1940s and as a people whose written history did not go beyond the British rule.

It vowed to follow a peaceful method to achieve its independence though in practice however it attempted a *coup d'état*. The MNF organized a parallel anti-*vai* movement at the civil level which indulged in intimidatory tactics and physical assault on Indians living in Mizoram as a part of its de-Indianization process. The MNF declaration of independence, similar to that of the American Declaration of Independence (1776), was as follows:

> In the course of history, it becomes invariably necessary for mankind to assume their social, economic and political status to which the laws of the nature's God entitle them. We hold this Truth to be self-evident that all men are created equal and that they are endowed with inalienable fundamental human rights, governments are instituted among men deriving their just powers from the consent of the government and whenever any from of government becomes destructive of this it is the right of the people to alter, change, modify and abolish it and institute a new government laying its foundation on such principles and to organize its powers in such forms as to them shall seem most likely to effect their right and dignity. The Mizos (were) created and moulded into a nation and nurtured as such by nature's God, have been intolerably dominated by the people of India in contravention to the laws of nature.[54]

The MNF described its attempt to be free of Indian rule as a 'nationalist movement' and 'freedom struggle'. After the Mizo Accord Laldenga rejected the term insurgency to describe its earlier activities. It preferred to call it a 'revolt'. As in Nagaland, here too the following anthem, composed by poet Rokunga, was adopted (unlike Nagaland, it was in Mizo language):

Kan ram mawi, eho lo la parin vul leh zbal la
Thangthar hmatiang sawnna tur khua sei zual se
Tin, lo varin lo thangin lo sang zel ila
Chvng pathian malsawmna pawh kukhuain awm zel rawhse

Mizoram,
My beautiful country, blossom and never wither
May there be room to grow for the young people
Then let there be light to straighten you growth
May the blessings of God be with you forever.

LIMITS TO RHETORIC

Independence, as we have just seen in the case of these communities, was sought as a necessary condition for attaining the ability to govern themselves for self-development. The ideal of sovereignty was projected for the people as a remedies for all ills that would lead to a perfect society. The respective territorial areas which they were fighting for, were projected as prized possessions—so valuable that a mighty power like India not only wanted to retain possession of these areas but eager to exploit them. This was achieved by the projection of its economic viability. The attainment of sovereignty, it was believed would be the beginning of a happy life, and usher in a society free of exploitation, discrimination, oppression of minority groups, and conflicts with neighbouring states. In fact, the theoretical, ideal image of independence was presented as a fact. The capacity of the new leadership to fulfil the demands of the people was projected as unlimited. The state was also projected as a unified entity without an opposition despite the fact that the independence movement itself was already faction-ridden. In fact, all the Naga underground outfits announced that if they came to power their party would brook no opposition. The MNF was hostile to the Congress and did not dare go for outright election. It secured power after the Mizo Accord by making a democratically elected government step down from power. Though it was its first election after the accord it neither could sustain itself for the stipulated five-year period nor could it emerge a victorious party with enough MLAs to form the government. In Manipur despite wide sympathy, the insurgents could never bring about a poll boycott and often had to resort to threats to accomplish their designs. Though these insurgents fought for their own independence they had in sympathy with others seeking it within their own states. The PLA chief Bisheshwar was vehemently opposed to surrendering the Naga and Mizo inhabited areas to Nagaland and Mizoram to allow the latter to form a state covering their entire population. The Nagas resented the surrender of Dimapur to the Dimachas. They were also opposed to the Zeliangrong Movement for a separate state and were hostile to the Kukis. In fact, there has been acute inter-tribal hostility described as 'tribalism' and attributed to be one of the reasons for the failure of the Naga Movement. In other words, the insurgent leaders were hostile to the opposition and minorities. While they took away the independence of minorities, and attempted to eliminate all political opposition either by an administrative act or a political device. Even before coming into power they resorted to the art of building majorities. While these leaders projected themselves as the protectors of the Christian population in Nagaland and Mizoram secularism was not projected as the guiding principle for the non-Christian minorities. In Manipur the tribals had to reconcile themselves with being second class citizens. The possibility that minorities might well demand separate independent states was at scorned. The insurgent groups never reflected on the fact that minorities were hardly likely to be enthusiastic about their forcible incorporation into a totally alien pattern of social, cultural and political behaviour.

The struggle for independence has always been garbed in romantic idealism and the insurgent leaders of north-east India were no exception to it. They could not afford to project it otherwise. Any talk or challenge that independence could mean the end of heroism and the fact that sovereignty might become fiction soon was not encouraged. In Nagaland and Mizoram, any talk of economic 'viability' was countered with the proposition that there could be initial problems but international aid could see them through the crisis. Besides, the feeling among these leaders was that it other 'worsity endowed' countries could survive, they could also manage. In other words, all forms of rhetorical tactics were used to impress the idea that sovereignty would be workable be and not result disappointment. Even models were presented to show that no such possibility existed. It is curious that though the entire Naga population is ostensibly Americanized its tastes and attitudes, the borrowed political models were that of Socialism and Communism. India was always projected as a colonial power and an aggressor and its development efforts in the region were seen as bribery and as unscrupulous attempts at purchasing the loyalty of the people of the north-east. And there has also been a sustained counter-propaganda against the Indian family planning campaign that the tribes should have more children in order to increase their population and foil Indian attempts at marginalizing them numerically.

THEORETICAL ANALYSES

A group of scholars belonging to the communities in question view the insurgency in the north-east as a part of the overall national question in India and describe the Naga, Mizo and Meithei movements as 'national movements'. This group of academician-turned local elite see the inherent plainsmen-tribal hostility and Indian 'imperialism' as the root causes of secessionism in the hills.

A Mizo intellectual emphathising with the Naga cause wrote:

> Why do the Mizos or Nagas have a deeper feeling of separate nationhood. . . . That the Nagas, the Mizos or other hill tribes of north east India are ethologically different from the rest of India, is a scientific and historical fact [*sic*]. They are Mongoloid and are physically, culturally, religiously and linguistically different from that of Aryans or Dravidians. While India claims to be a strictly secular state

at the top, the man in the street is not very conscious of it. Communal relations show a very little improvement and many (Mizos) began to wonder [*sic*] if we were not better-off during the British period. What, they ask, is this freedom we have when a man cannot even eat the food (beef) he likes. The tribals asked where lies the so-called mainstream of national life in Hindi or Hindu? or whether in one political party through which the Government of India tries to create national integration?

To the *Vais* (non-Mizos), these Mizos are jungle-wallah, dog eater and semi-human-beings, To Mizos all *Vais* appeared as witty cheats, whose words and promises cannot be depended upon. They were sensitive enough to face the insulting gestures and despising tones.

It has been claimed that Assam is the most neglected state in India. The then Mizo district was undoubtedly the most neglected and undeveloped district in undivided Assam. To get things done at Silchar the only door for Mizo people to the rest of India, they found corruption was widely prevalent to their great expense [*sic*]. This created exasperation and a desire to deal as little as possible with the *Vais*.

. . . Government often conducted public examinations on Sundays, official dignitaries visited Mizoram on Sundays—these were interpreted as attempts to restrict their freedom of public worship for those involved officially. Restrictions of Missionaries entry into Mizoram was interpreted as an attempt to restrict Christian enterprise. So the MNF brought out the religious issue. They considered India to be a land of the Hindus and Mizoram of Christians.

In their search for safeguarding the Mizo identity and socio-religious aspirations the MNF had no choice but to take arms. . . .[55]

The primary factors of Naga nationalism can be traced from the memorandum submitted by the Naga Club to the Simon Commission on 10 January 1929. The 'negative scores' highlighted in the memorandum are:

(1) That the Nagas are historically independent.
(2) Different in racial stock.
(3) They fear domination of foreigners from the plains, and are suspicious of their immemorial rights and customs being snatched away.

Historically, Nagas originated from the east, a nomadic tribe of the Mongoloid race. The historical evidence of origin ascertained that Nagas are not Indians. Nagaland was and is not Indian territory. . . . (They are) in far distance to Indian mass culture [*sic*]. To them Hindus are worshippers of idols and devil. This crated a deep sense of difference. To the Indians, Nagas are primitive and superstitious people who deserve contempt and violence rather than reason and understanding. . . .

Even at present, Nagas are little known and much less understood. Many in Delhi do not even know that India has a large population with Mongoloid racial traits. . . . India must come forward to settle the existing affairs otherwise the issue will go to the United Nations which India cannot block everytime.

Also, it is a historical fact that India was never politically united in the past . . . But India as a cultural unity had been existing since the past. This India as a cultural entity did not include the Nagas and other peripheries of present India. . . . (Thus, it is only) forcefully and powerfully (sic) the present India emerged as one political entity. . . .

The concept of nation is a contractual entity. In this content, the Nagas in general argue that they were not even a party to the contract of Indian nationhood. Therefore, they state that, they have every national right 'to determine their future as sovereign, which were once part of the one administrative entity of India.[56]

On the Meithei separatism it was said:

When rulers are racially, culturally and linguistically different from the rules, when there in exploitation; in short when nature of Government is neo-colonialism, it is natural that the rulers should mistrust the ruled. At some stage, the veneer of a free, self-administrated democratic Government wears off and the people are forced to take a stand: whether they will remain content with the trappings of a puppet or they will assert in defence of their self-respect, their distinctive identity and for the future of their children. Among the Meitheis the most Indianized of the minor nationalities in the region, it appears, the days of the innocent uncommitted of the fence sitters are at last coming to an end.[57]

A slightly sophisticated interpretation of insurgency in Manipur is as also available.

The movement of insurgency in Manipur has not been an event, preceded exclusively by an efficient cause; it has become a social phenomenon—a process in itself. . . . Manipur always stood as a country or nation—state with its territorial integrity, population, distinct cultural heritage, self-reliant economic structure, a government under rule of law for more than 10 or 15 centuries and a national, mental attitude during these centuries and its merger with the newly born Indian Union on 15 October 1949. The events that rolled by, led to erosion of the national question, dominance of Manipuri nation by others, destruction of economic stability and a trend leading towards permanent, irrevocable national subjugation.

The Manipuris have been a stable nationality with a territory, a government, a written constitution, a distinct ethnic population, comprising of the Meitheis in the valley and the Mongolian ethnoses in the hills, a distinct cultural heritage and civilization, a unique national psychological attitude (or spirit)—over and above this an independent political personality of its own acquired through the ages. It was an Asiatic sovereign, which the British Crown honoured by not annexing it even when all the historical circumstances favoured the annexation.[58]

As against this, it was said:

Even after the birth of the Indian Republic, India remained a multi-national and multi-racial country. In as much as the constituent unity posses the attributes of a distinct nationality, man has its own distinct and national person, which cannot be submerged under the person of any other dominant person.

Therefore, (Manipuri) insurgency or national liberation movement is a by-product of national oppression, subjugation, dominance, racism and apartheid mentality (by Indian nation against the Meitheis).[59]

Implicit in these theoretical analyses is the belief that these groups in question were already evolved as 'nations' and their merger with the Indian Union amounted to their colonial subjugation. Therefore, these movements which were categorized as insurgency by India were in reality nationalist movements fighting for liberation from the colonial yoke of India.

A plausible explanation of the Meithei insurgency was sought to be provided in terms of *nationalism* (national question), *dominance* (imbalance in the intra-nationality relationship), *national suppression* (extreme form of nationality relationship) and *economic dominance* (formation of economic classes). It was claimed that the Manipuris had been a nation which was subjected to national subjugation and oppression by India. The Meithei insurgency was therefore described as a national liberation movement.[60]

ABSTRACTION OF THREAT TO NATIONAL EXISTENCE

There have also been attempts to characterize the threats that confront these communities: One, at the level of rhetoric and the other at the level of an abstraction. In the following analysis we have a combination of both.

According to sociologists the question of identity involves two sets of issues:[61] Super-structural and organic. The first issue deals with the traits and marks which separate a particular group of people from others on the basis of uniformity and distinction. It is said that a primitive predisposition of the human groups has been the urge for cumulation and unification of all their kinsmen to facilitate the goal of reproduction of the species. This unification was generally achieved by isolating traits, either genetic or cultural or both, which are common to constituent individuals of a social group who in turn emerge as differentiable from other groups. And this form of unification was perceived to be necessary to sustain and perpetuate the existence of a biological group. The projection of such unified entity becomes a necessary counter as well as bargaining point in the changing political scenario where smaller groups are threatened, persecuted, suppressed and likely to be driven out of political existence. The latter affected the constitution as well as degeneration of a group aspiring for political recognition as a equal entity. While the first was an attempt to achieve unity and therefore superficial in nature the second was more real involving production and biological reproduction of the group involved. Since it takes place at the structural level it is concealed and even the group in question might not always be aware of the process till the results begin to show.

Production of material things has been defined as the actualization of, 'what is not' from 'what is always there' through the use of concrete (physical) and abstract (mental) labour. In other words, appropriation of natural resources for subsistence. In this process of extraction out of the physical universe, man creates a world of his own based on the image of the given universe. At a given time, this world consists of the current technology of production, distribution, communication, ideas and images, tradition, folk tales, songs and dances and myths. In other words, home, community, village, locality perceived as man's real world is the basis on which his worldview is developed. Such a society generates surplus production to prevent the penetration of exogenous forces.

Biological reproduction in a society has been seen as a process of renewal of its workforce through a natural course of replacement. In other words, the old generation renewed itself in the gene and chromosome of the new generation. To protect the unhindered perpetuation of this reproduction process has been an important urge in primitive societies. Endogamy, exclusivity, insularity, concept of purity and pollution, fear of exogenous forces, etc. were organically structured parts of such societies as a defence mechanism to sustain this reproductive cycle.

Any perceived threat to any one of these above components of the identity structure could be taken as a threat to identity or a crisis of identity. This threat can come from the spilling in of an excess population from sources external to a society which could endanger the process of biological renewal. As such these groups would be wary of societies which in terms of population have greater numerical strength and hence greater absorbing power.

Secondly, it was also theorized that a society whose technology was perceived to be of a superior order could easily disrupt the production process of these primitive societies, and flood their markets with its own produce. Thereby even disrupt and distort the process of tradition-making, leaving the primitive societies totally dependent on the superior society. Such a move could result in total destruction of the small group.

This group of scholars felt that the Meitheis, Mizos and Nagas were currently facing a crises. In view of the inherent weakness of these loosely connected tribes and ethnic groups, small and weak as they were, it was perceived that they were under perpetual threat of being driven out of existence. It foresaw that in the absence of substantial surplus production in these societies there would be an influx of products from India as a result of which their own production would suffer. And it did happen that these self-sufficient autochthons were made to depend on the supply of foodgrains and vegetables from other parts of India. For example, in Manipur rice production had declined substantially over the years and that Naga Hills and Mizoram might starve if the supply of foodgrains was delayed by the Centre.

It has been observed that in these primitive communities as a cumulative consequence of the cessation of the production process, the organic, old tradition-making process had almost stopped. As a result their entire world was lost. They found themselves in an alien new world that did not reflect their own images. The cessation of tradition-making was seen as a crisis which was in turn seen as a fall out of Indian rule. The crisis in tradition-making was said to be so acute that people had to resort to revivalist movements. Overwhelmed by the alien world of commodities and bogged down by alien structures, functioning without their participation, it was said that these groups felt themselves to be strangers in their own tradition. Nor was there any new tradition, characteristic of these societies, being offered to compensate the loss. So the revival of old traditions was the only available alternative. Lai-Heraoba and Raslila for the Manipuris, Cheraw of the Mizos and various Naga folk dances and songs as some of the remnants of their tradition.

There were perceived threats to the continuation of the species too. It was said that the influx of Indians and the consequent mixed breeding between the indigenous females and exogenous males, had markedly changed the racial features of the new generation: that the Mongoloid features were fast disappearing and caucasoid features becoming more pronounced. There was also a perceived threat to the democratic structure of these societies from a numerically strong India which could result in the degeneration of the socio-economic system. The Land Transfer Act has not prevented the transfer of land and agricultural and rural lands were being abandoned in favour of urban land. The returns from the already low-yielding *jhoom* cultivation had been showing a diminishing return. At the same time the tribal economy was being exposed to the proto-capitalist money-economy since independence, despite the Inner Line Regulations and laws of the Autonomous District Councils. There was a growing impact of monetization and consumerist market economy in some urban hill areas. The results were quite disquieting and economic disequilibrium was the consequence. It was argued that the alien government had allowed these economic ills to prevail in order to cripple the economic position of the tribals.[62]

THE COUNTER DISCOURSE

In 1944, Jawaharlal Nehru was depressed over the Cripps Mission proposal to give the princes the right to withdraw from the Indian Union.[63] For him any proposal to cut up India into parts was painful. But the democrat and the socialist within him was against keeping any territorial unit in the Indian Union against the declared will of its people. This was the view held by Nehru in 1944 when the Cripps Mission formulated the proposal of a future Indian federation. The Congress Working Committee Resolution on the Cripps Mission proposal was in consonance with his view. Nehru was not even against the principle of the Right to Secession. But his only condition was that 'before any such right of secession is exercised there must be properly constituted functioning in free India. . . . Thus, it may be desirable to fix a period, say ten years after the establishment of the free Indian state at the end of which the right to secede may be exercised through proper constitutional process and in accordance with the clearly expressed will of the inhabitants of the area.'[64]

But when a tiny Naga population declared their will be withdraw from the Indian Union in 1947 itself, Nehru at the helm of affairs in the Indian State machinery was taken aback. He preferred not to deny nationhood to the Nagas but raise the question of 'viability'. But the Naga resistance also stiffened his attitude when he declared that 'not an yard of India is going out'.[65]

Since then the post-colonial Indian State has tried to negotiate with the forces that sought withdrawal from India by adopting a two-pronged strategy: one at a rhetorical level and the other at the practical level. At the rhetorical level it did not initially deny the Naga, Mizo or Meithei tribes their right to self-determination nor their claims to nationhood. But it argued that the withdrawal of these groups from the Indian State would be detrimental to their own interests. As against this, they offered that these communities could stay within India where their nationality rights and aspirations would be protected and satisfied, and that adequate institutional safeguards and privileges would be provided to take care of their fears and misgivings.

Jawaharlal Nehru, getting wind of the NNC plan contemplating withdrawal wrote to T. Sakhrie, the secretary of NNC as early as 1 August 1946 that he was 'glad that the Naga National Council stands for the solidarity of all the Nagas Tribes'.[66] But at the same time he felt that the 'Naga territory in Eastern Assam is much too small to stand by itself politically or economically.' Moreover rather precariously it 'lies between two huge countries—India and China and part of it consists of rather backward people who require considerable help. Thus, the solution would be that the Naga territory should be an integral part of Assam Province and yet should have a certain measure of autonomy for its purposes.' Allaying the misgivings of the Nagas, Nehru reiterated that the policy of the Indian National Congress (which would be the policy of post-colonial India) had always been that the 'tribal areas should be given as much freedom and autonomy as possible so, that they can live their own lives according to their customs and desires'. In a tactical support of the Naga cause he agreed with the Naga leaders that the Naga Hills should constitutionally be included in an autonomous Assam in a free India with local autonomy and due safeguards of the interests of the Nagas. He made it clear that there would not be any interference in their social, cultural beliefs and they would be given opportunity to participate in the administration of the country. He promised that all possible help would be given for all round development of the Naga people and in fact a special department both at the centre and province could be opened to oversee the welfare of the tribals.

The tribal insularity and exclusivity of north-east India was attributed by Nehru to British rule which 'completely cut off (the tribals) from the rest of India during British rule. Few of them came out of their areas and few from outside went there.'[67] As a consequence

> they never experienced the sensation of being in a country called India and they were hardly influenced by the struggle for freedom or other movements in India their chief experience of outsiders was that of the British officers and Christian missionaries who generally tried to make them anti-Indian. As Indian independence gradually approached and it had become obvious that the British rule was coming to an end in India, some of these British officers and Christian missionaries induced them to think in terms of independence. This had some effect on some section of the Nagas.

Diagnosing the problem of the area as 'fear and apprehensions' about the Indian rule which would deprive them of their freedom and identity Nehru said that

> it was imperative on the part of Indian State to make the people feel that they have perfect freedom to live their own lives, and to develop according to their wishes and genius. India to them, should signify not only a protecting force but a liberating one. Any conception that India is ruling them and that they are ruled or that the customs and habits with which they were unfamiliar are going to be imposed on them, will alienate them.[68]

Talking about the Naga's he felt that the situation in the Naga Hills would not have deteriorated to such an extent if it 'had been handled little more competently'. The Nagas, he found, respond fairly easily to a friendly approach. 'They are proud and sensitive and do not like being treated as subject people.' Therefore, the 'tribals should be given largest measure of autonomy so that they did not feel being ruled by outsiders.' Nehru it has to be conceded, went out of his way to grant statehood to the Nagas. Despite the inherent contraction and consequent opposition in the Lok Sabha, this state was under the direct supervision of the Ministry of External Affairs which was the demand of the Naga People's Convention. Even the name 'Nagaland' which was not acceptable to many was granted at the behest of Nehru, to satisfy the Naga nationalist aspirations, 'to make them feel they were one with us'.[69]

In 1951, when a Naga delegation led by Phizo met Nehru to impress upon him the political aspiration of the Nagas, he sympathized with the Naga cause and appealed to them to see reason:

> I consider freedom very precious; I am sure that the Nagas are as free as I am, in

fact more free in a number of ways. For while I am bound down by all sorts of laws, the Nagas are not except to customary laws and usages. But the independence the Nagas are after is something quite different from the individual or group freedom. In the present context of affairs both in India and the world, it is impossible to consider, even for a moment, such an absurd demand for independence of the Nagas. I am doubtful whether the Nagas realize the consequence of what they are asking for.[70]

Reacting to the argument that the Naga Hills were never a part of India which justified their demand for independence Nehru told the NNC leaders that the 560 Princely States which were not legally part of India during British rule had acceded to India or Pakistan. The Nagas too were free like other Indians. The question of India colonizing the Naga Hills did not even arise as India did not believe in forceful occupation of any foreign territory. But Nagaland as an independent state was simply absurd, impractical and unfeasible. When the extremist faction of the Naga leadership led by Phizo organized the self-sponsored plebiscite in the Naga Hills which claimed a result of 99 per cent votes in favour of independence met him again (March 1952) seeking freedom, Nehru lost his temper and is reported to have burst out saying that even if the heavens fell and India went to pieces, Nagas would not be given independence. Nehru's words even had implicit warnings: 'We can give you complete autonomy but not independence. You can never hope to be independent. No state, big or small in India will be allowed to remain independent. We will use all our influence and power to suppress such tendencies.'[71]

Accordingly India refused to recognize the Naga (unilateral) declaration of independence on 14 August 1947. Neither did it agree to a plebiscite in the Naga Hills. The Naga leadership sponsored plebiscite was rejected by the Indian State. To counter such tendencies it attempted to cash in on the Naga popular desire for peace and in conciliating the moderate leadership, by granting statehood to the Naga Hills. While it initiated what it called a democratic and development process, it sent its army to the hills to deal with the movements and operations which it dismissed as 'secessionism and insurgency'. Jayaprakash Narayan's suggestion that 'it is far more important to have friendly Nagas on our frontier closely associated with us in some new constitutional manner rather than unfriendly and discontented Nagas kept forcibly within Indian Union' was taken as seditious. In fact, after Jayaprakash Narayan made this suggestion

(22 November 1965) many Members of the Parliament demanded his immediate arrest. The same strategy was employed in the case of the Mizos as well as the Meitheis. An Indian official described it as a 'carrot and stick' policy. But though the phrase seems apposite, there was really no policy. In a similar battle of discourses that took place between the nationalists and colonialists in pre-independent India the freedom seekers were also described as hostiles, 'insurgents and extremists' by the Indian State.

As a part of the discourse of the Indian State on the Naga issue, Fazl Ali, attempted to provide a philosophical perspective on freedom and the pragmatic aspect of how freedom of the Nagas was inseparable from India's freedom.

> The freedom India has attained is ultimately in the best interest not only of India but of the Nagas themselves. This freedom is indivisible and has been embodied in an inviolable constitution under this constitution. Our Naga fellow countrymen enjoy equality of citizenship and equal opportunities with any other Indian national. Freedom is already there, if only it is understood alright and properly availed of.
>
> The great and diverse peoples of India, who have throughout campaigned against exploitation coercion and domination, can be relied upon to uphold. The traditions of freedom in all parts of India with their last breath. There is not the slightest desire on behalf of anyone for domination or exploitation. On the other hand, what is sought is fraternal co-operation and mutual prosperity. The Naga Hills being a part and parcel of India, we have always been prepared to accord to our Naga fellow countrymen the fullest assistance and opportunities for development, freedom in a narrow and fissiparous sense of the word is really no freedom at all. For it cannot then be concretely transformed into cardinal freedom that is freedom from want.[72]

Another section, representative of the Indian States, viewed the demand for Naga freedom to be the handiwork of few ambitious Naga leaders in connivance with the foreign Christian missionaries 'to keep them isolated from the rest of India'.[73] There was also a view which held one individual—Phizo—responsible for it. Even Nehru, for all his profound understanding of the Naga situation, often gave in to this view. There was even a shade of opinion which saw the Naga movement as a conspiracy of Communist China who were racially close to the Nagas. As a result during the Chinese invasion of India (1962) there was a fear that the Naga rebels would side with the Chinese.[74] In this discourse pattern the Indian State however did not deny nationhood to the Nagas in theory. But in practice it treated it as one of the many subnational movements that post-independence India had seen. Jayprakash Narayan a member of the Naga Peace Mission presenting the perspective of the Indian State wrote:

> India is a family made up of equal nations: a multinational union. The Naga people are unquestionably a nation . . . while there can be no doubt that the Naga problem was not a law and order question but a question of freedom for the Nagas, I have also tried to show that the Naga freedom Movement may take a different character if it is placed in the context of a union of self-governing state.[75]

While the grant of statehood to the Nagas was in pragmatic terms, an attempt to satisfy the Naga aspirations and bring peace in the hills, in theoretical terms, was to channelize the Naga freedom movement 'to take such a different character'. The new state was given maximum possible autonomy, along the lines of Kashmir, in the hope that as an unit of the Indian federation, its urge for sovereignty would be satisfied or neutralized by this autonomy. While doing so Nehru could not but concede that it was not an indulgence on the part of the Indian State but legitimate sanctions.

> The fact is that the area that is going to be called Nagaland has been separate, a separate entity all along. Nothing is being separated. It was separated some time back, some years back it has been functioning like that. Now that separate entity is being given a certain name. The separation does not take place now. It took place years ago, but it is being given some autonomy. . . .[76]

Nehru also could not hide his impression of the Naga movement vis-à-vis the Indian State in his remark to the Assam ministers, who insisted in retaining the administration of the Naga Hills District. 'When a limb has become gangrenous for God's sake cut it off at once before the whole body is infected. Can't you see you will be doing yourself more harm than good by trying to cling on to the Nagas?'[77]

But this discourse pattern slowly changed its character and reached its climax when Prime Minister Morarji Desai reported to have threatened to 'exterminate the Nagas'. Though Desai claimed that he had been misquoted his remarks 'in the parliament by way of clarification only reinforced the account released by Phizo'.

The display of such 'extreme aggressiveness' by the prime minister was striking in contrast to the past official rhetoric. Although it had engaged its military might it crushing the Nagas, it never used language acknowledging coercion. Morarji Desai not only did it, but even hinted at the power at the disposal of the Indian State as well as its intention in dealing with the rebels. This also highlighted the fact that right from Nehru to Morarji Desai, the Indian statesmen continued to view the Naga issue as a problem crated by 'few Nagas'. Although the Indian State had been able to win over the loyalty of a large section of the Nagas through conciliatory measures, this admission was also an acknowledgment of its failure to tackle those few Nagas even after decades of sustained military counters.

This implied acknowledgement of failure to control the Nagas was, rightly, viewed by the Naga rebels as an ideological victory. Even in their exchanges the Indian State indeed treated these communities as foreign even though in its rhetoric it did not recognize their independent status. The Indian State entered into accords with all these communities as if they were foreign powers. Nagaland was granted statehood under the External Affairs Ministry. Foreigners like Burmese Premier U Nu, British citizens Michael Scott and David Astor were brought in to deal with its own people. All these factor were a moral victory and a tacit recognition of the claims forwarded by the Nagas, Mizos and Meitheis.

Unlike the Nagas, the Mizo and the Meithei movement were not accorded any status higher than that of a law and order problem. These two latter movements had the disadvantage of being late starters. Since these movements were launched after their respective mergers with the Indian Union, their nationalist content was not recognized and were condemned as secessionism and insurgency which the Indian State felt could be countered and over-powered by the military might of the state.

In this interaction the discourses on the nationality question were used as an instrument of self-assertion by the Nagas, Mizos and Meitheis while in India State used it for absorbing them. These discussions on the nationality question have been an academic exercise by intellectuals and political thinkers. A number of ruling regimes have used it to resolve their respective nationality issues. But for a group leading a liberation movement it was a hard-core political practise. The nationality question as a theoretical exercise might often be a vague academic exercise but as a political discourse it exudes power—strong enough for self-assertion and to secure liberation from the powerful state that a group has to fight against. It is this enormous power that enabled even a tiny community like the Nagas, Mizos or Meitheis to challenge the might of the Indian State. From an amorphous structureless mass of people, the Nagas, Mizos, Meitheis thus became a nation with the conferment of nationhood on themselves. This became a means of its defence. The acknowledgement of Indian suzerainty and the acceptance of the constituent status by these small communities would have qualified them for small sanctions but the conferring of nationhood on themselves have legitimized their struggle as a nationalist struggle as well as their demand for independence. At the same time it has rendered illegitimate the Indian occupation of tribal territory and the subjugation of the people.

This power has emanated from two directions: One, nationhood implied the united strength of its people and two, recognition of its status and grievances by international bodies. The League of Nations had already granted all 'nations' right to sovereignty which was also the position of the UNO. Even other international bodies like the Amnesty International, Unrepresented Nations and People's Organization, International Working Group for Indigenous Affairs provided support to the struggling people while condemning Indian repression. India itself had undergone a similar situation. The diverse and divided people of India gained strength to challenge the British colonial state in India only after it accorded itself nationhood. It not only empowered them to fight for independence but even provided legitimacy to their struggle. The basic issue was therefore of empowerment. The Nagas, Mizos and Meitheis wanted to empower themselves to decide their own future according to their own will and aspiration through the political use of the nationalist discourse. The use of this discourse proved to be so powerful that the Indian State had to use its armed strength to counter it. The denial of nationhood to them by the Indian State and its treatment as subnational affair and law and order problem was a counter discourse, often translated into repressive measures, aimed at rendering the struggling communities powerless. By doing so it was not only trying to rob the ideological strength of these movements but also giving itself the legitimate power to tackle it militarily. As earlier the counter to these movements were developed in terms of strategies—a combination of rhetoric and practise. As a part of the rhetoric it treated all insurgencies as monolithic structures even though these arose in different parts, in different times and among different people. The Naga insurgents were called 'hostile' while the Mizos were described as 'rebels'. The Meitheis as insurgents while the Sikhs were extremists and terrorists and the Kashmiris as subversives. It was never recognized the fact that Secessionist Movements were generated by nationalist considerations. Insurgency was seen as uncharacteristic of the 'peace loving' tribal people, even though the tribals concerned here had a century's history of violent insurrections and resistance. The current unrest was viewed as a product of the manipulations of a few. It has always been seen as a threat to national integration which as a concept is not older than 1947-8, when it was used to secure the merger of the Princely States into the Union of India. This afforded the Indian State to address the crisis from the point of view of the power-holders and not the struggling people and deal with them accordingly. On the one hand, its strategy emphasized the spread of ideas that would prohibit the insurgents from securing power and on the other pursued the policy of pacification of a section of the people. Again 'pacification' was a tactic that the British had evolved during its conquests of small powers in India in the eighteenth century. As far as pacification was concerned it appropriated the tactics of WHAM (win heart and minds). It sought to do so by pumping money into the region, and proceeded on the presumption that such unrests were a consequence of lack of economic development. Hence, the Indian State sanctioned a development projects, central aid to an extent that the entire Naga Mizo and Meithei population were made totally dependent on central funds. Simultaneously, a more effective package of attractive amnesty programmes for secessionist leaders and their rank and file members were offered. This 'kill by dollar' policy had the desired consequence.

> Least of all Naga economic development, the central monetary aids have brought several serious consequences. For one it explains the emergence of certain neo-elites and symptoms of class characteristics, mainly as a consequence of certain mechanisms of anomaly in distribution of the monetary assistance, conspicuously placed against the backdrop of underdevelopment. A serious development took place in such a situation when the traditional Naga economy lost its autonomy and became a dependent and integral part of the complex Indian economy. It is this phenomenon which may explain for the contemporary lack of 'inner motivation' within the Nagas to be self-generative, so much so that they now view themselves as a 'sponsored society'. All these have resulted in a situation in which Nagaland is in the process of being economically peripheral to the Indian social core and its metropolitan capital intensive economy.

This policy was practiced by the Americans in Vietnam and Britishers in Malaya. There were other counter-insurgency measures too that the Indian State banned from these two countries. The techniques of concentration camps' and 'cordoning system' that had been evolved by the British during the Boer War were profitably used now in north-east India. Ironically the British had described the tribal uprisings as insurgency and used the technique of 'promenades' (for punitive expeditions) and economic blockade on the same Naga and Mizo people, a hundred years ago which was now being repeated by the Indian State.

In a reflective encounter of discourses, Minaketan, a senior Manipuri poet in a pro-state celebration of the silver jubilee of India's independence recited this poem,

> Bhagat, Kshudi, Subhash and their
> Numberless sons
> sacrificed their lives for thy
> freedom, Mother
> now the tricolour flag of
> freedom flies
> Let it remain flying as long as the
> Sun and the moon
> victory be to thee, mother.

Padmakumar a young Meithei poet representing the current generation, on the same occasion reacted:

> While loitering in the desolate heath
> from the sky
> a bird shouted down on my head
> you are not yet free
> not yet free. . . .[78]

NOTES

1. Phizo to H. Boland, President, UNO, 8 October 1960.
2. Manifesto of the National Socialist Council of Nagaland, Preface, 31 January 1980.
3. 'Rectification of basic Erroneous Views' in ibid.
4. Ibid.
5. 'Nagaland and the Influx of Indian Capital and Indian National', Nagaland and the Effect of Indian and Burmese Culture and Their Faith', in ibid.
6. NSCN, *A Brief Political Account of Nagaland*, (n.m., n.d.), pp. 43-4.
7. MNF, Memorandum submitted to the Prime Minister of India, MNF Headquarters, Aizawl, 30 October 1965.
8. MNF, Declaration of Independence, 1 March 1966.

9. PLA, *Dawn*, Vol. III, Imphal, 1979, p. 12.
10. Ibid.
11. Ibid., pp. 14-15.
12. Ibid., Vol. I, Imphal, 1979, p. 12.
13. Ibid.
14. Ibid., Vol. II, Imphal, 1979 p. 12.
15. Ibid.
16. PLA, '*Minai Oibagee Cheinakhol*', pamphlet in Manipuri, cited in Kshetri Rajendra Singh, 'Social Movements in Manipur: A Study of Two Movements Among the Meitheis', unpublished Ph.D. thesis, Surat: Centre for Social Studies, 1987.
17. PLA, *Dawn*, Vol. I, Imphal, 1979, p. 12.
18. Ibid., Vol. II, pp. 28-9.
19. Ibid.
20. Ibid., Vol. III, Imphal, 1979, pp. 21-2.
21. Bisheshwar in *New Delhi Journal*, 9-22 June 1980, pp. 14-15.
22. Ibid.
23. *Dawn*, Vol. I, p. 5.
24. Op. cit.
25. Op. cit.
26. N. Bisheshwar, *The Last Expression in My Death Bed*, Imphal: Pax Publication, 1986, pp. 11-12.
27. Ibid.
28. Ibid., p. 10.
29. Ibid.
30. Ibid.
31. Ibid.
32. Ibid.
33. Ibid., pp. 18-19.
34. Ibid., p. 29.
35. Ibid., p. 24.
36. Ibid., p. 49.
37. N. Sanjaoba, 'Genesis of Insurgency', *Manipur: Past and Present*, Delhi: Mittal, 1989, pp. 245-90.
38. Gangumei Kabui, 'Insurgency in Manipur Valley', in B.L.A.B.I. (ed.), *North Eastern India: Problem and Perspective of Development*, Chandigarh: CPRID, 1984, pp. 233-9.
39. Memorandum of the Naga Hills to the Indian Statutory Commission by Naga Club, 10 January 1929.
40. Phizo to H. Boland, President, UNO, 8 October 1960.
41. 'Nagaland and the System of Socialism' in Manifesto of the National Socialist Council of Nagaland, 31 January 1980.
42. Ibid.
43. Ibid.
44. Interview by R.L. Raising, NSCN, 15 February 1991 in *The Sun* (North-

East), Vol. XIV, No. 34, 23 March 1991, pp. 26 I-26 VII.

45. Manifesto of the National Socialist Council of Nagaland, January 1980.
46. Memorandum of the Assam Hill Tribal Leaders Conference held in October 1954, 1955, at Aizwal. Also MNF declaration of independence 1.3.1966.
47. Ibid.
48. Ibid.
49. Ibid
50. John V. Hluna, *Church and Political Upheaval in Mizoram*, Aizawl, 1985, p. 88.
51. Laldenga, *Mizoram Marches Towards Freedom*, Aizawl: MNF, 1973.
52. John V. Hluna, op. cit., pp. 91-2.
53. Ibid.
54. MNF, Declaration of Independence, Aizawl, 1 March 1966.
55. John V. Hluna, 'Mizo Problem and Some Fact', in *Souvenir*, National Seminar on Futurology, 28-30 April 1987. Also his 'Mizo Problems Leading to Insurgency', Proceedings of the North-East India History Association, Agartala, 1985, pp. 442-9.
56. Zavier Mao, 'Secessionism and Historical Inevitability with Special Reference to Nagaland', paper read in *North East India History Assocaition*, Imphal, 1990.
57. *Resistance*, Imphal, 1 May 1979.
58. Naorem Sanjaoba, op. cit.
59. Ibid.
60. Ibid.
61. Soyam Lokendrajit, 'Identity and Crisis of Identity', in *Proceedings of North East History Assocaition*, Pashighat Session, 1986.
62. Visier Sanyu, 'What Nagaland State Did to the Nagas: A Historical Perspective', in Subhadra Mitra Channa (ed.), *Nagaland: A Contemporary Ethnography*, Delhi: Cosmo, 1992, pp. 265-74; Hector D'Zouza, 'The Emergent Self of Nagaland', in ibid., pp. 275-90.

    I. Lanu Iyer, 'Conteporary Naga Social Formation and Ethnic Identity: A Case of Development or Decay', unpublished Ph.D. thesis, Shillong: North-Eastern Hill University, 1985, pp. 122-4 and 180-9.
63. Jawaharlal Nehru, *Discovery of India*, Centenary Edition, Delhi: OUP, 1989, p. 458.
64. Ibid.
65. Jawaharlal Nehru, speech at Shillong, *The Hindu*, 31 December 1957, cited in S. Gopal, *Jawaharlal Nehru: A Biography*, Vol. 3, Delhi, 1983, p. 30.
66. Nehru to T. Sakhrie, New Delhi, 1 August 1946.
67. Jawaharlal Nehru, 'A Note on the North Eastern Frontier Tracts 18th to 25th October 1952', Appendix—Speech of Jawaharlal Nehru at the opening Session of the Scheduled Tribes and Scheduled Areas conference in New Delhi on 7 June 1952.
68. Ibid.
69. Debate on the Lok Sabha on the Nagaland State Bill, August 1962,

Appendixed in Hokishe Sema, *Emergence of Nagaland*, Delhi: Vikas, 1986, pp. 206-37.

70. Cited in Asoso Yunou, *The Rising Nagas: A Political and Historical Study*, Delhi: Vivek, 1974, p. 203.
71. Cited in S. Gopal, op. cit.
72. Fazl Ali, Governor of Assam, Republic Day Message cited in ibid., p. 197-8.
73. It was floated by the Assam administration without providing substantial evidence. As a consequence, suspicion on the missionaries were so strong that they had to issue public statements that they were apolitical and had nothing to do with insurgency. Even if we assume that pre-independence missionaries who were ethnic Europeans had encouraged anti-Indian feeling on the ground that other European administrators of the hills did so, it has to be conceeded that post-independence missionaries have largely been Indian themselves. In other words, the character of the missionaries themselves had changed colonialist to nationalist. It is amply proved by the fact that both the Shillong Accord and the Mizo Accord were possible due to the untiring efforts of these missionaries themselves. See Jayaprakash Narayan, *Nagaland Ka Sawal* (in Hindi), Varanasi, 1965, pp. 26-8; John Hluna, 'Peace in Mizoram: A Study of the Contributions of the Churches', in *Proceedings of the North-East India History Association*, Kohima, 1987, pp. 497-509.
74. During the Chinese Aggression in 1962, there were absurd but strong suspicions in Delhi that the Naga, Mizo and other Mongoloid tribes of north-east would join the Chinese due to their racial affinity.
75. Jayaprakash Narayan quoted in 'Exterminating Angles', editorial, *Economic and Political Weekly*, 27 August 1977.
76. Jawaharlal Nehru participating in the Lok Sabha debate on the Thirteenth Amendment Bill and the State of Nagaland Bill, 28 August 1962; see n. 69 above.
77. Nehru to Assam ministers in Nari Rustomji, *Imperiled Frontiers*, Delhi: OUP, 1989, p. 55.
78. Cited in Homes Borgohain, 'Manipur: Anatomy of Despair', *Economic and Political Weekly*, 13-20 November 1982, p. 1858.

Epilogue

There have also been academic attempts to characterize the Naga, Mizo and Meithei movements. The most striking aspect of this endeavour has been that such characterizations have varied according to particular political beliefs or ideological predilections of the scholars. The paradigm of nationhood chosen also varied accordingly, For example, the Naga, Mizo or Meithei scholars generally subscribed to the theory that these movements were nationalist movements. According to them, the definition of a nationalist movement was a movement of groups or people who had achieved or were trying to achieve the status of nations or nation states largely through revolutionary and violent efforts where the group was incorporated, allegedly against its will, in a wider unit, and sought to severe the bond through an act of secession. Such nationalist movements, were based on either ethnic nationalism or territorial nationalism. A variant of ethnic nationalism was secession which was seen as the commonest route to nationhood.[1]

The position of the other scholars on the subject can be categorized into two groups: one, those who rejected nationhood for these insurgent groups and supported the rhetoric and practice of the Indian State vis-à-vis the Nagas, Mizos and Meitheis. Two, scholars with a radical bent who accepted and even perpetuated the form nationhood constructed by the struggling communities. Significantly, in their eagerness to do so, their theoretical framework often came in conflict with the ground realities presented by the tribals scholars who obviously have a better understanding of their own respective societies. Here we find an extremely interesting interplay of theories, empirical facts and ideological positions.

CHARACTERIZATION OF THE NAGA MOVEMENT

The scholars of the radical school described the Naga movement as a struggle against nation suppression and made a case for the Naga right to self-determination and secession.[2] Essentially a critique of the thesis that the Nagas were a non-nation and hence their struggle for independence lacked the merit of being described as a national movement. It rejected the theory that the Naga struggle was a mere 'secessionist movement' inspired and aided by foreign missionaries who have been exploiting the hill people's passion for independence to breakup the Indian nation. It tried to accommodate the Naga case into the Stalinist definition of nationhood.[3] According to Udayan Mishra, Nagas have many of the features that go to make a nation: a common descent, a distinct territory, common political and economic pattern of life, customs and traditions, and a psychological structure on which a common Naga culture is based. The only missing feature is a common language. But for the Nagas it has not been an insurmountable factor in the growth of nationalism. As for national consciousness and corporate will, the Nagas have a common religious belief contrary to that of the Hindus; they also have a collective will separate from India and have their own 'home-rule'. The Nagas have solved the problem arising out of the large number of mutually unintelligible tribal languages by evolving a pidgin called Nagamese, which is used as a lingua franca. It cannot be called a dialect, as it is not the local patois of any standard Naga language, which are all independent of each other. Despite the absence of a common religion or culture, which is one of the prerequisites of nationhood, there existed one 'uniform principle' underlying the cross section of the Nagas. There commonalities were visible in their religious practices which were different from Hinduism.

There is general agreement that the word 'Naga' is a generic term used by non-Nagas to describe the Naga community which consists of at least sixteen major tribes. A Naga scholar coined the term 'Nagaland'—the name of the sixteenth state of India which is a controversial issue both among Nagas and non-Nagas.[4] 'The expression Naga is (only) useful as an arbitrary term to attribute to the tribals living in particular parts of north-east India.' The Nagas refer to people in their community by their respective tribal names, viz., Ao, Angmai Sema, Lotha, Rengma, etc. And the feeling of oneness among the Nagas referred to as *Naganess* or *Nagaland* is only the result of the Naga response to the 'larger Indian arrogance'.

Contrary to Mishra's understanding of the Naga, the Naga scholars are in agreement with the theory that the Nagas did not have a common descent.[5] The folk tales offer different stories of descent of the respective tribes. The Semas trace their origin to the south while a certain section amongst them claim that they have a western origin and most certainly have close affinity with the eastern Angami Nagas.

The Sangthams trace their origin to the south and south-east. The Angamis are principally of a southern origin though we find a strong indication of mixed origin. They maintain that they were from the south-east and reached their present habitat through the Tangkhul lands. A group of the Chang Naga tribe also claims that it came in from the south while others claim the Aos as their ancestors. The Rengma Nagas migrated from the Kezami-Angami country. Tangkhuls point to the south-east of Rengma and Angami country as the home of their ancestors: the diversity of their origin can also be corroborated from the level of their respective technological development.

Similarly, the theories about Nagas belonging to one common territory are of recent origin. The traditional frontier of each Naga was his own village and agricultural land. Since raids into the frontier plains was also a part of the Naga mode of production the frequently raided territory also was imagined to be an extended territory of the raiding tribes. Any trespassing into the territory of a particular tribe by an alien tribal could result in fierce tribal warfare and bloodshed. It is true that even in the post-1950 period, the practise of shifting cultivation compelled the tribes to migrate from one site to another, which meant that the tribes did not have a fixed territory. Even now an Angami Naga cannot win an assembly election from the Ao Naga area. Therefore, the traditional loyalty of a particular person was to his tribe not the cross-community. It is also not true that the unintelligibility of languages spoken among the different tribes did not pose any problem to the Nagas.

The Nagas did not even have a common economic life because the level of technological development was not the same among all the tribes. *Jhoomming* or the method of shifting, slash and burn cultivation has been the primary mode of agricultural production, the other being terrace cultivation. The Angamis, Zemis, Rengmas, Chakesangs, Tangkhuls, Maos and Marams practise terrace cultivation elaborately whereas other Naga tribes practise the slash and burn method. Under the method of shifting cultivation, large tracts of land usually on forested slopes of the hills are first slashed by choppers. After cutting down all the large trees and bushes, the clearing is set on fire. On this charred site the farmers sow a crop for just one or two seasons at the most, after which they move on to a fresh hillside. The law of diminishing returns also prompted the tribes to sow in a new field. Earlier the *jhoom* cycle spanned for at least ten to fifteen years but with the increase in population the cycle has been reduced to a period of three to five years.

The terrace cultivation on the other hand, involves the setting up of wet rice fields which are cut along the hills depending on the availability and proximity of stream water. Hill slopes are cut and leveled into plain steps down to the level from where the hill rises. Then a canal system is dug which links plots in such a manner that after the required water level is retained in a particular plot, the rest of it is drained to the next plot. A system typical to the plains, this was a technological improvisation introduced to practise we rice cultivation in the hilly terrains.

Political patterns too varied from tribe to tribe again reflecting the different stages of civilizational development. The hereditary chiefs among the Konyaks and Semas enjoy almost the position of a feudal landlord having the final say over every aspect of village life. The Ao and Tangkhul villages have chiefs whose position and powers were several notches below those of the Sema and Konyak chiefs who were called kings. An incipient concept of kingship was visible among these two tribal groups. Among the Aos and Tangkhuls however, the actual power rested in the village council—a body of village elders drawn from the clans residing in the village and who in turn represented the principal kindred in the villages. The life of the Angamis, Chakesangs, Rengmas and Maos are run on even more democratic lines. The Angamis, however, have a hereditary priesthood, the office being handed down the line of the founder of the village in question. Therefore, it is a fallacy that all Nagas had a democratic political setup in its purest from something like the Greek city states as claimed by the protagonist of Naga independence. It would be incorrect to assume that the Nagas had a uniform political practice.

Now that we have a basic idea of the diversity among the different Naga tribes, it would be redundant to emphasize the fact that they did not have a common culture and tradition. It is too obvious that the tribes, so different from each other in terms of place of origin, ancestry, economic and political life, level of technological development, would have had unique social customs and tradition of their own. How can such diverse and even hostile tribes have a common psychological structure? As for the insularity, sensitivity to outsiders and xenophobia, these are typical to all tribal groups anywhere in the world. As shown earlier, the concept of Naga identity was a Naga middle class construct and as far as the masses were concerned the identity formation process had just began. For Naga villagers his identity did not extend beyond affiliation to his own tribe, language and village. The argument that Naga religious beliefs as a whole were different from the religious practices of the rest of India, like Vaishnavism and Saktism, is too far fetched. While the Nagas did not practice those two forms of Hinduism, they also did not share each others religious practises and their uniformity of practise end at the point that, diverse through they all were, they all could be categorized as animists. A Naga scholar points out, that: 'There is no Naga nation in the sense that there is, say, a British, Chinese or French Nation. . . . The Nagas are neither homogenous nor unified and Nagaland is a veritable tangle of clans and tribes, dialects, local traditions and customary laws.'[6]

But this Naga scholar would still call the Nagas a nation and the Naga movement a nationalist movement:

> The Nagas do share a common homeland and belong broadly speaking, to Mongoloid race group. They also share a common faith—majority being Christians today and all practising a common religion in the past, their dialects all spring from Tibeto-Burman group. . . . The nationalist doctrine of the Nagas is based not so much in what they have in common as in the respects in which they differ from the Indians. Despite these diversities and considerations which often drive wedges between the various tribes, racially the Nagas are closer to one another than the rest of India. . . . Naga nationalists sentiment is based on the fact that Nagas are different from Indians.[7]

The corporate will of having a separate state for the Nagas was activated by this consciousness. As pointed out by the Naga scholars themselves that Naga nationalist sentiment was, based on the fact that they are different from Indians. These were some of the factors that helped in the unification of the Naga tribes and in streamlining them into a nationality.

A Trotskyite scholar found that 'much of the debate on national question in India has got bogged down in a terminological morass of competing definitions which produce(d) no higher synthesis'. Rejecting the above model,[8] he asserted that there is no nationality question in India because it has already solved it and has become a nation state politically, but culturally still a nation-in-the-making. This nation-in-the-making seeks a stronger cultural-emotional foundation for a pan-Indian identity. The Naga independence movement is then seen as a nationalist struggle. To be more precise the Naga nationalist struggle originated against the oppression and absorption of the tribals by Indians as well as the great Indian chauvinism. The Naga nationalist movement was national because 'a nationality is formed by the decision to form a nationality and nationalism in a state of mind striving towards transforming this consciousness into the political fact of nation-state'. In this sense Nagas are a nationality wherein a significant number of people in the community feel that they belong to or want to have a nation. The Naga nationalist struggle was described as a 'low-intensity insurgency' whose protagonist had failed to translate the broad sympathy from a war-ravaged Naga population into a qualitatively higher level of mass or even guerrilla struggle. This failure of the Naga leadership was compounded by the carrot and stick policy of the Indian State which succeeded in reducing the political aspirations of the Nagas from independence to regional autonomy: a process by which a nationalist struggle was turned into a sub-nationalist movement. Same was the case with Mizos.

The challenges posed to the Indian Nation State in recent times and the consequent heating up of the debate whether India is a nation or the remains of a nation, had prompted a prominent historian to claim that India should be characterized as a civilizational state rather than a nation or union of nations.[9] A Naga scholar used a recent political coinage to describe the Naga situation without taking away the nationalist content of the Naga struggle. He characterized the Naga as a 'non-state nation' which has grown out of tribalism. In fact, the dealings of the Indian State with the Nagas itself signify the tacit approval of this non-state nation status.[10]

Another school of historians sought to strike a balance between the two extreme positions. It sees India itself as a union of nationalities rather than a nation and the struggling groups as constituent nationalities aspiring for self-rule. According to these historian, the awakening of Indians under the British colonial rule had two parallel streams: one based on the pan-Indian identity and the other based on the regional identity.[11] India is a country which contains a number of emerging nationalities with different cultures and languages of their own. While the pan-Indian sentiment gave rise to a pan-Indian nationalism, which provided the strength to combat colonialism, the regional identities provided the basis for nationality formation. The pan-Indian sentiment was described as great nationalism and regionalist sentiment and aspirations as little nationalism or regionalism. The Naga or Mizo movements were of the regionalist or little nationalistic variety, which in turn constitutes a part of the all-India configuration. But neither of the processes—either great nationalism or little nationalism are complete yet. In other words, neither the process of the making of the Indian nation or the process of the nationalities emerging as nations are complete yet. Implied here is the fact that India has not yet emerged as a nation—it is a union of nationalities; nor have these nationalities yet attained the status of a nation. The process is on. As of now the aspirations of the nationalities for self-rule is satisfied by the grant of regional autonomy within a federal structure.

Within this broad framework the Naga, Mizo and Meithei movements in north-east India are seen as part of the over-all scenario wherein these movements are of the 'regionalist' or little nationalistic variety. The processes of pan-Indianism and regional nationality formation in this area had been delayed because of its geographical distance and political exclusion. But one the process was underway it had both these dimensions at work. The exclusion of north-east India was strengthened by the 'growth of Christianity' which gave a different orientation to the search for identity in the Naga-Mizo areas. As such secessionism has been an 'irrational' reaction to the wider integrative process. The positive and progressive contributions of these movements have been that they have integrated the disunited tribes into a nationality and despite the presence of secessionism gradual integration with pan-Indianism has been visible. These twin processes form the configuration of the nationality question in north-east India.

THE SITUATION

The Naga nationality formation was delayed because of the late and restricted entry of capitalism as well as the protracted decay of tribalism. As a result there was a slow decline of the tribal institutions and idea. But the Nagas were fortunate to have a early emergence of a weak but articulate middle class to lead its nationality formation process.

The case of the Mizos and Meitheis is qualitatively different from that of the Nagas. The Mizos are a conglomeration of a number of tribes, but lesser than that of the Nagas. Though multi-lingual, these tribes had already accepted the language of the Lushai tribe as their lingua franca. Since the oppressive institution of chieftainship was common to all the tribes the united fight against the chiefs had brought about a common sentiment. The Mizo middle class that emerged did not demand immediate secession from India but facilitated the nationality formation process. They used 'Mizo' as a generic term for all the tribes within that area and encouraged the use of the term, facilitated the adoption and usage of the dominant Lushai language as the common language and unified the people not on the basis of common cultural traits, but their sentiment against the oppressive chiefs. The mobilization of the people against the chiefs was a significant phase in the nationality formation process of the Mizos. Tribalism had disintegrated faster in Mizoram as a result of the opening up of the society due to capitalist penetrations.

Though the nationality formation process was started, simultaneously in both the Mizo and Meithei areas, worked faster in the case of the Mizos. But it has not yet resolved its contradictions to be able emerge as a nationality. Tribalism has not yet collapsed entirely and capitalist relations have not entered completely. Although primitive economic pursuits are fast disappearing and tribal political institutions are being replaced by modern ones, tribalism still works at the level of ideas and consciousness. At the same time total transformation to capitalism is not possible in Mizoram. Its terrains are such that neither capitalist agriculture nor industrial pursuits can have a foothold in Mizoram. It can only function as a market economy aiding Indian capitalism. As for the present the Hmars and Chakmas are demanding separation from the Mizos. The greater Mizoram Movement also failed due to lack of response from Mizo tribes in Manipur and Tripura as well as the lack of enthusiasm from the Mizos themselves.

The Meitheis were at a much advanced stage of history as compared to the Nagas and Mizos. They practiced an economic activity which was feudal in character but still retained some features of primitivism. They had developed a language of their own with a script and a rich literature. They had a common cultural tradition, a common economic life and a mental make up. In other words, they had emerged as a stable community of people before the advent of colonialism. Colonialism ushered in capitalist relations in Manipur. Increased production of commodities resulted in the flourishing of trade and mercantile activities. A rich history of social movements streamlined its nationality formation and the Meitheis were a nationality like any of the other nationalities which constituted the Indian Union. But political processes that resulted in the absorption of Manipur into India and the ambivalence involving the question of identity complicated the nationality question. There was dilemma, confusion and ambivalence, which gave birth to secessionism. It has to be remembered that Meithie secessionism was not older than that of the Nagas and Naga secessionism with its functional role as a means to secure concessions was always an example to others. Meithei secessionism we find was a result of the oppressive political and economic processes, which complicated the unresolved nationality question in Manipur. The unresolved nationality question of the Meitheis can also be seen in its chauvinism, oppression and attempts at depriving the tribals living in the periphery of Manipur. The colonial rule had stopped the process of absorption of these tribals into the Meithei category. But the Meitheis tried to continue to retain their hegemony over them. Even though the community had progressive ideological affiliations, tribals like the Tangkhuls, Zeliangrougs, Kukis, Pawis, Lakhers suffered political and economic deprivation and social discrimination. Despite refusing to be identified as Hindus, the Meitheis considered these tribals as 'impure' and barbaric—a typical Hindu practice. The aggressive retaliatory measures against the move for Greater Nagland and Greater Mizoram also testified to their reactionary behaviour. The PLA was totally against surrendering any of these tribal areas to the protagonists of greater Nagaland or greater Mizoram. Under any scheme of political reorganization of north-east India in accordance with the principle of nationality, the state of Manipur is liable to be broken up and reduced to just one tenth of its present area if Naga or Mizo aspirations are to be accommodated. The reactionary chauvinism of the Meitheis is also evident in their raising the question of identity and claiming that it was a danger. This has been the reaction of the same Meitheis who had projected themselves as a 'nation'. They considered as a source of danger the small migratory Nepalese population consisting of essentially ex-servicemen of the Imperial army who had been settled there by the British.[12] A large section of these Nepalis have been assimilated by absorption and intermarriage as Meitheis, which has in fact strengthened the nationality status of the Meitheis. But these marginal groups were still considered a threat and the Meitheies carried out repeated violent attacks on them, terrorized and attempted to evict them. Such chauvinism is characteristic of a nationality whose political and economic aspirations have not been fulfilled, and criss-crossed by modern class-formation, a great number of whose lower classes suffer acute deprivation.

Even though the professed goal has been political independence and setting up of a sovereign state, the Naga, Mizo and Meithei uprisings were essentially a rejection of the marginal status offered by the Indian State, and a refusal to accept the *status quo*. Under the changed times and modern environment these conscious conglomeration of tribes, which were being harnessed to form a modern nationality on par with the other nationalities of the Indian sub-continent, foresaw difficult times for themselves. With the setting in of the decolonization process a transformation in the nature of the polity was underway where the dominant partner of the polity would be the majority community. In fact, the emerging majoritarianism had also boosted the nationality making process of these tribes. The accent on numbers had dwarfed them in the modern system. There were insecurities, fears and paranoia about the prospective attachment to a people about whom nothing much was known. The separatism of the Muslims and Sikhs and even the dalits provided enough concerns as well as reinforced their insecurities. And by now even these tribes were not the same people. They were Christians, while the Meitheis were conscious of being Hindus but still suspect in the eyes of the Hindus. They had no idea about how things would be in the new polity. There were possibilities of their being wiped out of their political existence. They could be further marginalized in the Indian polity. Their race, language religion and civilization could be the potential cause of their further marginalization. They were Mongoloids and as such differentiable physical types to begin with. They spoke Tibeto-Burma languages that were unintelligible to the Indo-Aryan Indians. They were Christians and animists whereas the majority were dominant Hindus. Most of them were tribals or semi-tribals in contrast to the advanced people of the plains. The indications of the things to come was already there on the eve of Indian with independence, sections of the Indians demanding that the protective devices and reservation given to them by the British should be withdrawn exposing them to unfair and unequal competition. In numerical terms too these tribals constituted only a tiny drop in the vast sea of Indian population which could easily be swallowed up. In this number based polity they were lonely travelers who could neither form any pressure group nor would be heard. Despite the rhetoric of equality and democracy these tribals could never hope to attain any high important political position unless the dominant community offered them one. These tribes and ethnic groups have all along lived independently and preferred a king of egalitarian society and communal living arrangement which was antithetical to the class and caste-based lifestyle of the Indians. Hence, they were both against assimilation and loss of autonomy. They could visualize such incompatibility and marginalization and therefore were against joining a world where their own world would be drowned. Their secessionism was a refusal to be a part of a system in which they would continue to constitute a marginal component and for every small 'mercy' would have to look up to an alien people. It was an attempt to protect their own world and its autonomy: cultural, political and economic. They wanted the retention of a world where they could form the system, neither be a marginal factor in a system, nor a participant in a system formed by others. The clauses of the 9-point Akbar Hydari-NNC Agreement, the Shillong Agreement, the MNF Accord, terms of the Sixth Schedule all were vivid reflections of the fears and apprehensions of the tribals and an all-out attempt to safeguard their interests. But despite these constitutional safeguards and preferential policies some of these tribal and ethnic groups still found themselves to be a marginal component of the Indian polity and their worst fears came true. When the constitutional safeguards declare that those areas would be left uniterferred, it did not mean that no development work would be undertaken. But in reality these poor areas were left to fend for themselves as far as development processes were concerned. The detribalization process had delinked them from their basic economic pursuits. Shifting cultivation was discouraged but no alternatives were provided; traditional craftsmanship disappeared but no industrial pursuits were forthcoming. The conditions were so bad that most of these areas depended on Delhi for even basic necessities such as rice and vegetable. The economic foundation of these tribal communities was totally shattered resulting in a void. Detribalization was by the British encouraged which made the people of these areas to discard their own customs and adopt western dresses. Since Indian dresses were rejected by the tribals considered un-Indian. These people had long functioned as a tribal polity and in the modern political sense they could neither participate in the contemporary political system efficiently nor appreciate such participation. Corruption, nepotism, and the ability to manoeuvre, which were alien to these tribals now became an inevitable corollary of the their life. Alien languages were imposed on them—Hindi and Assamese. Employment was scarce for this proletarianized people. The 'pristine' tribal societies were exposed to the modern vices of theft, rape, dishonesty, and other forms of crimes. A new value system replaced the old tribal values. Since their food habits had changed, cooking too was altered; communal living disintegrated, housing pattern changed, and consumerism invaded their societies. Their rituals were transformed, as religion had changed; animism gave way to institutionalized religion. A quick process of detribalization in all spheres did not have corresponding substitutes. The change ranged from institutions to value systems, from geography to food habits in a span of half century when the same process had taken several centuries for other communities. The tribal world was lost without a substitute to fill the void. Colonialism had initiated this process of change, which the Indian State reinforced and hastened. The tribal world experienced wide ranging changes: from an egalitarian society to a stratified one; from chieftainship and communal living to class and number based politics; from tribes to ethnicity; from animism to institutionalized religion; from nudity to European dress as; from being a neolithic people to a consumerist society, from fire-making to a gas cooking technology; from food gathering to pressure cooking; from forest herbs to modern medicines. These tremendous changes taking place in tribal societies are unimaginable to a casual observer. It might seem a developmental change which is untrue, because if it has done them a world of good it has also deprived the tribals of their own world and left them in a void as they are not yet equipped—psychologically, morally, politically or culturally—to adjust and identify with the present. The present has been oppressive for the tribals and the reason why insurgent leaders have often promised to return them the lost world which proved to be an effective slogan. In fact, there have been occasional revivalist movements in search of the old world. Identity crisis is a result of this transformation too. So acute has been the problem of such transformation, that a school of historians believe the turmoil in the north-east to be closely connected to this 'change'.

> While inability to meet basic needs in a changed economic environment is the principal cause of discontent, the problems of north east India need to be viewed in the context of history, demographic change, the existing political system, security requirements and aspirations of the people of the region. One also has to appreciate the role of modernization, which has sharpened encounters between the imperatives of the present and future—political scientific and economic. The process of shaping a collective conscious in north east India, which was slow in the push, has became rapid and strident in the present circumstances.[13]

These changes not only resulted in protest and revolt movements, but have also created tensions within the tribal societies. And insurgency reflects the tensions within these societies.

Thus, another member of the 'change school' observed that the harbingers of change 'sought to pack into a couple of decades, changes which should normally have taken centuries even in an alert country like Europe. This was introducing abrupt change and forced growth at the abnormal pace and the results have been more revolutionary than evolutionary.'[14] Further, he added, 'it is this revolutionary aspect of social change which are the causes for various separatist tendencies in north east India.'

After the merger of tribal communities with India these changes were hastened but the fears of the people were ignored. For example, in Mizoram the dominant Assamese first tried to impose their language on the tribals. Despite repeated appeals of the Mizo Union, the Mizos were not granted autonomous status within Assam. In spite of the warning of the Mizo leaders, the Government of Assam encouraged the transformation of Mizo National Famine Front to Mizo National Front to counter the influence of the Mizo Union. While declaring the desire for independence, the MNF president Laldenga pointed out that the experience of the Mizos after their merger with India was not a pleasant one. Even Manipur a 'C' category state initially, later made into a union territory, was reeling under grinding poverty and food scarcity before insurgency broke out full-scale.

But it was Nagaland, which was granted statehood not Manipur. It seemed New Delhi only understood the language of violence. The Nagas and Mizos were provided protection under the Sixth Schedule but not the Meitheis on the plea that they were Hindus. The essentially subsistence level peasant economy of Manipur could not cope with the demands of a modern economy. The rampant corruption, unemployment and nepotism affected the emerging middle classes who felt that though they constituted about 69 per cent of the population, it has always been a Tangkhul hegemony in Manipuri politics. Very few of Meitheis could enter the all-India services while a small tribal population had the benefit of the Centre's reservation policy. There has been a feeling among the Meitheis that though they are educationally forward, there is discrimination against them because of their identification with Hinduism. The Miethie language is rich in its history and literature unlike the Nagas or Mizos. But yet despite their repeated appeal and agitation the government has refused to include it in the Sixth Schedule. They gave vent to their anger and discontent two ways—one, reject the merger and seek secession from India to form a Socialist state of their own. Two, reject Hinduism and revive their traditional faith. Thus, there was a very strong de-Hinduization and de-Sanskritization movement in Manipur, which was accompanied by an effort to revert to their pre-

Hindu animist religion and marginalize the adherents of Hinduism.

The word 'insurgency', despite being in frequent use in the modern world, has not been given a separate entry in the *Oxford Dictionary of English Language* until recently. The *Encyclopaedia of Social Sciences* too does not include it. The *Random House Dictionary* defines 'insurgency' as an act of rejection. It is further amplified to mean an insurrection against an existing government by a group not recognized as having the status of a belligerent. The governments of various states use it from a standardized legal point of view. The *Dictionary of International Law*, defines 'insurgents' as 'Rebels, resistance, detachments participants in a civil war or national liberation war who control certain territory in their country, wage around struggle against colonialists, dictatorial fascists and other antidemocratic regimes for self-determination of their people and have been recognized as insurgents by other subjects of international law.'[15]

Academically, insurgency has been defined 'as a struggle between a non-ranking group and the ruling authorities in which the former consciously employs political resources and instruments of violence to establish legitimacy for some aspect of the political system it considers illegitimate'.[16] Here legitimacy and illegitimacy have been used to refer to whether or not existing aspect of polities are considered moral or immoral by the population or selected elements therein. Hence, insurgency may break out against a particular regime, particular persons of a regime, particular structures and salient values a regime upholds or particular policies or biases of a regime. In all such possible cases, the prime objective of insurgents would be to capture power and replace the political community. The broad categorization of all the above mentioned cases can be nationalistic, ideological, factional or preferential.[17]

Although insurgency can take two forms, conspiratorial and warlike, which include terrorism, *coup d'êtat* guerrilla tactics, kidnapping, hijacking, etc., it can be classified under these six types of insurgencies: Secessionist, Revolutionary, Restorational, Reactionary, Conservative and Reformist.[18] The variables that determine the culmination of an insurgent movement include popular support, organizational cohesion, external support, geography and environment.

There is complete agreement that insurgency is a form of political violence and is a means to an end.[19] The cases that we have examined in this study show that the groups which wanted to secede from India were going through acute and traumatic social and political changes and were to be absorbed in the Indian polity. They already formed a marginal part of the Indian polity and now with detribalization and modernization these groups were nationalities in the making, and refused to be marginal components anymore. Since the India State did not grant these communities their desired status and failed to recognize their nationality aspirations, they questioned the legitimacy of the Indian State to rule over them. All of them rejected a political community (the Indian State) in which they would be marginal components. They sought to severe this link and withdraw from such a political community and form a new one that would provide them with the legal authority to act and make decisions for their own people. It was an attempt on the part of groups to empower themselves, to live according to their own free will and fulfil their aspiration.

A historian's intervention in writing a history of the nationalist movement can be participatory, i.e. provide nations, existing or potential, a past because a nation without a past is a contradiction in terms and it is the past that justifies one nation against others.[20] As such this historical practise turns into a political practice and an essential component of nationalism. Renan wrote that the progress of historical studies is often dangerous to a nationality because forgetting history or even getting history wrong is an essential factor in the formation of a nation.[21] The other intervention could be of the critical type: examining the claim of nationhood by the established parameters and pass a judgement on the legitimacy of a given movement. In the present case, the former intervention has been made by the regional historiography and the ideologues sympathetic to the Naga, Mizo or the Meithei cause. The latter type of intervention, which I intended to do, has become redundant in the context of the rapidly changing world environment as well as the ever increasing fluidity of the concept and perception of nationhood. The post-enlightenment Eurocentric parameters, attributes and ancestry of nationness have been rendered partisan in the post-modern world. For instance, Tribalism and nationness were traditionally seen as contradictions in terms and principles because nationness was seen to be a capitalist occurrence. But the Naga and Mizo struggles were legitimized as nationalist movement condoning the historicity of their overwhelming tribalness. But testing this framework might also take out the 'nationalist content' of many a anti-colonial movements in Africa and South-East Asia. It would also imply the unequivocal acceptance of the nineteenth century liberal-rationalist discourse of nationness even when we are on the threshold of the twenty-first century. By this time nationness has already acquired different meanings. The nationalist discourse today denotes 'power' and its appropriation has often been purported to obtain a shift of political power from one political community to another. The current nationalist discourse therefore is beginning to base itself on primordialist premises: community rather than nationality, ethnicity rather than community, tribe rather than ethnicity. The shift from civilization to tribe, the lowest possible unit, as the basis of nationalist discourse has been a significant development in the history of nationalism. A similar return to primordialist premises have been seen in the following: indigenousness *versus* enogenousness; language *versus* languages; nation state *versus* civil-society; roots and traditions *versus* modernity and modernization; locals *versus* outsiders; Xenophobia, anti-foreigner violence, fundamentalism, localism, provincialism and regionalism *versus* internationalism.

In India the nationalist discourse on 'Indian nationalism' was derived from the post-enlightenment nineteenth century Euro-American sources and was an inextricable part of the nationalist movement. As such it had to struggle and counter the imperialist discourse of nationness which was also based on the same sources and was similarly an inextricable part of the imperialist structure. Ironically, the post-independent Indian polity, faces a similar situation vis-à-vis some of its own constituent communities. The tables are now turned.

NOTES

1. A.D. Smith, 'Formation of Nationalist Movement', in A.D. Smith (ed.), *Nationalist Movement*, London: Macmillan, 1976, pp. 1-30.
2. Dev Nathan, 'Varieties of National Oppression', *Economic and Political Weekly*, 2 July 1988, pp. 1356-7.
3. Udayan Mishra, 'Naga National Question', in Andhra Pradesh Radical Students Union, *Nationality Question in India*, Hyderabad: APRSU, 1982, pp. 61-82.
4. M. Horam, *Thirty years of Naga Insurgency*, Delhi: Cosmo, 1990, pp. 4-10.
5. Ibid.
6. Ibid., p. 33
7. Ibid.
8. Achin Vanaik, *The Painful Transition: Bourgeois Democracy in India*, London: Verso, 1990, pp. 113-38.

9. Ravinder Kumar, *India: A Civilizational-State*, Delhi: UBS and NMML, 1991.
10. C.L. Imchen, 'Naga Politics: Regionalizm or Non-state Nation', in B. Pakem (ed.), *Regionalism in India*, Delhi: Har Anand, 1993, pp. 103-12.
11. Amalendu Guha, *Nationalism: Pan Indian and Regional in Historical Perspective*, Presidential Address, Indian History Congress, Burdwan, 1983.
12. Soyam Lokendrajit, 'Identity and Crisis of Identity', in *Proceedings of the North East History Association*, Pasighat Session, 1986. Also N. Bisheshwar, *Battle of Waterloo*, Imphal: Pax Publication, 1987.
13. B.P. Singh, *The Problem of Change: A Study of North East India*, Delhi: OUP, 1987, p. 26.
14. B. Pakem, 'Separatist Movement in North East India', in T.L. Bose (ed.), *Indian Federalism: Problem and Issues*, Calcutta: K.P. Bagchi, 1987, p. 207.
15. Cited in B. Sharma, Review ofVenkata Rao's book on *Government and Politics in Manipur*, in *Souvenir*, 95th Birth Anniversary of Irabat Singh, 30 September 1991, Imphal, pp. 4-6.
16. Bard O'Neil, 'Insurgency: A Framework for Analysis', in Bard O'Neil et al. (eds.), *Insurgency in Modern World*, Colarado: The Social Science Foundation for Graduate School International Studies, Monograph Series for World Affairs, University of Denver, 1980, p. 1.
17. Ibid., pp. 1-42.
18. A.D. Smith, 'The Formation of Nationalist Movement', in A.D. Smith (ed.), *Nationalist Movement*, London: Macmillan, 1976, pp. 1-30.
19. Bard O'Neil, op. cit.
20. E.J. Hobsbawm, 'Ethnicity and Nationalism in Europe Today', *Anthropology Today*, Vol. 8, No. 1, February 1992, p. 3.
21. Renan cited in ibid.

Bibliography

PRIMARY SOURCES

Archival Sources

Activities of the Mizo Union (148/C 1950).
Administrative Report of the Lushai Hills for the years 1945-6, 1946-7, 1947-8.
Administrative Reports of Manipur 1891-1950.
Assam Government Reports Regarding Tribes and Scheduled Areas (55/C, 1947).
CID, 1931-40 (Manipur).
Collection of personal interviews by the Mizoram State Archives, File Nos. m-1, m-2, m-3.
D. Ronghaka, *Zoram Independent,* Aizawl, 1946.
Delegation of powers to tribal authorities in Lushai Hills (200/C1, 1945).
Files regarding correspondence between the District Superintendent and the Mizo Union Office Bearers.
Fortnightly Reports on the excluded areas 1946, File No. 27C, 1946.
Fortnightly reports on the excluded areas 1947.
Intelligence Summaries: Lushai Hills (66/C, 1942).
K. Zawla, *Zoram Din Hmun Dik Hmuh Chuah Thelhna Tur* (A guide towards making the right political decision for future Mizoram).
Kohima Raj Bhavan Records (Special Files Sereis on the Nagas).
List of Number of Representatives from the area of Mizo Chiefs, 1946.
'Memorandum of the case of Mizo' Memorandum of the Mizo Union to the Sub-Committee on North East India excluded and partially excluded areas (Assam) known as 'Bordoloi Committee'.
Memorandum submitted to the Government of India by the Mizo National Council.
Memorandum submitted to the Government of India by the Naga National Council.
Mizo Union Constitution and the Presidential Speech.
Mizo Union General Assembly Proceedings, General Department files belonging to the office of the District Superintendent.
Mizo Union Mite Hnena Thuchah (Memorandum of the Mizo Union), Aizawl, 1947.
Naga Hills: Dossiers on Naga leaders and members of Naga National Council (No. 196/C, 1950, Governor's Secretariat, Confidential).
Naga National Councils: Reports of Threats to Assam (No. 157/C, 1950).

Pachunga, Dahrawka and Hmartawnphunga, *Independence*, Aizawl: Authors,1947.
———, *Mizoram Dindantur Ngaituahhuna Vant lang* (A Public meeting dealing with the future political state of Mizoram), Aizawl, 1947.
Political activities on the border of the Lushai Hills, 1946 (128/C, 1946).
Political Movements of Congress in Manipur C/Pol/1/8.
Post-war reconstruction on the tribal areas in Assam (251/C,1945).
Proceedings of the accredited lectures of all Lushai Political Leaders, Aizawl, 14.8.47 (in Mizo).
Proceedings of the Manipur Praja Sangha Working Committee.
Proceedings of the Manipur State Dorbar.
Proceedings of the Naga National Council.
Proceedings of the Working Committee Meeting of Manipur Krishak Sabha, 28.9.1948.
Propaganda among the Hill tribes by the Congress MLA's (Governor's Confidential (36/C,1938).
Proposed action against Thanga Lushai who joined INA (144/C, 1945).
Report on the North Eastern Frontier (Assam) Tribal and Exlcuded Areas, 3 vols.
Reports and Pamphlets (published).
Reports on the Local Self Government among the Hills Tribes (257/1945).
Resolutions of the Manipur State Dorbar.
Resolutions of the Manipur State Congress.
Resolutions of the Manipur State Council.
Resolutions of the Naga National Council.
Resolutions of the Working Committee of Nikhil Manipur Mahasabha.
Separation Movement in the Lushai Hills (Government's Secret Confidential (118/C, 1940).
Shillong Raj Bhavan Records 1946-50 on the Naga Issue (Special File).
The Assam Lushai Hills District (Acquisition of Chiefs Right) Act, 1954.
United Mizo Freedom Party Constitution and its Correspondence with the Superintendent, Lushai Hills.
Vanlawma, R., *The Mizo Union*, Aizawl, 1946.
Weekly Confidential Reports of the Lushai Hills District for the years 1946, 1947.

MEMOIRS, REPORTS, ACCOUNTS AND MANUSCRIPTS

Evidences on the report on the North East Frontier Tribal and Excluded Areas, Vol. 3 by eminent Mizo Leaders.
Imti T., Aliba, *Reminiscences: Impur to Naga National Council*, Mokokchung: Author, 1988.
IWGIA, The Naga Nation and Its Struggle against Genocide, Copenhagen: IWGIAP, 1986.
Laldenga, *Mizoram Marches Towards Freedom*, Aizawl: MNF, 1973.

MNF, *Declaration of Independence*, 1.3.1966, Aizawl.

NSCN, *A Brief Account of Nagaland*.

Pahlira, C., 'Mizo Hills in the Indian Union', in *Tribal Mirror*, Vol. 6, Karimganj, 1970.

Phizo, A.Z., *The Fate of the Naga People: An Appeal to the World,* London: Author, 1960.

———, *Nagaland: A Strange Country in Asia*, Kohima: NNC, 1950.

Ch. Saprawnga, *Ka Zin Kawng* (My Journey), Aizawl: Zoram Printing Press, 1973.

———, 'Factors Contributing to the Mizo Problem', in *Tribal Mirror*, Karimganj, Vol. 3, 1967.

Singh, N. Bisheshwar, *Last Expression on my Death Bed*, Imphal: Pax Publications, 1986.

Thanlira, R., 'Mizo Union Nawrh' (unpublished) (in English).

———, 'Reminiscence of Gopinath Bordoloi', in Lili M. Barua, *Lokpriya Gopinath Bordoloi,* Delhi: Gian, 1992.

Vanlawma, R., *Ka Ram Le Kei* (My Country and I): *Political History of Modern Mizoram*, Aizawl: Zoram Printing Press, 1972.

———, 'Lokpriya Gopinath as I Know him', in Lili M. Barua, *Lokpriya Gopinath Bordoloi,* Delhi: Gian, 1992.

NEWSPAPERS

Naga Nation

Peoples Age

Peoples War

Resistance

The Dawn

The Sentinel

INTERVIEWS

Interview with R. Vanlawma on 8 July 1997, at his home Venglui, Aizawl. He was born in the year 1915. This Octogenarian was the first matriculate among the Mizos. He was the leader of the Young Lushai Association and later the Mizo Union. At present he is staying with his son and his grandchildren in Aizawl at 'Zalen cabin', a beautiful two storeyed bungalow surrounded by thick plants and flowers. He was awarded The Padmashri on 26 January 1998, by the President of India.

SECONDARY SOURCES

BOOKS

Abbi, B.I., *North Eastern Region: Problem and Perspective*, Chandigarh: CRRID, 1985.

Aram, M., *Peace in Nagaland*, Delhi: Arnold Heineman, 1974.

APRSV, *Nationality Question in India*, Hyderabad, APRSV, 1982.

Barpujari, H.K., *Problems of the Hill Tribes: North East Frontier*, Vol. I, Gauhati: Lawyers, 1970; Vol. II, Gauhati: United, 1976; Vol. III, Gauhati: Spectrum, 1981.

Baruah, A., *Lokpriya Gopinath Bordoloi*, Delhi: Gian, 1992.

Bose, T.C. (ed.), *Indian Federalism: Problem and Issues*, Calcutta: K.P. Bagchi, 1987.

Bhatt, S., *The Challenge of North East*, Bombay: Popular Prakashan, 1975.

Chatterjee, S., *Mizoram Under British Rule*, Delhi: Mittal, 1985.

———, *Mizo Chiefs and Chiefdom*, Delhi: MD Publication, 1995.

———, *Mizoram Encyclopedia*, 3 vols., Delhi: Jaico, 1990.

Chaube, S.K., *Hill Politics in North East India*, Delhi: Orient Longman, 1973.

Choudhary, P. Roy, *The North East: Roots of Insurgency*, Calcutta: Firma KLM, 1986.

Choudhury, S., *Social Background of Mizo Insurgency*, ICSSR, North Eastern Regional Centre, Mimeographed, 1988.

Constantine, R., *Manipur: Maid of the Mountains*, Delhi: Mittal, 1980.

Dev, B.J. and D. Lahiri, *Manipur: Culture and Politics*, Delhi: Mittal, 1981.

Desai, A.R. (ed.), *Repression and Resistance in India*, 2 vols., Bombay: Sangam Books, 1990.

Elwin, Verrier, *Nagaland*, Shillong, Research Dept. Govt. of Assam, 1961.

Gait, E., *History of Assam*, Calcutta: Thacker Spink & Co., 1906 (reprint 1984).

Galula, D., *Counter Insurgency Warfare: Theory and Practise*, Delhi: Sagar, 1982.

Gopal, S., *Jawaharlal Nehru: A Biography*, 3 vols., Delhi: OUP, 1979-80.

Goswami, B.B., *The Mizo Unrest: A Study of Politicisation of Culture*, Jaipur: Alekh, 1979.

Govt. of India, *Collected Works of Mahatma Gandhi*, Delhi: Publication Division, 1983.

Guha, Amalendu, *Planter Raj to Swaraj: Freedom Struggle and Electoral Politics in Assam*, Delhi: ICHR, 1977.

Hansaria, B.L., *Sixth Schedule to the Indian Constitution: A Study*, Gauhati: Author, 1983.

Hluna, J.V., *Church and Political Upheaval in Mizoram*, Aizawl: Author, 1988.

Horam, M., *Thirty Years of Naga Insurgency*, Delhi: Cosmo, 1990.

International Seminar on the Mizos held at Aizawl, 7-9 April 1992, Proceedings, Aizawl, 1992.

Kabui, G., et al., *Modern Manipur*, Imphal: Modern Book, 1991.

Kumar Girija and V.K. Arora (eds.), *Documents on Indian Affairs*, Bombay: Asia, 1965.

Lalbiakthanga, *The Mizos: A Study in Racial Personality*, Gauhati: United, 1978.

Lalchungnunga, *Mizoram Politics of Regionalism*, Gauhati: United, 1996.

Luithui and N. Haksar, *Nagaland Files*, Delhi: Lancer International, 1984.

Manserg, N. (ed.), *Transfer of Power, 1942-47*, Vol. X, London: HMSO, 1981.

Maxwell, N., *India, the Nagas and the North East London*, MRG, 1980.

McCall, A.G., *Lushai Chrysalis*, London: Luzac & Co., 1949.

Menon, V.P., *Integration of Indian States*, Hyderabad: Oreint Longman, 1956, reprint 1961.

Moore, R.J., *Endgames of Empire: Studies in Britain's Indian Problem*, London: OUP, 1988.

Narayan, J.P., *Nagaland ka Sawal* (in Hindi), Varanasi: Sarva Sewa Sangh, 1965.

Nag, A.K., *The Mizo Dilemma*, Silchar: Tribal Misson Publication, 1984.

Nag, C.R., *The Mizo Society in Transition*, Delhi: Vikas, 1994.

Nag, S., *Roots of Ethnic Conflict: Nationality Question in North-East India*, Delhi: Manohar, 1990.

———, *India and North-East India: Mind, Politics and the Process of Integration, 1946-50*, Delhi: Regency, 1998.

———, *Nationalism, Separatism and Secessionism*, Jaipur: Rawat, 1999.

Nibedan, N., *Mizoram: Daggers Brigade*, Delhi: Lancer, 1980.

———, *North East India: The Ethnic Explosion*, Delhi: Lancer, 1981.

———, *Nagaland: Night of the Guerrillas*, Delhi: Lancer, 1989.

O'Neil, Bard, *Insurgency in Modern World*, Denver, Colorado: SSFGSISMSWF (The Social Science Foundation for Graduate School for International Studies), Monograph Series for World Affairs, University of Denver, 1980.

Phadnis, Urmilla, *Ethnicity and Nation-Building in South Asia*, Delhi: Sage, 1990.

Phanjonbam, Tarapot, *Insurgency Movement in North East India*, Delhi: Vikas, 1983.

Prasad, R.N., *Government and Politics in Mizoram 1947-1986*, Delhi: Northern Book Centre, 1987.

———, *Autonomy Movements in Mizoram*, Delhi: Northern Book Centre, 1994.

Proceedings of the North East India History Association, Shillong, NEIHA, 1979 onwards.

Ray, Animesh, *Mizoram: Dynamics of Change*, Calcutta: Pearl, 1982.

Ray, B. Datta, *Emergence and Role of Middle Class in North East India*, Delhi: Uppal, 1989.

Rao, V.V., *Century of Tribal Politics in North East India*, Delhi: S. Chand & Co., 1976.

Rao, V.V., et al., *Century of Government and Politics in North East India*, 6 vols., Delhi: S. Chand & Co., 1987-91.

Rustomji, Nari, *Enchanted Frontiers*, Delhi: OUP, 1971.

———, *Imperilled Frontiers*, Delhi: OUP, 1989.

Samuelson, R. Sena, *Love Mizoram*, Imphal: Goodwill Press, 1985.

Sangma, Milton (ed.), *Essay on North East India*, Delhi: Indus, 1994.

Sanjaoba, N., *Manipur: Past and Present*, Delhi: Mittal, 1990.

———, *Manipur: Treaty and Documents*, 2 vols., Delhi: Mittal, 1992.

Sarkar, Sumit, *Modern India*, Delhi: Macmillan, 1983.

Sareen, H., *Insurgency in North East India*, Delhi: Sterling, 1982.

Singh, B.P., *The Problem of Change: A Study of North East India*, Delhi: OUP, 1987.

Singh, Chandrika, *Political Evolution of Nagaland*, Delhi: Lancer, 1989.

Singh, K.S. (ed.), *Tribal Movements in India*, Simla: IIAS, 1982.

———, *Tribal Situation in India*, Shimla: IIAS, 1972.

Singh, K.M., *Hijam Irabot Singh and Political Movement in Manipur*, Delhi: B.R. Publishing, 1989.

Singh, N. Joykumar, *Social Movements in Manipur*, Delhi: Mittal, 1992.

Singh, N. Bisheshwar, *Battle of Waterloo*, Imphal: Pax Publication, 1987.

Singh, N. Lokendra, *Unquiet Valley*, Delhi: Mittal, 1998.

Singh, T. Bir, *Comrade Inabot*, Imphal: Irabat Memorial Library and Information Centre, 1983.

Sinha, Surajit (ed.), *Tribal Politics and State Formation in North Eastern India*, Calcutta: K.P. Bagchi, 1987.

Spear, P., *History of India*, Vol. 2, Penguin, reprint 1990.

Stracey, P.D., *The Nagaland Nightmare*, Bombay: Allied, 1965.

Smith, A.D., *Nationalist Movement*, London: Macmillan, 1976.

Vumson, *Zo History*, Aizawl, Author, n.d.

Yonou, Asoso, *The Rising Nagas: A Political and Historical Study*, Delhi: Vivek, 1974.

Zinyo, M., *Phizo and the Naga Problem*, Dimapur: Author, 1979.

Dissertations

Bharati, M., 'Insurgency in Manipur', M.A. Dissertation, Vadodra: M.S. University of Baroda, 1993.

Iyer, I. Lanu, 'Contemporary Naga Social Formation and Ethnic Identity: A Case of Development or Decay', Ph.D. Dissertation, Shillong: North Eastern Hill University, 1985.

Pautu, S.H., 'Mizoram: Seperatist Politics', M.Phil Dissertation, Shillong: North Eastern Hill University, 1989.

Singh, Kshetri Rajendra, 'Social Movements in Manipur: A Study of Two Movements', Ph.D. Dissertation, Surat: Centre for Social Studies, South Gujarat University, 1993.

Singh, N. Lokendra, 'Socio-Economic Roots of Popular Movements in Manipur Valley', Ph.D. Dissertation, Imphal: Manipur University, 1990.

Articles

Banerjee, Sumanta, 'Dangerous Game in Nagaland', *Economic and Political Weekly*, 18 July 1992.

Borgohain, Homen, 'Manipur: Anatomy of Despair', *Economic and Political Weekly*, 13-20 November 1982.

Ch. Saprawnga, 'Factors Contributing to the Mizo Problem', *Tribal Mirror*, Vol. III, 1967.

Downs, Frederick, 'Study of Christianity in North East India', *North Eastern Hill University Journal of Social Sciences and Humanities*, Vol. IX, No. 3, July-September 1991.

Hardgrave, R.L., 'The North East, Punjab and the Regionalisation of Indian Politics', *Asian Survey*, Vol. 23, No. II, November 1983.

Kabui, Gangumei, 'Leftist Movement in Manipur: A Case Study of Comrade Irabat Singh', *Indian History Congress Proceeding*, Jadavpur Session, 1974.

Lokendrajit, Soyam, 'Identity and Crisis of Identity', in *North East India History Association Proceeding*, Pasighat Session, 1986.

Nunthara, C., 'Grouping of Villages in Mizoram: Its Social and Economic Impact', *Economic and Political Weekly*, 25 July 1981.

Pahlira, C., 'Mizo Hills in the Indian Union', in *Tribal Mirror*, Vol. VI, 1970.

Rangaswami, Amrita, 'Mizoram: Tragedy of Our Making', *Economic and Political Weekly*, 15 April 1978.

Singh, K.R., 'From PLA to MLA', *Frontier*, Vol. 19, No. 20, 3 January 1987.

Singh, K.S., 'Merger of Manipur with India', *North East India History Association Proceeding*, Imphal Session, 1982.

Singh, N. Joykumar, 'Movement for Responsible Government in Manipur 1938-48', in *North East India History Association Proceeding*, Barapani Session, 1983.

———, 'The Merger of Manipur into India: A Study of Political Integration of a Kingdom into Indian Union', in *North East India History Association Proceeding*, Agartala Session, 1982.

Singh, Y.S., 'Nupilan: Manipur Womens Agitation', *Economic and Political Weekly*, Vol. II, No. 8, 21 February 1978.

Syiemlieh, D.R., 'The Crown Colony Scheme for North East India 1928-1947', in *North East India History Association Proceeding*, Dibrugarh Session, 1981.

———, 'Responses of the North Eastern Hill Tribes of India Towards Partition and Independence', *Indo-British Review: Journal of History*, Vol. 17, September-December 1989.

Index